Shojo Beat

Skip·Beat!

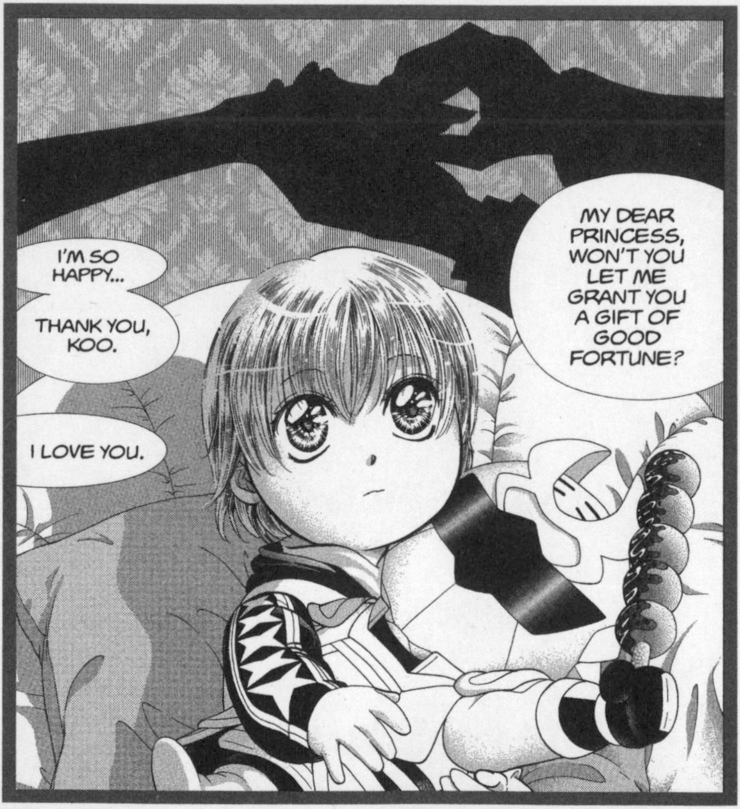
MY DEAR PRINCESS, WON'T YOU LET ME GRANT YOU A GIFT OF GOOD FORTUNE?
I'M SO HAPPY...
THANK YOU, KOO.
I LOVE YOU.

43

Story & Art by Yoshiki Nakamura

Skip·Beat!

Volume 43

CONTENTS

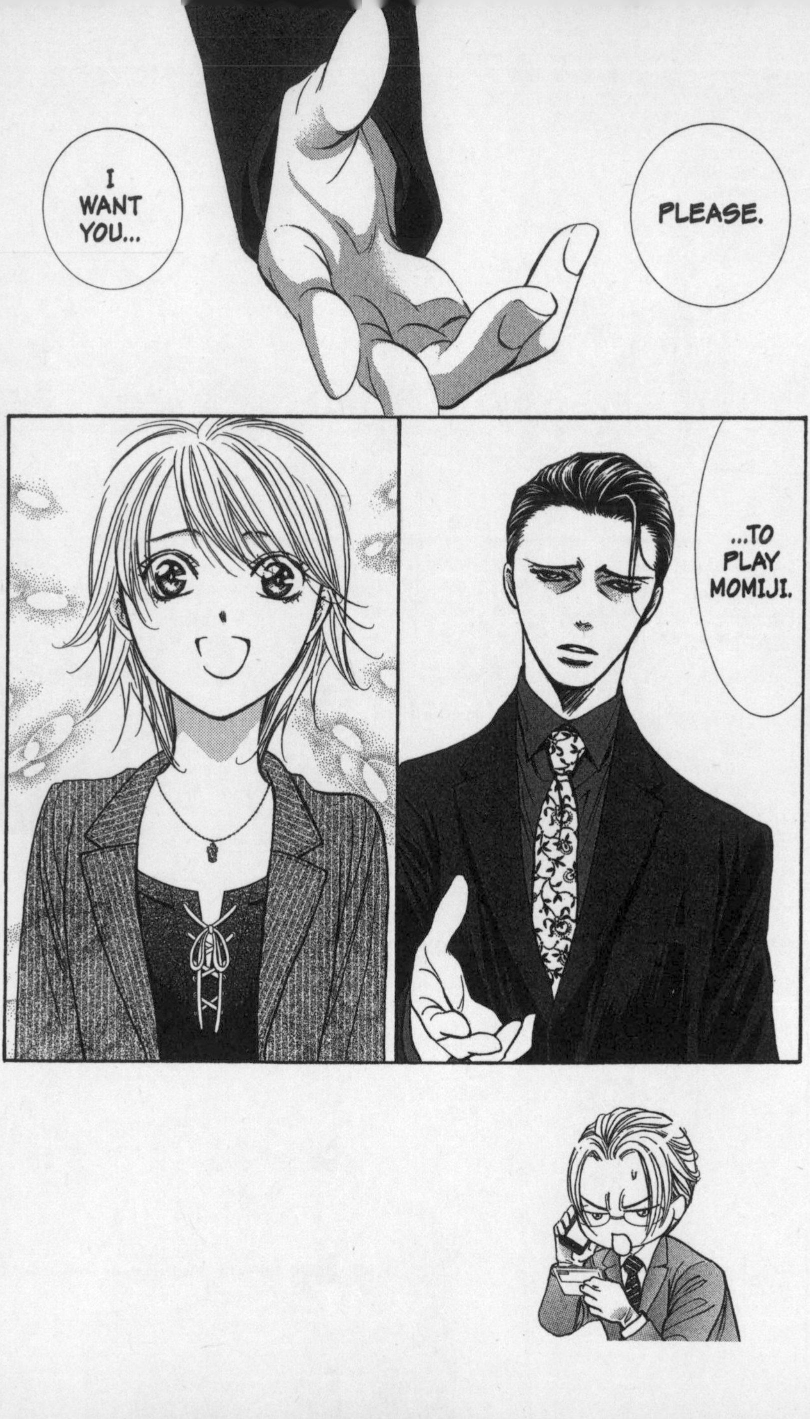
PLEASE.
I WANT YOU...
...TO PLAY MOMIJI.

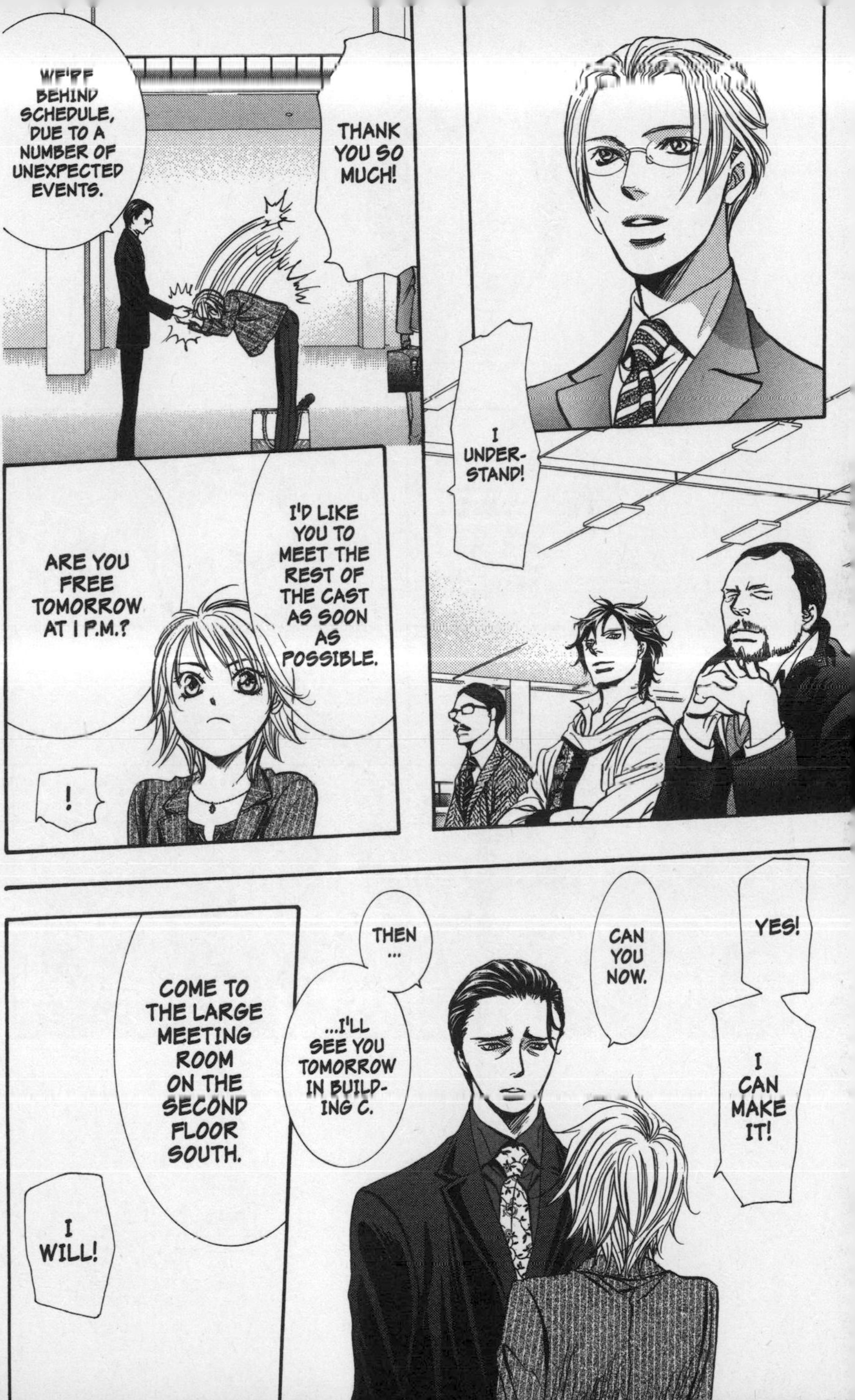
WE'RE BEHIND SCHEDULE, DUE TO A NUMBER OF UNEXPECTED EVENTS.
THANK YOU SO MUCH!
I UNDER-STAND!
I'D LIKE YOU TO MEET THE REST OF THE CAST AS SOON AS POSSIBLE.
ARE YOU FREE TOMORROW AT 1 P.M.?
!
YES!
I CAN MAKE IT!
CAN YOU NOW.
THEN ...
...I'LL SEE YOU TOMORROW IN BUILD-ING C.
COME TO THE LARGE MEETING ROOM ON THE SECOND FLOOR SOUTH.
I WILL!

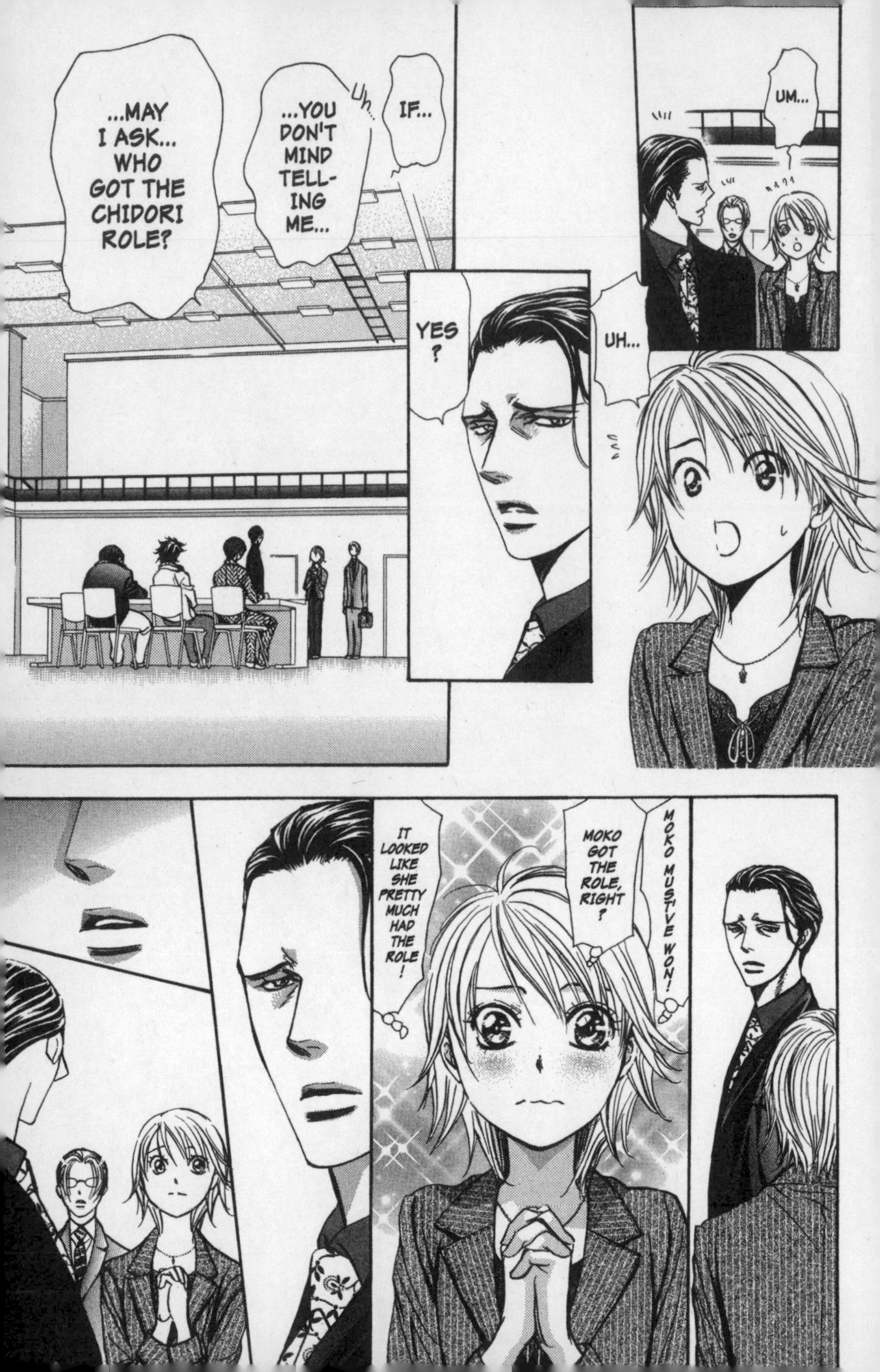
UM...
UH...
YES?
IF...
Uh...
...YOU DON'T MIND TELLING ME...
...MAY I ASK... WHO GOT THE CHIDORI ROLE?
MOKO MUST'VE WON!
MOKO GOT THE ROLE, RIGHT?
IT LOOKED LIKE SHE PRETTY MUCH HAD THE ROLE!

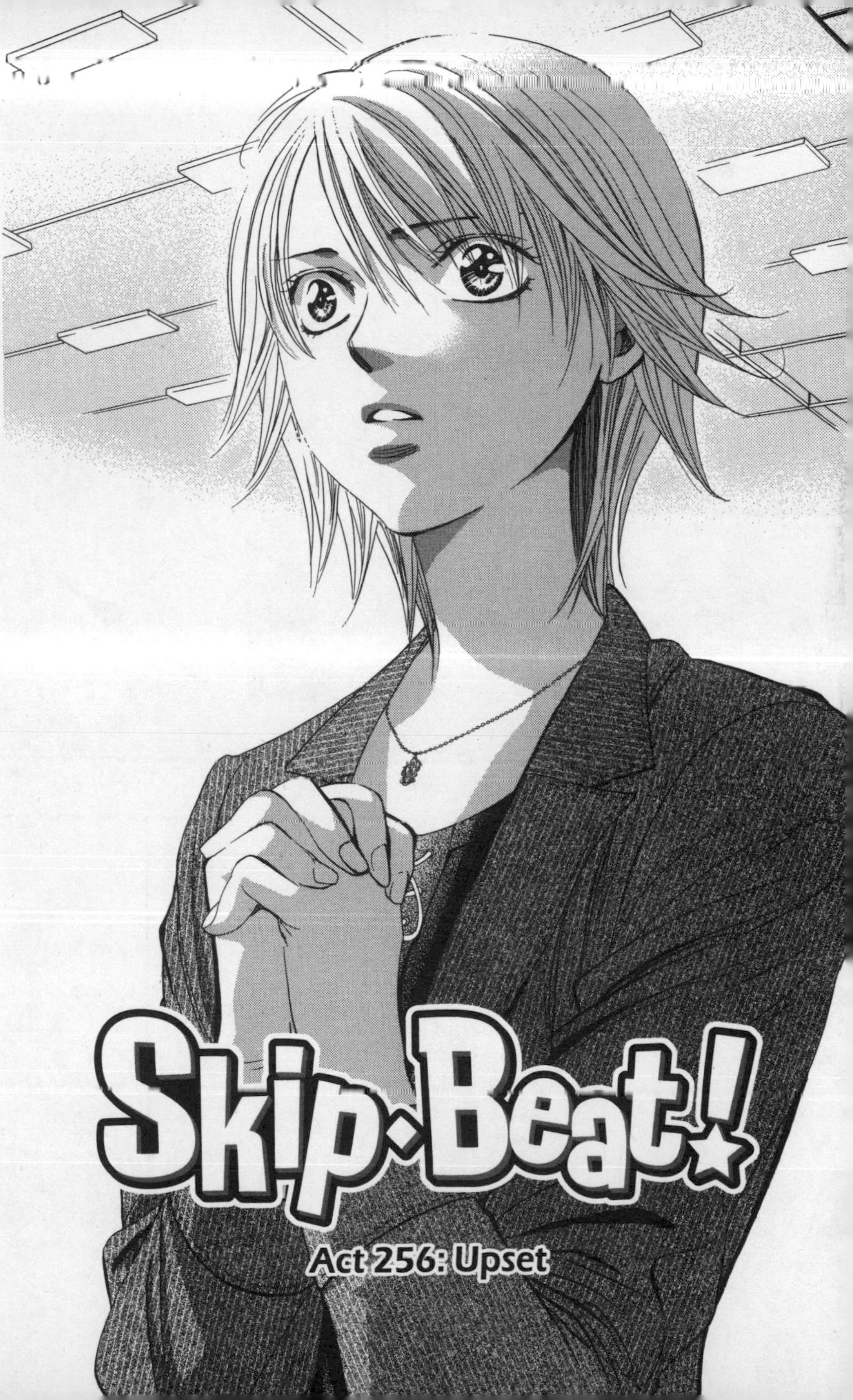
Skip·Beat!
Act 256: Upset

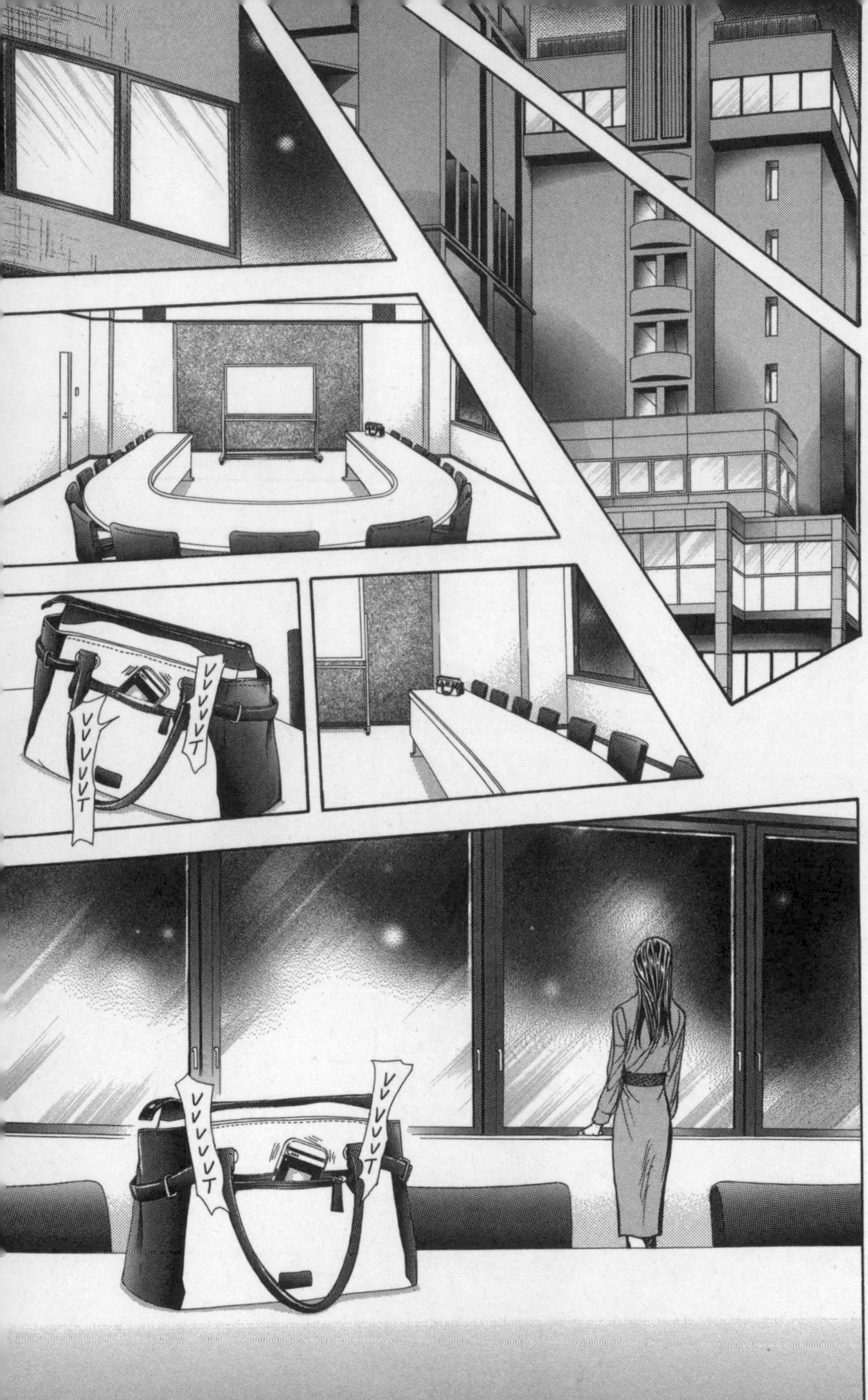
VVVVVT
VVVVVT
VVVVVT
VVVVVT

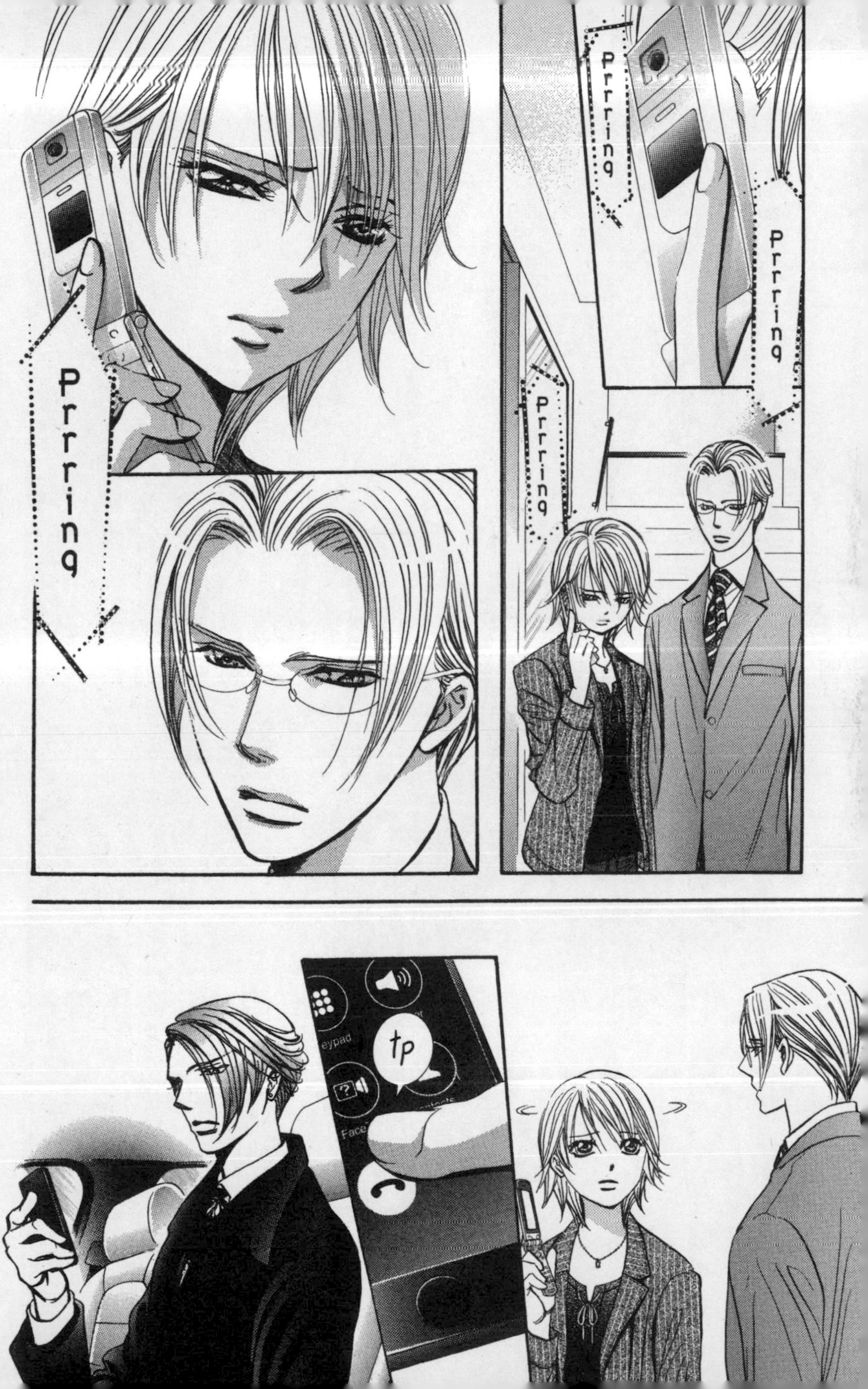
Prrring
Prrrring
Prrrring
Prrrring
tp

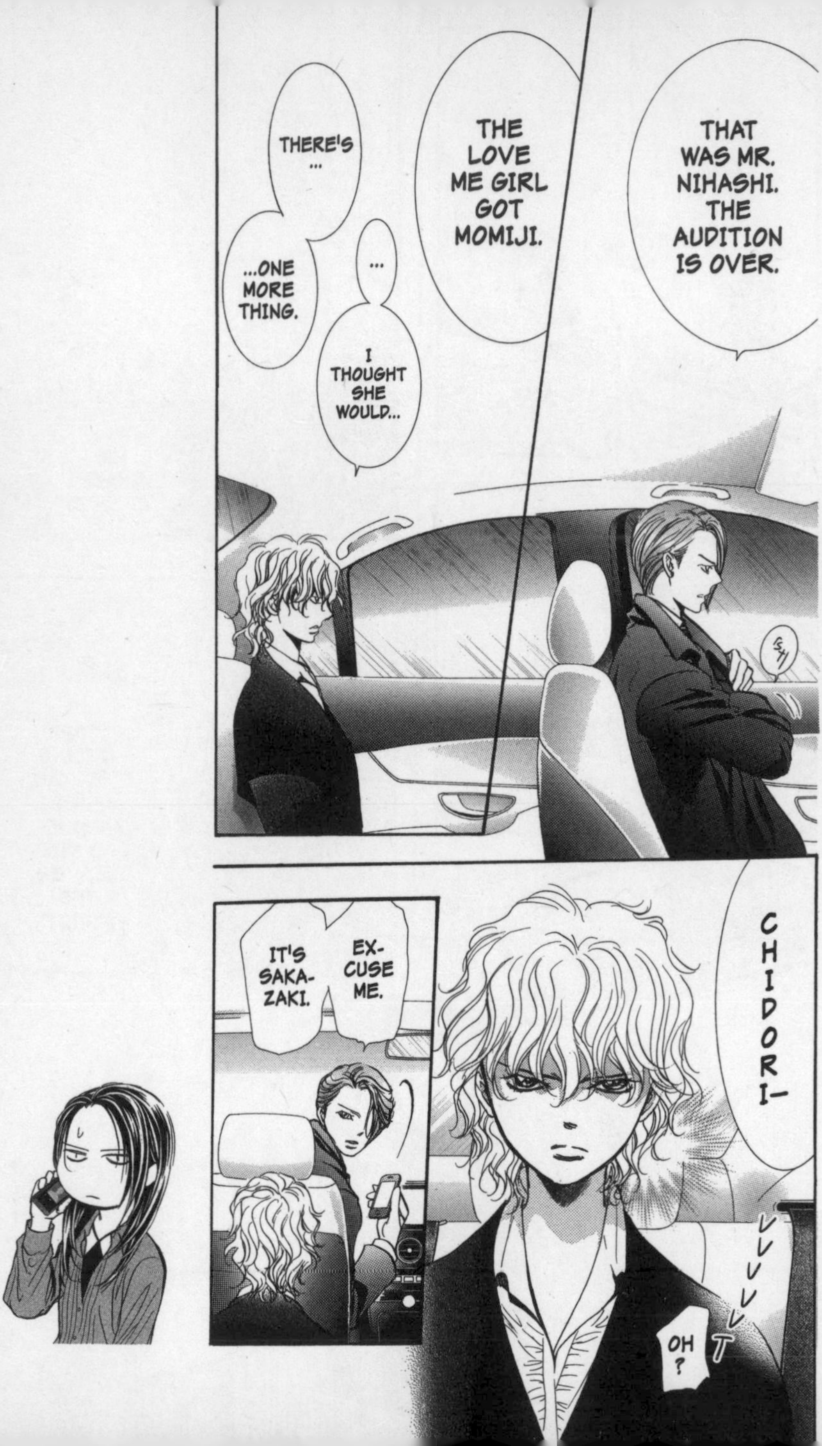

THAT WAS MR. NIHASHI. THE AUDITION IS OVER.
THE LOVE ME GIRL GOT MOMIJI.
...
I THOUGHT SHE WOULD...
THERE'S ...
...ONE MORE THING.
CHIDORI—
VVVVVVVT
OH?
EXCUSE ME.
IT'S SAKAZAKI.

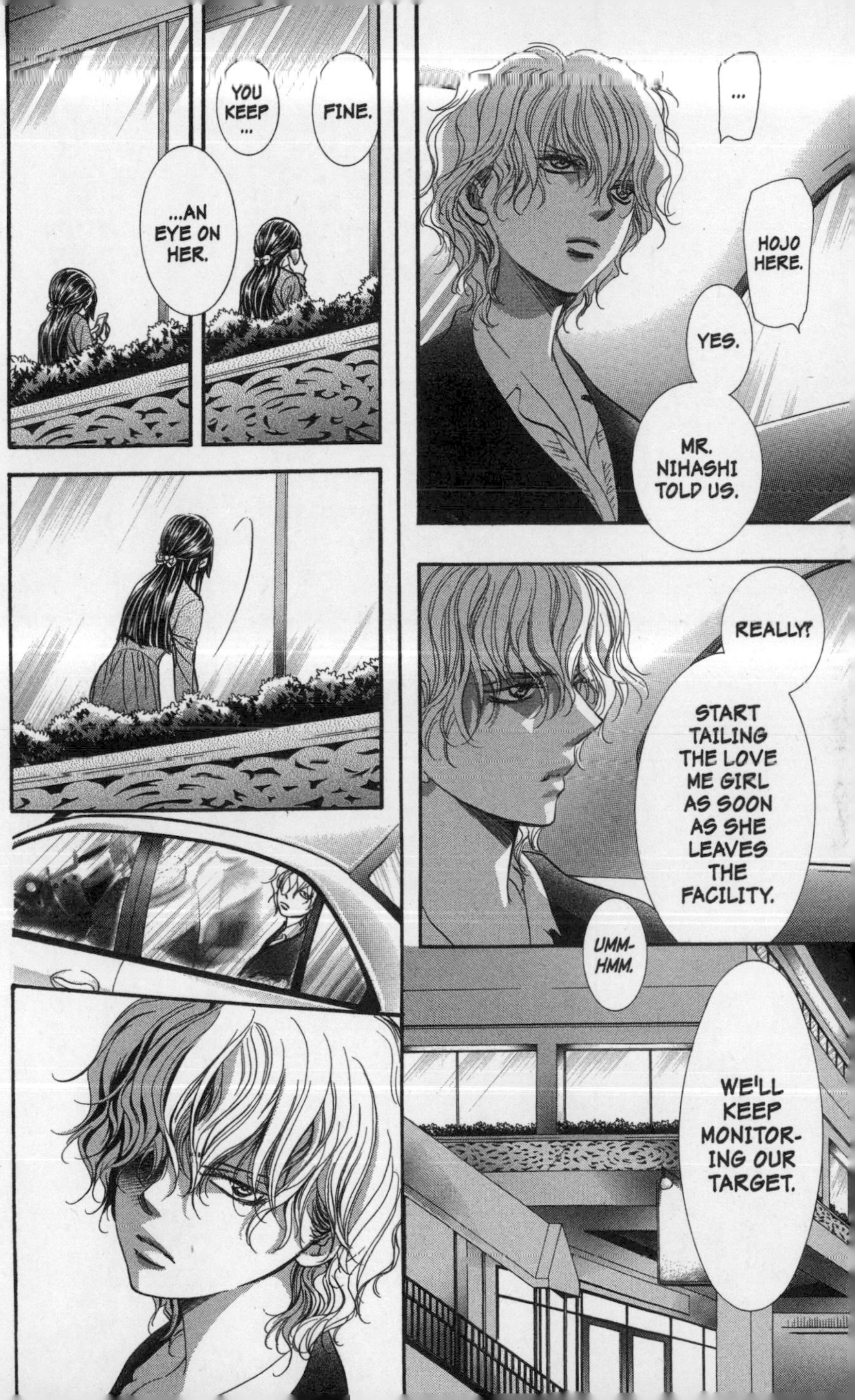
...
HOJO HERE.
YES.
MR. NIHASHI TOLD US.
REALLY?
START TAILING THE LOVE ME GIRL AS SOON AS SHE LEAVES THE FACILITY.
UMM-HMM.
WE'LL KEEP MONITOR-ING OUR TARGET.
FINE.
YOU KEEP ...
...AN EYE ON HER.

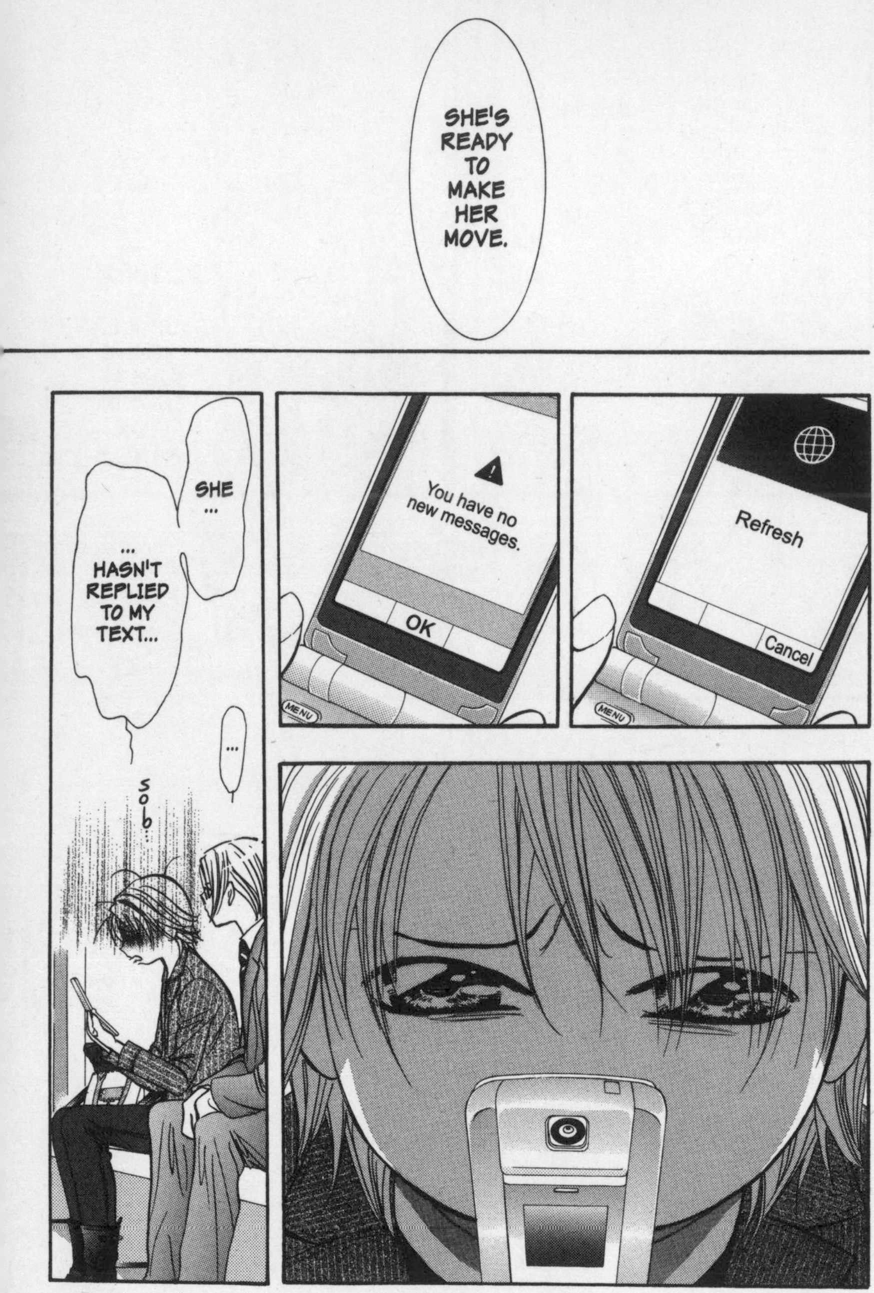
SHE'S READY TO MAKE HER MOVE.
Refresh
Cancel
You have no new messages.
OK
SHE ...
... HASN'T REPLIED TO MY TEXT...
...
sob...

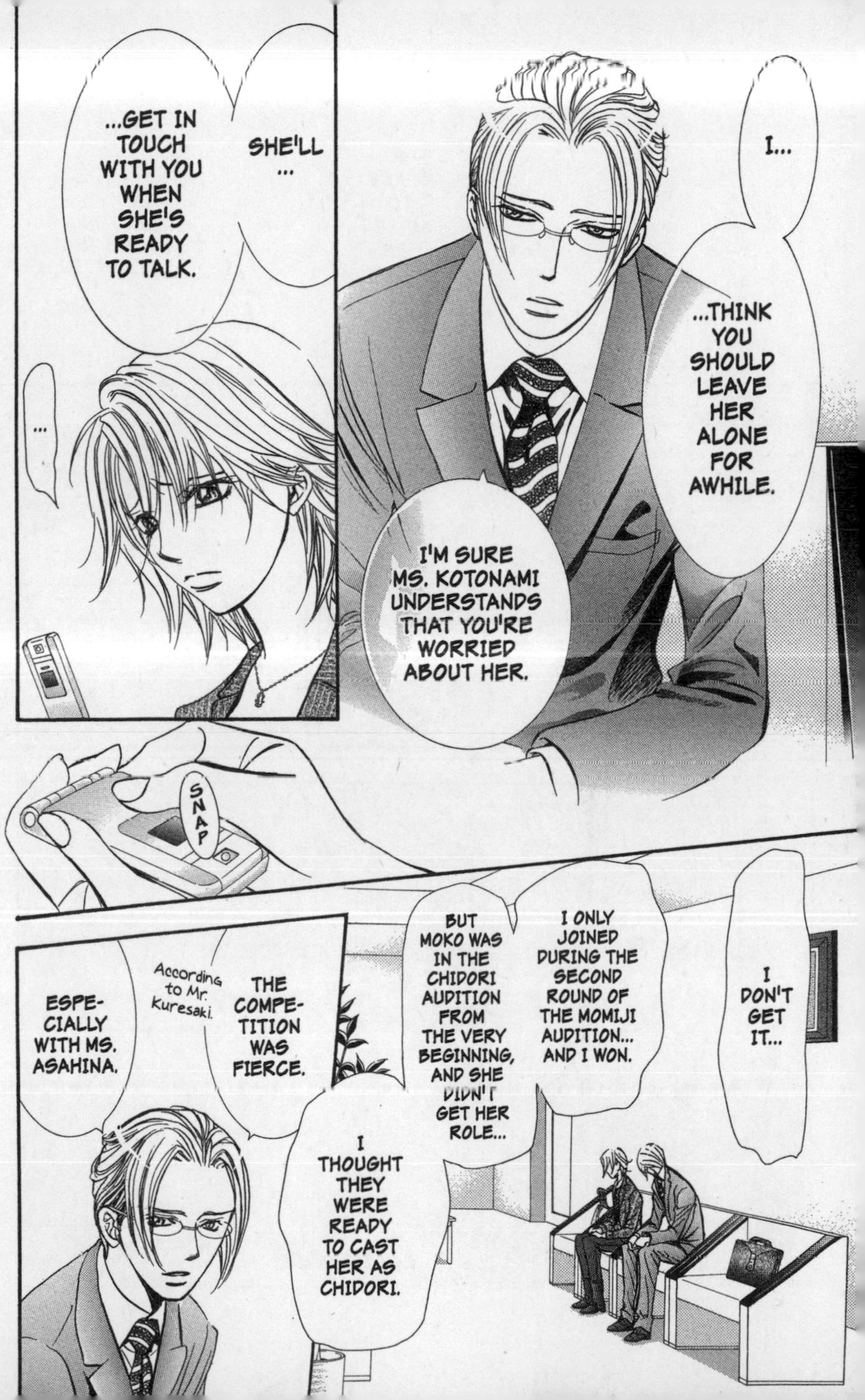
I...
...THINK YOU SHOULD LEAVE HER ALONE FOR AWHILE.
I'M SURE MS. KOTONAMI UNDERSTANDS THAT YOU'RE WORRIED ABOUT HER.
SHE'LL ...
...GET IN TOUCH WITH YOU WHEN SHE'S READY TO TALK.
...
SNAP
I DON'T GET IT...
I ONLY JOINED DURING THE SECOND ROUND OF THE MOMIJI AUDITION... AND I WON.
BUT MOKO WAS IN THE CHIDORI AUDITION FROM THE VERY BEGINNING, AND SHE DIDN'T GET HER ROLE...
I THOUGHT THEY WERE READY TO CAST HER AS CHIDORI.
THE COMPETITION WAS FIERCE.
According to Mr. Kuresaki.
ESPECIALLY WITH MS. ASAHINA.

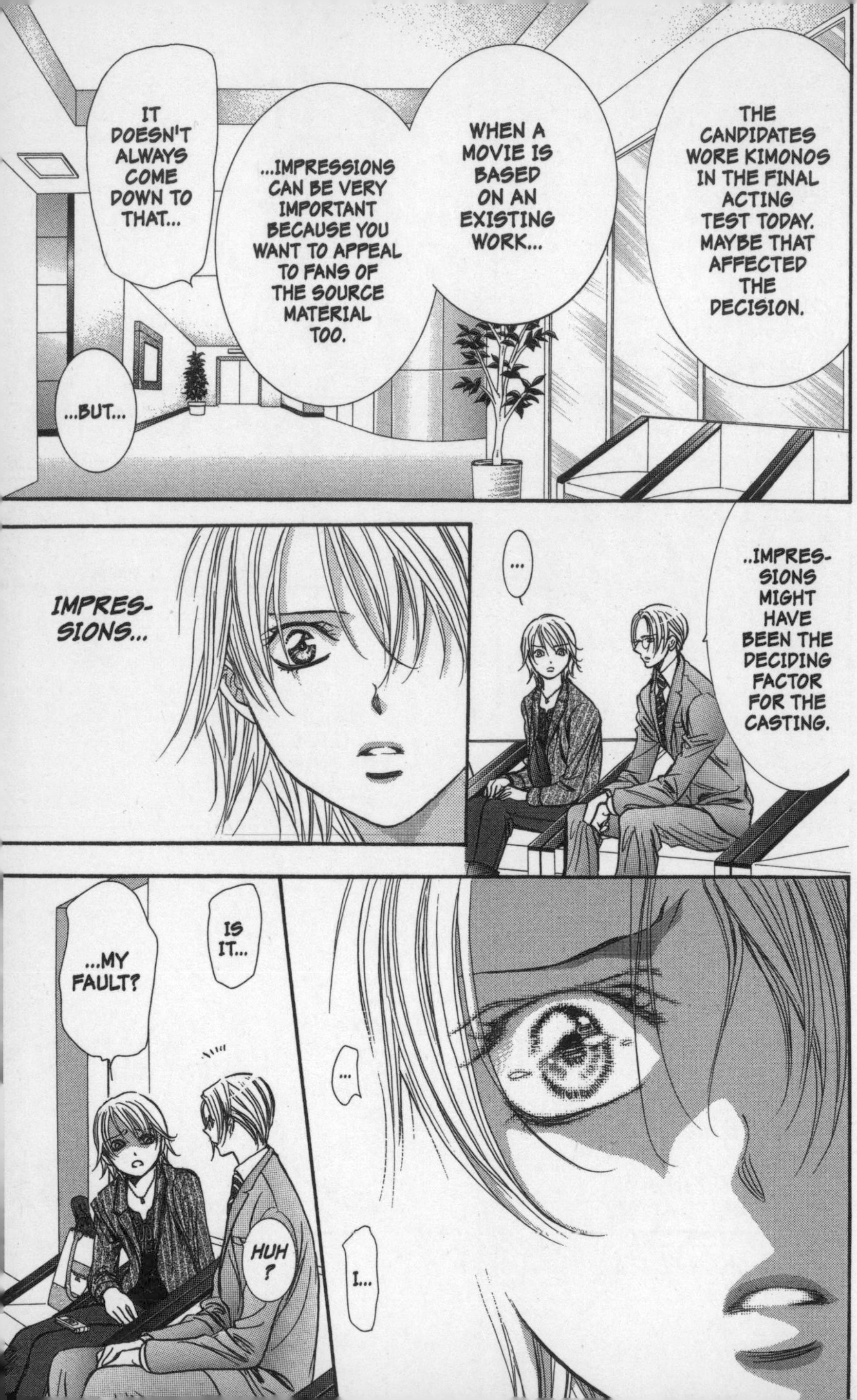
THE CANDIDATES WORE KIMONOS IN THE FINAL ACTING TEST TODAY. MAYBE THAT AFFECTED THE DECISION.
WHEN A MOVIE IS BASED ON AN EXISTING WORK...
...IMPRESSIONS CAN BE VERY IMPORTANT BECAUSE YOU WANT TO APPEAL TO FANS OF THE SOURCE MATERIAL TOO.
IT DOESN'T ALWAYS COME DOWN TO THAT...
...BUT...
..IMPRESSIONS MIGHT HAVE BEEN THE DECIDING FACTOR FOR THE CASTING.
...
IMPRES-SIONS...
...
I...
IS IT...
...MY FAULT?
HUH?

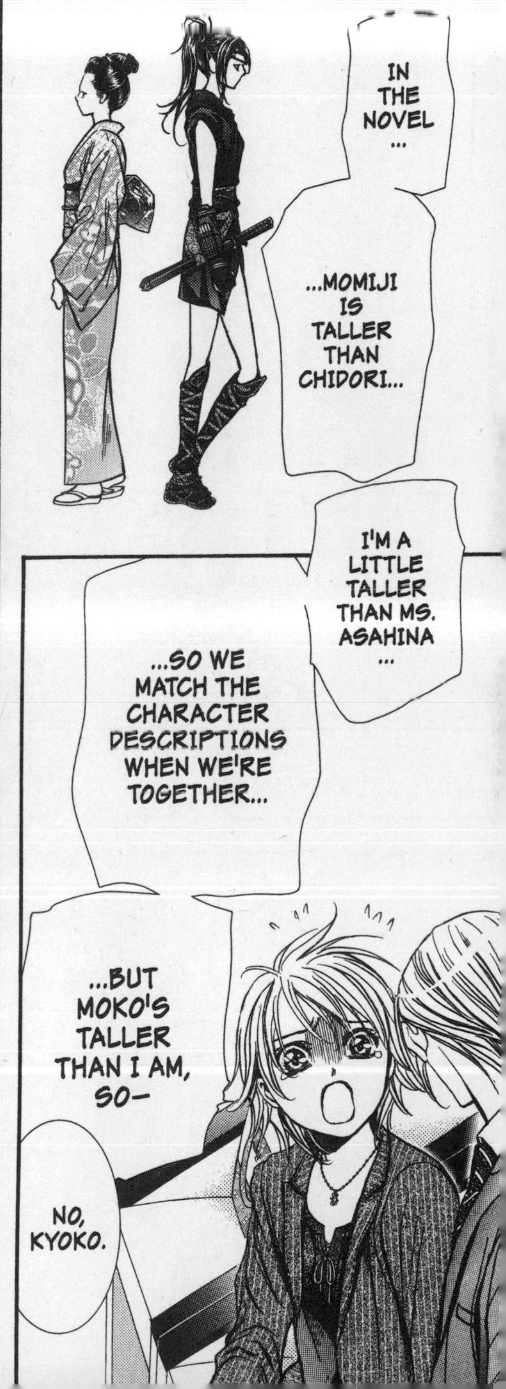
IN THE NOVEL...
...MOMIJI IS TALLER THAN CHIDORI...
I'M A LITTLE TALLER THAN MS. ASAHINA...
...SO WE MATCH THE CHARACTER DESCRIPTIONS WHEN WE'RE TOGETHER...
...BUT MOKO'S TALLER THAN I AM, SO–
NO, KYOKO.
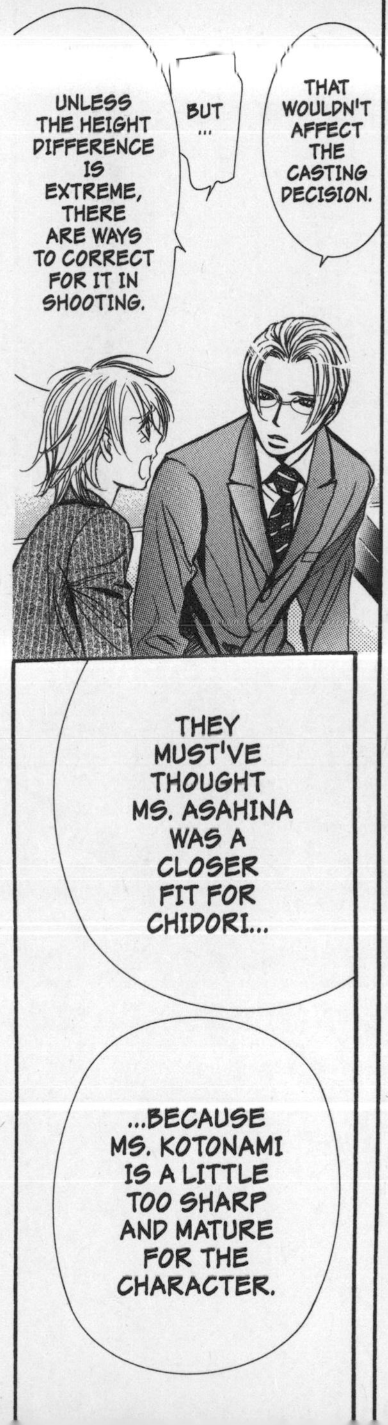
THAT WOULDN'T AFFECT THE CASTING DECISION.
BUT...
UNLESS THE HEIGHT DIFFERENCE IS EXTREME, THERE ARE WAYS TO CORRECT FOR IT IN SHOOTING.
THEY MUST'VE THOUGHT MS. ASAHINA WAS A CLOSER FIT FOR CHIDORI...
...BECAUSE MS. KOTONAMI IS A LITTLE TOO SHARP AND MATURE FOR THE CHARACTER.

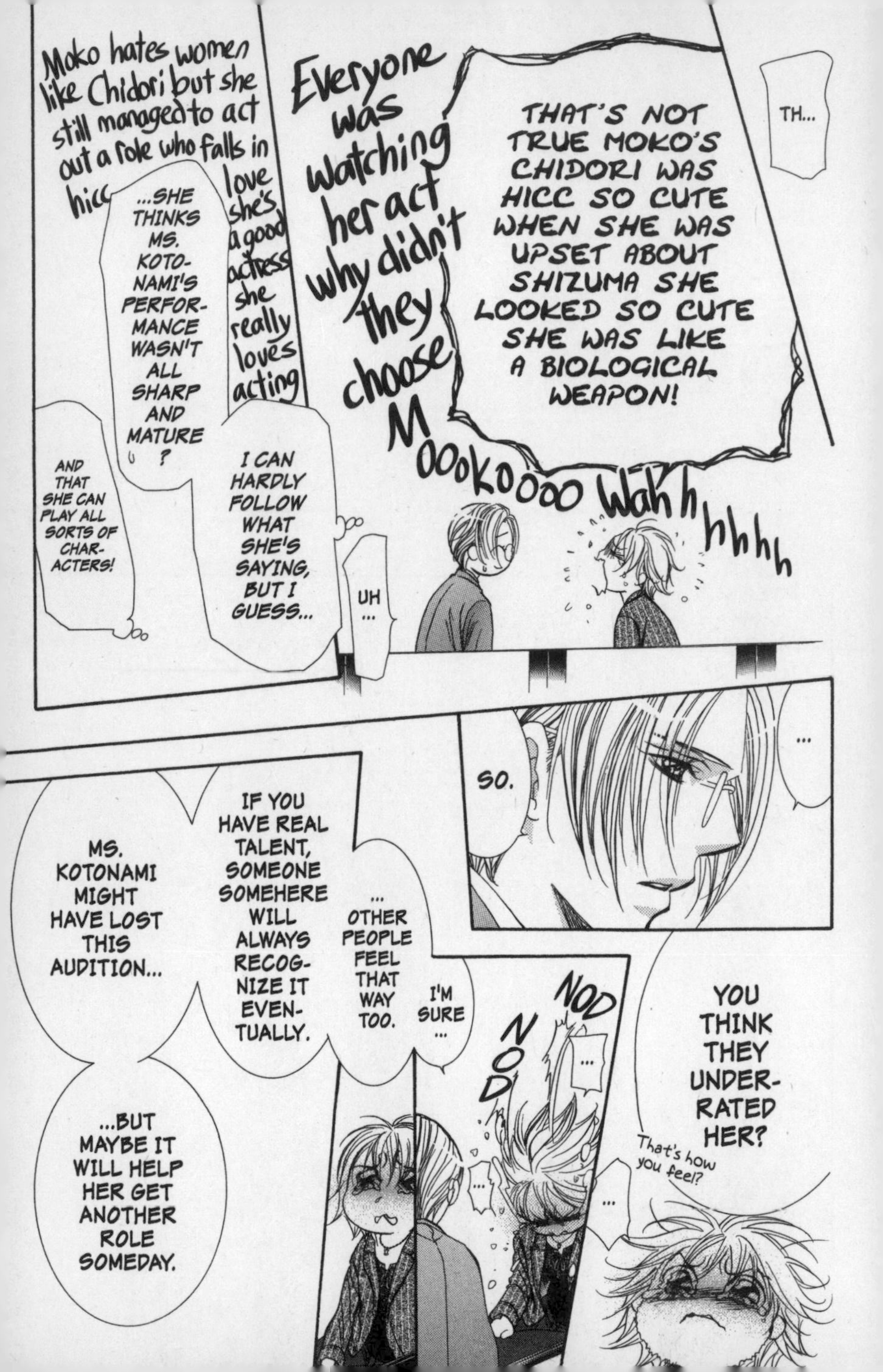
TH...
THAT'S NOT TRUE MOKO'S CHIDORI WAS HICC SO CUTE WHEN SHE WAS UPSET ABOUT SHIZUMA SHE LOOKED SO CUTE SHE WAS LIKE A BIOLOGICAL WEAPON!
Everyone was watching her act why didn't they choose Moooko
Wahhhhhh
Moko hates women like Chidori but she still managed to act out a role who falls in hicc love she's a good actress she really loves acting
UH ...
I CAN HARDLY FOLLOW WHAT SHE'S SAYING, BUT I GUESS...
...SHE THINKS MS. KOTONAMI'S PERFORMANCE WASN'T ALL SHARP AND MATURE?
AND THAT SHE CAN PLAY ALL SORTS OF CHARACTERS!
...
SO.
YOU THINK THEY UNDER-RATED HER?
That's how you feel?
...
NOD
NOD
...
...
I'M SURE ...
... OTHER PEOPLE FEEL THAT WAY TOO.
IF YOU HAVE REAL TALENT, SOMEONE SOMEHERE WILL ALWAYS RECOG-NIZE IT EVEN-TUALLY.
MS. KOTONAMI MIGHT HAVE LOST THIS AUDITION...
...BUT MAYBE IT WILL HELP HER GET ANOTHER ROLE SOMEDAY.

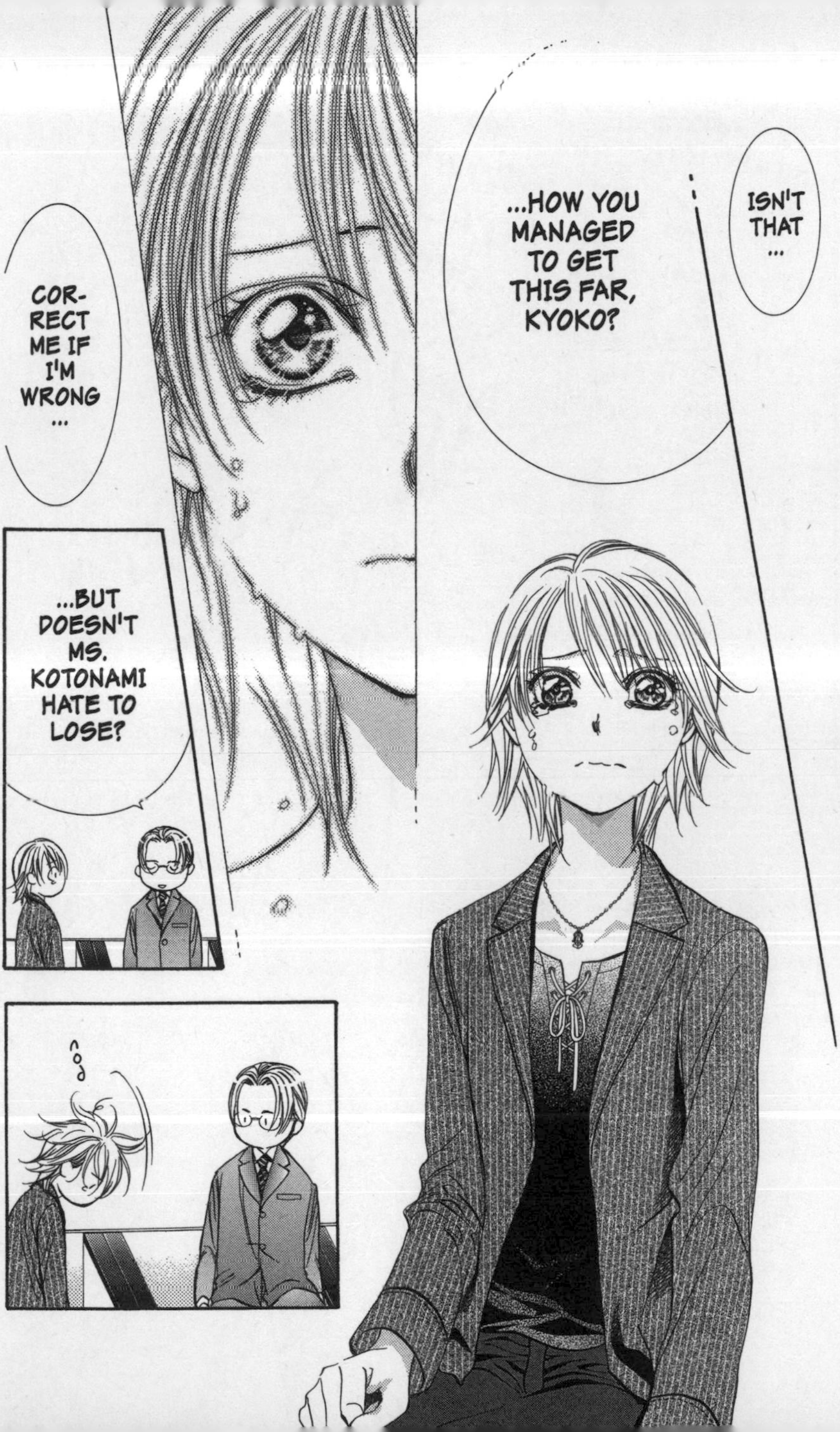
ISN'T THAT ...
...HOW YOU MANAGED TO GET THIS FAR, KYOKO?
COR-RECT ME IF I'M WRONG ...
...BUT DOESN'T MS. KOTONAMI HATE TO LOSE?

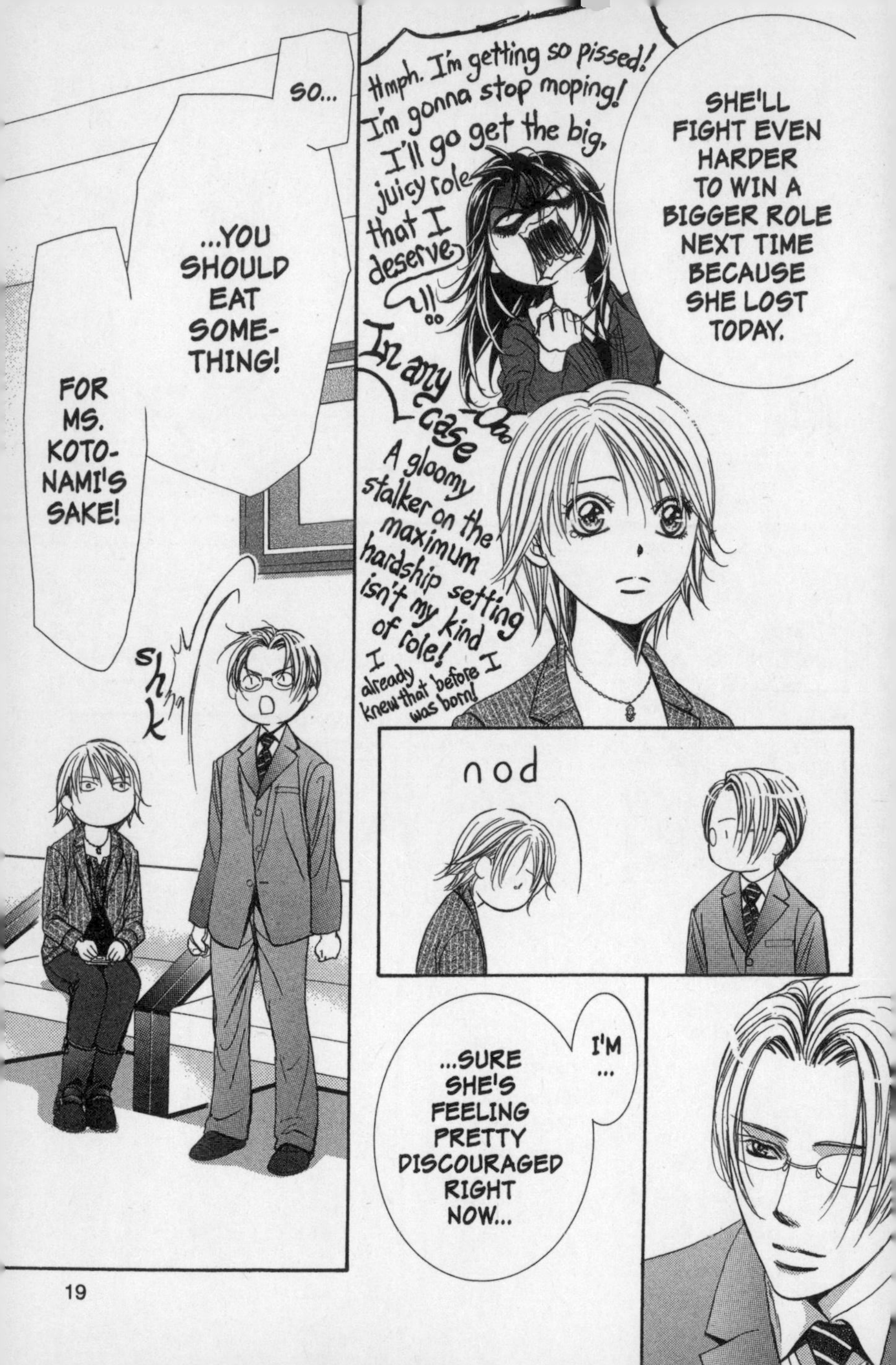
SHE'LL FIGHT EVEN HARDER TO WIN A BIGGER ROLE NEXT TIME BECAUSE SHE LOST TODAY.
Hmph. I'm getting so pissed! I'm gonna stop moping! I'll go get the big, juicy role that I deserve!!
In any case
A gloomy stalker on the maximum hardship setting isn't my kind of role! I already knew that before I was born!
nod
I'M...
...SURE SHE'S FEELING PRETTY DISCOURAGED RIGHT NOW...
SO...
...YOU SHOULD EAT SOMETHING!
FOR MS. KOTONAMI'S SAKE!
shhk

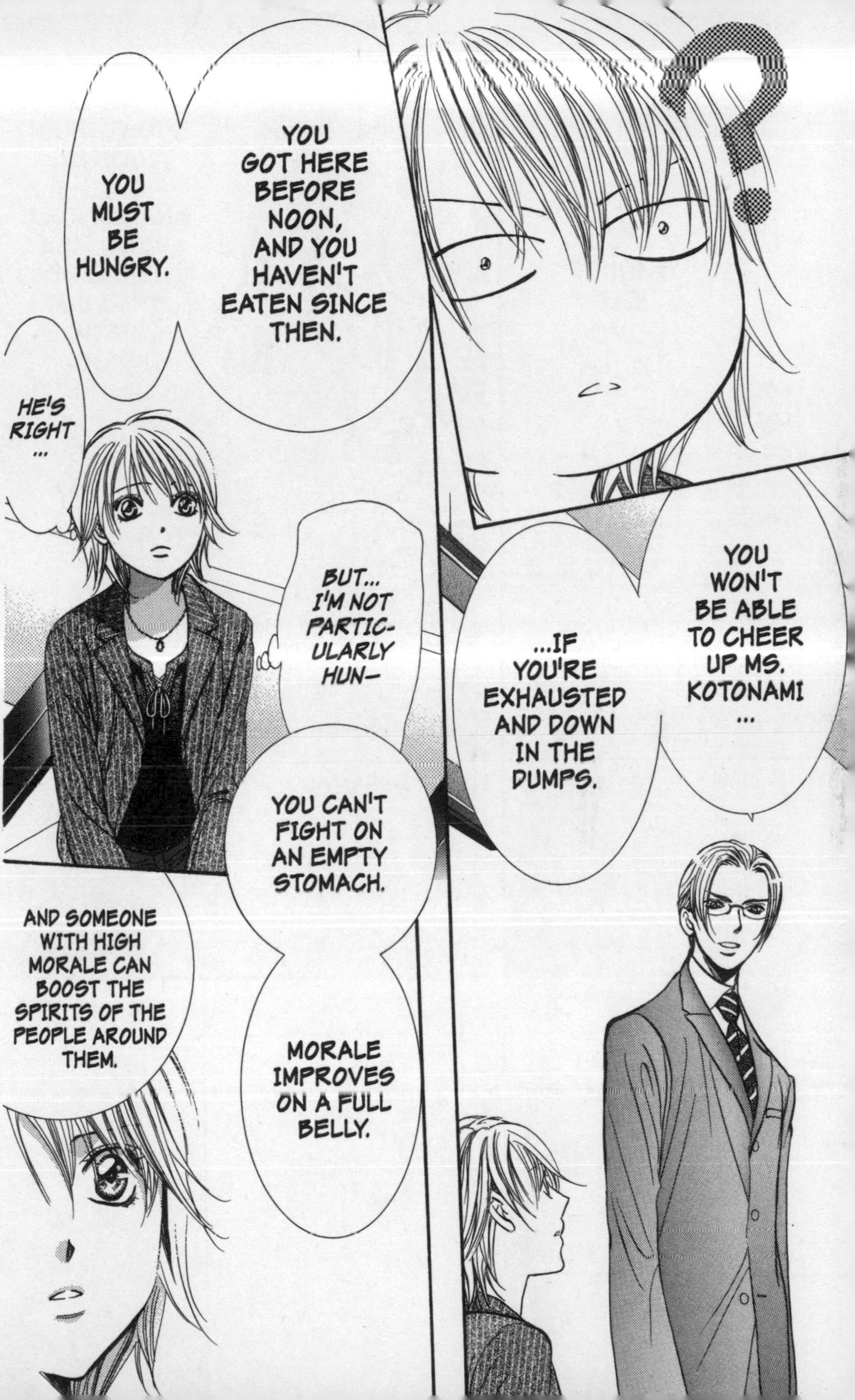
?
YOU GOT HERE BEFORE NOON, AND YOU HAVEN'T EATEN SINCE THEN.
YOU MUST BE HUNGRY.
HE'S RIGHT...
BUT... I'M NOT PARTICULARLY HUN—
YOU WON'T BE ABLE TO CHEER UP MS. KOTONAMI...
...IF YOU'RE EXHAUSTED AND DOWN IN THE DUMPS.
YOU CAN'T FIGHT ON AN EMPTY STOMACH.
MORALE IMPROVES ON A FULL BELLY.
AND SOMEONE WITH HIGH MORALE CAN BOOST THE SPIRITS OF THE PEOPLE AROUND THEM.

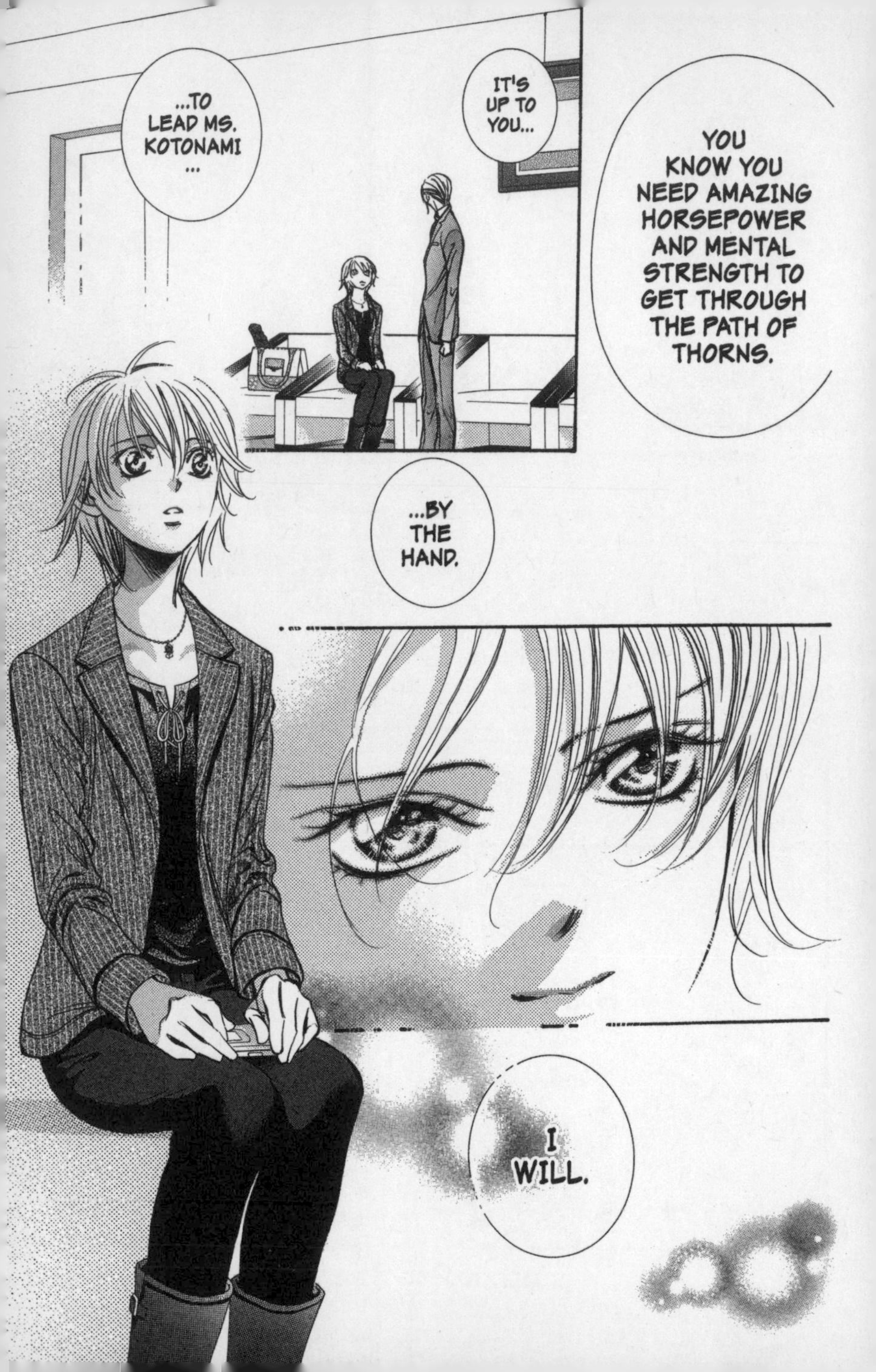
YOU KNOW YOU NEED AMAZING HORSEPOWER AND MENTAL STRENGTH TO GET THROUGH THE PATH OF THORNS.
IT'S UP TO YOU...
...TO LEAD MS. KOTONAMI ...
...BY THE HAND.
I WILL.

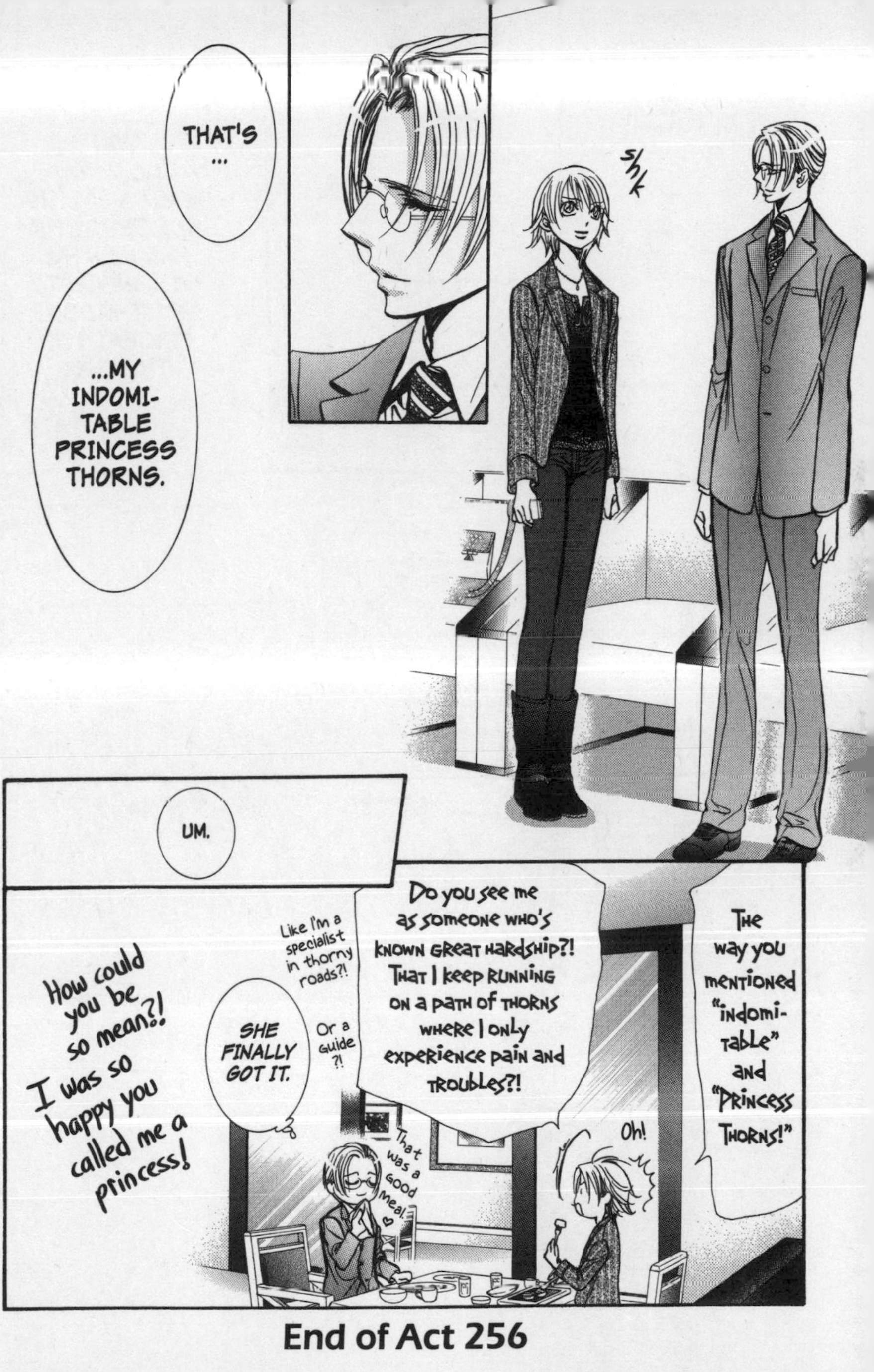
SHK
THAT'S ...
...MY INDOMITABLE PRINCESS THORNS.
UM.
The way you mentioned "indomitable" and "Princess Thorns!"
Oh!
Do you see me as someone who's known great hardship?! That I keep running on a path of thorns where I only experience pain and troubles?!
That was a good meal. ♡
Like I'm a specialist in thorny roads?!
Or a guide?!
SHE FINALLY GOT IT.
How could you be so mean?! I was so happy you called me a princess!

End of Act 256

Mailboxes
Inbox
Search
Edi
Misuzu Soga
Thank you so much
Hello, I went to the shop you told me
about.
Masato Takahashi
So what do you want to do?
Hi, I got in touch with everyone. If you want
to go ahead, I'll arrange everything, so...
airi Ohara
for your flowers
quite a while.
you for sending flowers to the theater...
sumi
thanks! ♪
quite a while.
meant to to email you
Edit
tmp
this spring
useful apps
Satoshi Takagi
Select All
tmp
Flag
tmp
Mark as Read
Cancel
Search
fwip
fwip
fwip
scrolling
Mobile News
Having Trouble with Spam
An Email filtering service can help you
more convenience for the consumer than
Serika Natori
Lovely strawberry sweets
The other day, I went to a confectionery that
even adults can enjoy. The interior was tasteful
Hitoka
Hello (´ ▽`)
Mr. Tsuruga, your advice to me the other day
success! (≧▽≦)
Yuzuha
Do you have time late next month?
Takahashi got touch in with me the
fine with it! Will you be available to
Motoki Kaneya
Hello
I think that'd do regarding that matter
will need some more time to consider
ptt
ptt
ptt
ptt
ptt
ptt
ptt
ptt

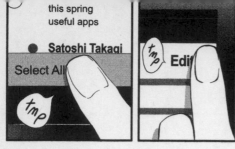

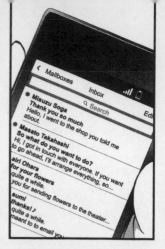

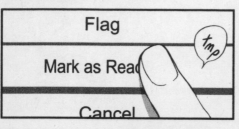

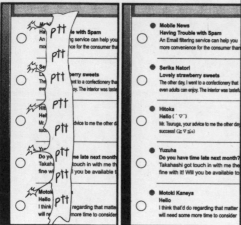

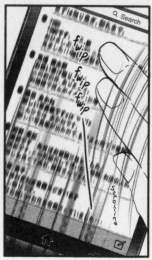

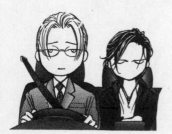

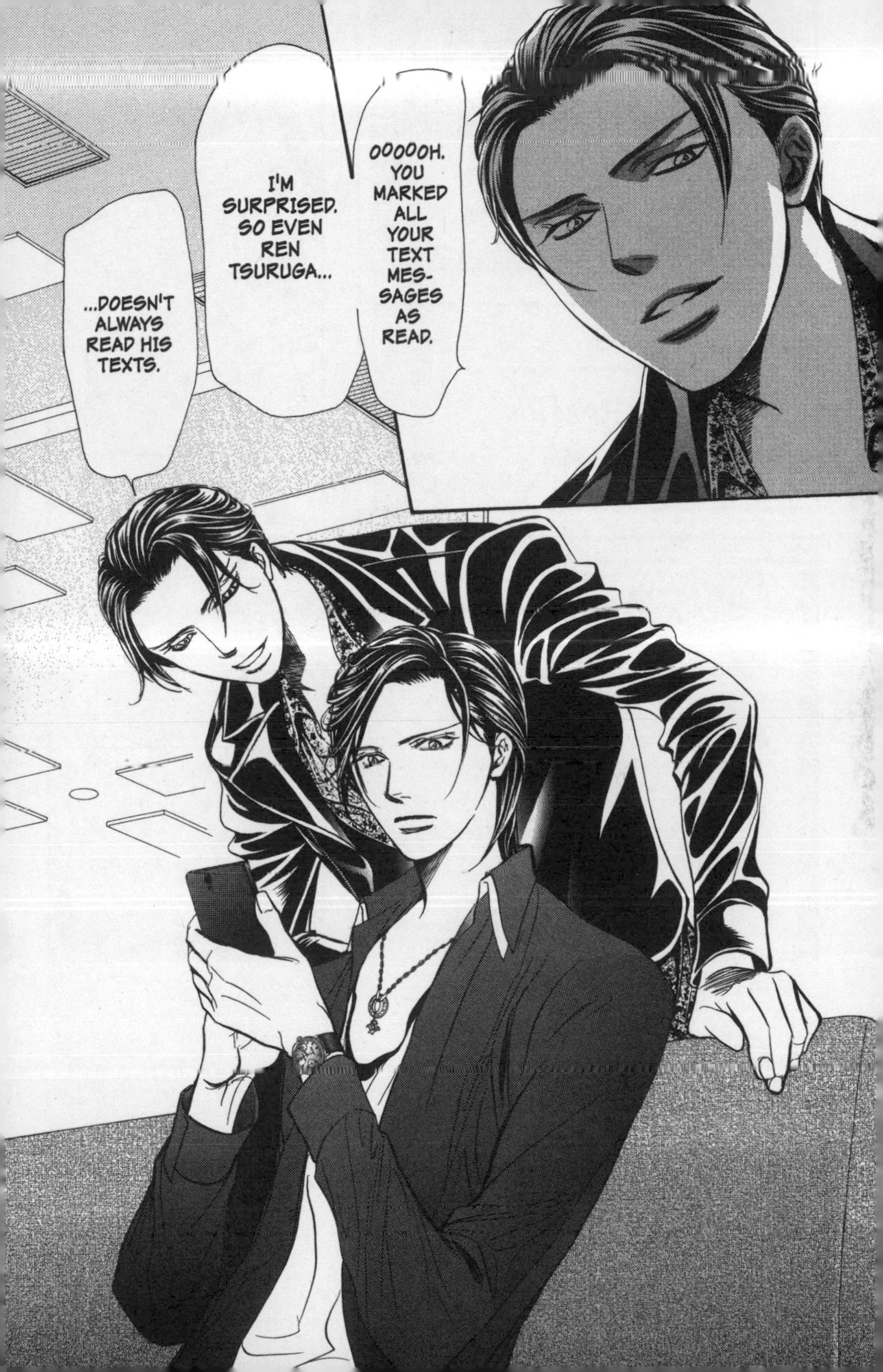
OOOOOH. YOU MARKED ALL YOUR TEXT MES-SAGES AS READ.
I'M SURPRISED. SO EVEN REN TSURUGA...
...DOESN'T ALWAYS READ HIS TEXTS.

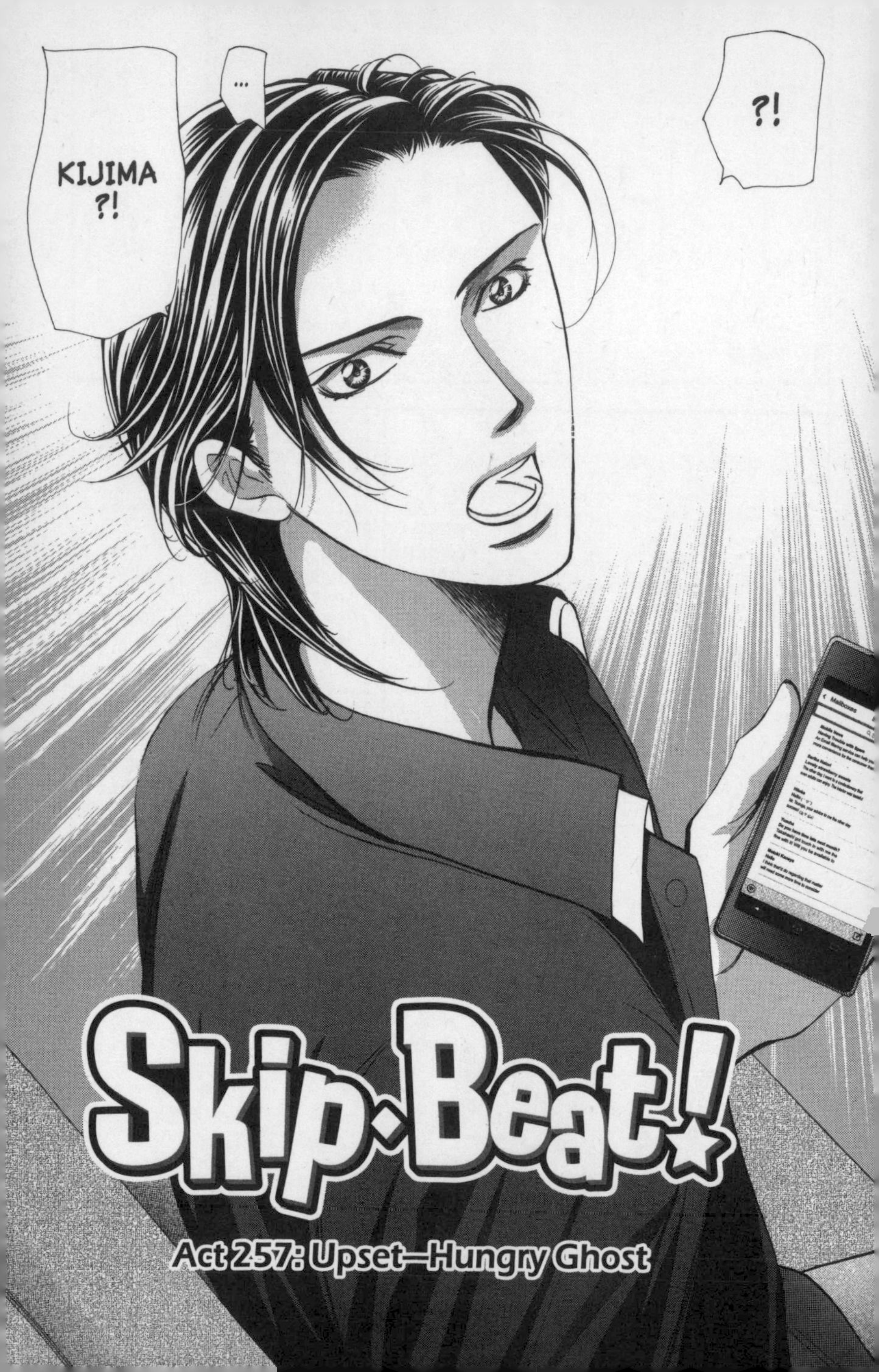
?!
...
KIJIMA ?!
Skip·Beat!
Act 257: Upset—Hungry Ghost

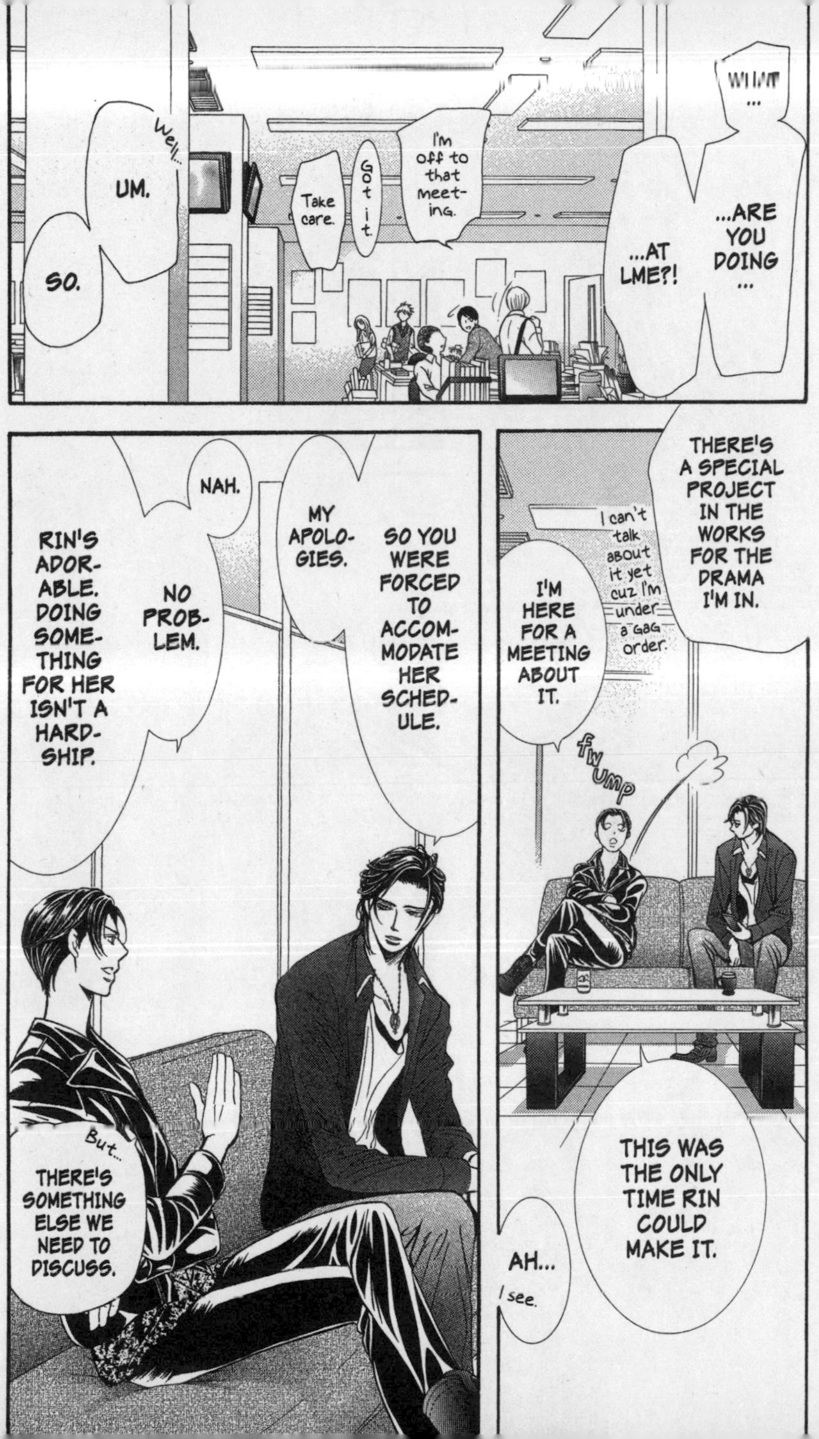
WHAT ...
...ARE YOU DOING ...
...AT LME?!
I'm off to that meet-ing.
Got it.
Take care.
Well...
UM.
SO.
THERE'S A SPECIAL PROJECT IN THE WORKS FOR THE DRAMA I'M IN.
I can't talk about it yet cuz I'm under a gag order.
I'M HERE FOR A MEETING ABOUT IT.
fwump
THIS WAS THE ONLY TIME RIN COULD MAKE IT.
AH...
I see.
SO YOU WERE FORCED TO ACCOM-MODATE HER SCHED-ULE.
MY APOLO-GIES.
NAH.
NO PROB-LEM.
RIN'S ADOR-ABLE. DOING SOME-THING FOR HER ISN'T A HARD-SHIP.
But...
THERE'S SOMETHING ELSE WE NEED TO DISCUSS.

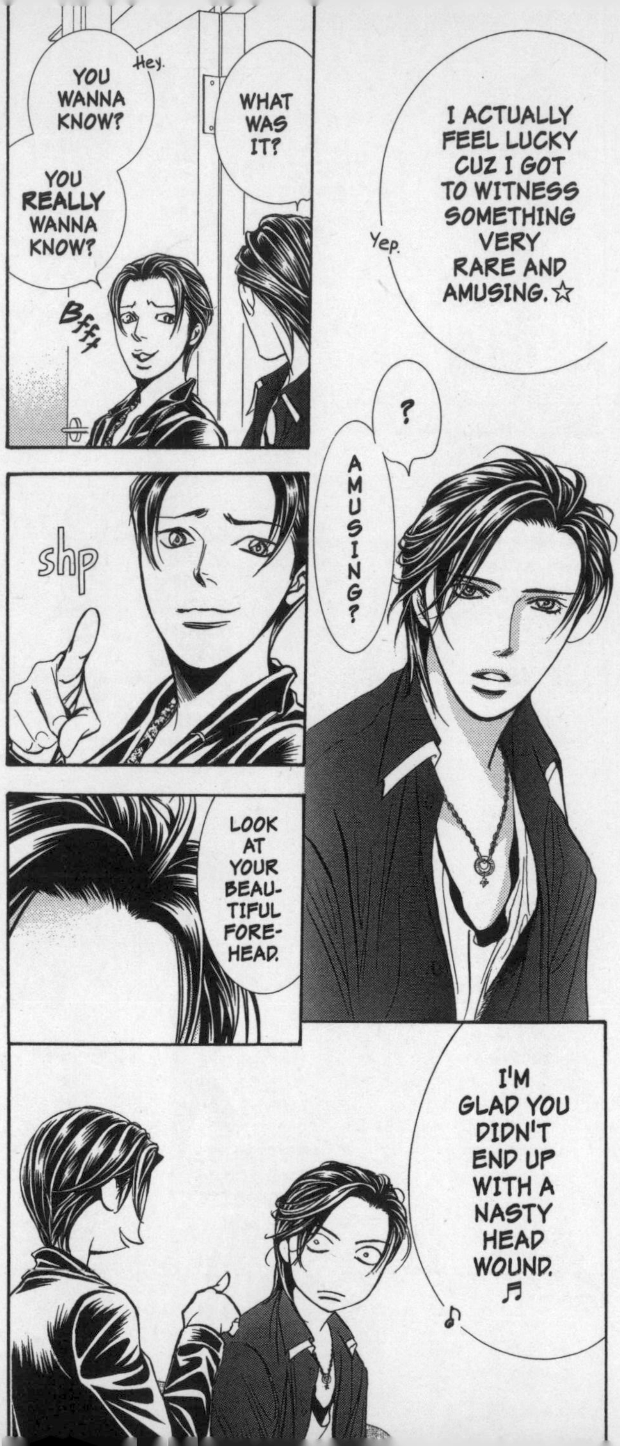
Yep.
I ACTUALLY FEEL LUCKY CUZ I GOT TO WITNESS SOMETHING VERY RARE AND AMUSING.☆
?
AMUSING?
WHAT WAS IT?
Hey.
YOU WANNA KNOW?
YOU REALLY WANNA KNOW?
Bfff
shp
LOOK AT YOUR BEAU-TIFUL FORE-HEAD.
I'M GLAD YOU DIDN'T END UP WITH A NASTY HEAD WOUND. ♬
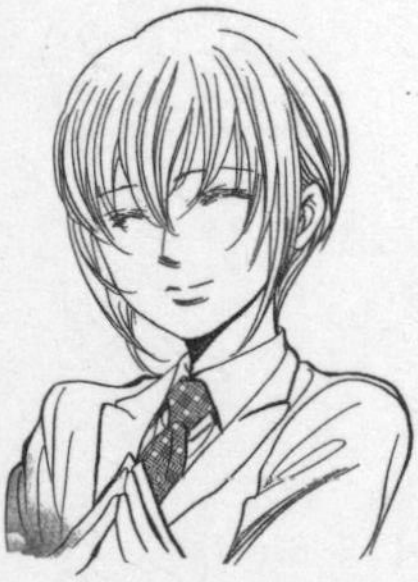

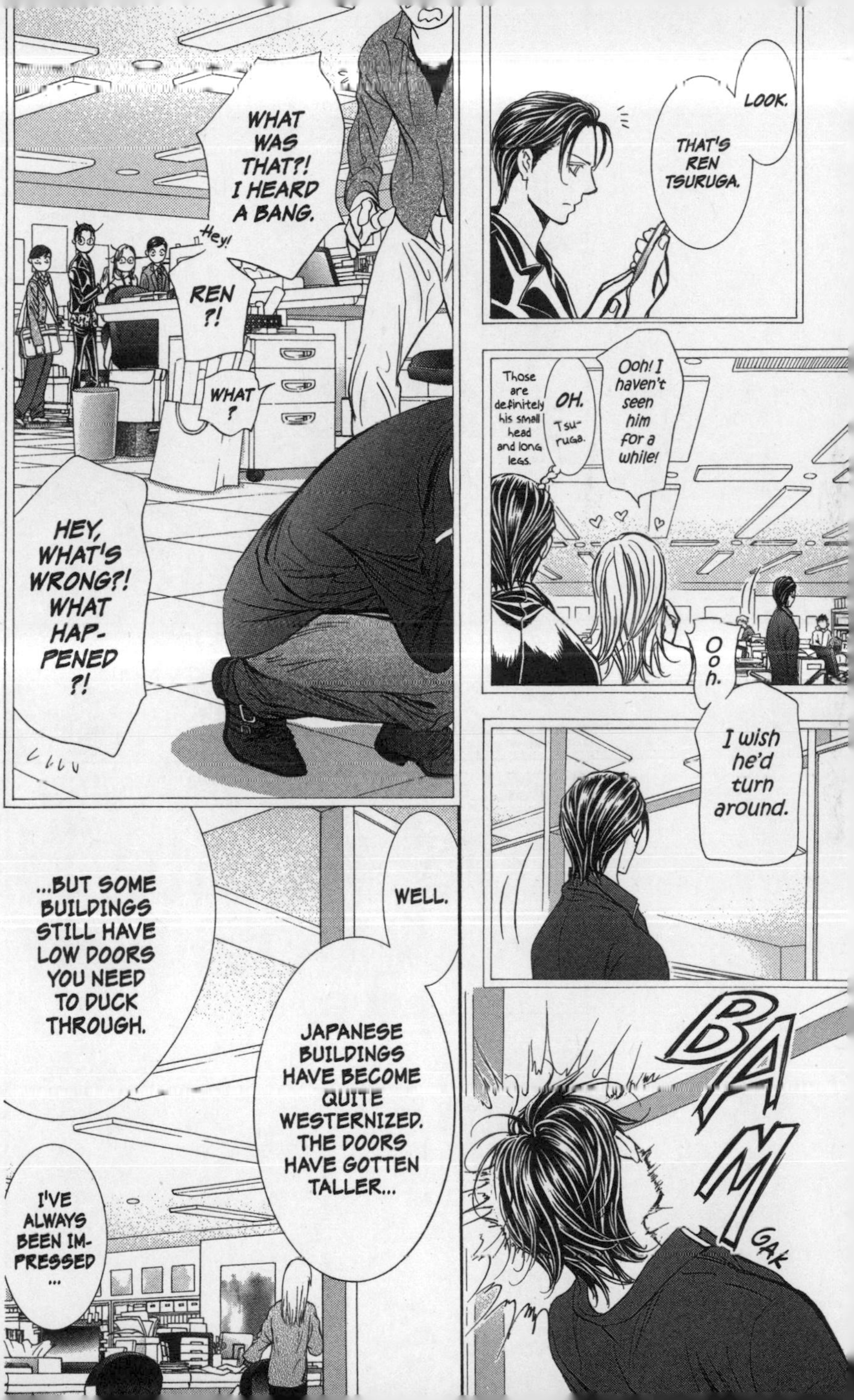
LOOK.
THAT'S REN TSURUGA.
Ooh! I haven't seen him for a while!
OH.
Tsu-ruga.
Those are definitely his small head and long legs.
Ooh.
I wish he'd turn around.
BAM
GAK
WHAT WAS THAT?! I HEARD A BANG.
Hey!
REN ?!
WHAT ?
HEY, WHAT'S WRONG?! WHAT HAP-PENED ?!
WELL.
JAPANESE BUILDINGS HAVE BECOME QUITE WESTERNIZED. THE DOORS HAVE GOTTEN TALLER...
...BUT SOME BUILDINGS STILL HAVE LOW DOORS YOU NEED TO DUCK THROUGH.
I'VE ALWAYS BEEN IM-PRESSED ...

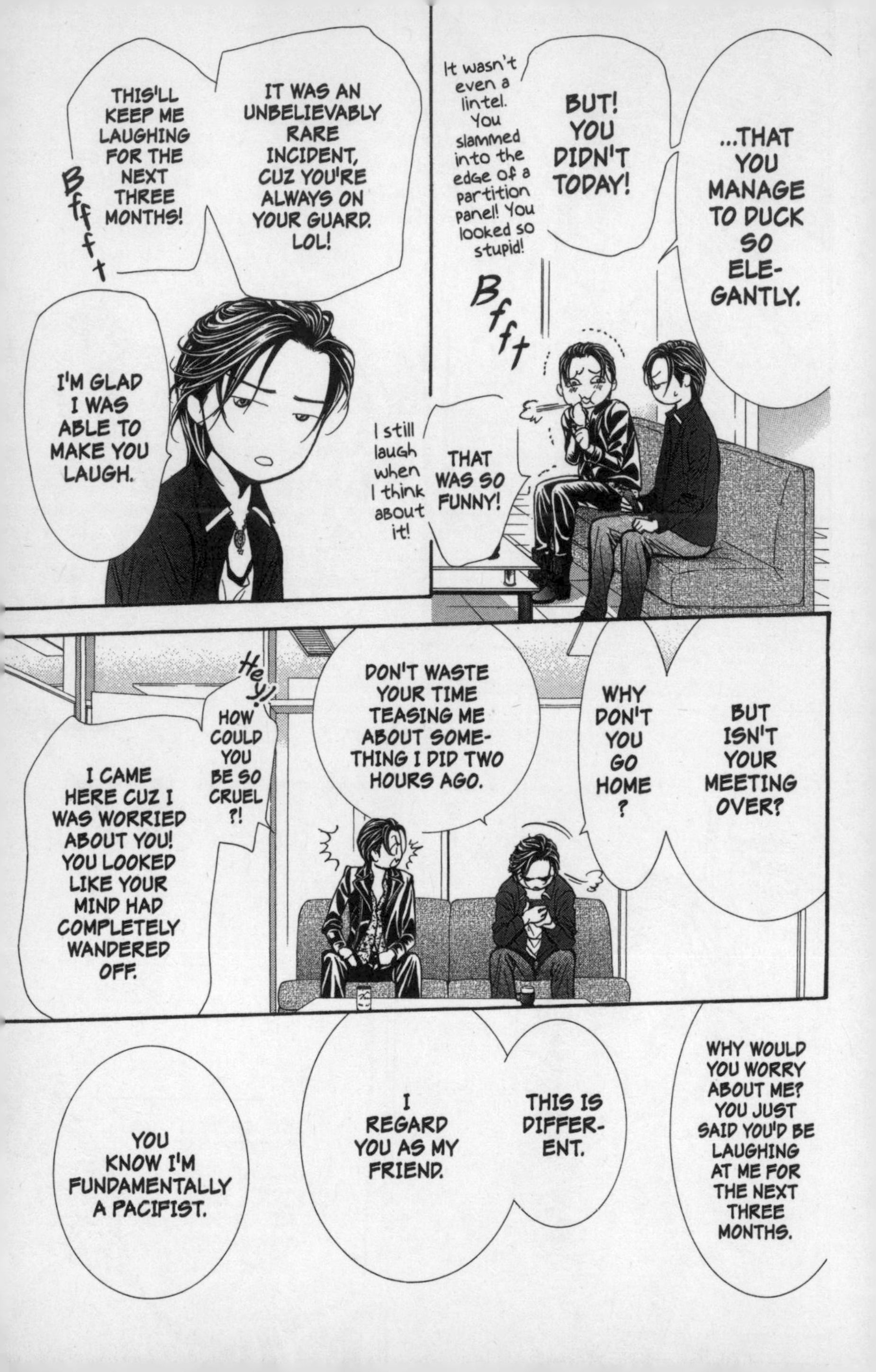
...THAT YOU MANAGE TO DUCK SO ELEGANTLY.
BUT! YOU DIDN'T TODAY!
It wasn't even a lintel. You slammed into the edge of a partition panel! You looked so stupid!
Bffft
THAT WAS SO FUNNY!
I still laugh when I think about it!
IT WAS AN UNBELIEVABLY RARE INCIDENT, CUZ YOU'RE ALWAYS ON YOUR GUARD. LOL!
THIS'LL KEEP ME LAUGHING FOR THE NEXT THREE MONTHS!
Bffft
I'M GLAD I WAS ABLE TO MAKE YOU LAUGH.
BUT ISN'T YOUR MEETING OVER?
WHY DON'T YOU GO HOME?
DON'T WASTE YOUR TIME TEASING ME ABOUT SOMETHING I DID TWO HOURS AGO.
Hey!
HOW COULD YOU BE SO CRUEL?!
I CAME HERE CUZ I WAS WORRIED ABOUT YOU! YOU LOOKED LIKE YOUR MIND HAD COMPLETELY WANDERED OFF.
WHY WOULD YOU WORRY ABOUT ME? YOU JUST SAID YOU'D BE LAUGHING AT ME FOR THE NEXT THREE MONTHS.
THIS IS DIFFERENT.
I REGARD YOU AS MY FRIEND.
YOU KNOW I'M FUNDAMENTALLY A PACIFIST.

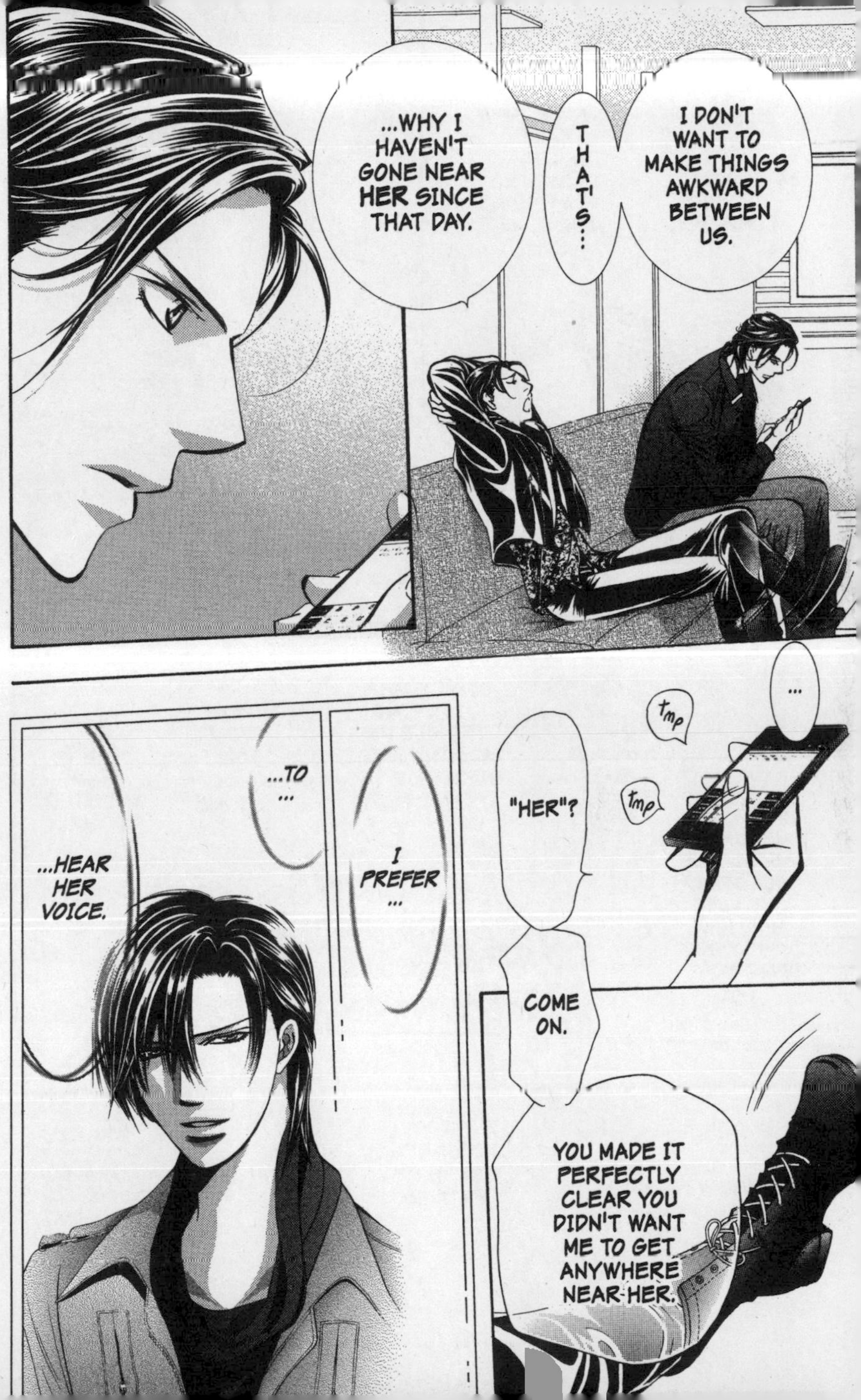

I DON'T WANT TO MAKE THINGS AWKWARD BETWEEN US.
THAT'S...
...WHY I HAVEN'T GONE NEAR HER SINCE THAT DAY.
...
tmp
tmp
"HER"?
COME ON.
YOU MADE IT PERFECTLY CLEAR YOU DIDN'T WANT ME TO GET ANYWHERE NEAR HER.
I PREFER...
...TO...
...HEAR HER VOICE.

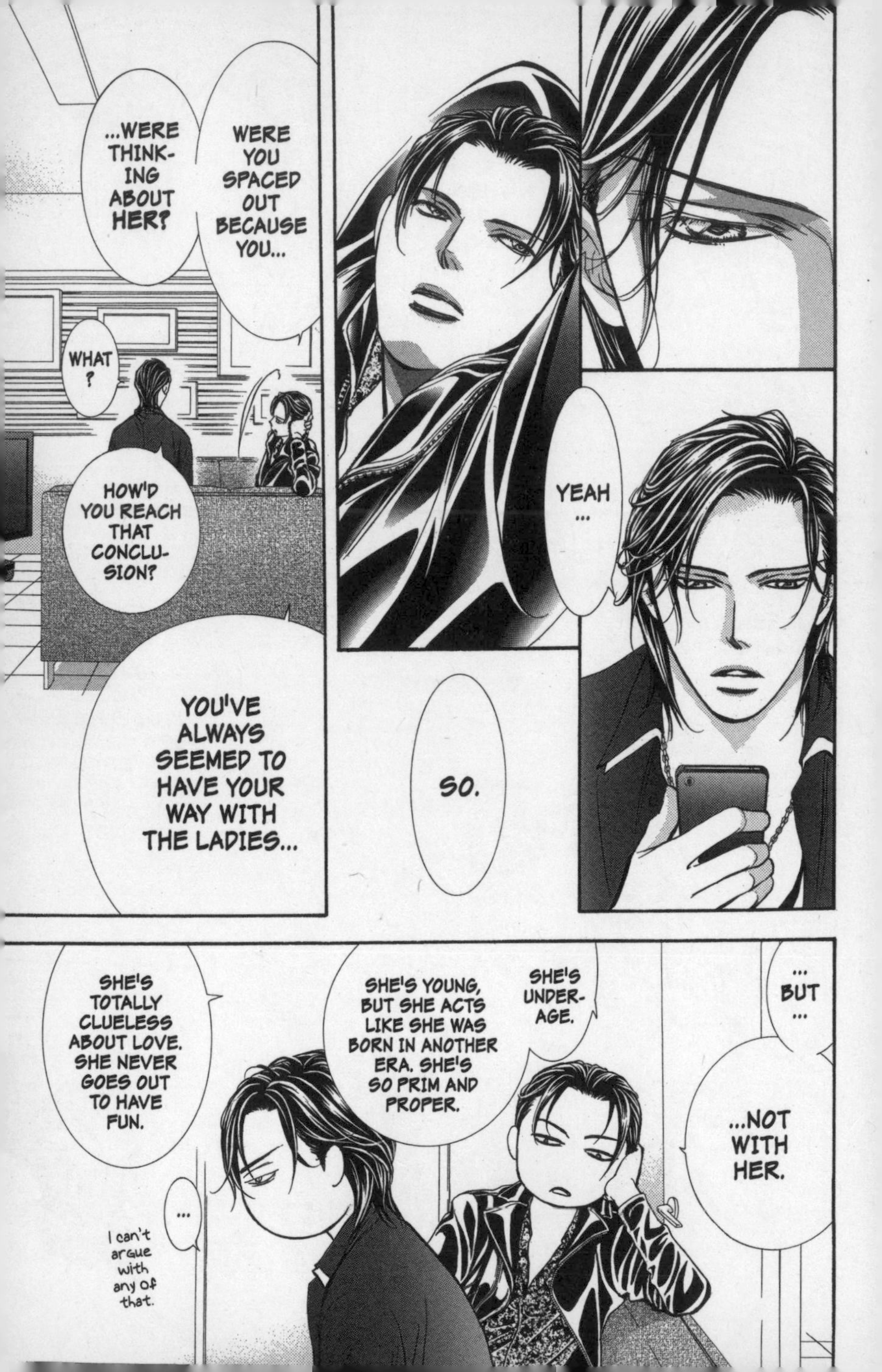
YEAH ...
SO.
WERE YOU SPACED OUT BECAUSE YOU...
...WERE THINKING ABOUT HER?
WHAT?
HOW'D YOU REACH THAT CONCLUSION?
YOU'VE ALWAYS SEEMED TO HAVE YOUR WAY WITH THE LADIES...
... BUT ...
...NOT WITH HER.
SHE'S UNDERAGE.
SHE'S YOUNG, BUT SHE ACTS LIKE SHE WAS BORN IN ANOTHER ERA. SHE'S SO PRIM AND PROPER.
SHE'S TOTALLY CLUELESS ABOUT LOVE. SHE NEVER GOES OUT TO HAVE FUN.
...
I can't argue with any of that.

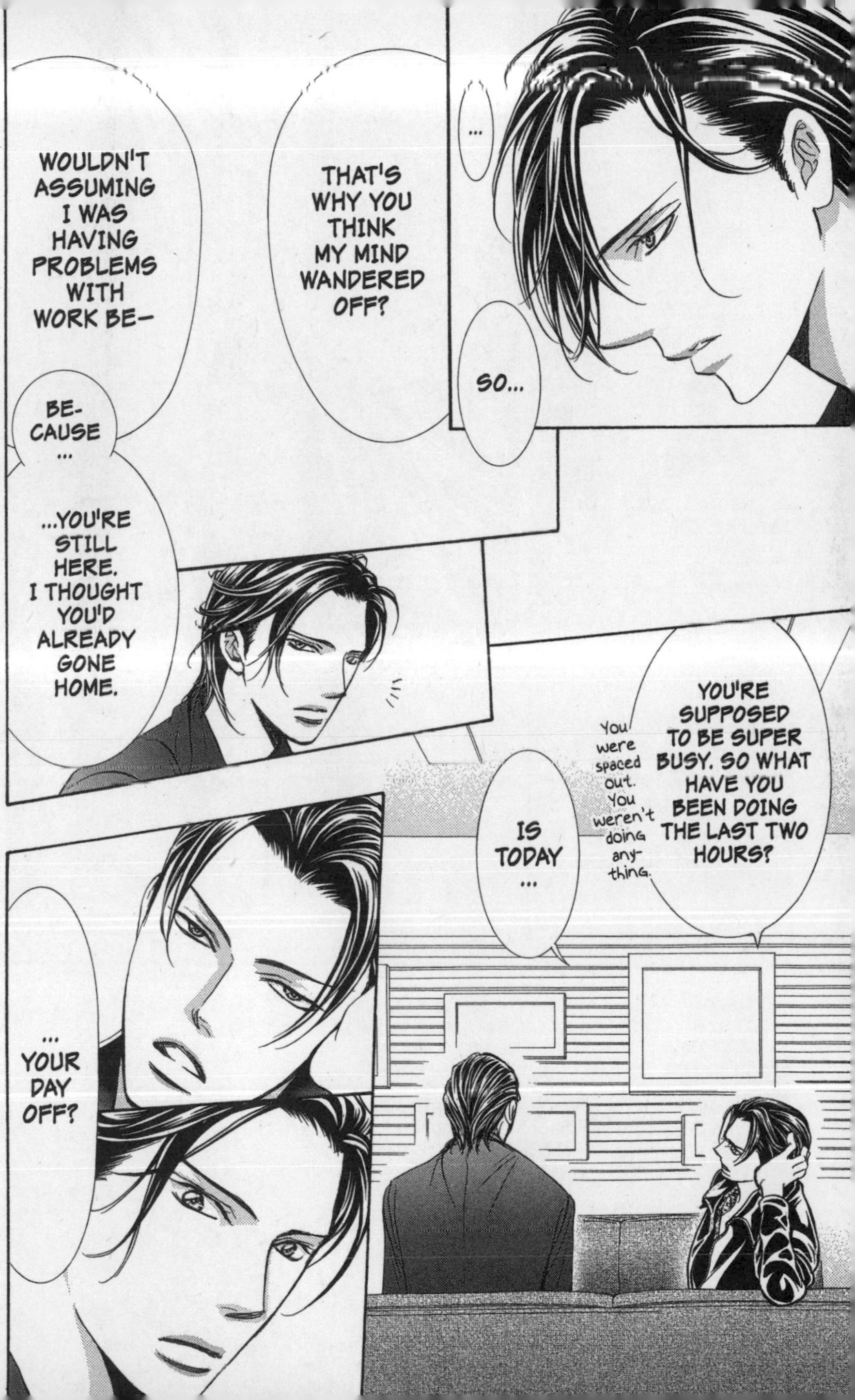
...
SO...
THAT'S WHY YOU THINK MY MIND WANDERED OFF?
WOULDN'T ASSUMING I WAS HAVING PROBLEMS WITH WORK BE—
BE-CAUSE ...
...YOU'RE STILL HERE. I THOUGHT YOU'D ALREADY GONE HOME.
YOU'RE SUPPOSED TO BE SUPER BUSY. SO WHAT HAVE YOU BEEN DOING THE LAST TWO HOURS?
You were spaced out. You weren't doing any-thing.
IS TODAY ...
... YOUR DAY OFF?

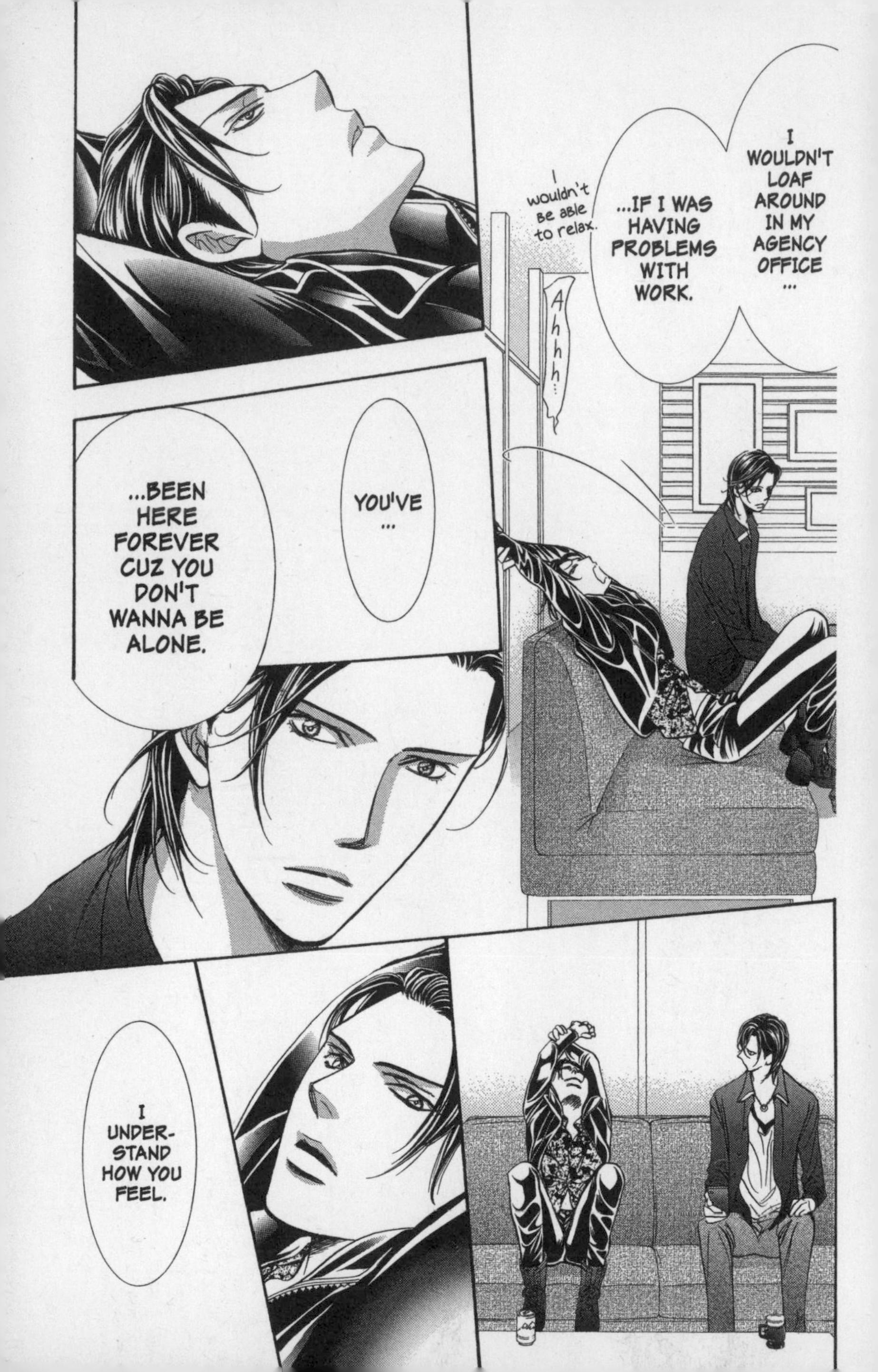
I WOULDN'T LOAF AROUND IN MY AGENCY OFFICE ...
...IF I WAS HAVING PROBLEMS WITH WORK.
I wouldn't be able to relax.
Ahhhh...
YOU'VE ...
...BEEN HERE FOREVER CUZ YOU DON'T WANNA BE ALONE.
I UNDER-STAND HOW YOU FEEL.

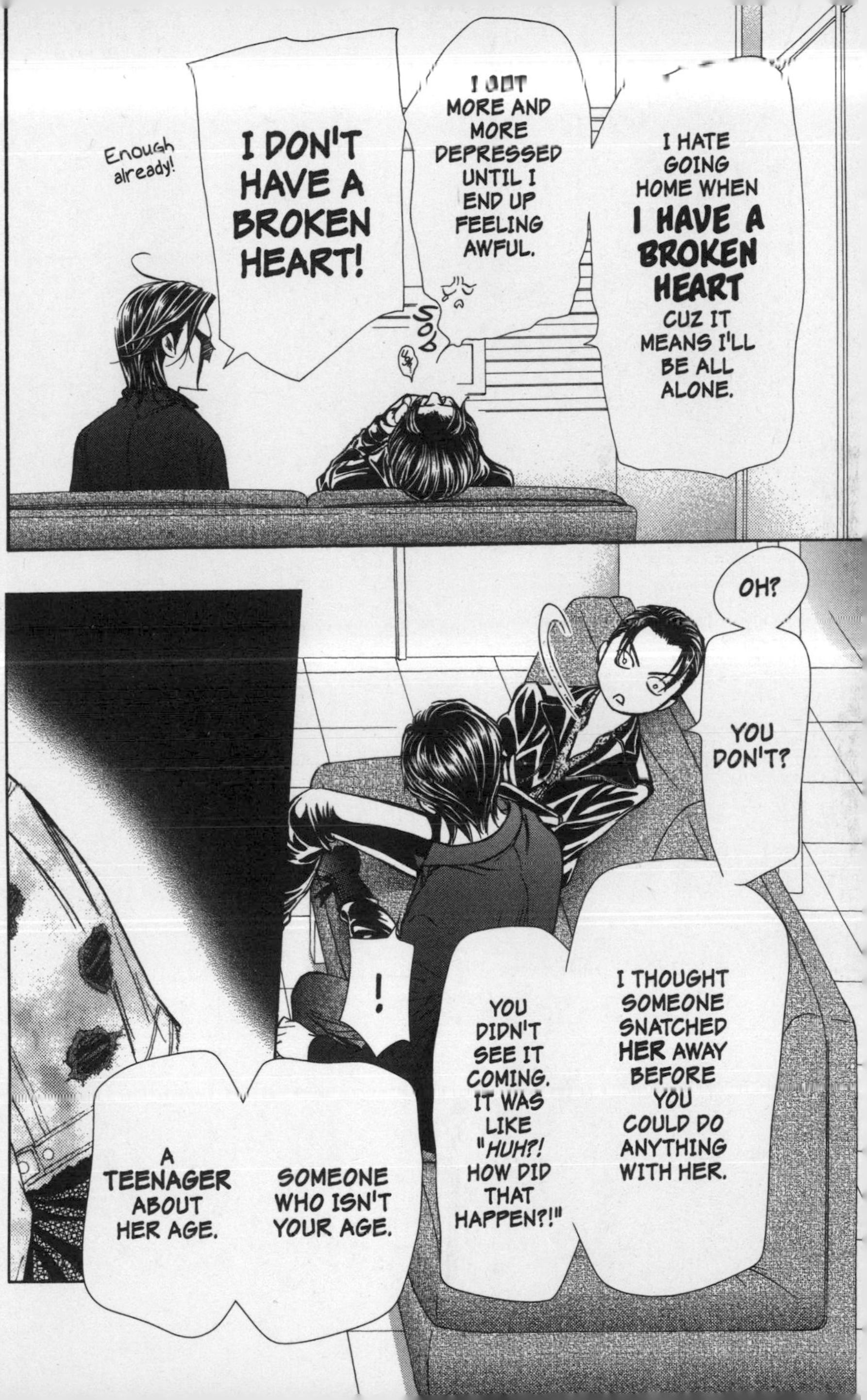
I HATE GOING HOME WHEN I HAVE A BROKEN HEART CUZ IT MEANS I'LL BE ALL ALONE.
I GOT MORE AND MORE DEPRESSED UNTIL I END UP FEELING AWFUL.
SOB
I DON'T HAVE A BROKEN HEART!
Enough already!
OH?
YOU DON'T?
I THOUGHT SOMEONE SNATCHED HER AWAY BEFORE YOU COULD DO ANYTHING WITH HER.
YOU DIDN'T SEE IT COMING. IT WAS LIKE "HUH?! HOW DID THAT HAPPEN?!"
!
SOMEONE WHO ISN'T YOUR AGE.
A TEENAGER ABOUT HER AGE.

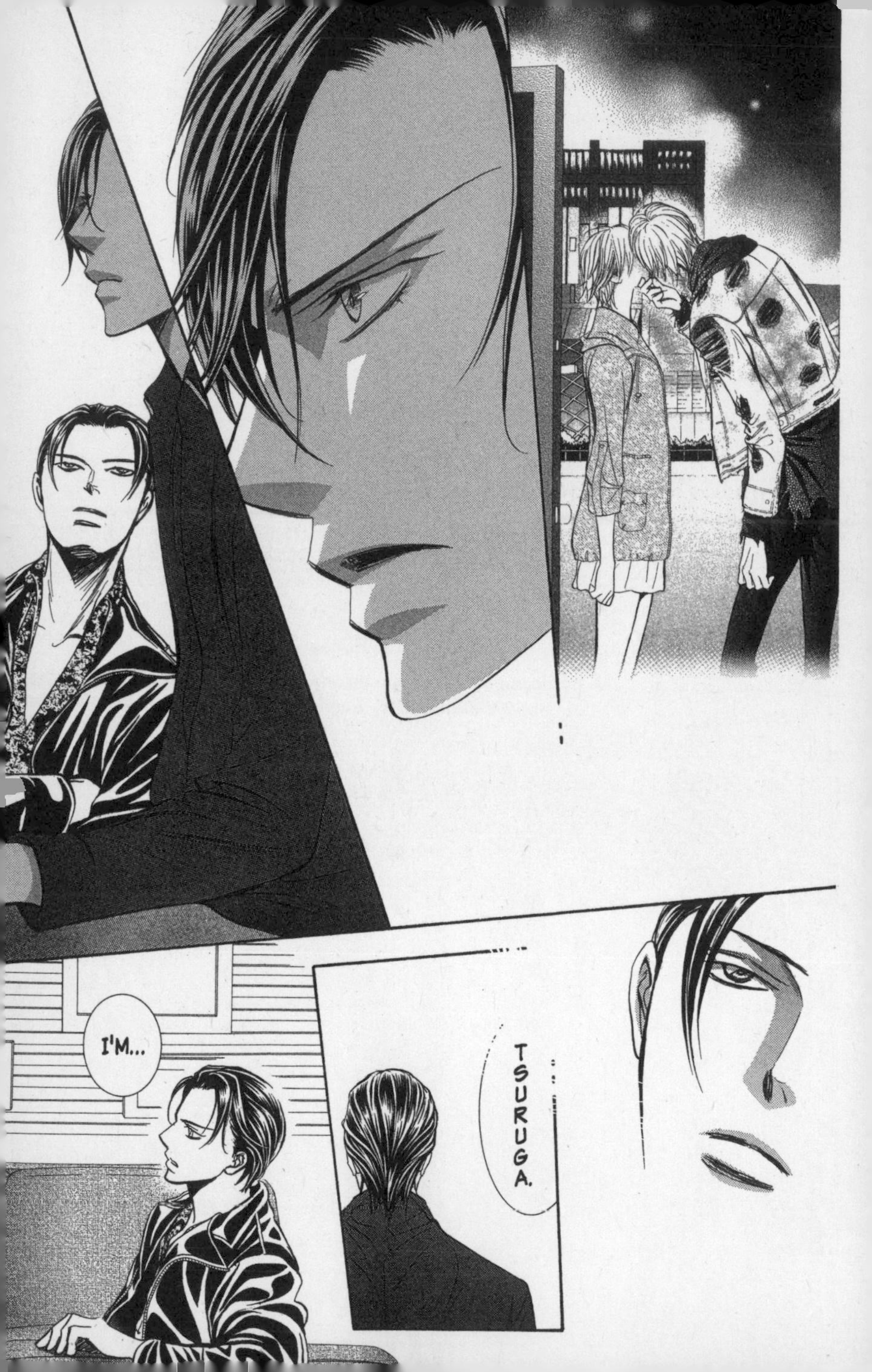
TSURUGA.
I'M...

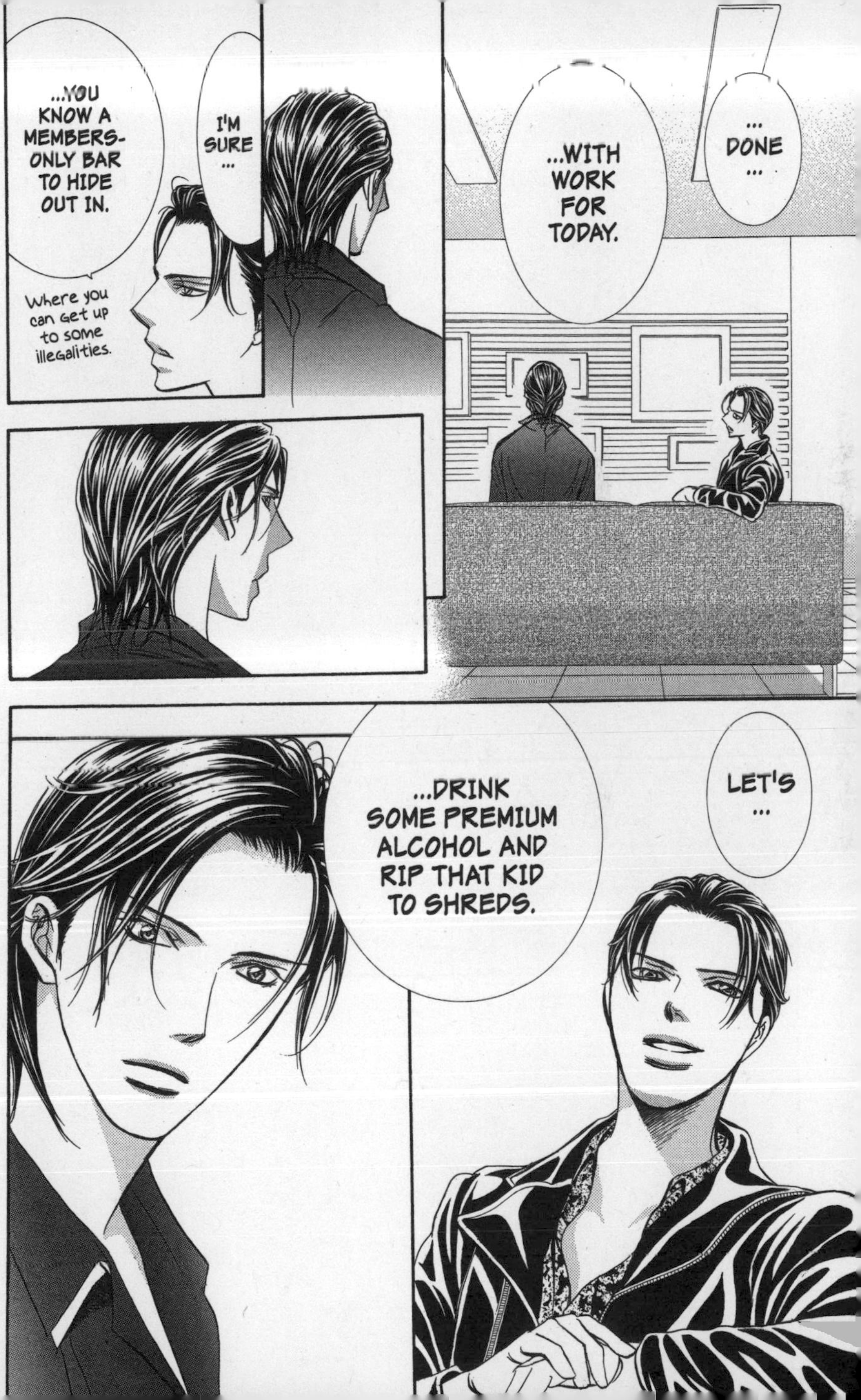
...DONE...
...WITH WORK FOR TODAY.
I'M SURE...
...YOU KNOW A MEMBERS-ONLY BAR TO HIDE OUT IN.
Where you can get up to some illegalities.
LET'S...
...DRINK SOME PREMIUM ALCOHOL AND RIP THAT KID TO SHREDS.

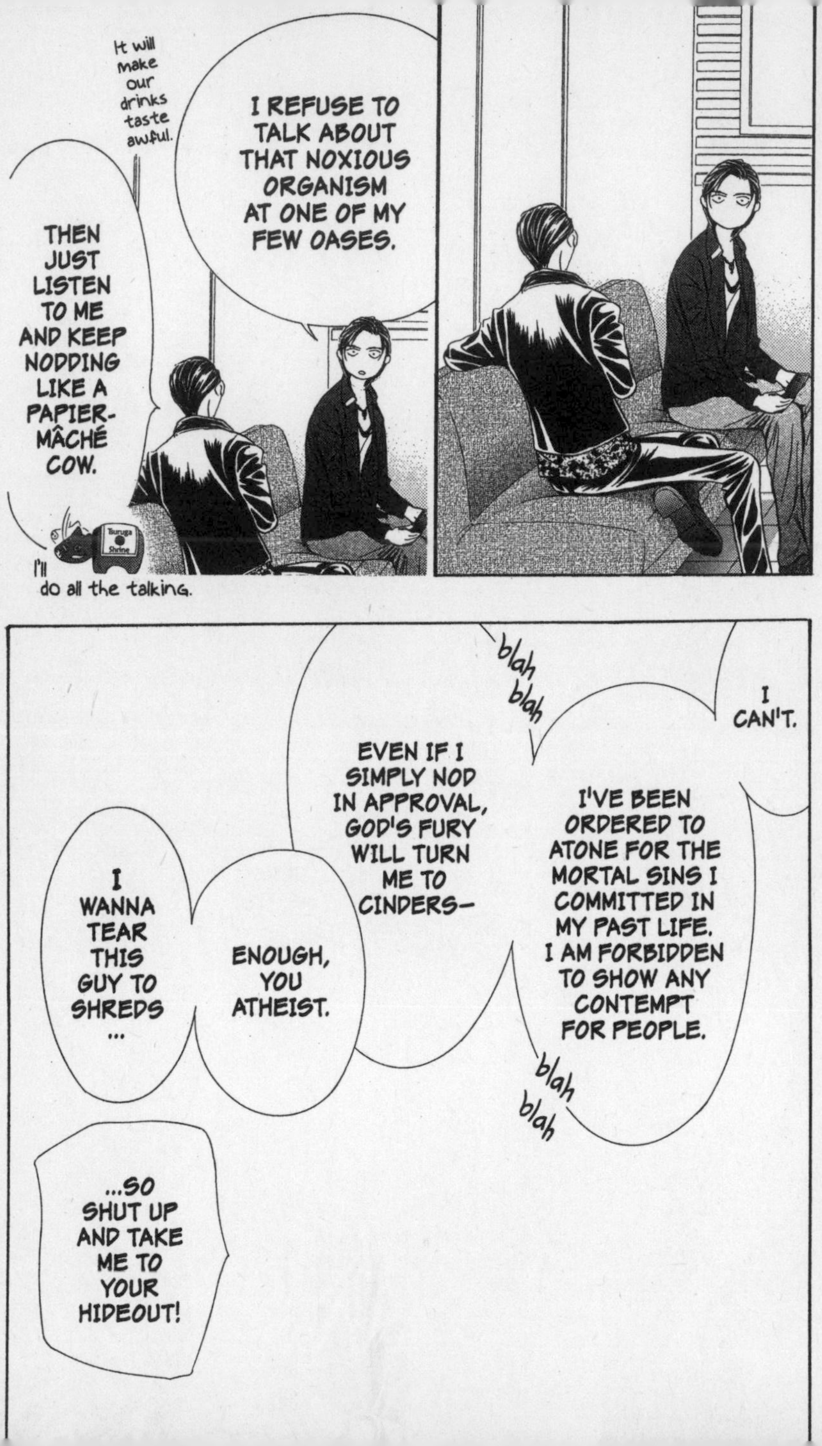

I REFUSE TO TALK ABOUT THAT NOXIOUS ORGANISM AT ONE OF MY FEW OASES.
It will make our drinks taste awful.
THEN JUST LISTEN TO ME AND KEEP NODDING LIKE A PAPIER-MÂCHÉ COW.
Tsuruga Shrine
I'll do all the talking.
I CAN'T.
blah blah
I'VE BEEN ORDERED TO ATONE FOR THE MORTAL SINS I COMMITTED IN MY PAST LIFE. I AM FORBIDDEN TO SHOW ANY CONTEMPT FOR PEOPLE.
EVEN IF I SIMPLY NOD IN APPROVAL, GOD'S FURY WILL TURN ME TO CINDERS—
blah blah
ENOUGH, YOU ATHEIST.
I WANNA TEAR THIS GUY TO SHREDS...
...SO SHUT UP AND TAKE ME TO YOUR HIDEOUT!

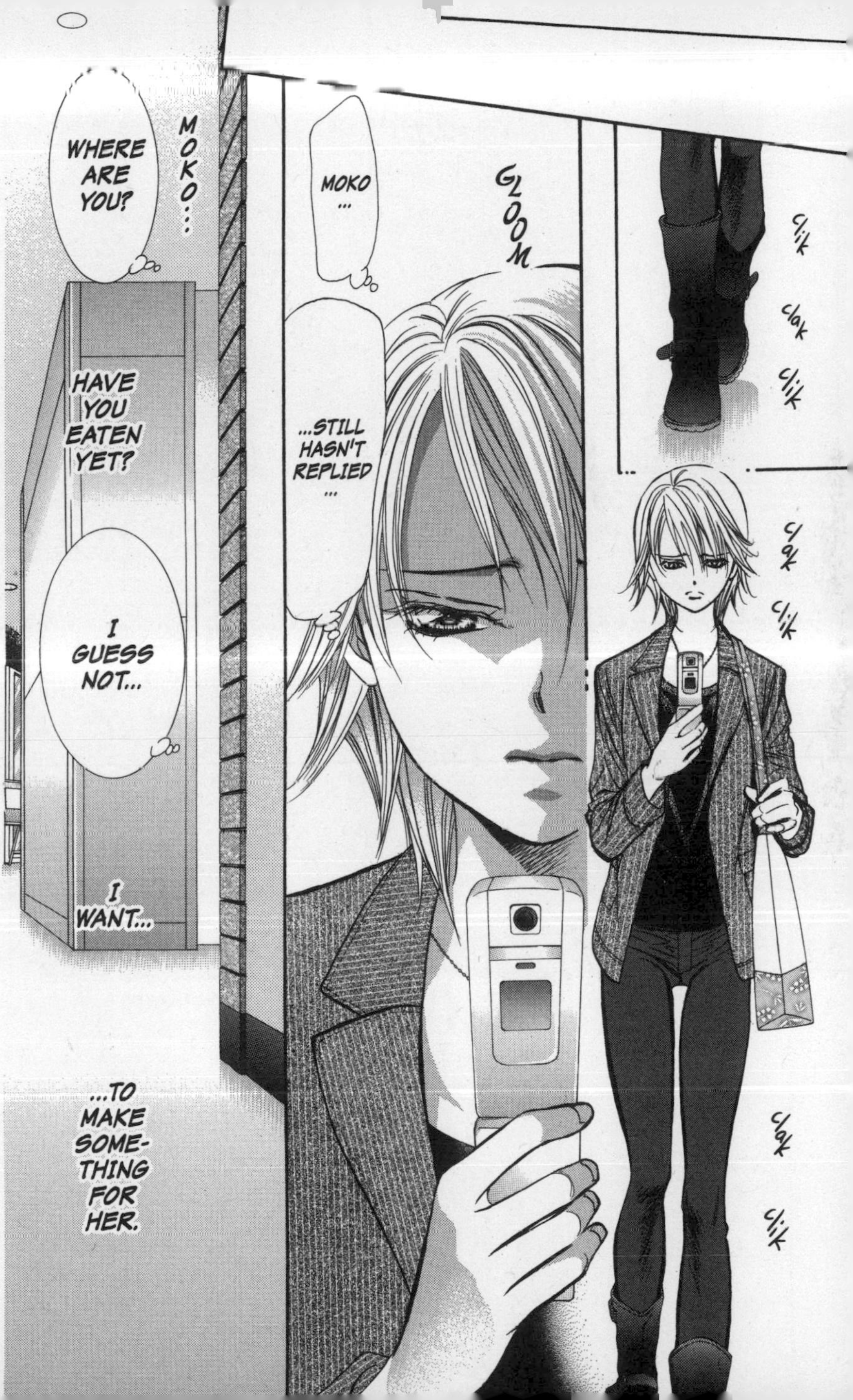
clik
clak
clik
clak
clik
clak
clik
GLOOM
MOKO ...
...STILL HASN'T REPLIED ...
MOKO...
WHERE ARE YOU?
HAVE YOU EATEN YET?
I GUESS NOT...
I WANT...
...TO MAKE SOMETHING FOR HER.

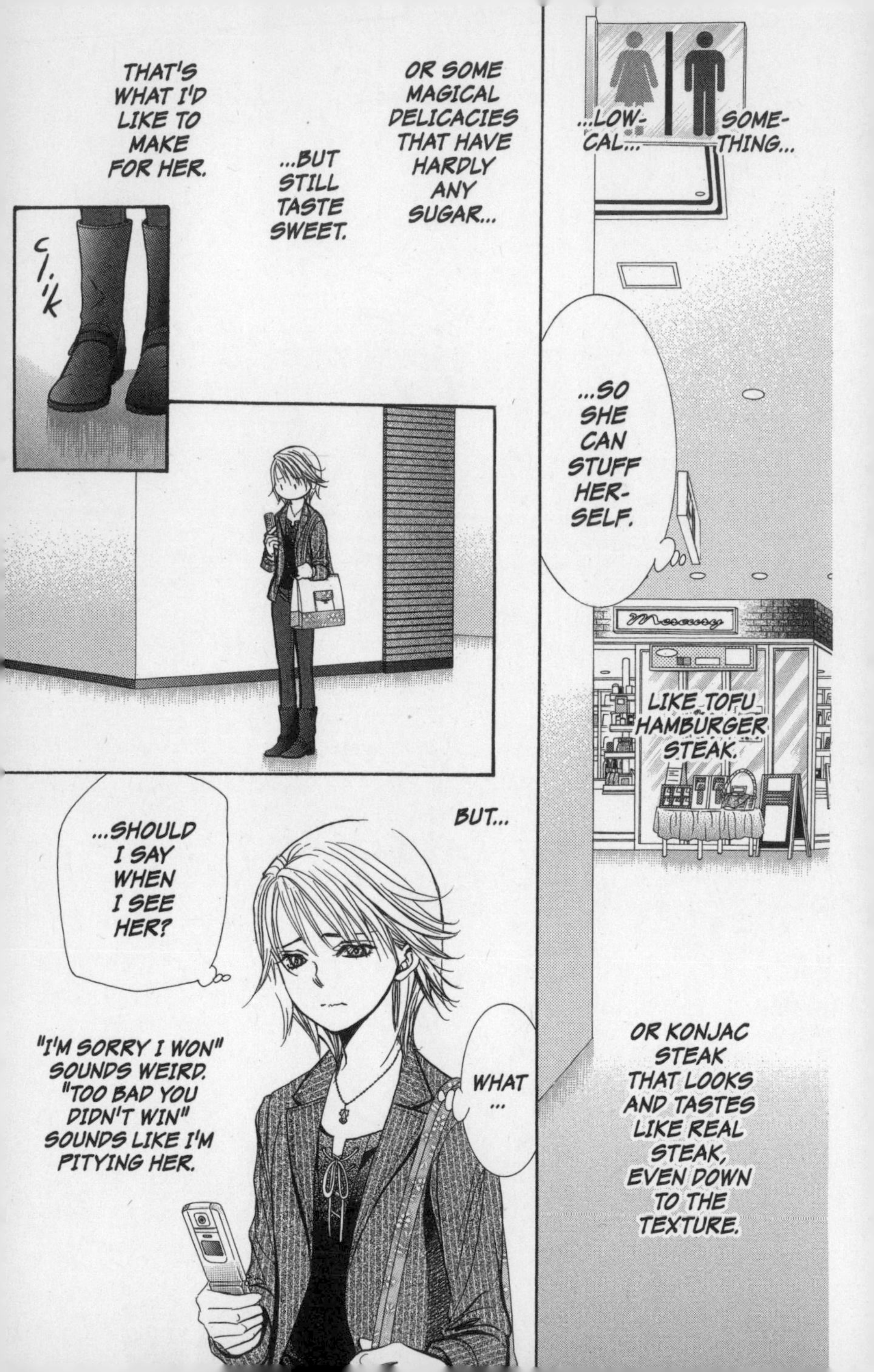
...LOW-CAL...
SOME-THING...
...SO SHE CAN STUFF HER-SELF.
LIKE TOFU HAMBURGER STEAK.
OR KONJAC STEAK THAT LOOKS AND TASTES LIKE REAL STEAK, EVEN DOWN TO THE TEXTURE.
OR SOME MAGICAL DELICACIES THAT HAVE HARDLY ANY SUGAR...
...BUT STILL TASTE SWEET.
THAT'S WHAT I'D LIKE TO MAKE FOR HER.
clik
BUT...
WHAT...
...SHOULD I SAY WHEN I SEE HER?
"I'M SORRY I WON" SOUNDS WEIRD. "TOO BAD YOU DIDN'T WIN" SOUNDS LIKE I'M PITYING HER.

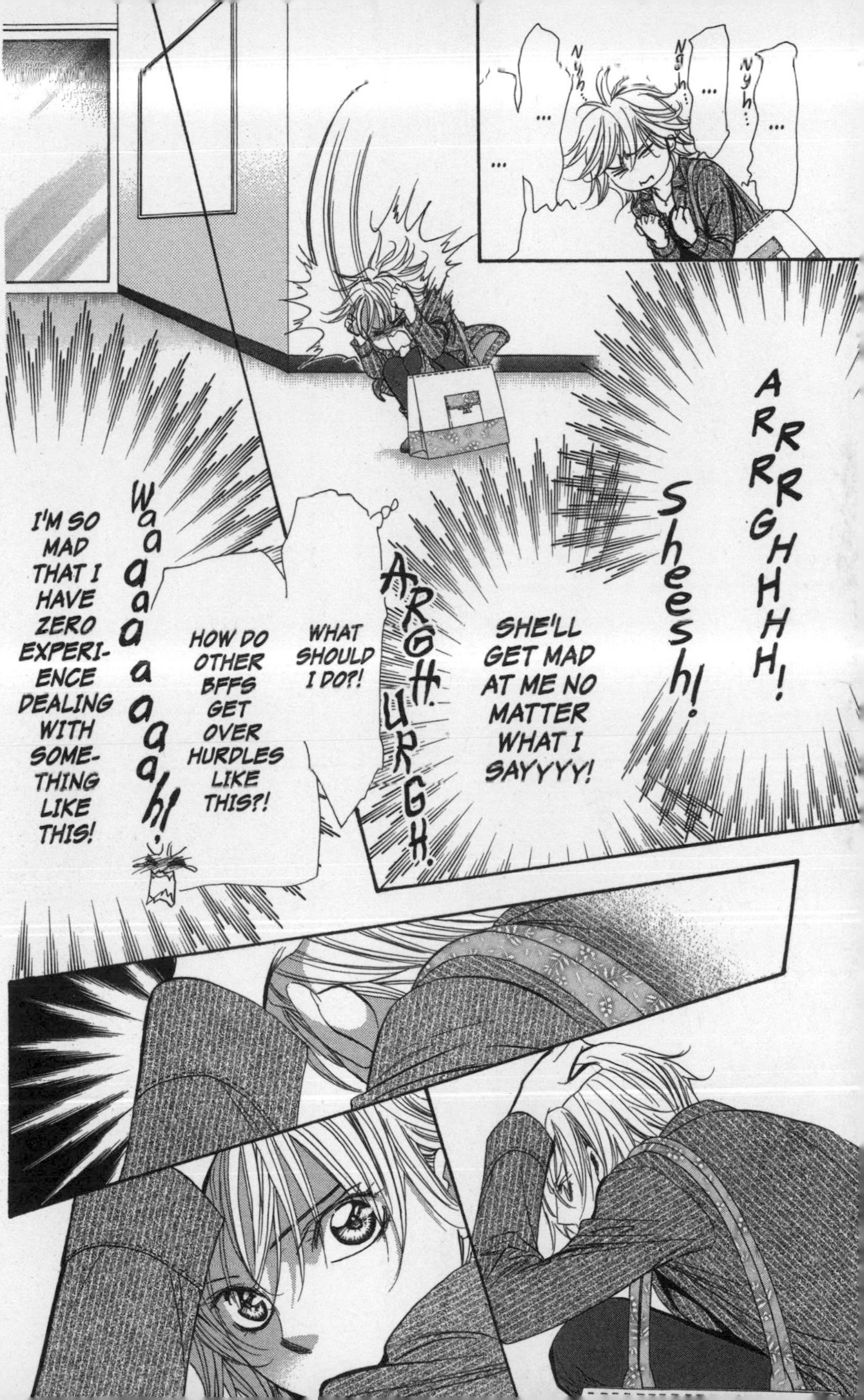
Nyh...
Ngh...
Nyh...
...
...
...
...
ARRRRGHHHHH!
Sheesh!
SHE'LL GET MAD AT ME NO MATTER WHAT I SAYYYY!
ARGH! URGH!
WHAT SHOULD I DO?!
HOW DO OTHER BFFS GET OVER HURDLES LIKE THIS?!
Waaaaaaaaah!
I'M SO MAD THAT I HAVE ZERO EXPERIENCE DEALING WITH SOMETHING LIKE THIS!

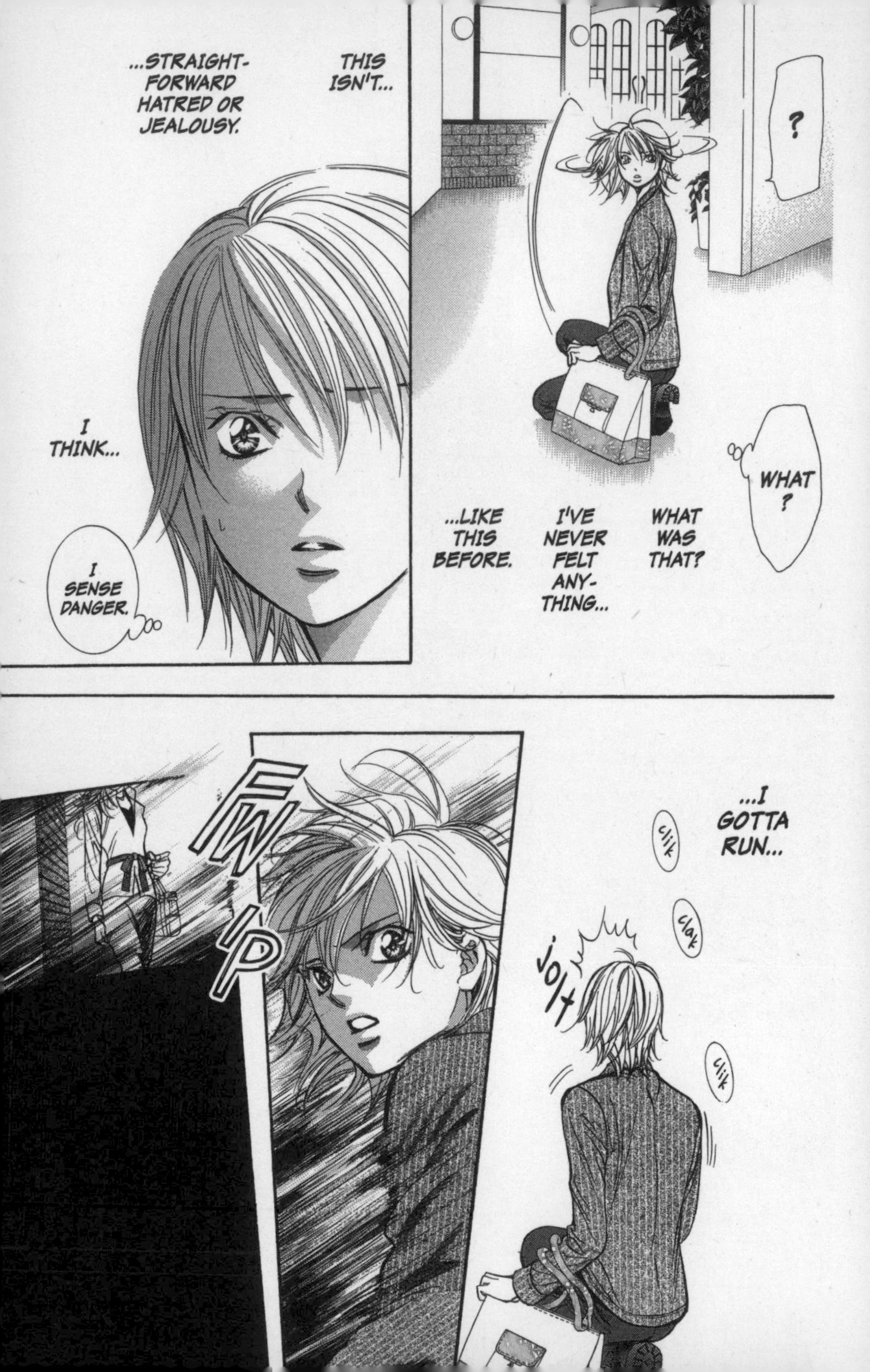
?
WHAT?
WHAT WAS THAT?
I'VE NEVER FELT ANYTHING...
...LIKE THIS BEFORE.
THIS ISN'T...
...STRAIGHT-FORWARD HATRED OR JEALOUSY.
I THINK...
I SENSE DANGER.
...I GOTTA RUN...
clik
clak
jolt
clik
FWIP

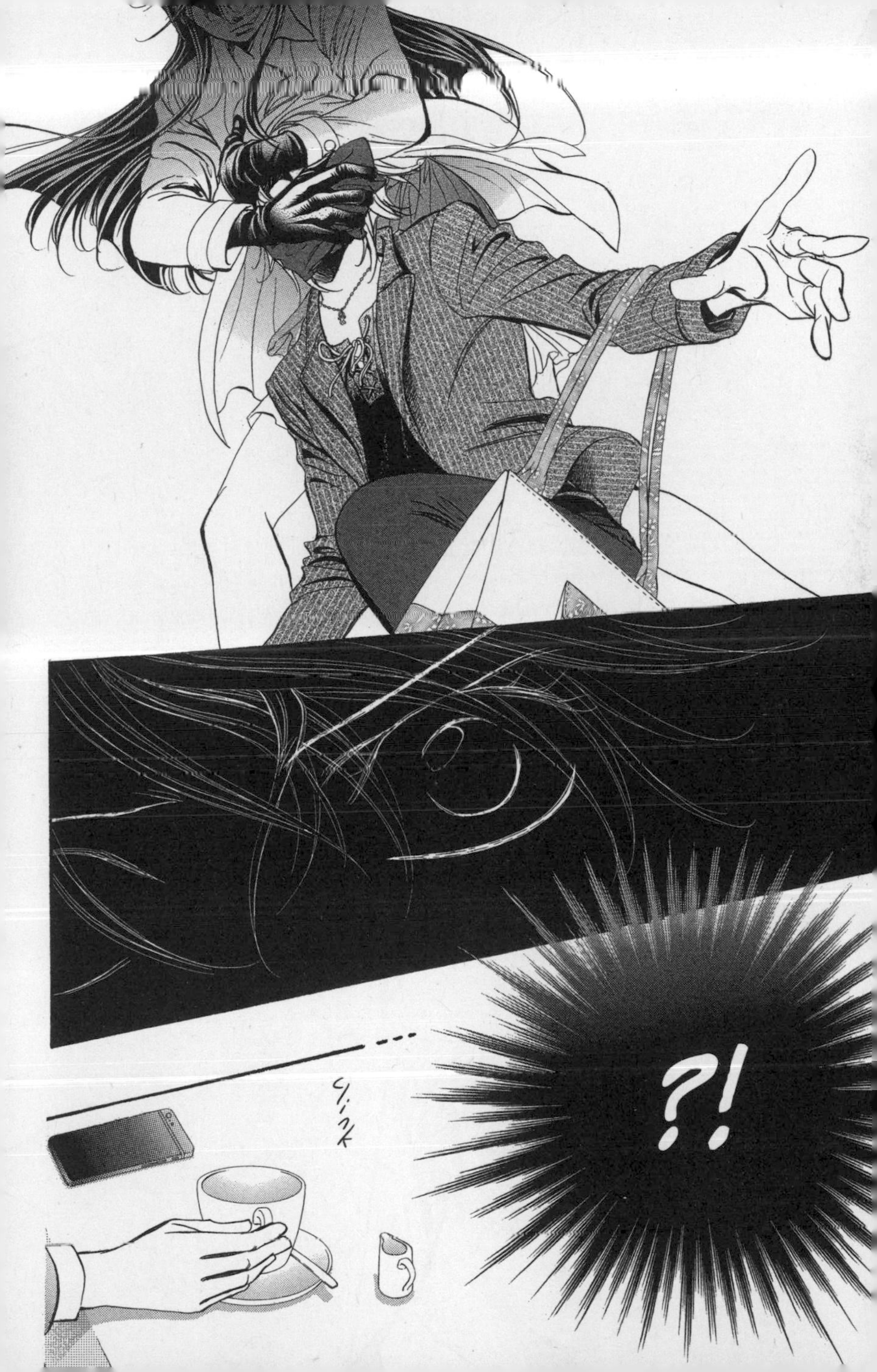
?!
clink

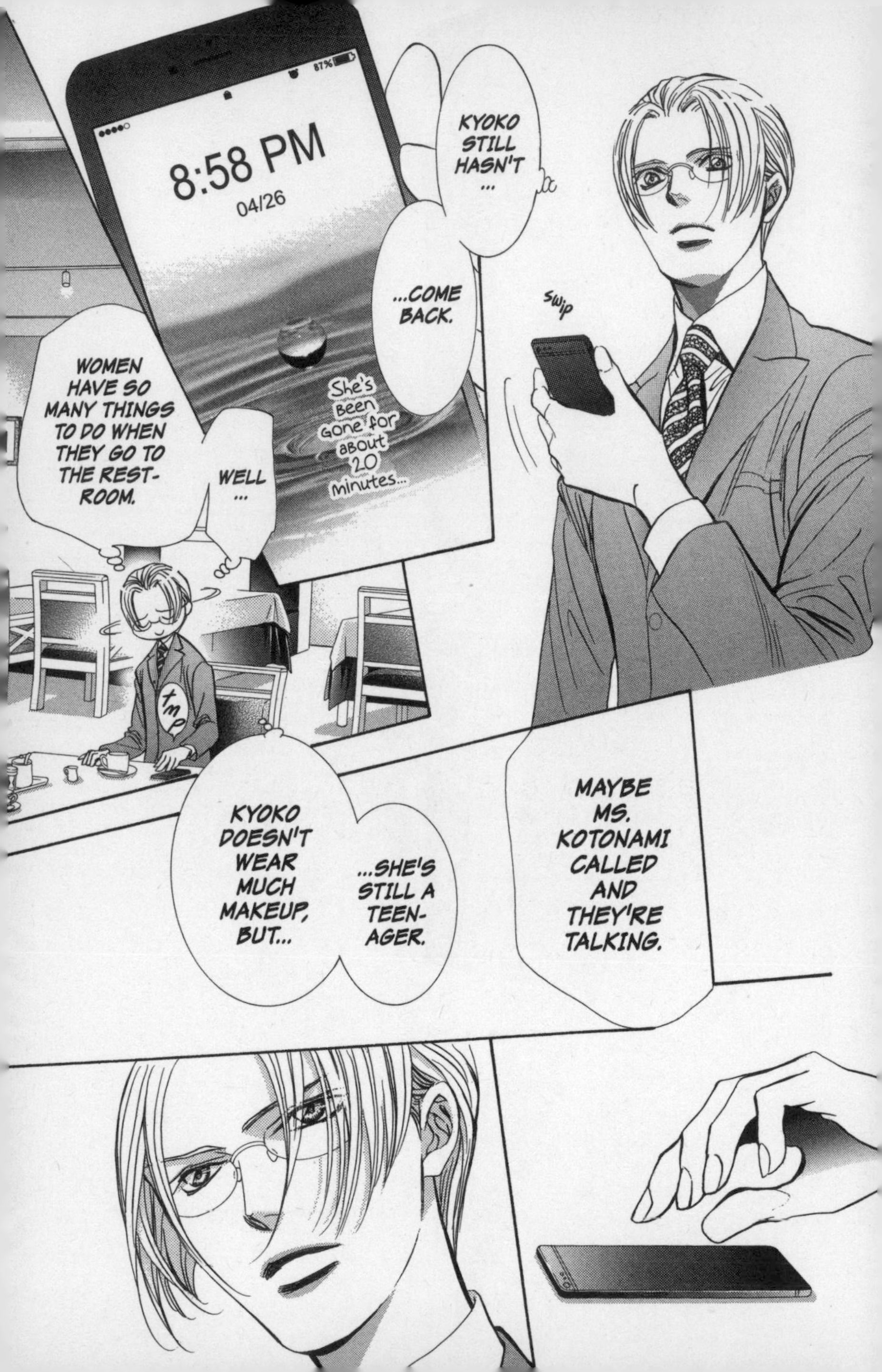

SWIP
KYOKO STILL HASN'T ...
...COME BACK.
87%
8:58 PM
04/26
She's Been Gone for about 20 minutes...
WELL ...
WOMEN HAVE SO MANY THINGS TO DO WHEN THEY GO TO THE REST-ROOM.
TMP
MAYBE MS. KOTONAMI CALLED AND THEY'RE TALKING.
KYOKO DOESN'T WEAR MUCH MAKEUP, BUT...
...SHE'S STILL A TEEN-AGER.

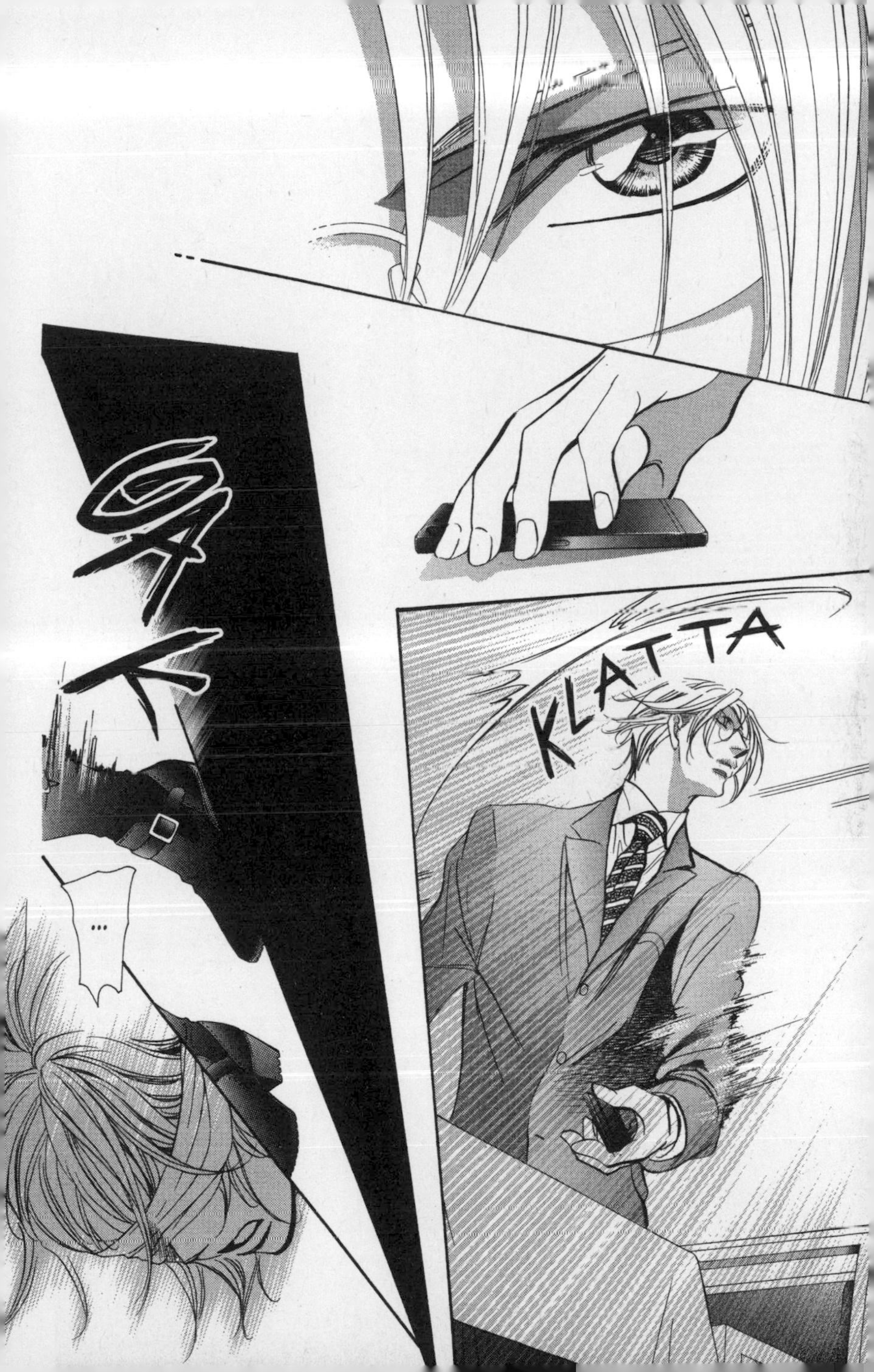
KLATTA
GAK
...

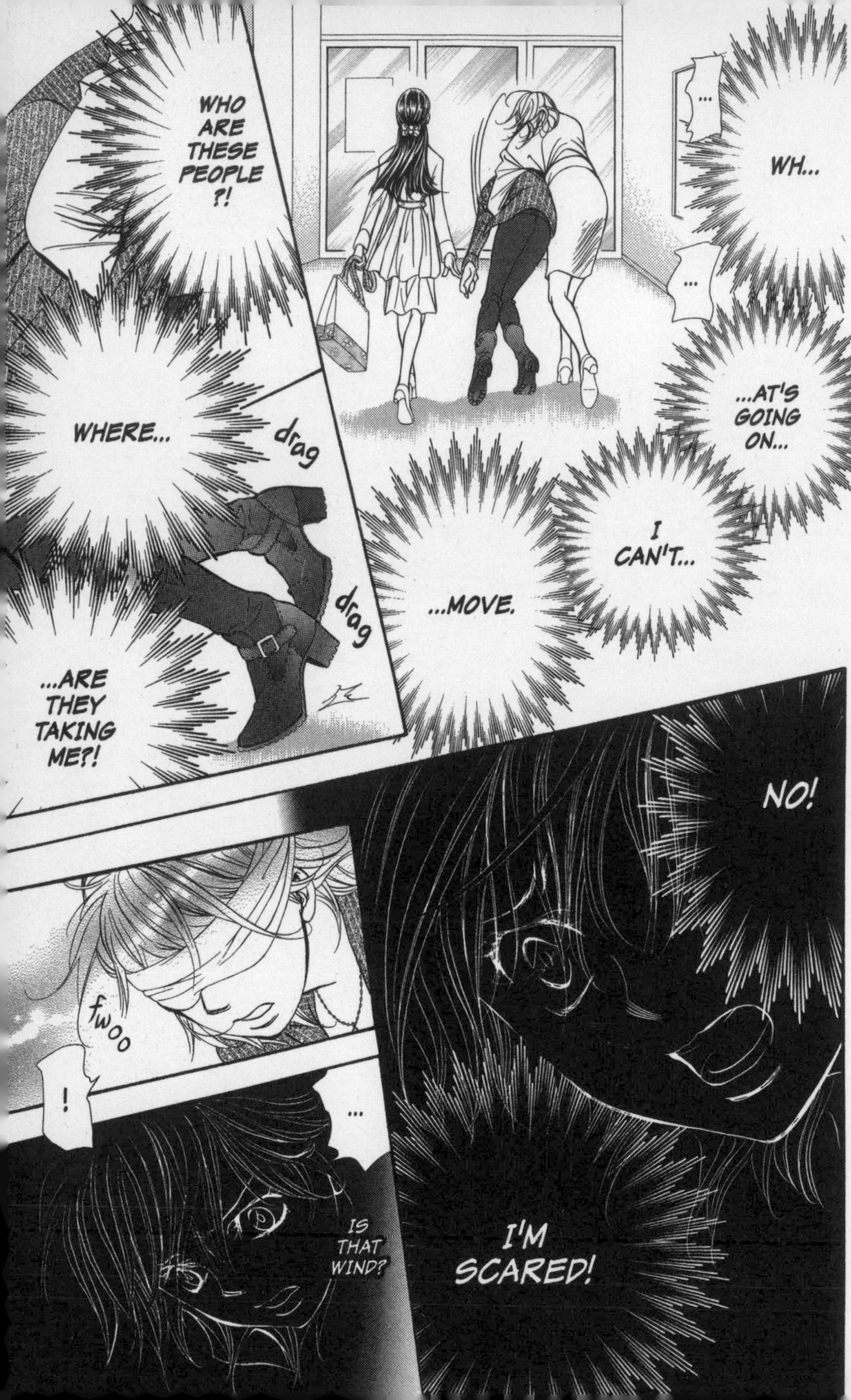
...
WH...
...
...AT'S GOING ON...
I CAN'T...
...MOVE.
WHO ARE THESE PEOPLE?!
WHERE...
drag
drag
...ARE THEY TAKING ME?!
NO!
I'M SCARED!
fwoo
!
...
IS THAT WIND?

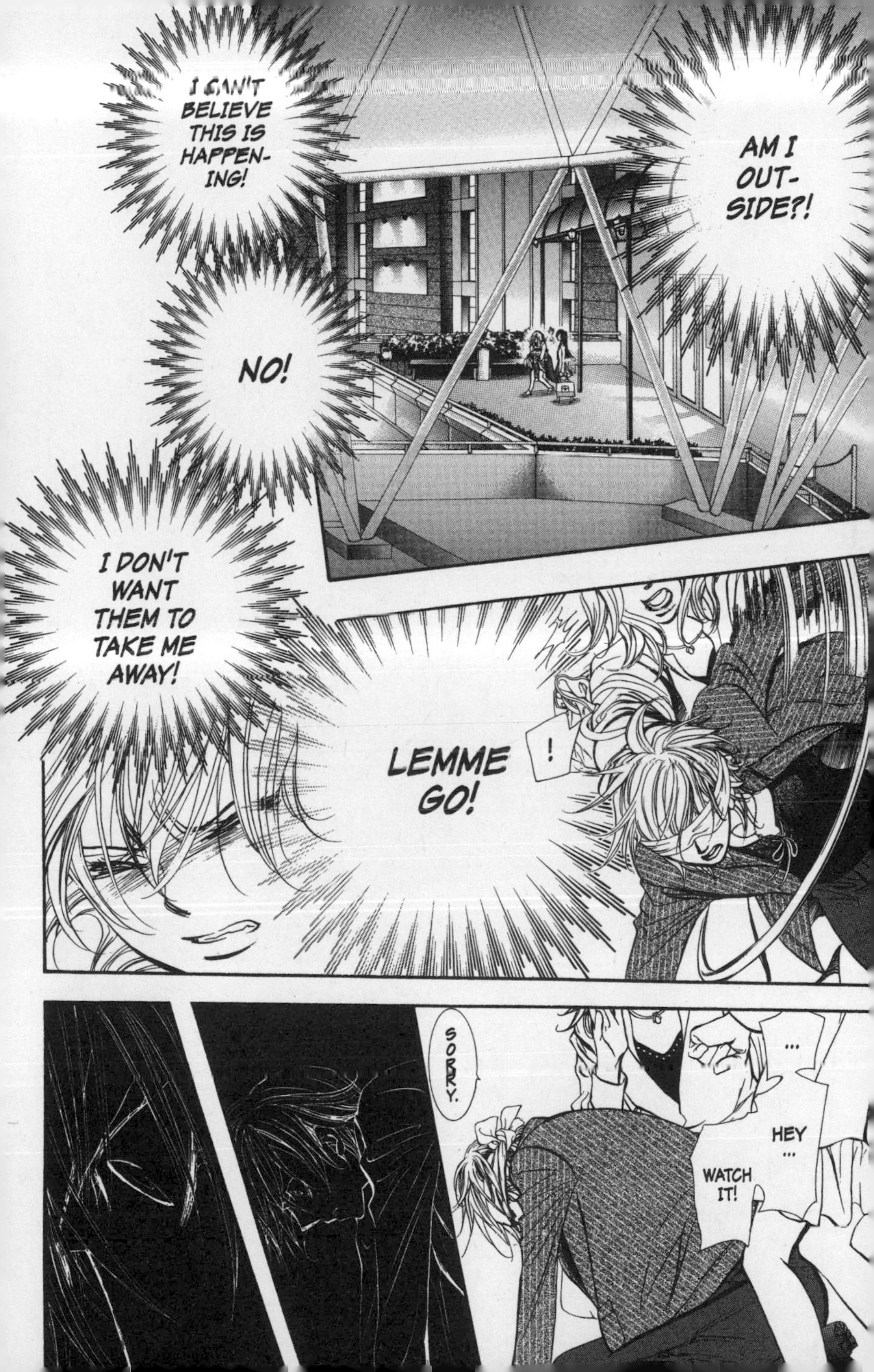
AM I OUT-SIDE?!
I CAN'T BELIEVE THIS IS HAPPEN-ING!
NO!
I DON'T WANT THEM TO TAKE ME AWAY!
!
LEMME GO!
...
HEY ...
WATCH IT!
SORRY.

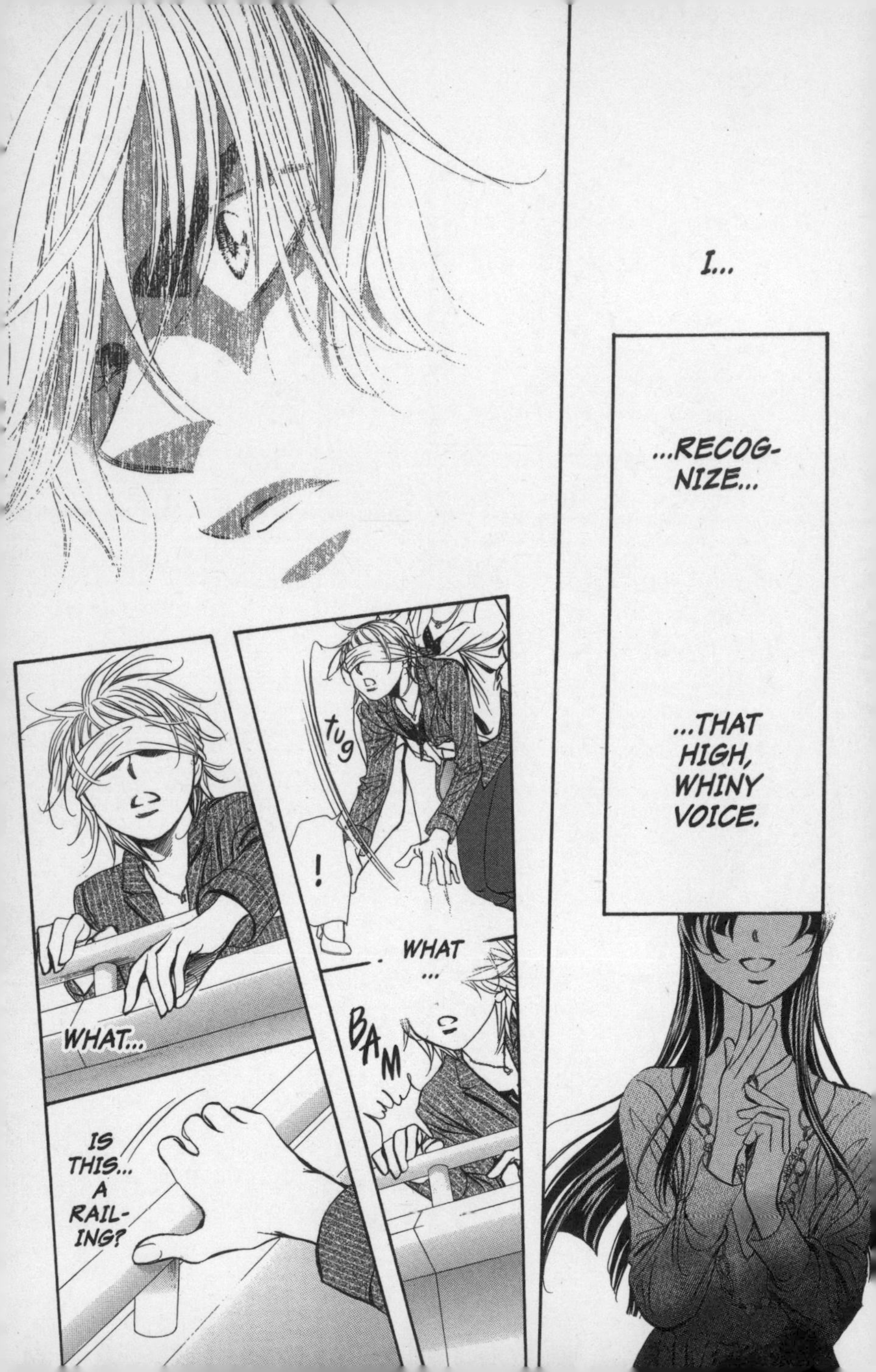
I...
...RECOG-NIZE...
...THAT HIGH, WHINY VOICE.
tug
!
WHAT ...
BAM
WHAT...
IS THIS... A RAIL-ING?

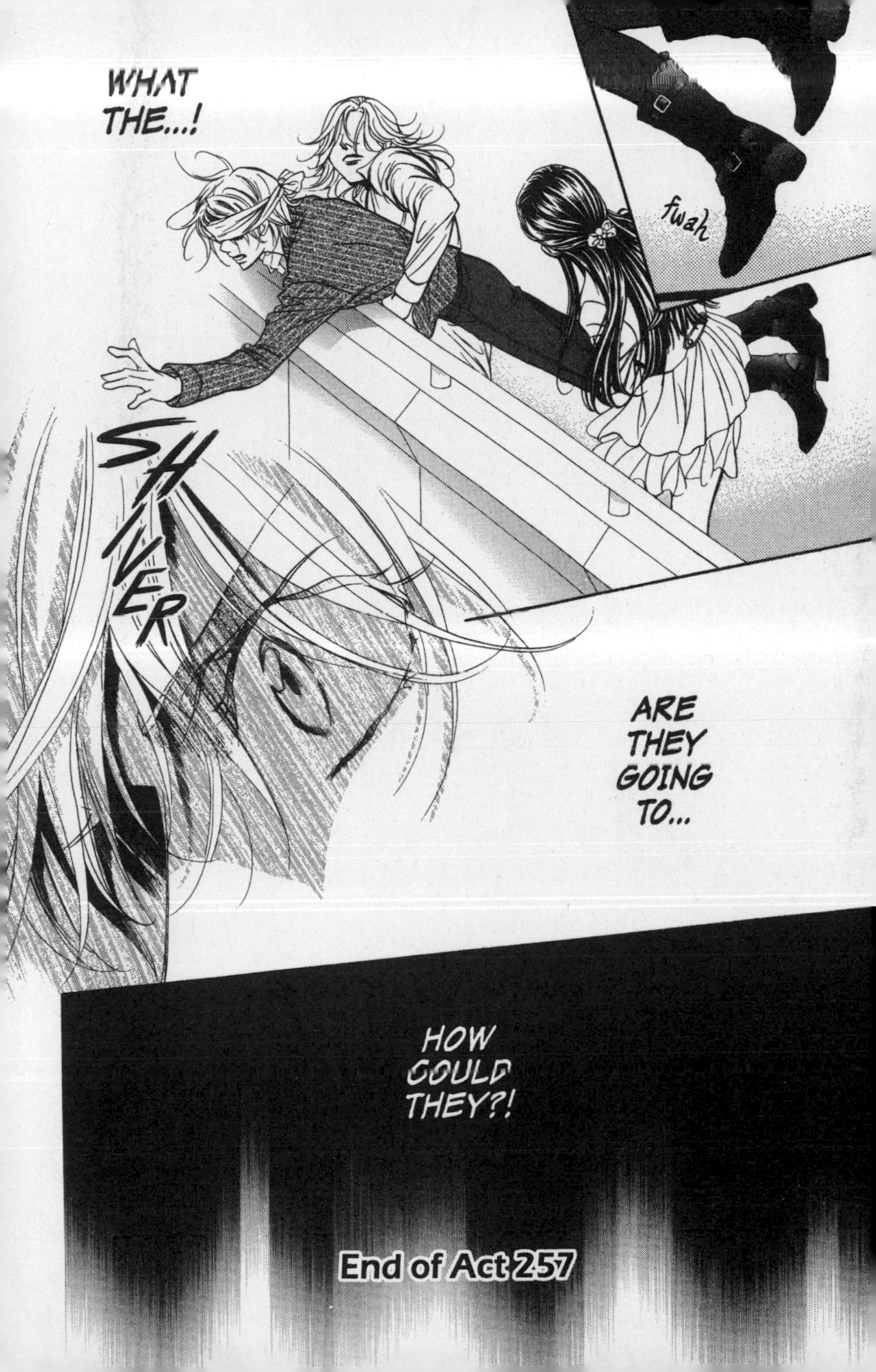
fwah
WHAT THE...!
SHIVER
ARE THEY GOING TO...
HOW COULD THEY?!
End of Act 257

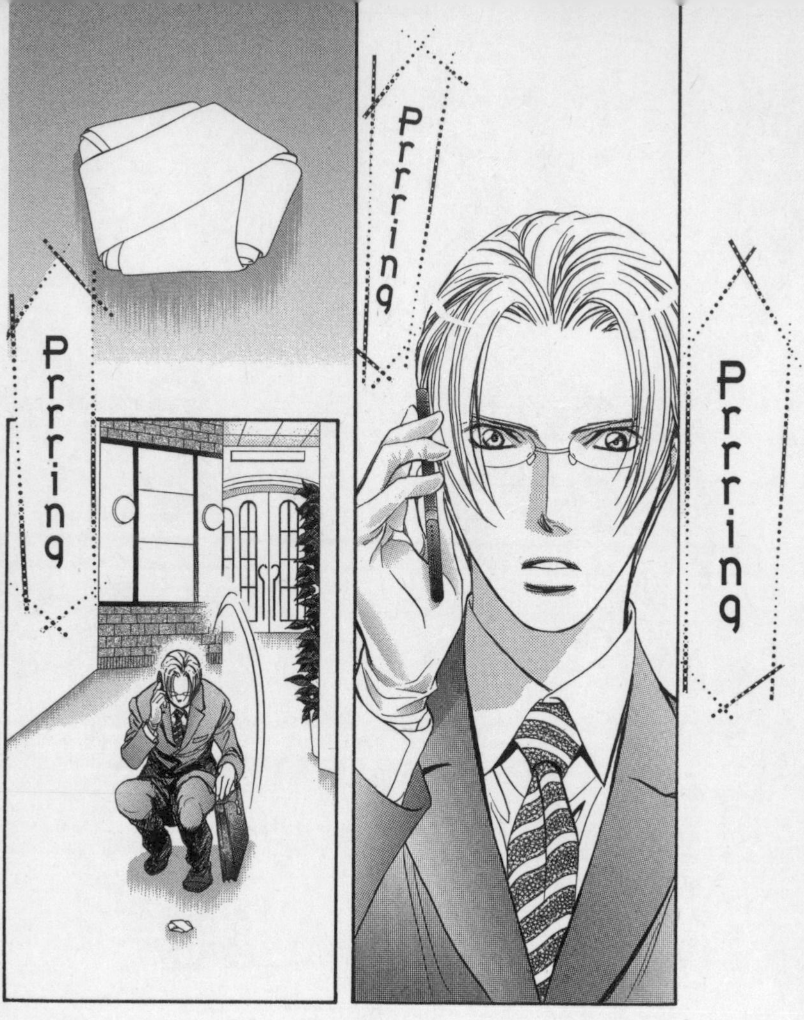
Prrring
Prrring
Prrring

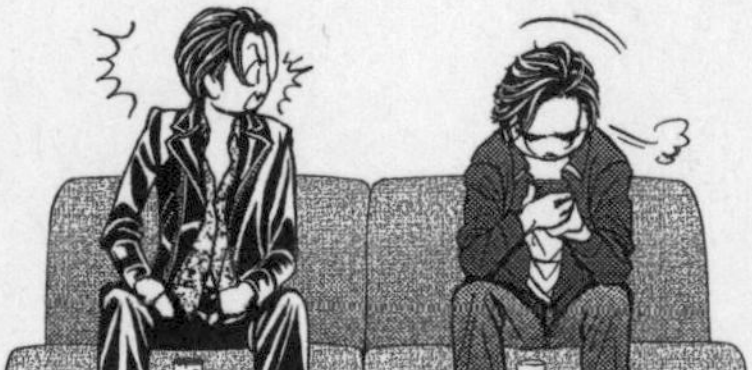

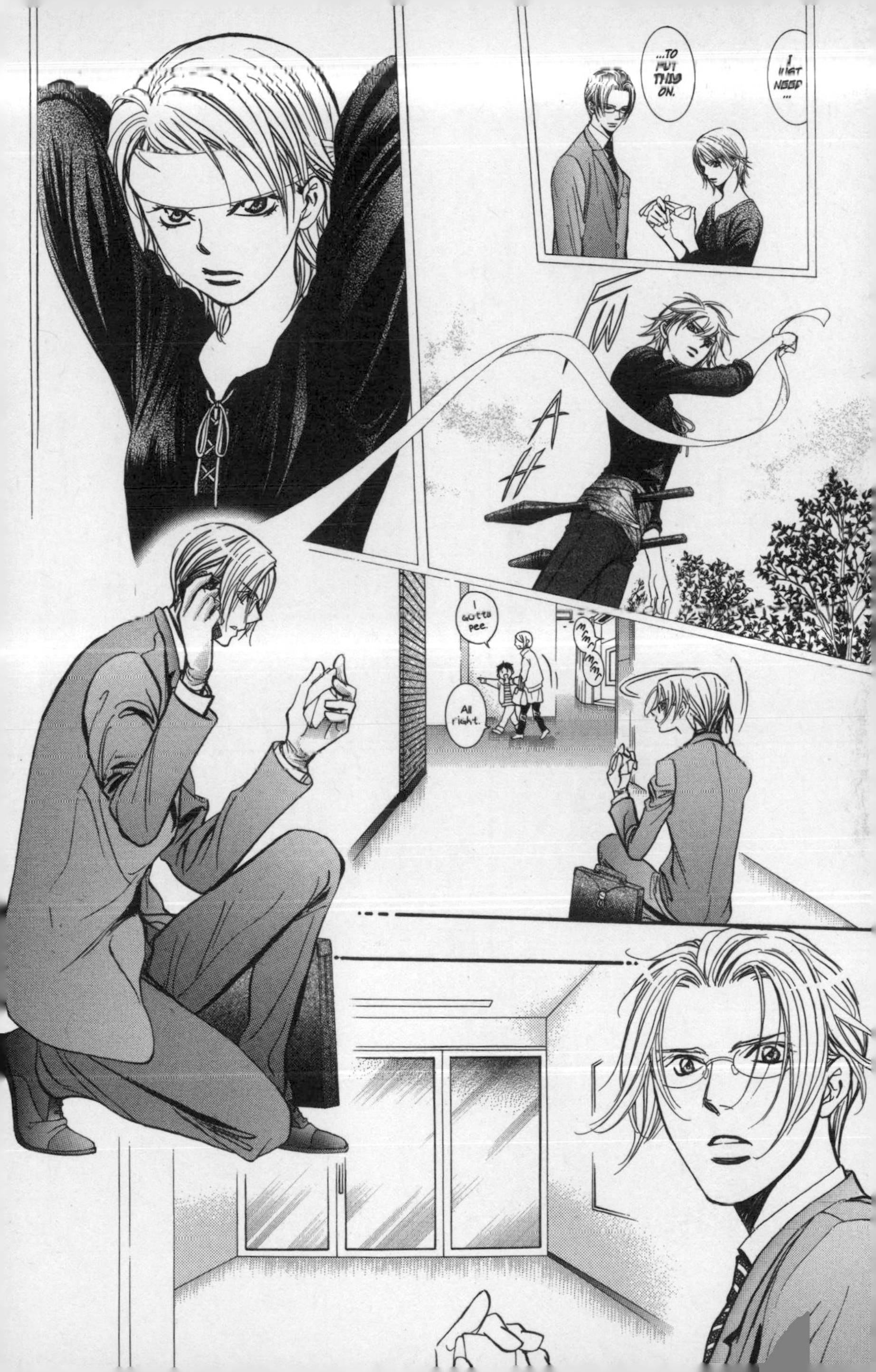
I JUST NEED...
...TO PUT THIS ON.
FWAHH
I gotta pee.
All right.

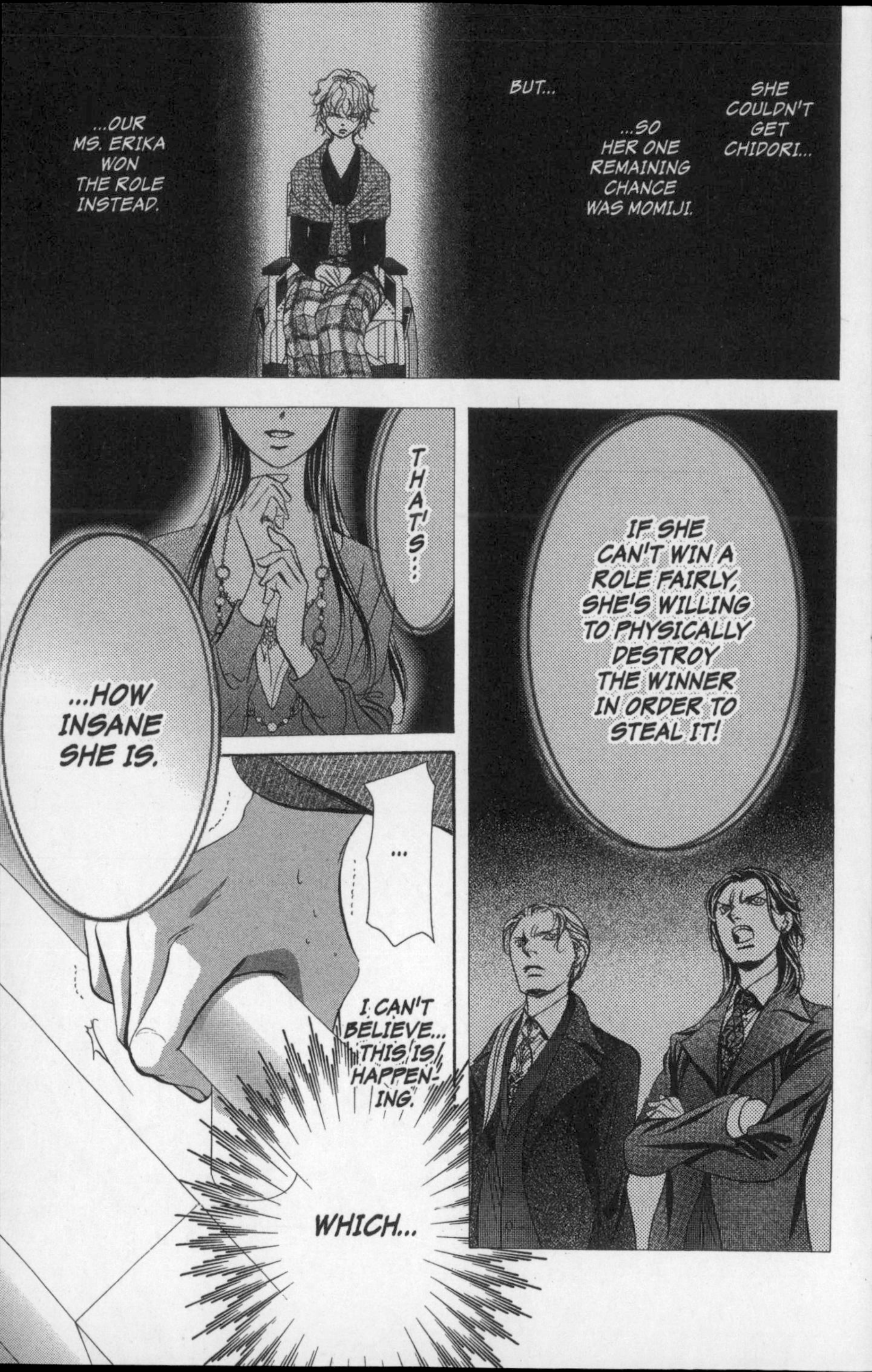
SHE COULDN'T GET CHIDORI...
...SO HER ONE REMAINING CHANCE WAS MOMIJI.
BUT...
...OUR MS. ERIKA WON THE ROLE INSTEAD.
IF SHE CAN'T WIN A ROLE FAIRLY, SHE'S WILLING TO PHYSICALLY DESTROY THE WINNER IN ORDER TO STEAL IT!
THAT'S...
...HOW INSANE SHE IS.
...
I CAN'T BELIEVE... THIS IS HAPPENING.
WHICH...

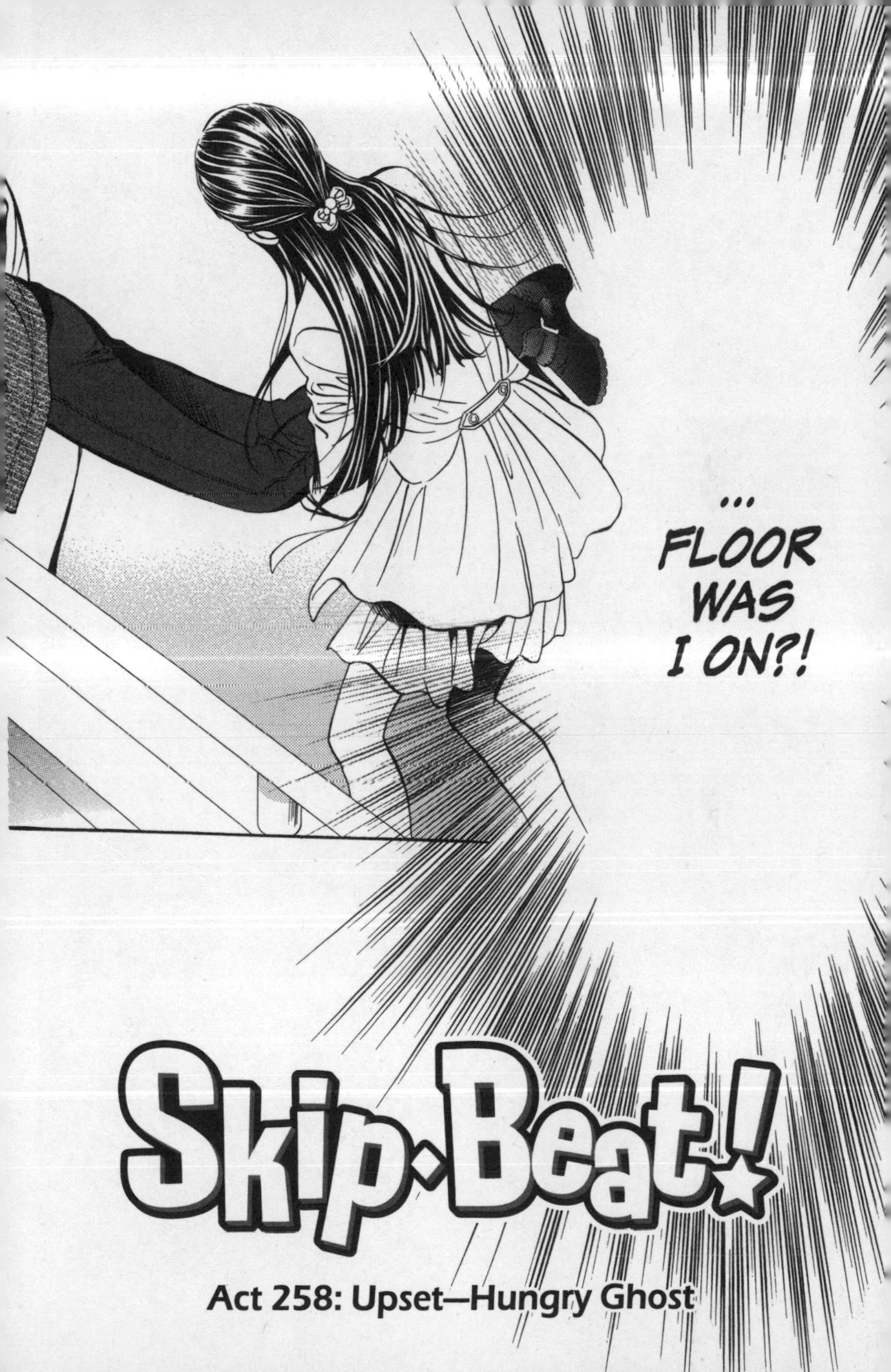
... FLOOR WAS I ON?!
Skip·Beat!

Act 258: Upset—Hungry Ghost

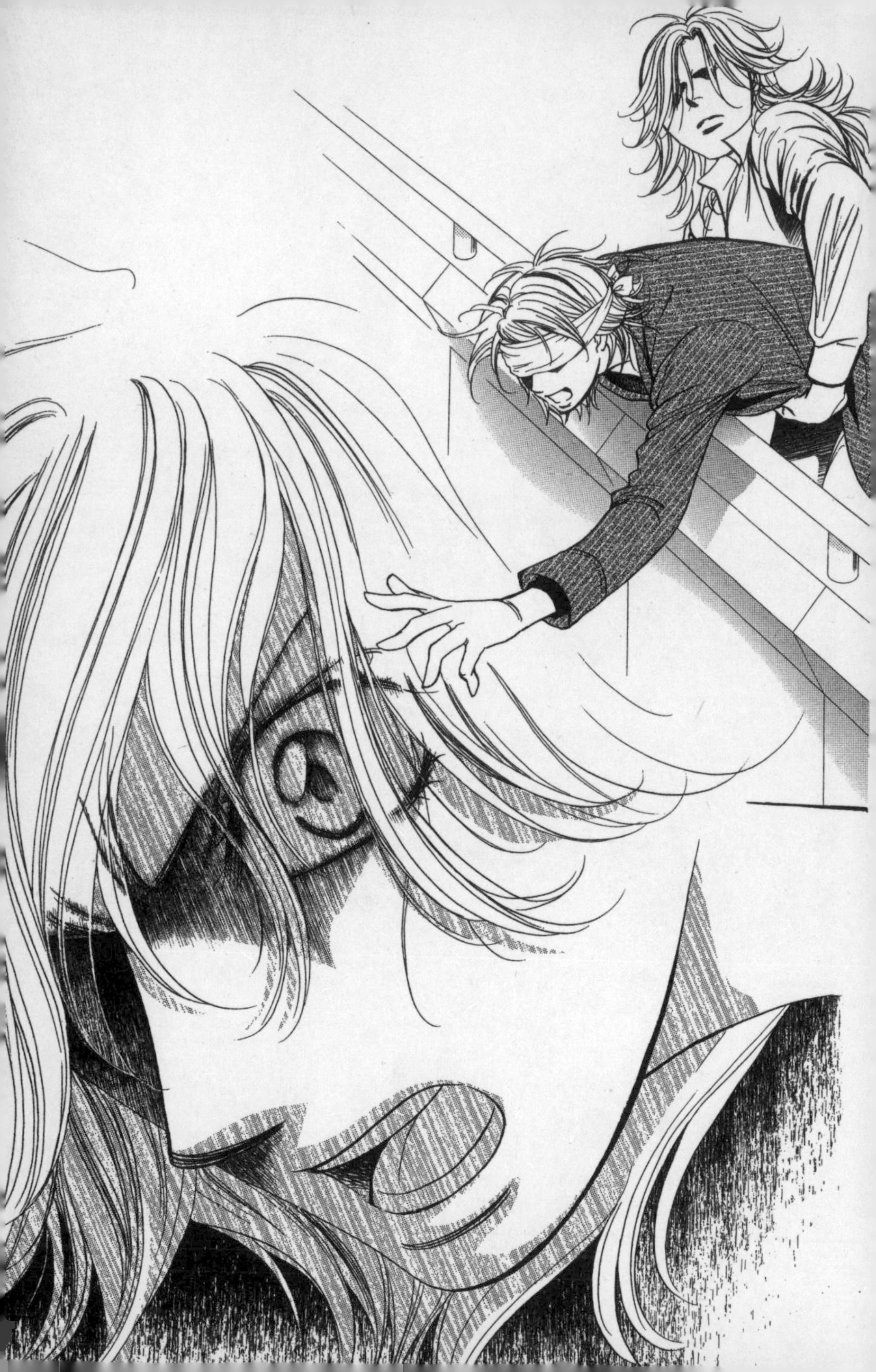

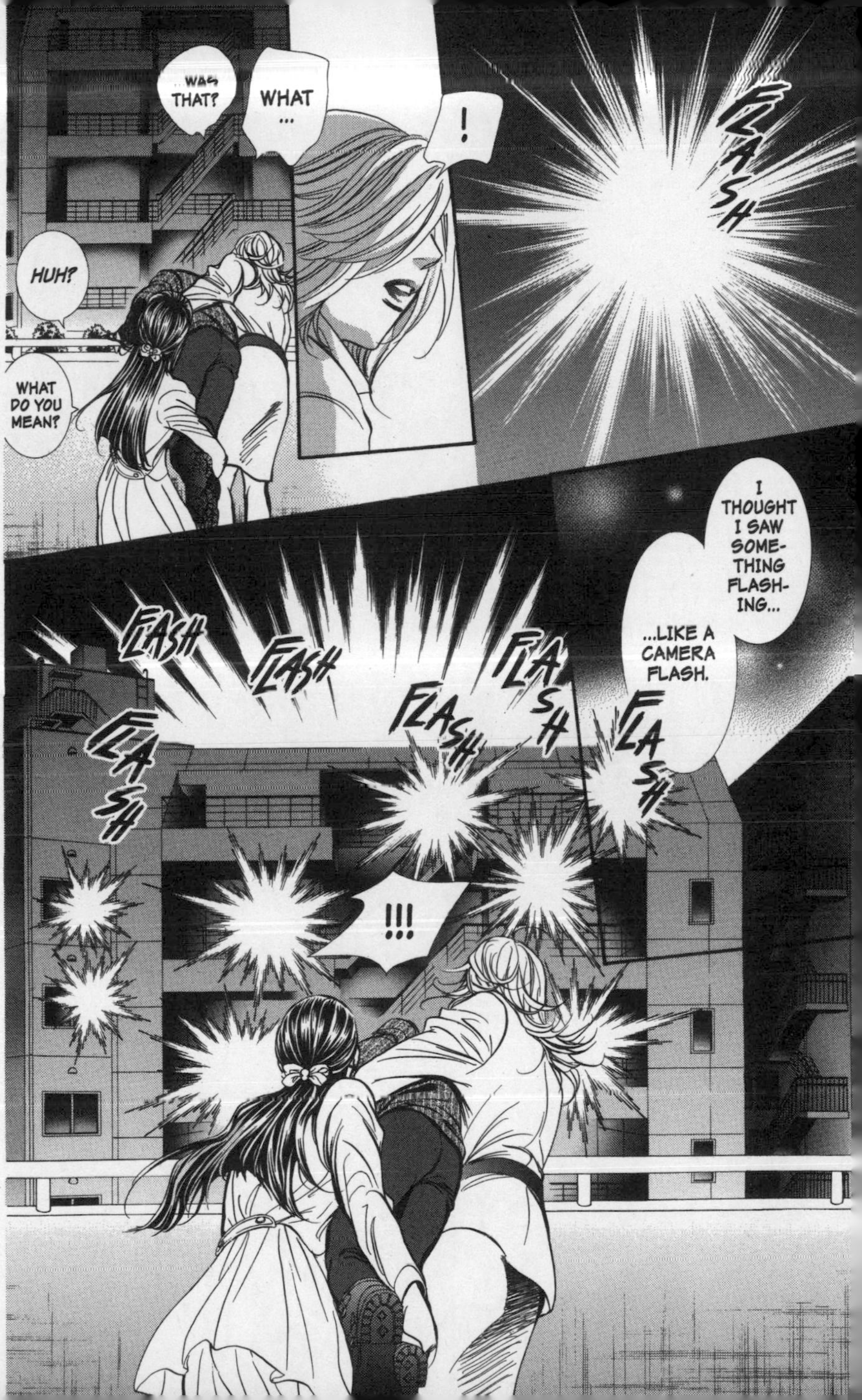
FLASH
!
WHAT ...
...WAS THAT?
HUH?
WHAT DO YOU MEAN?
I THOUGHT I SAW SOME-THING FLASH-ING...
...LIKE A CAMERA FLASH.
FLASH
FLASH
FLASH
FLASH
FLASH
FLASH
!!!

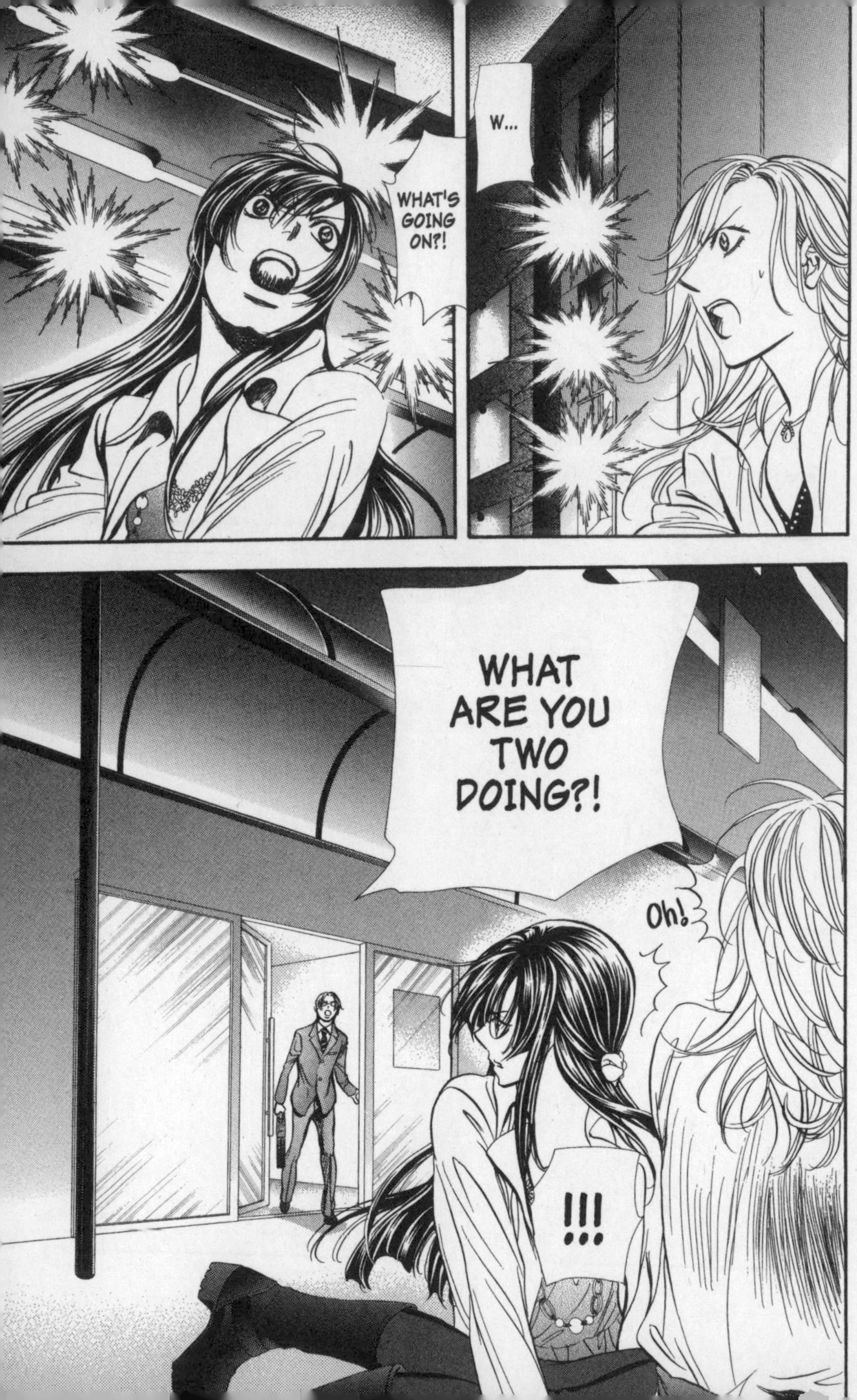
W...
WHAT'S GOING ON?!
WHAT ARE YOU TWO DOING?!
Oh!
!!!

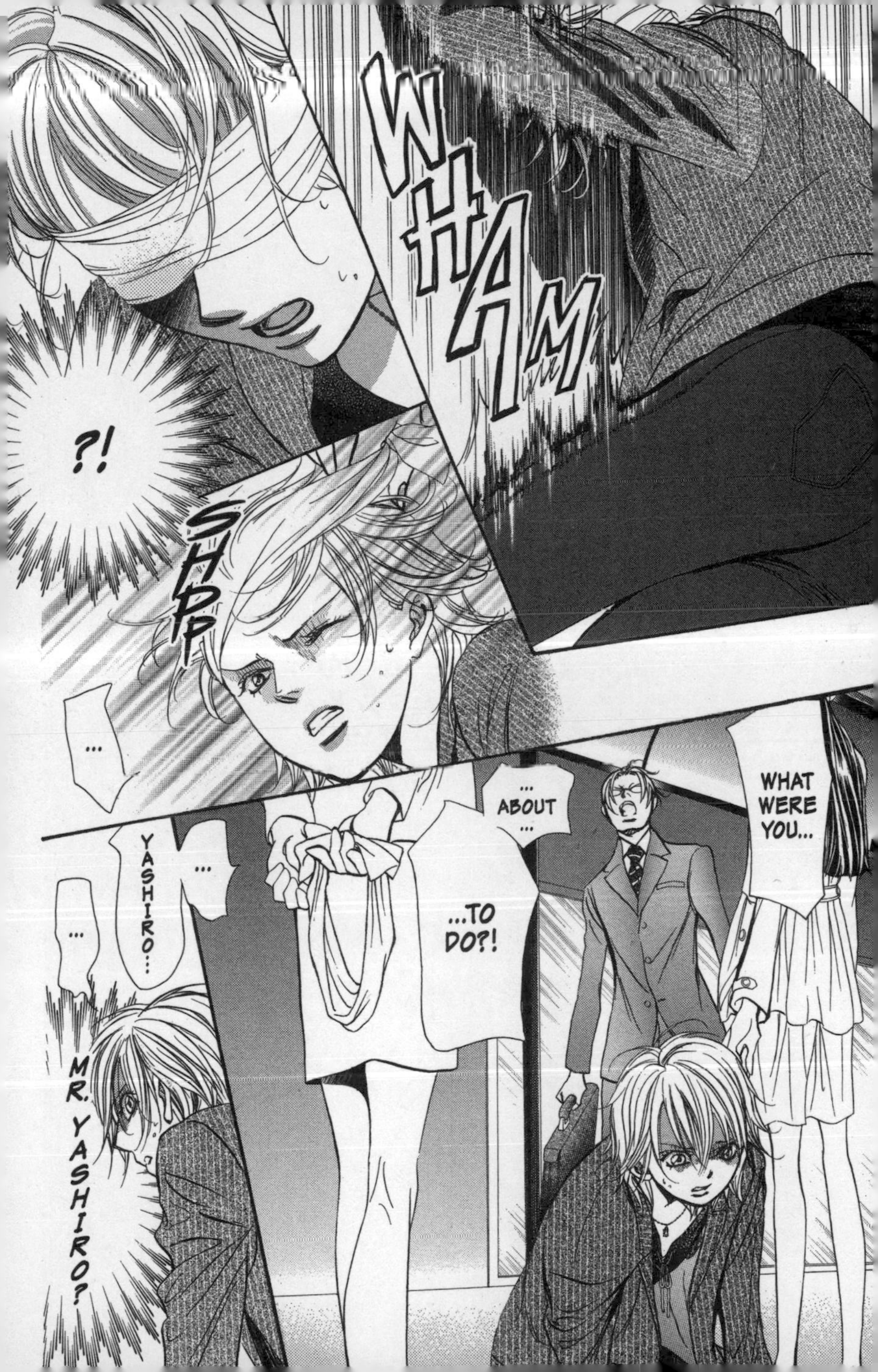
WHAM
?!
SHPP
...
WHAT WERE YOU...
...ABOUT...
...TO DO?!
...
YASHIRO...
...
MR. YASHIRO?

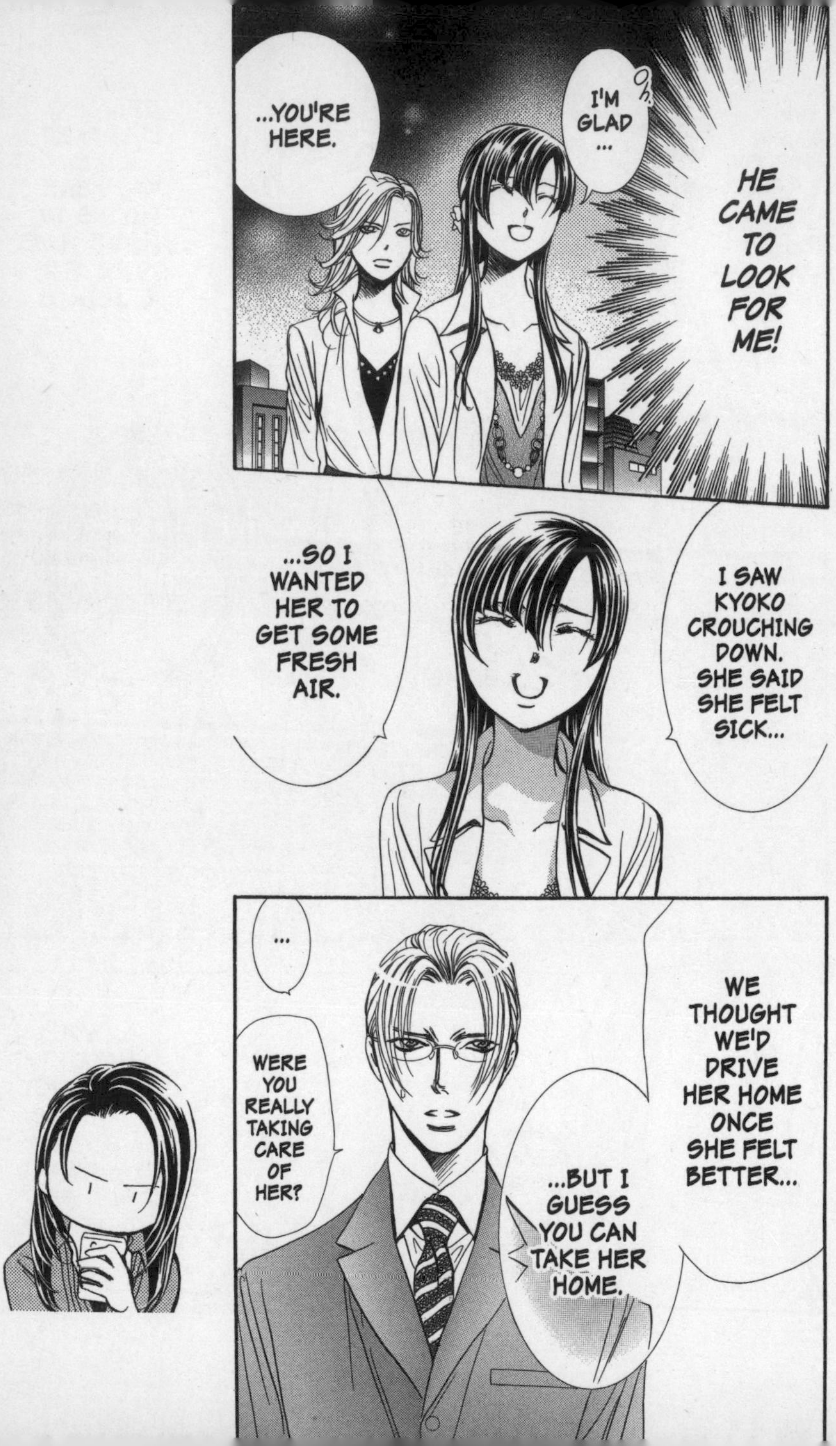
oh
I'M GLAD ...
...YOU'RE HERE.
HE CAME TO LOOK FOR ME!
I SAW KYOKO CROUCHING DOWN. SHE SAID SHE FELT SICK...
...SO I WANTED HER TO GET SOME FRESH AIR.
WE THOUGHT WE'D DRIVE HER HOME ONCE SHE FELT BETTER...
...BUT I GUESS YOU CAN TAKE HER HOME.
...
WERE YOU REALLY TAKING CARE OF HER?

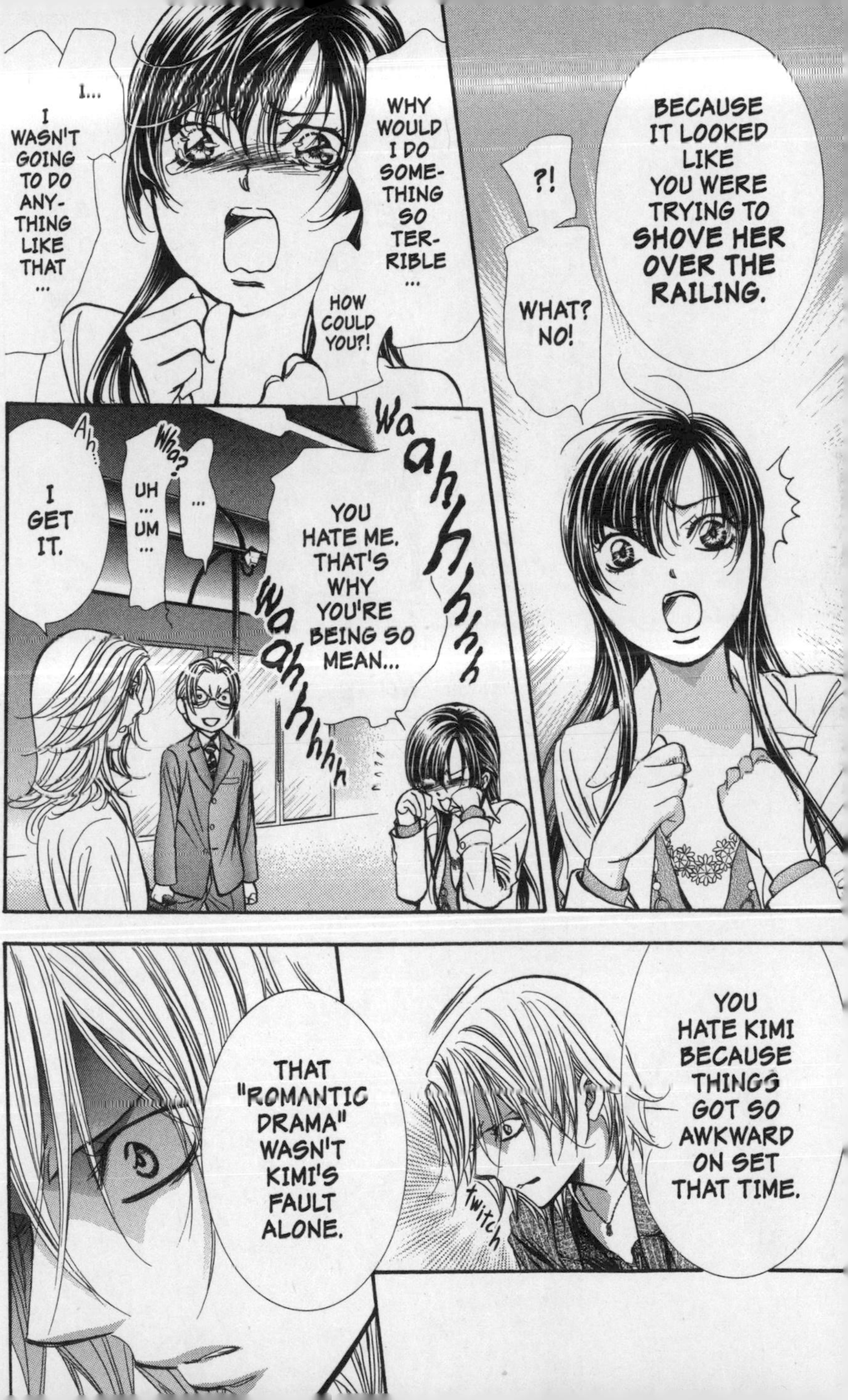
BECAUSE IT LOOKED LIKE YOU WERE TRYING TO SHOVE HER OVER THE RAILING.
?!
WHAT? NO!
WHY WOULD I DO SOME-THING SO TER-RIBLE ...
HOW COULD YOU?!
I...
I WASN'T GOING TO DO ANY-THING LIKE THAT ...
Waahhhhhh
YOU HATE ME. THAT'S WHY YOU'RE BEING SO MEAN...
Waahhhhhh
...
Wha?
UH ... UM ...
Ah...
I GET IT.
YOU HATE KIMI BECAUSE THINGS GOT SO AWKWARD ON SET THAT TIME.
twitch
THAT "ROMANTIC DRAMA" WASN'T KIMI'S FAULT ALONE.

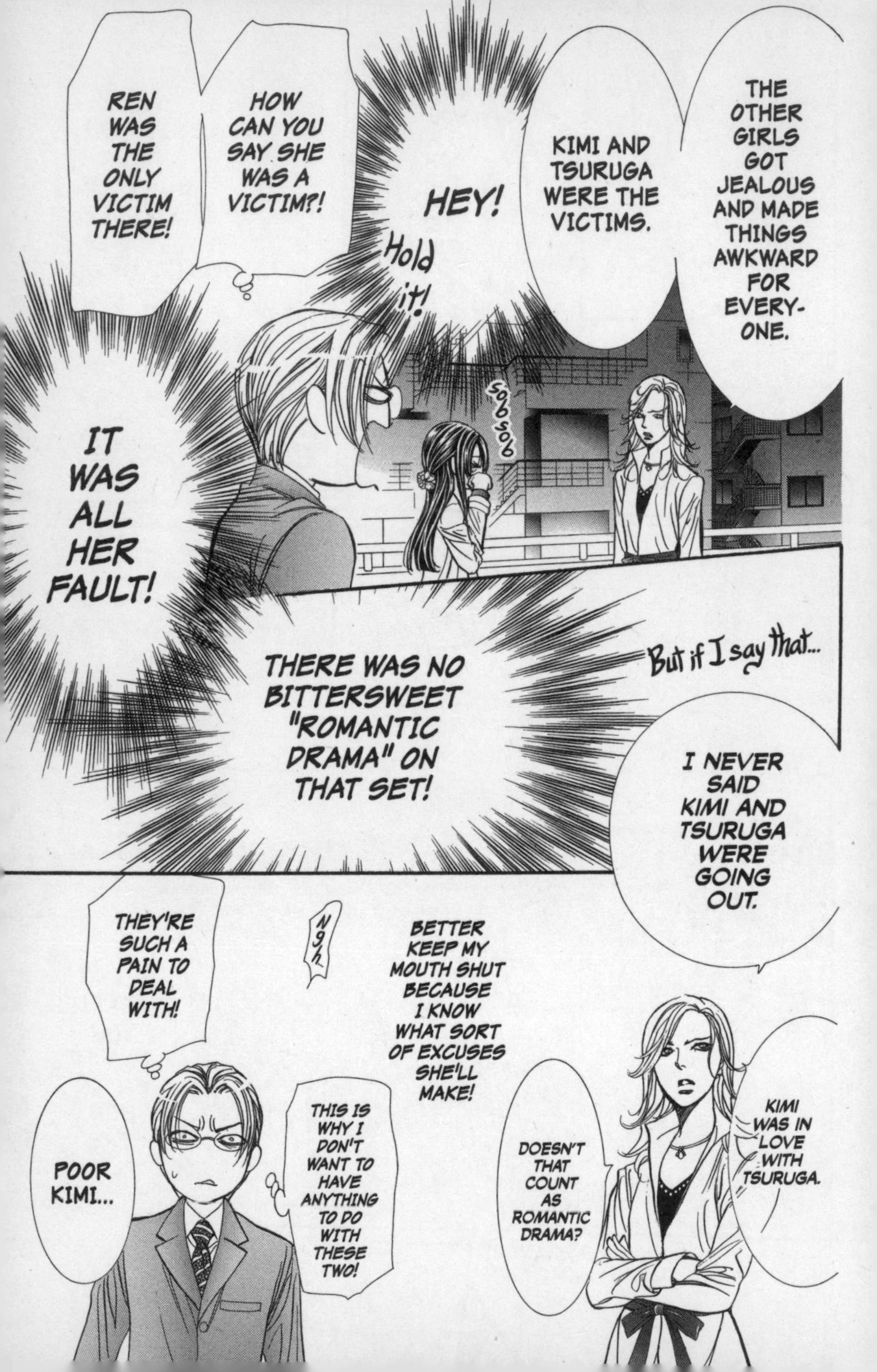
THE OTHER GIRLS GOT JEALOUS AND MADE THINGS AWKWARD FOR EVERY-ONE.
KIMI AND TSURUGA WERE THE VICTIMS.
HEY!
Hold it!
HOW CAN YOU SAY SHE WAS A VICTIM?!
REN WAS THE ONLY VICTIM THERE!
sob sob
IT WAS ALL HER FAULT!
THERE WAS NO BITTERSWEET "ROMANTIC DRAMA" ON THAT SET!
But if I say that...
I NEVER SAID KIMI AND TSURUGA WERE GOING OUT.
KIMI WAS IN LOVE WITH TSURUGA.
DOESN'T THAT COUNT AS ROMANTIC DRAMA?
BETTER KEEP MY MOUTH SHUT BECAUSE I KNOW WHAT SORT OF EXCUSES SHE'LL MAKE!
Ngh
THEY'RE SUCH A PAIN TO DEAL WITH!
THIS IS WHY I DON'T WANT TO HAVE ANYTHING TO DO WITH THESE TWO!
POOR KIMI...

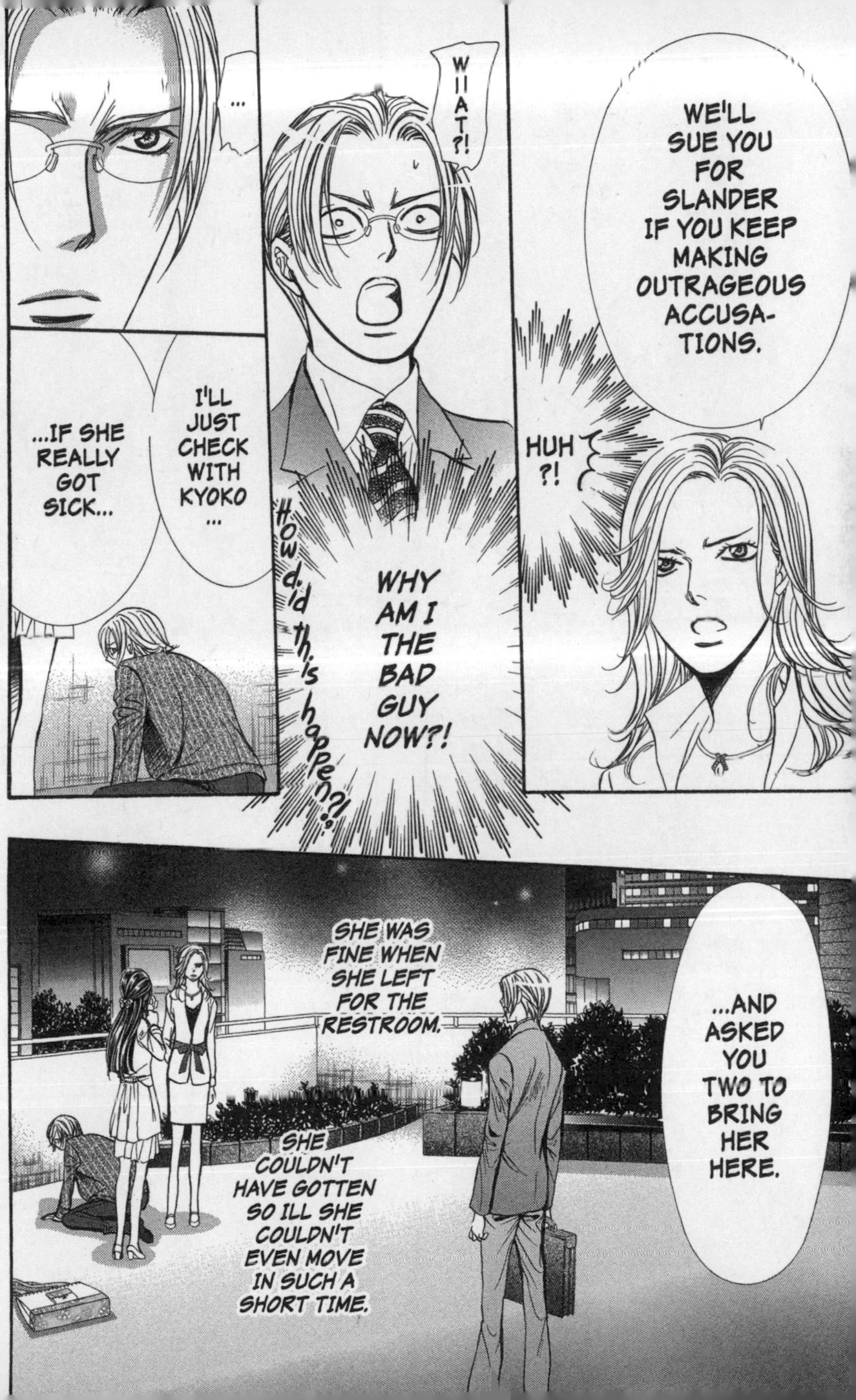
WE'LL SUE YOU FOR SLANDER IF YOU KEEP MAKING OUTRAGEOUS ACCUSA-TIONS.
HUH?!
WHAT?!
WHY AM I THE BAD GUY NOW?!
How did this happen?!
...
I'LL JUST CHECK WITH KYOKO...
...IF SHE REALLY GOT SICK...
...AND ASKED YOU TWO TO BRING HER HERE.
SHE WAS FINE WHEN SHE LEFT FOR THE RESTROOM.
SHE COULDN'T HAVE GOTTEN SO ILL SHE COULDN'T EVEN MOVE IN SUCH A SHORT TIME.

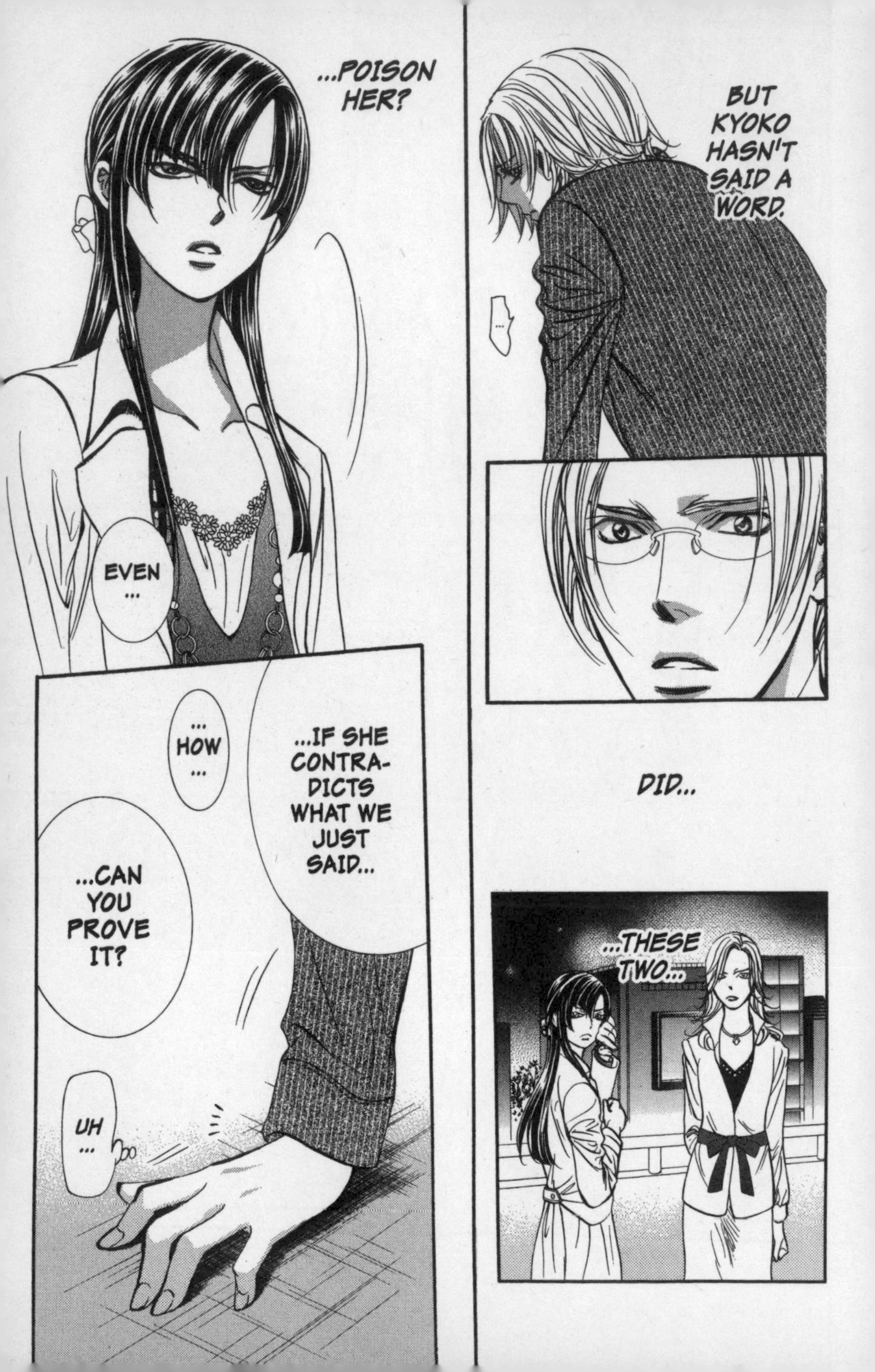
BUT KYOKO HASN'T SAID A WORD.
...
DID...
...THESE TWO...
...POISON HER?
EVEN ...
...IF SHE CONTRA-DICTS WHAT WE JUST SAID...
... HOW ...
...CAN YOU PROVE IT?
UH ...

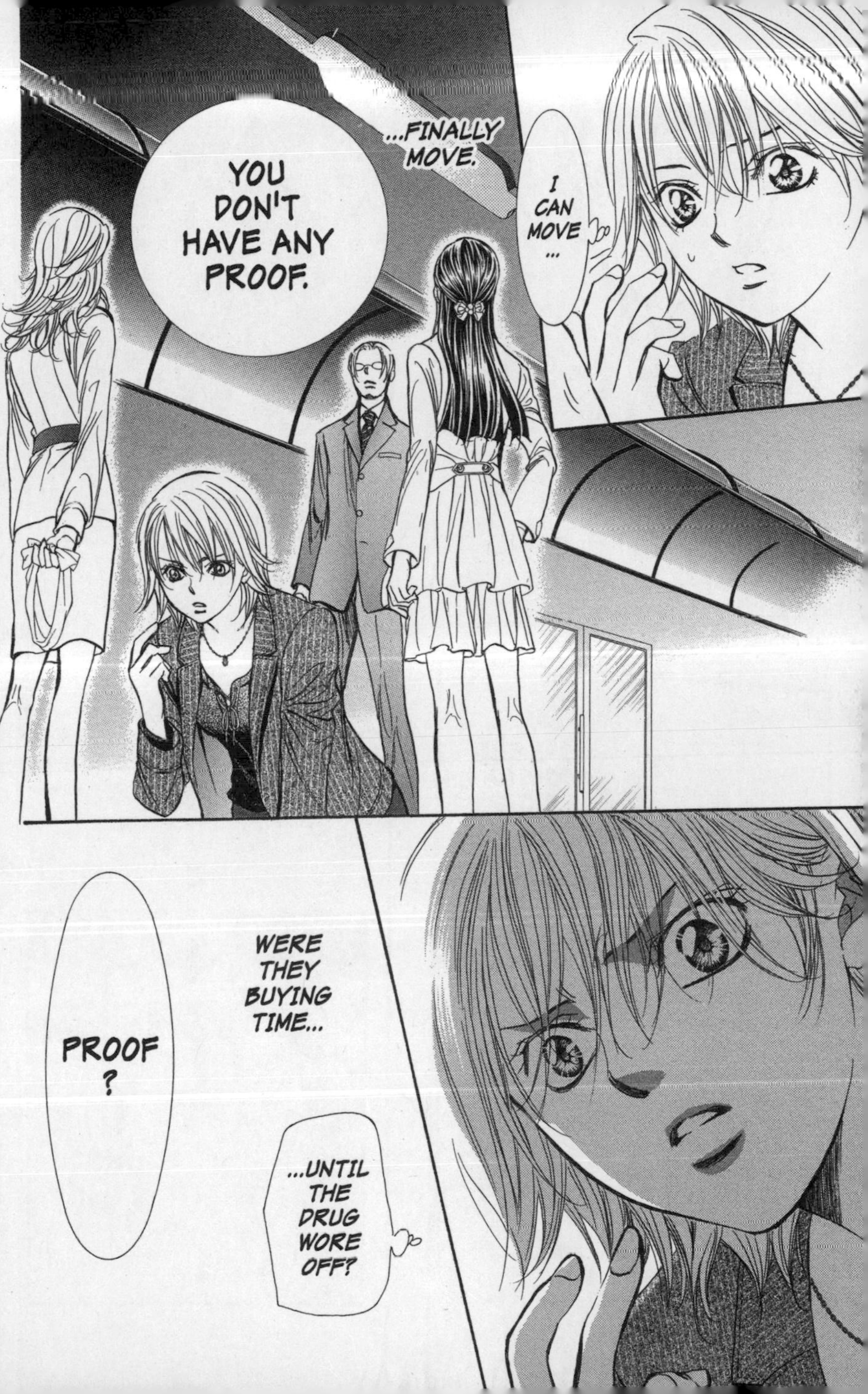
I CAN MOVE ...
...FINALLY MOVE.
YOU DON'T HAVE ANY PROOF.
PROOF?
WERE THEY BUYING TIME...
...UNTIL THE DRUG WORE OFF?

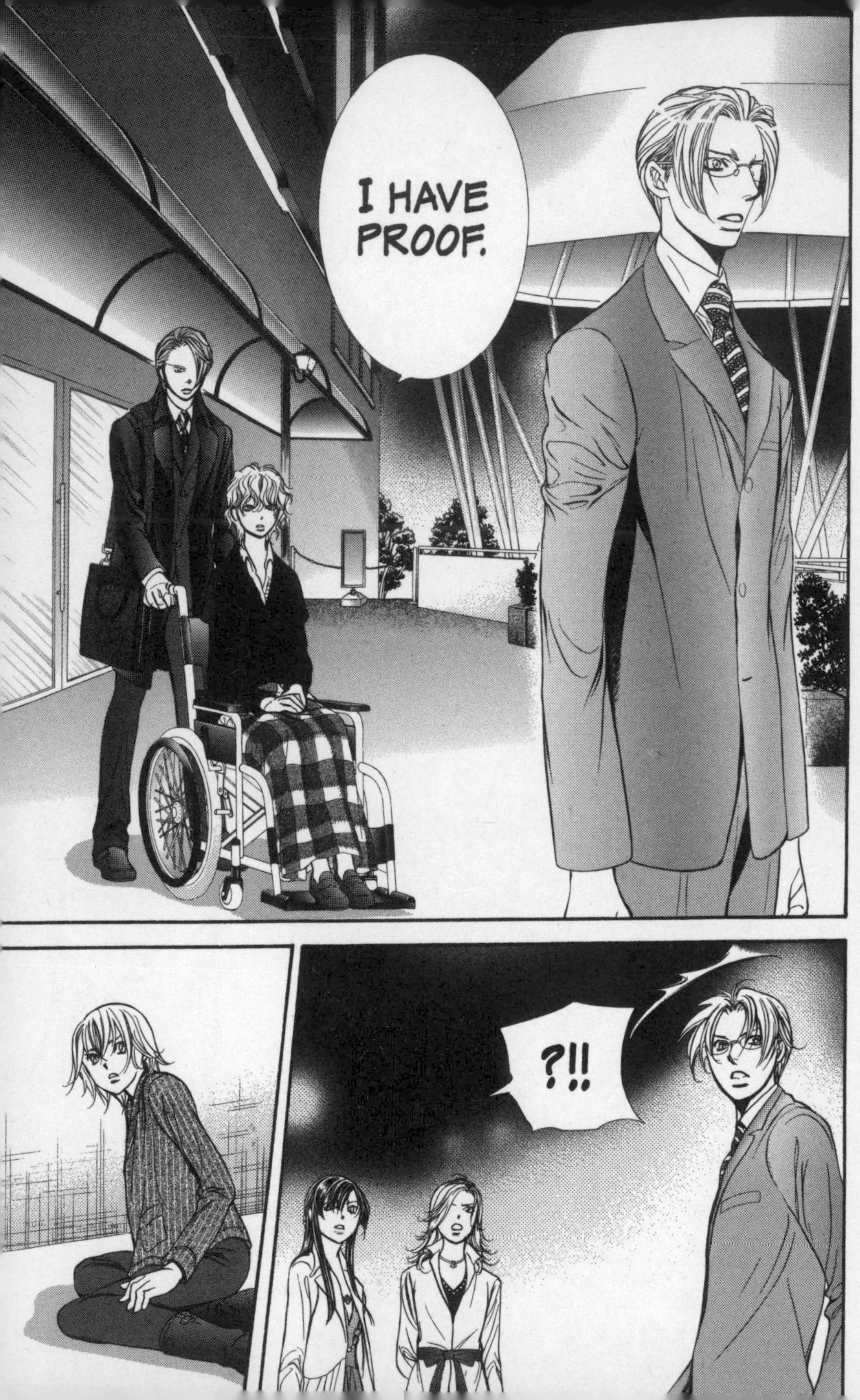
I HAVE PROOF.
?!!

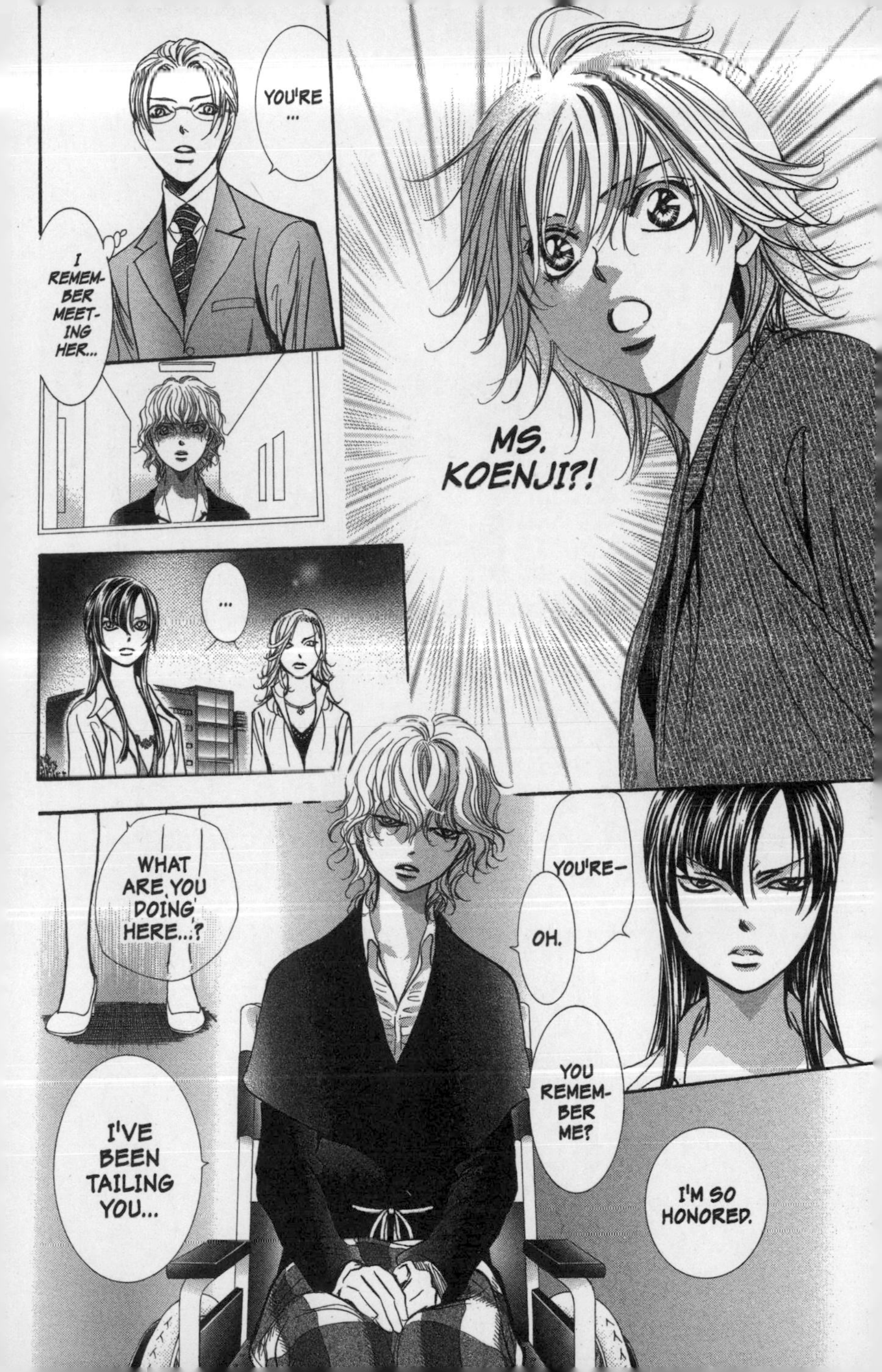
MS. KOENJI?!
YOU'RE ...
I REMEMBER MEETING HER...
...
YOU'RE—
OH.
YOU REMEMBER ME?
I'M SO HONORED.
WHAT ARE YOU DOING HERE...?
I'VE BEEN TAILING YOU...

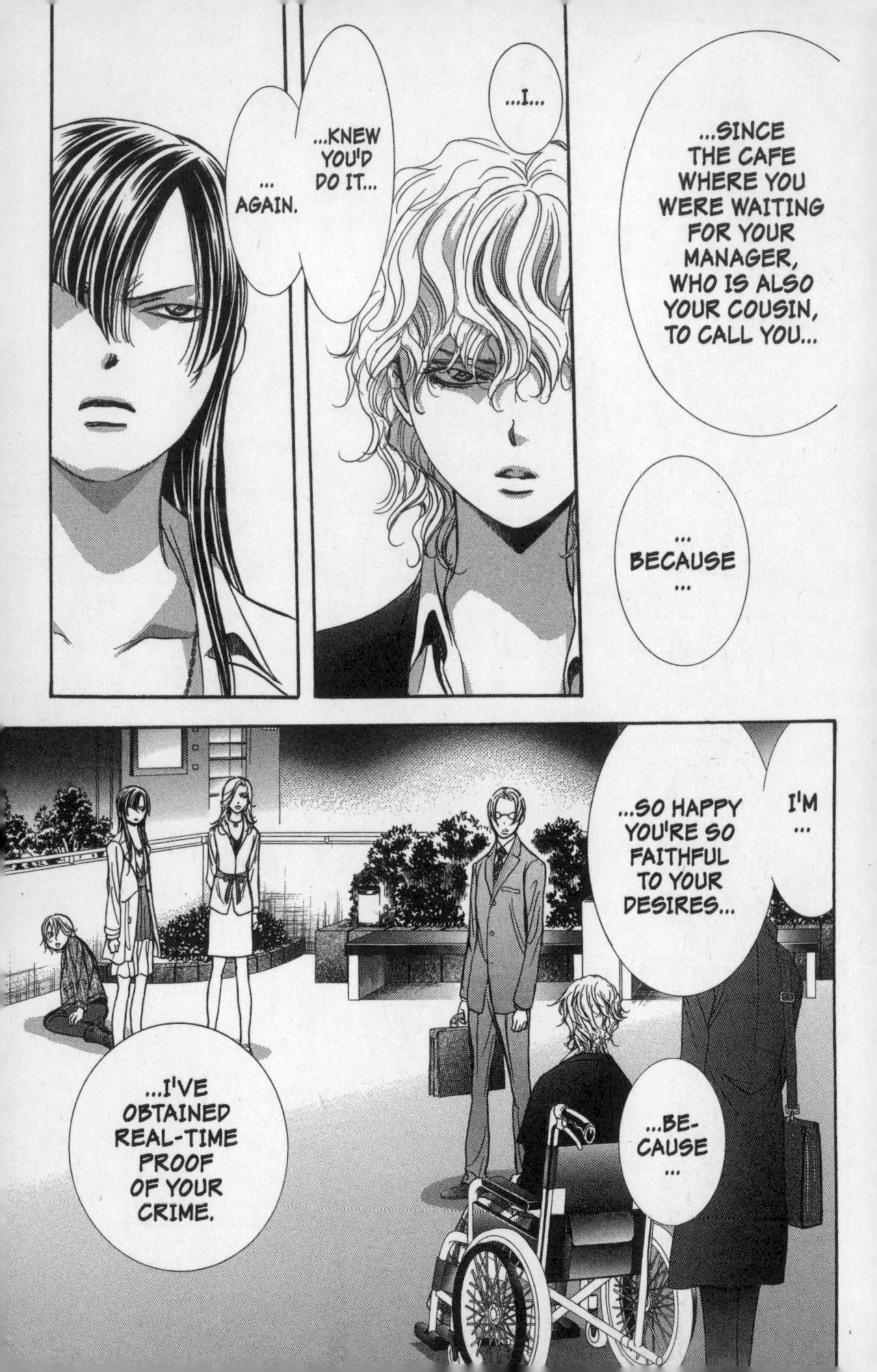
...SINCE THE CAFE WHERE YOU WERE WAITING FOR YOUR MANAGER, WHO IS ALSO YOUR COUSIN, TO CALL YOU...
... BECAUSE ...
...I...
...KNEW YOU'D DO IT...
... AGAIN.
I'M ...
...SO HAPPY YOU'RE SO FAITHFUL TO YOUR DESIRES...
...BE-CAUSE ...
...I'VE OBTAINED REAL-TIME PROOF OF YOUR CRIME.

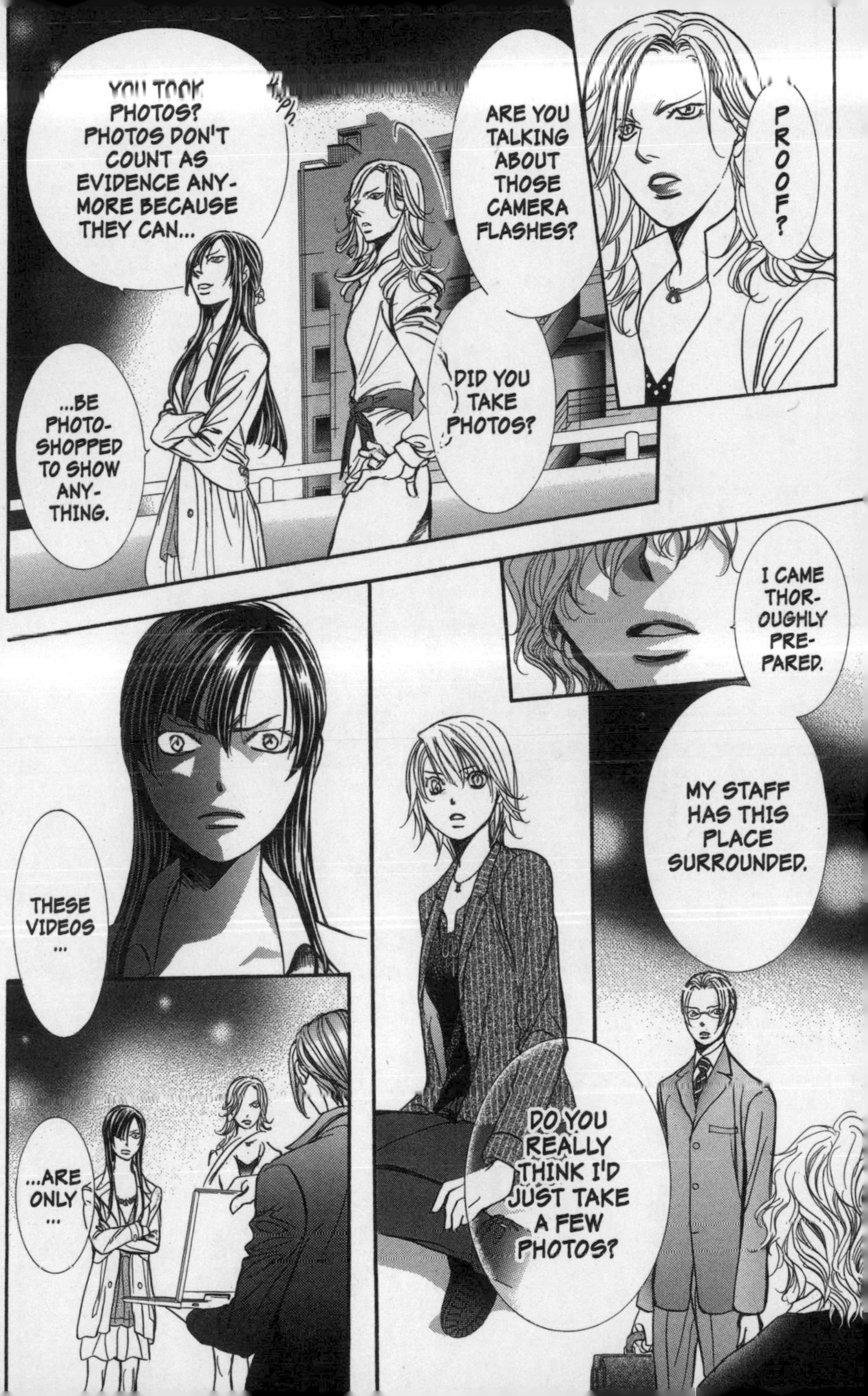
PROOF?
ARE YOU TALKING ABOUT THOSE CAMERA FLASHES?
DID YOU TAKE PHOTOS?
YOU TOOK PHOTOS? PHOTOS DON'T COUNT AS EVIDENCE ANY-MORE BECAUSE THEY CAN...
...BE PHOTO-SHOPPED TO SHOW ANY-THING.
I CAME THOR-OUGHLY PRE-PARED.
MY STAFF HAS THIS PLACE SURROUNDED.
DO YOU REALLY THINK I'D JUST TAKE A FEW PHOTOS?
THESE VIDEOS ...
...ARE ONLY ...

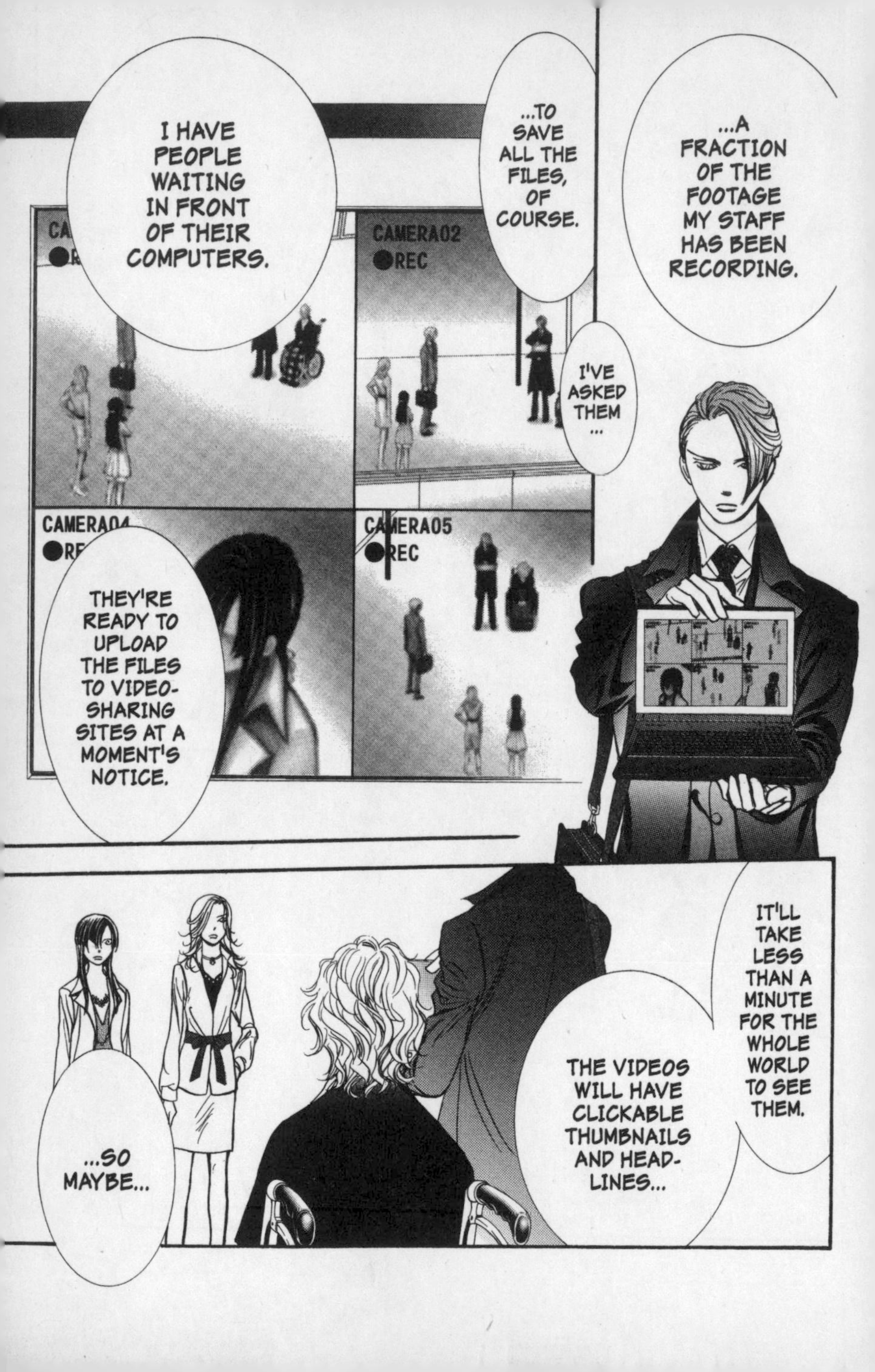
...A FRACTION OF THE FOOTAGE MY STAFF HAS BEEN RECORDING.
I'VE ASKED THEM...
...TO SAVE ALL THE FILES, OF COURSE.
I HAVE PEOPLE WAITING IN FRONT OF THEIR COMPUTERS.
CAMERA02
REC
THEY'RE READY TO UPLOAD THE FILES TO VIDEO-SHARING SITES AT A MOMENT'S NOTICE.
IT'LL TAKE LESS THAN A MINUTE FOR THE WHOLE WORLD TO SEE THEM.
THE VIDEOS WILL HAVE CLICKABLE THUMBNAILS AND HEAD-LINES...
...SO MAYBE...

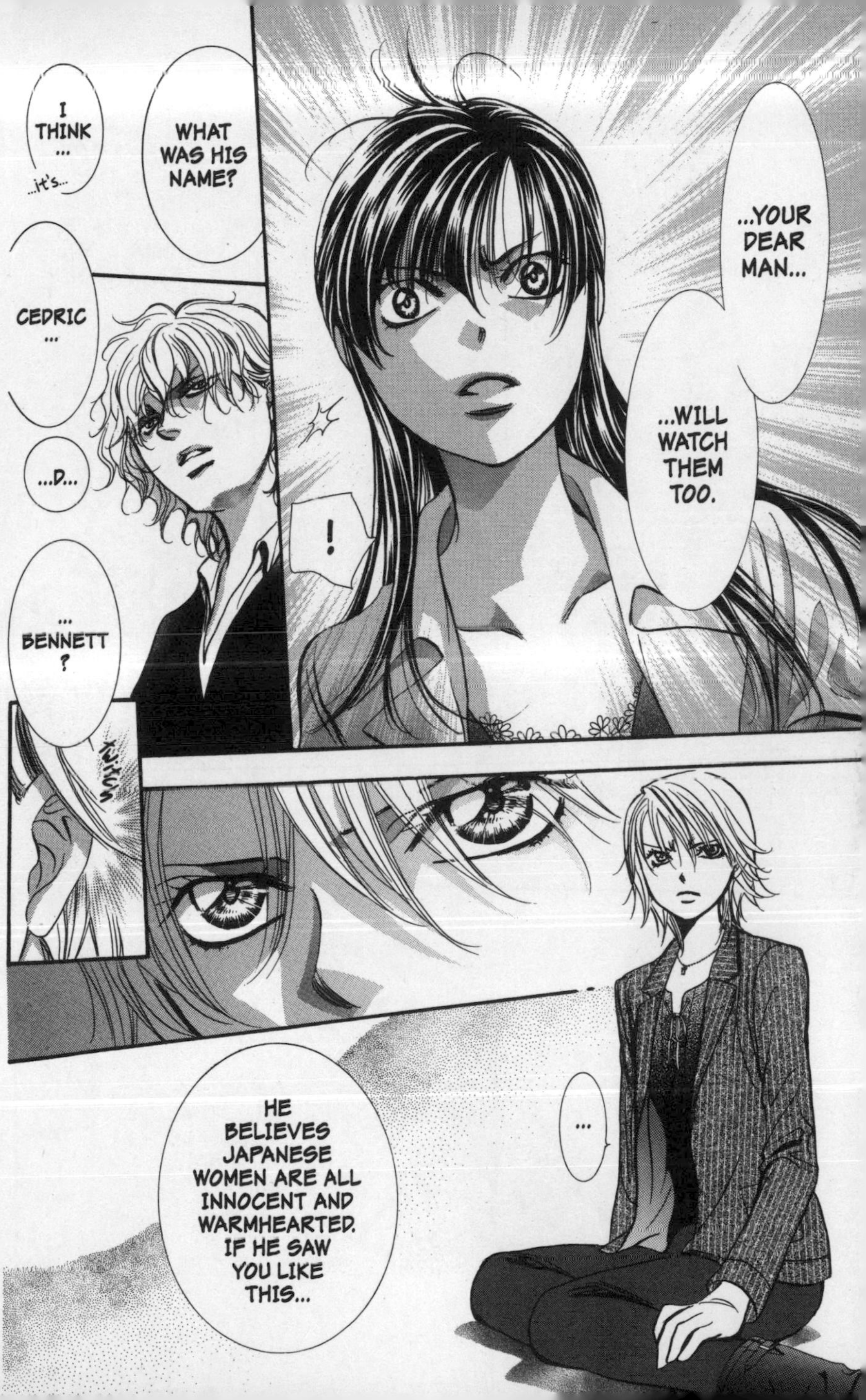

...YOUR DEAR MAN...
...WILL WATCH THEM TOO.
!
WHAT WAS HIS NAME?
I THINK ...
...it's...
CEDRIC ...
...D...
... BENNETT ?
twitch
...
HE BELIEVES JAPANESE WOMEN ARE ALL INNOCENT AND WARMHEARTED. IF HE SAW YOU LIKE THIS...

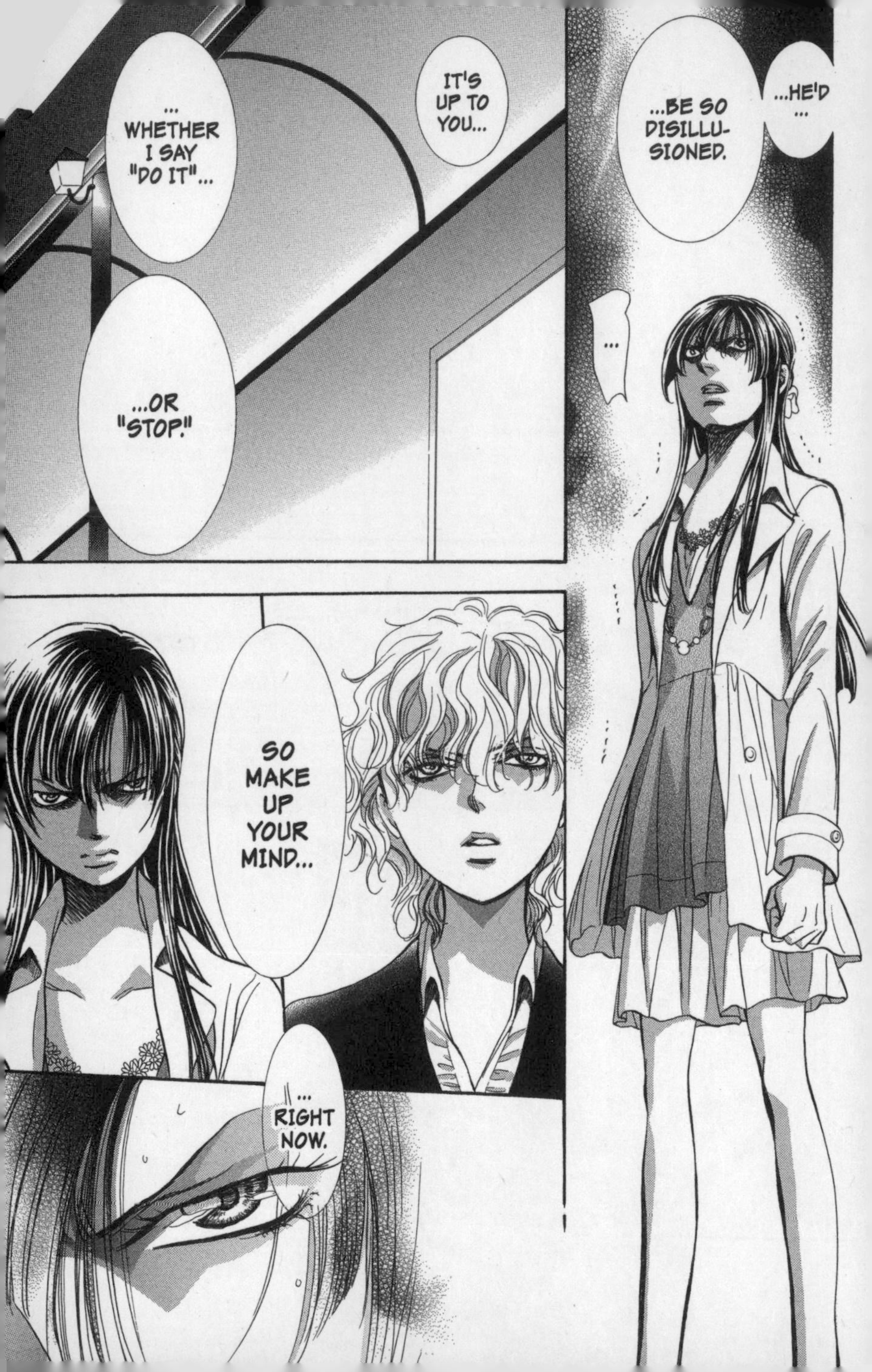
...HE'D ...
...BE SO DISILLU-SIONED.
...
IT'S UP TO YOU...
... WHETHER I SAY "DO IT"...
...OR "STOP."
SO MAKE UP YOUR MIND...
... RIGHT NOW.

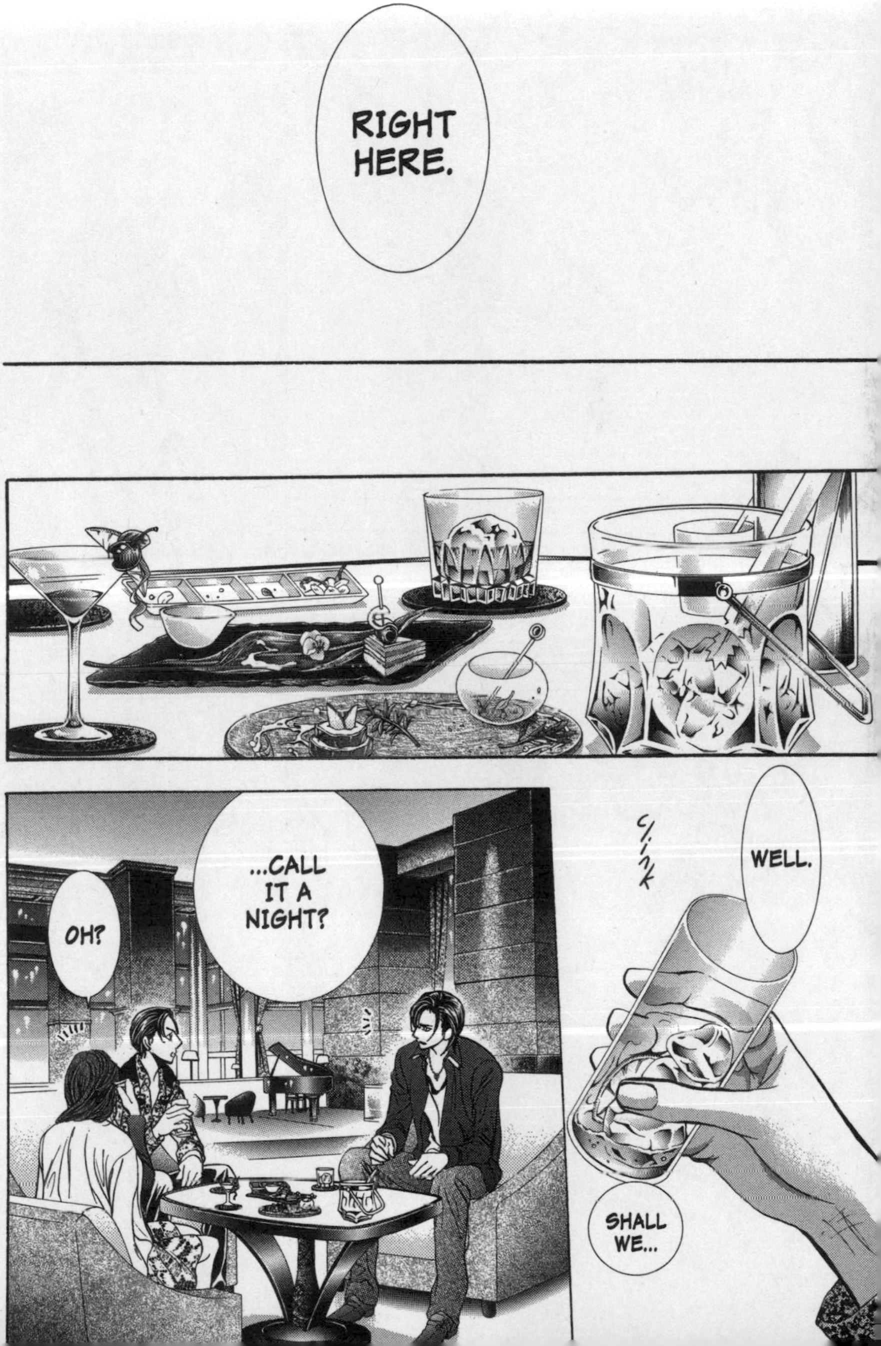
RIGHT HERE.
WELL.
CLINK
SHALL WE...
...CALL IT A NIGHT?
OH?

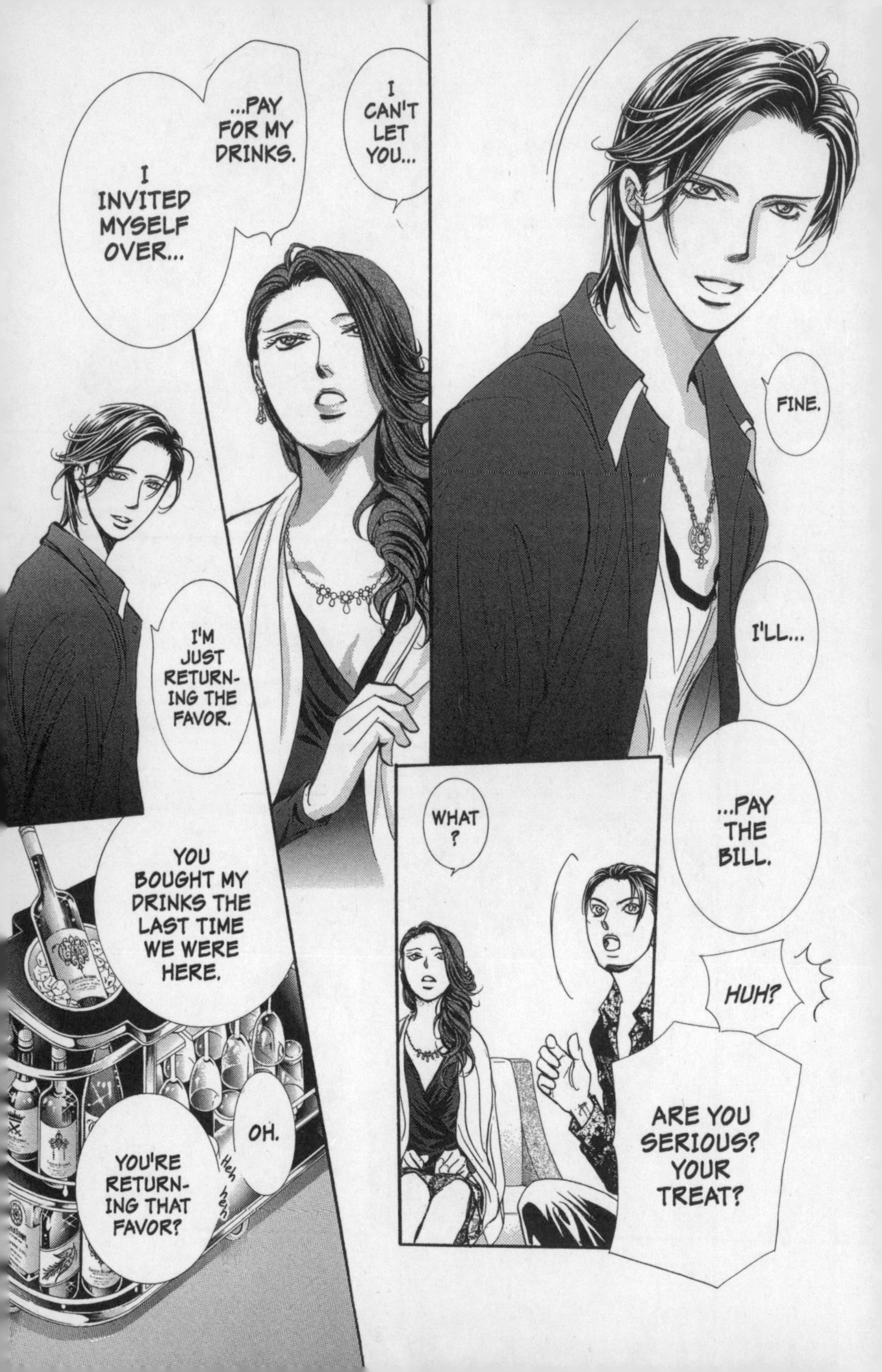
FINE.
I'LL...
...PAY THE BILL.
WHAT?
HUH?
ARE YOU SERIOUS? YOUR TREAT?
I CAN'T LET YOU...
...PAY FOR MY DRINKS.
I INVITED MYSELF OVER...
I'M JUST RETURNING THE FAVOR.
YOU BOUGHT MY DRINKS THE LAST TIME WE WERE HERE.
OH.
Heh heh
YOU'RE RETURNING THAT FAVOR?

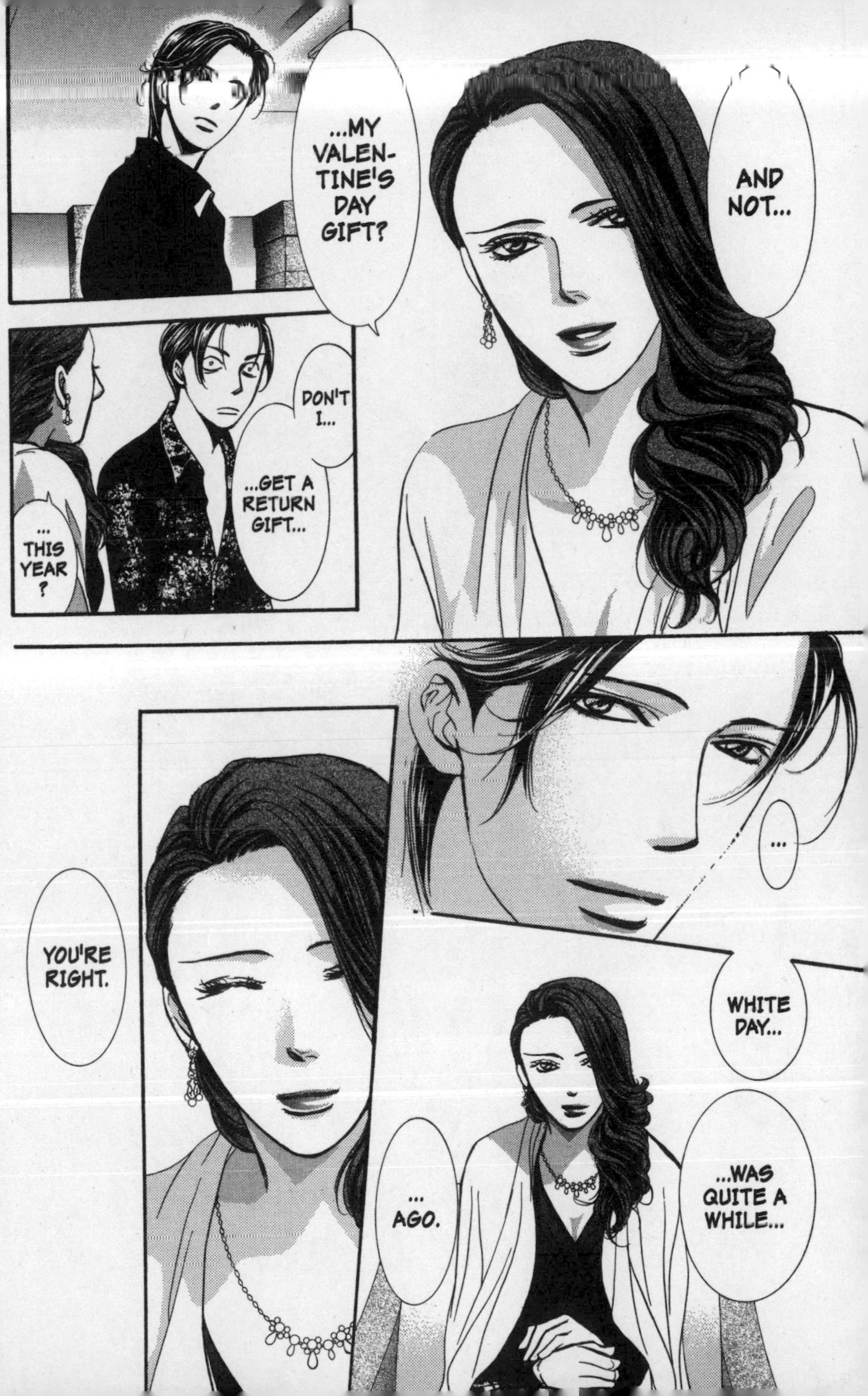
AND NOT...
...MY VALEN-TINE'S DAY GIFT?
DON'T I...
...GET A RETURN GIFT...
... THIS YEAR?
...
WHITE DAY...
...WAS QUITE A WHILE...
... AGO.
YOU'RE RIGHT.

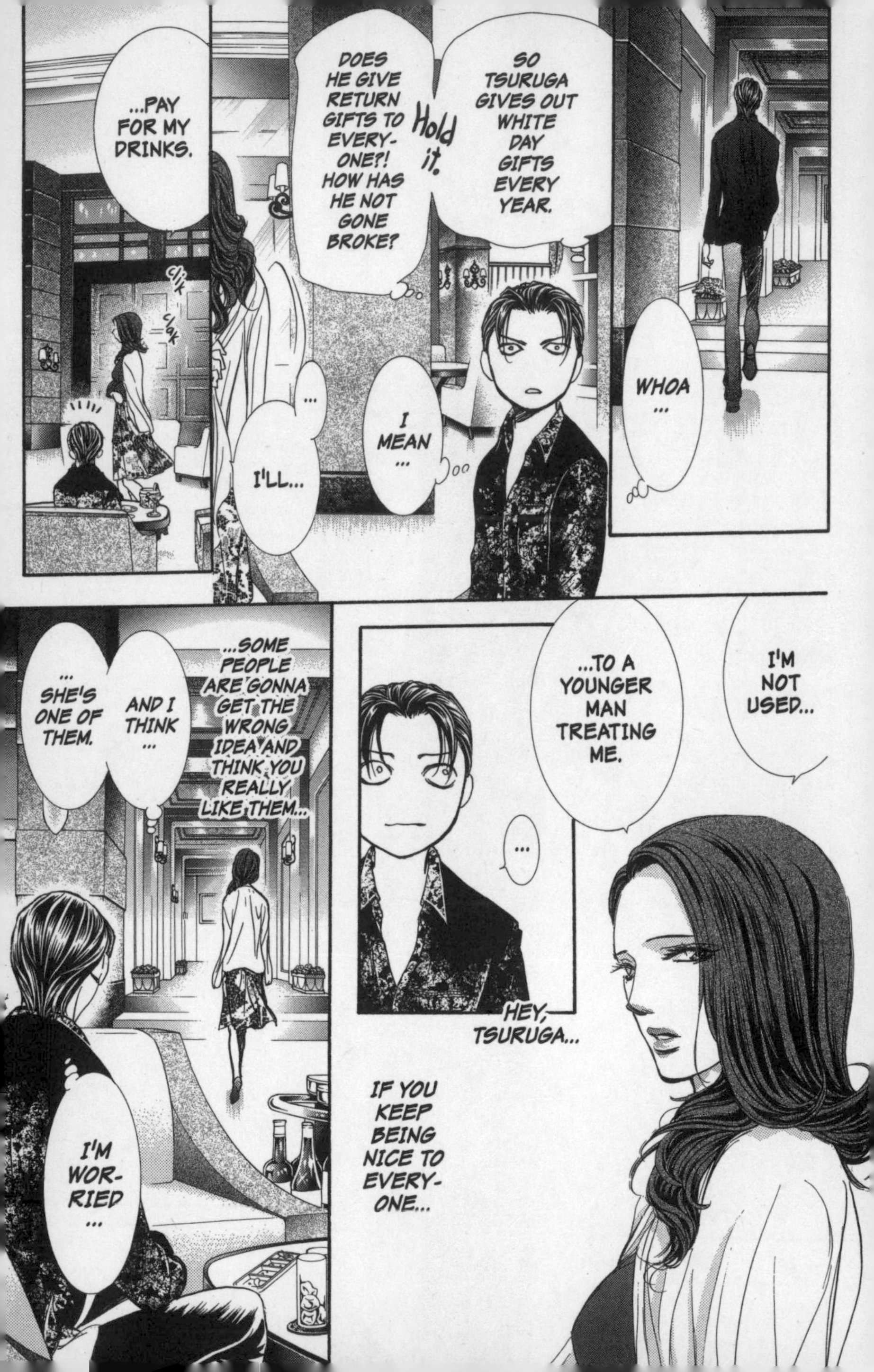
WHOA...
SO TSURUGA GIVES OUT WHITE DAY GIFTS EVERY YEAR.
Hold it.
DOES HE GIVE RETURN GIFTS TO EVERY-ONE?! HOW HAS HE NOT GONE BROKE?
I MEAN...
...
I'LL...
...PAY FOR MY DRINKS.
clik
clak
I'M NOT USED...
...TO A YOUNGER MAN TREATING ME.
...
HEY, TSURUGA...
IF YOU KEEP BEING NICE TO EVERY-ONE...
...SOME PEOPLE ARE GONNA GET THE WRONG IDEA AND THINK YOU REALLY LIKE THEM...
AND I THINK...
...SHE'S ONE OF THEM.
I'M WOR-RIED...

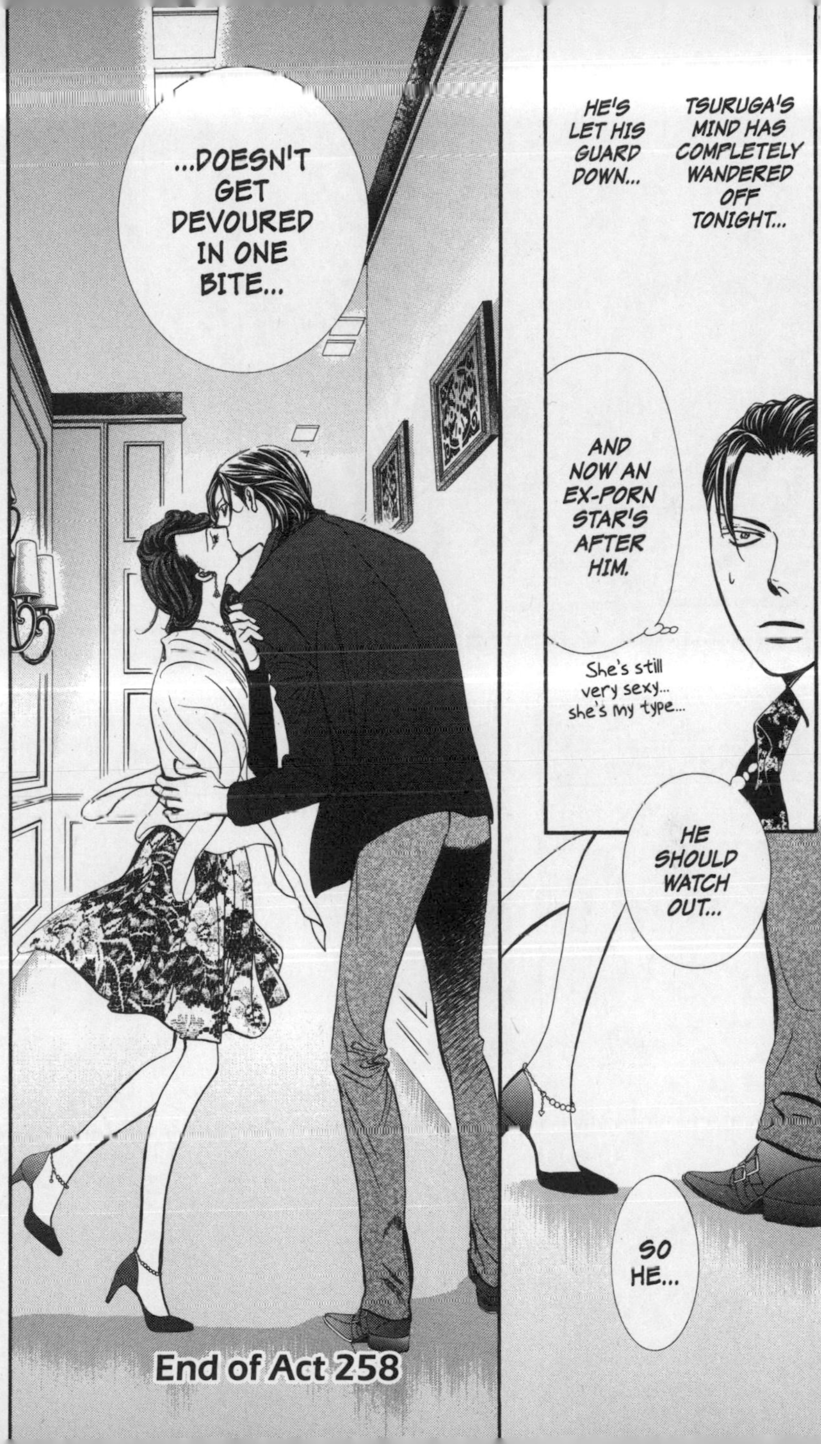
TSURUGA'S MIND HAS COMPLETELY WANDERED OFF TONIGHT...
HE'S LET HIS GUARD DOWN...
AND NOW AN EX-PORN STAR'S AFTER HIM.
She's still very sexy... she's my type...
HE SHOULD WATCH OUT...
SO HE...
...DOESN'T GET DEVOURED IN ONE BITE...

End of Act 258

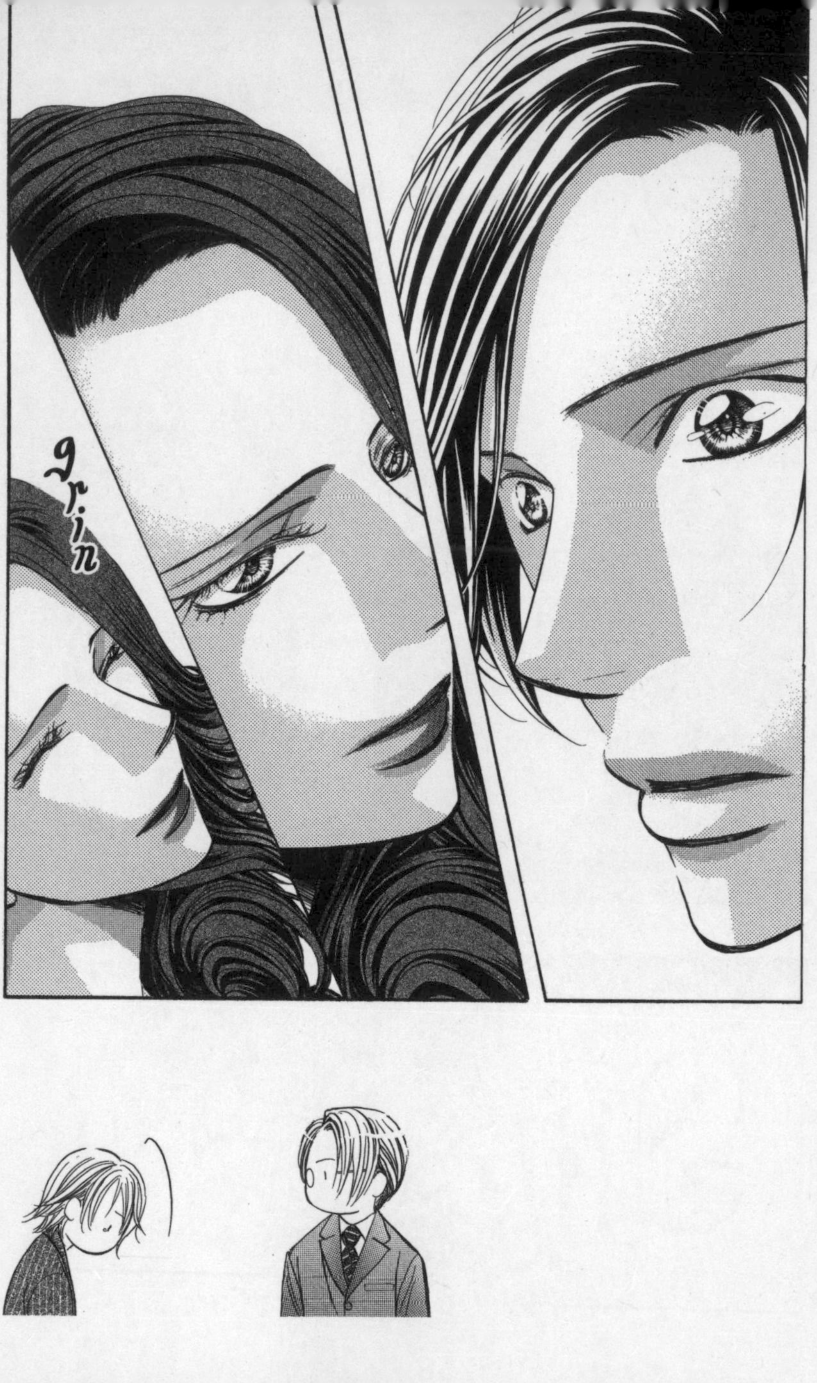
grin

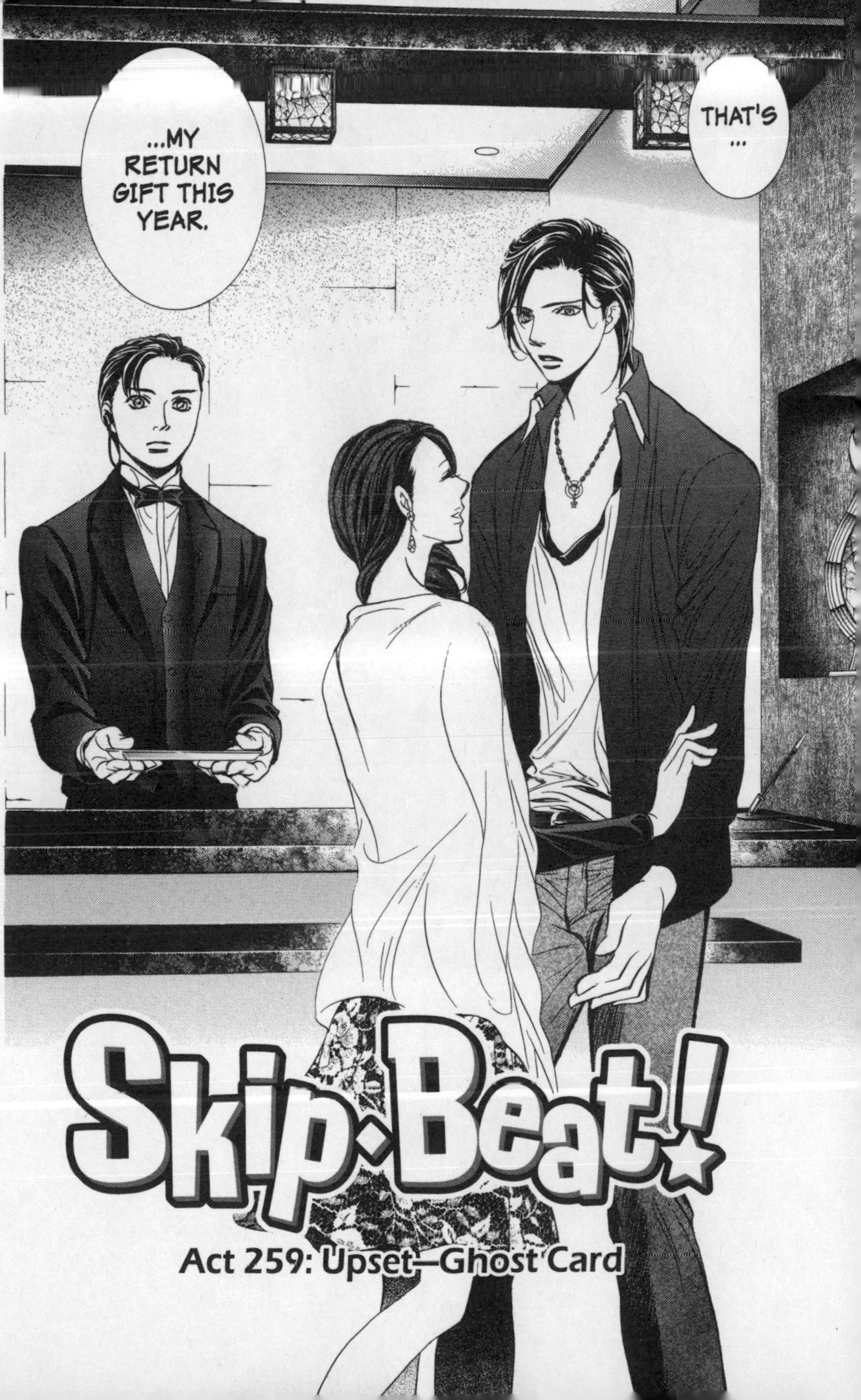

THAT'S ...
...MY RETURN GIFT THIS YEAR.
Skip·Beat!
Act 259: Upset—Ghost Card

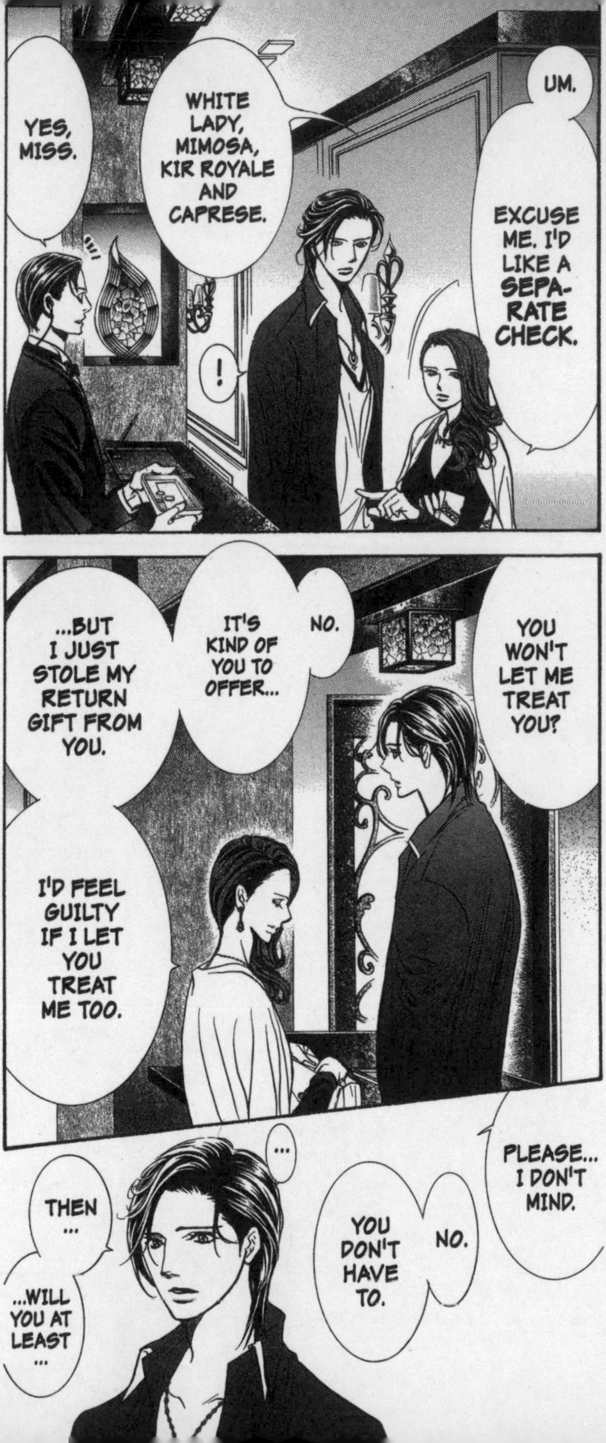
UM.
EXCUSE ME. I'D LIKE A SEPA- RATE CHECK.
!
WHITE LADY, MIMOSA, KIR ROYALE AND CAPRESE.
YES, MISS.
YOU WON'T LET ME TREAT YOU?
NO.
IT'S KIND OF YOU TO OFFER...
...BUT I JUST STOLE MY RETURN GIFT FROM YOU.
I'D FEEL GUILTY IF I LET YOU TREAT ME TOO.
PLEASE... I DON'T MIND.
NO.
YOU DON'T HAVE TO.
...
THEN ...
...WILL YOU AT LEAST ...

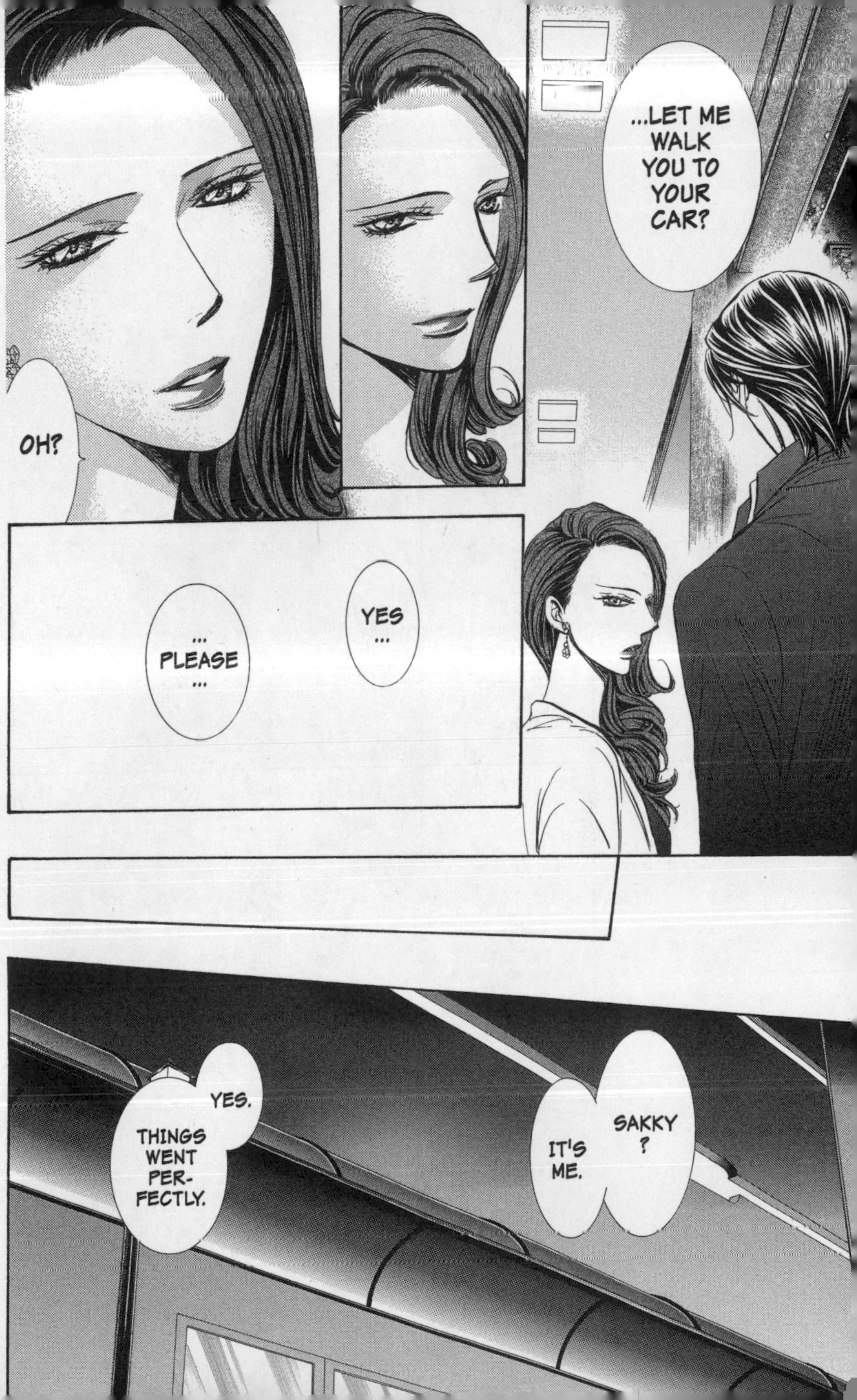
...LET ME WALK YOU TO YOUR CAR?
OH?
YES...
...PLEASE...
SAKKY?
IT'S ME.
YES.
THINGS WENT PER-FECTLY.

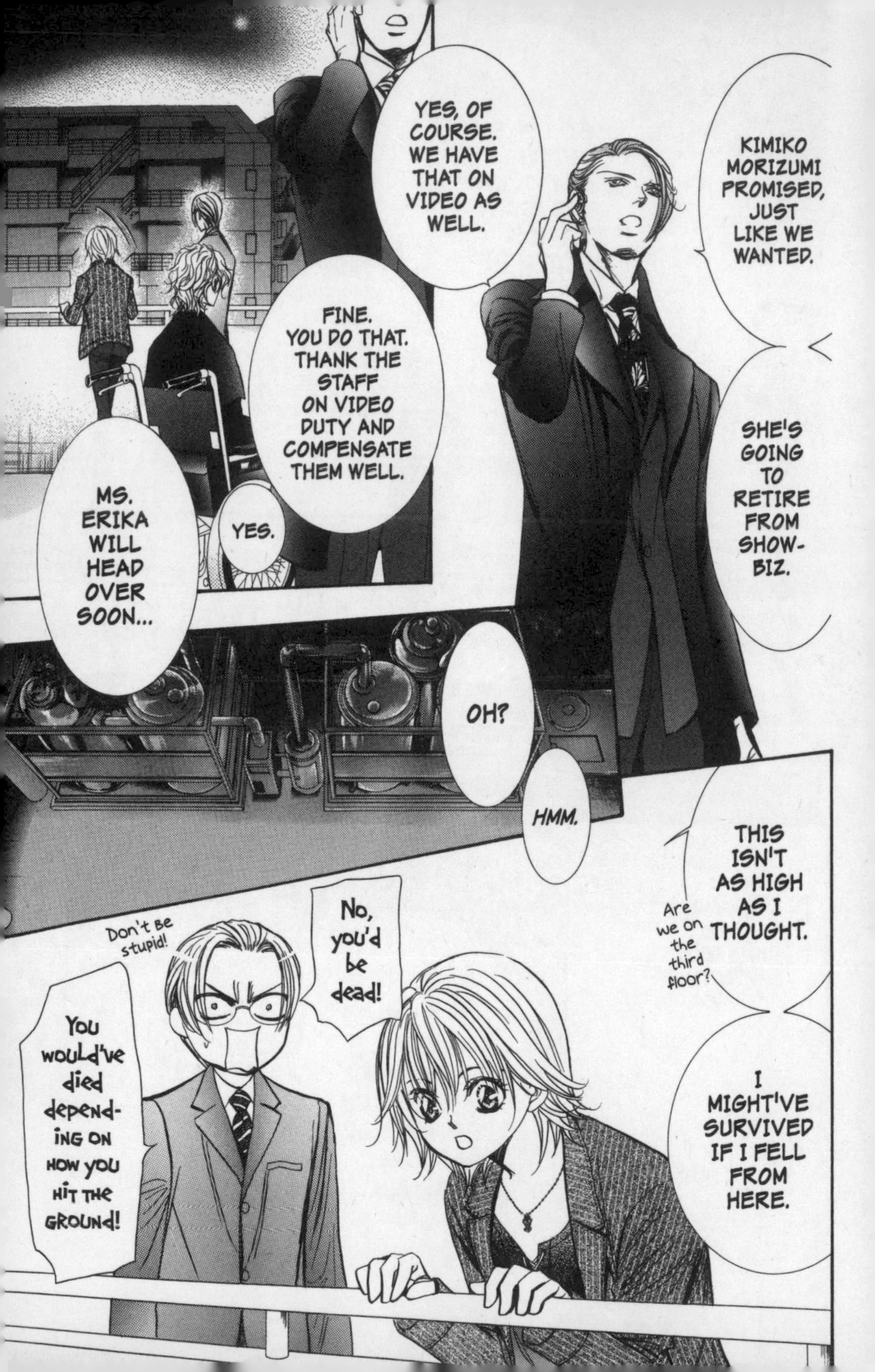
KIMIKO MORIZUMI PROMISED, JUST LIKE WE WANTED.
SHE'S GOING TO RETIRE FROM SHOW-BIZ.
YES, OF COURSE. WE HAVE THAT ON VIDEO AS WELL.
FINE. YOU DO THAT. THANK THE STAFF ON VIDEO DUTY AND COMPENSATE THEM WELL.
YES.
MS. ERIKA WILL HEAD OVER SOON...
OH?
HMM.
THIS ISN'T AS HIGH AS I THOUGHT.
Are we on the third floor?
I MIGHT'VE SURVIVED IF I FELL FROM HERE.
No, you'd be dead!
Don't be stupid!
You would've died depend-ing on how you hit the ground!

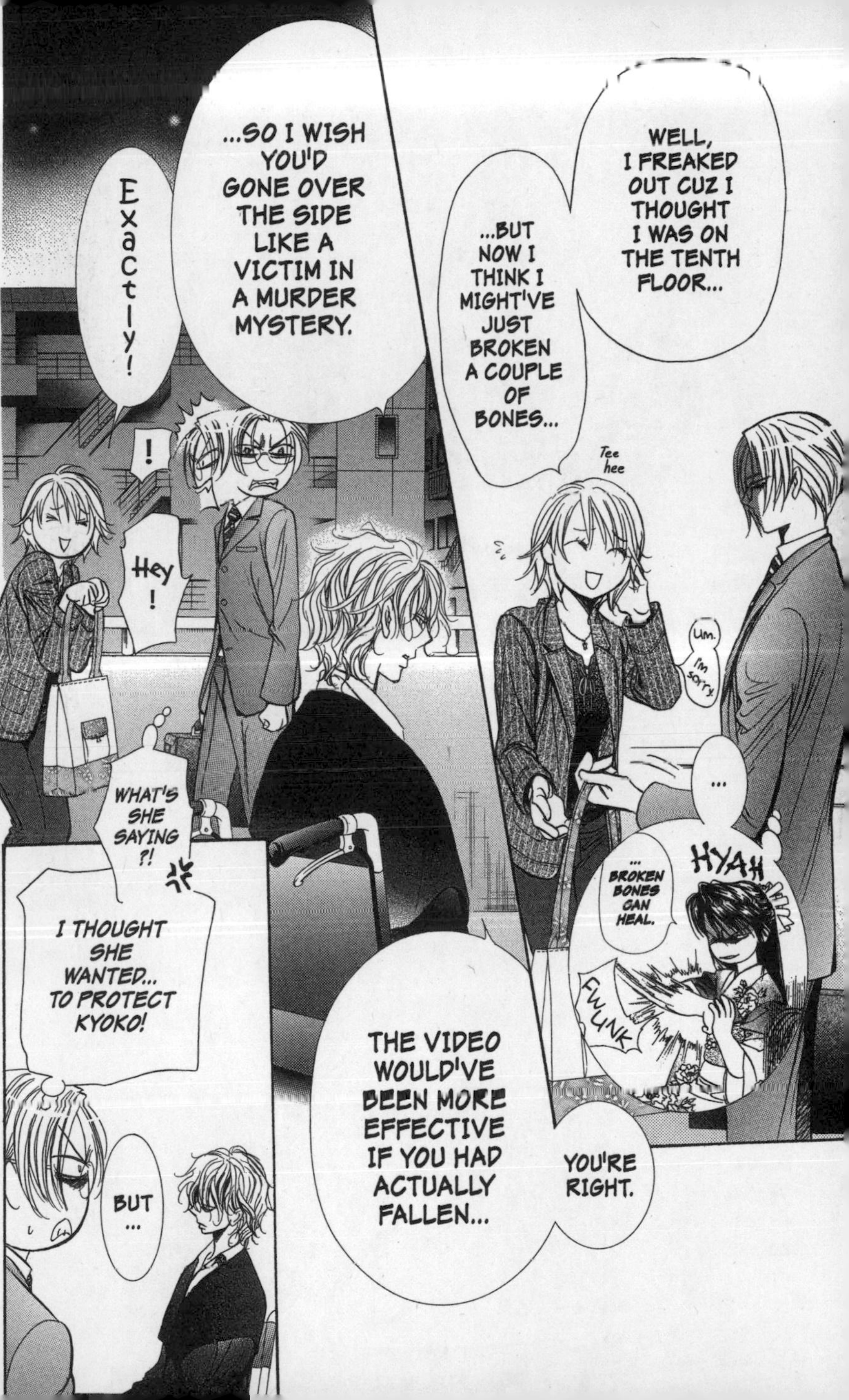

WELL, I FREAKED OUT CUZ I THOUGHT I WAS ON THE TENTH FLOOR...
...BUT NOW I THINK I MIGHT'VE JUST BROKEN A COUPLE OF BONES...
Tee hee
Um. I'm sorry.
...
HYAH
... BROKEN BONES CAN HEAL.
FWUNK
...SO I WISH YOU'D GONE OVER THE SIDE LIKE A VICTIM IN A MURDER MYSTERY.
Exactly!
!
Hey!
WHAT'S SHE SAYING?!
YOU'RE RIGHT.
THE VIDEO WOULD'VE BEEN MORE EFFECTIVE IF YOU HAD ACTUALLY FALLEN...
I THOUGHT SHE WANTED... TO PROTECT KYOKO!
BUT ...

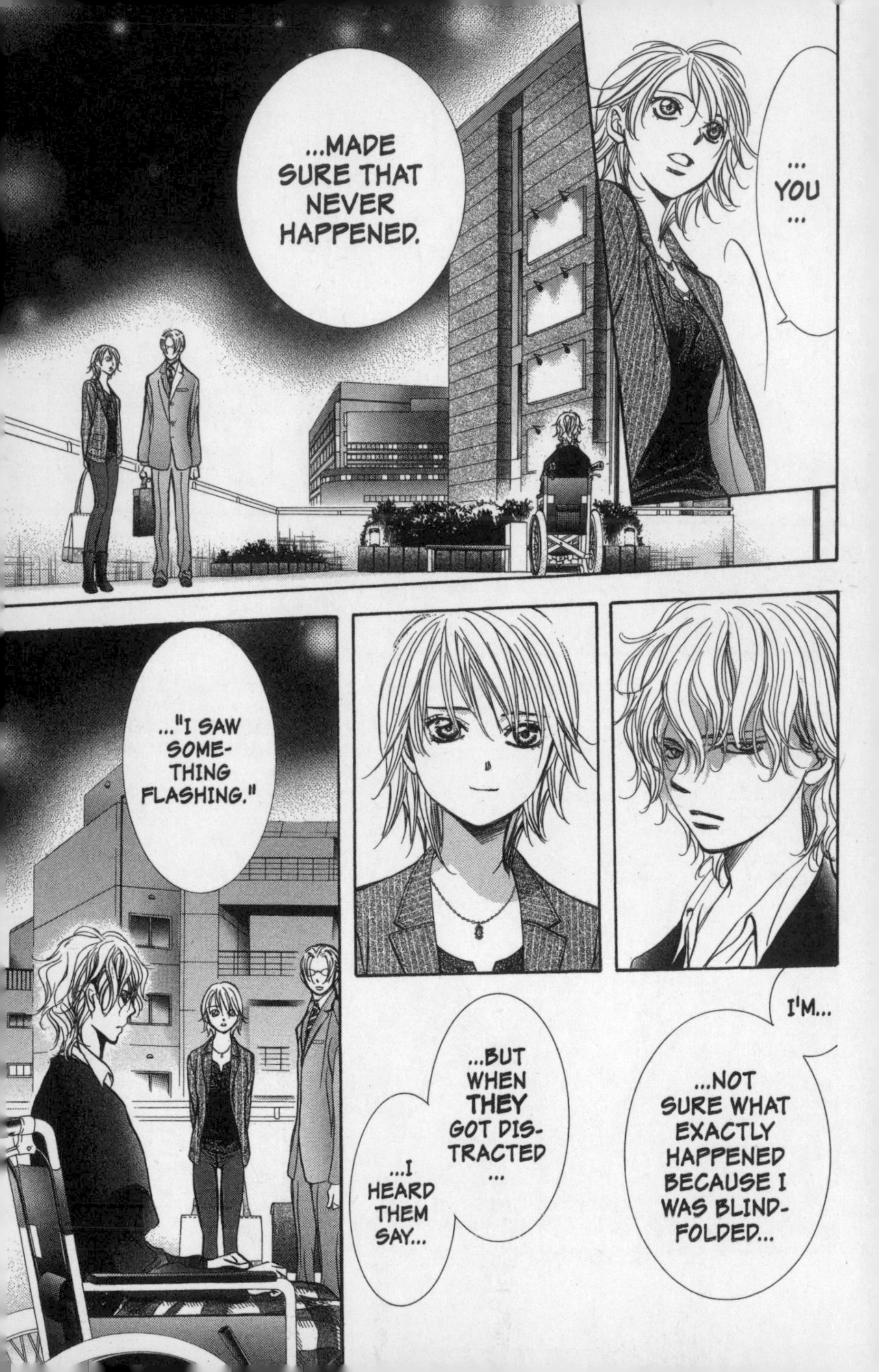
... YOU ...
...MADE SURE THAT NEVER HAPPENED.
I'M...
...NOT SURE WHAT EXACTLY HAPPENED BECAUSE I WAS BLIND-FOLDED...
...BUT WHEN THEY GOT DIS-TRACTED ...
...I HEARD THEM SAY...
..."I SAW SOME-THING FLASHING."

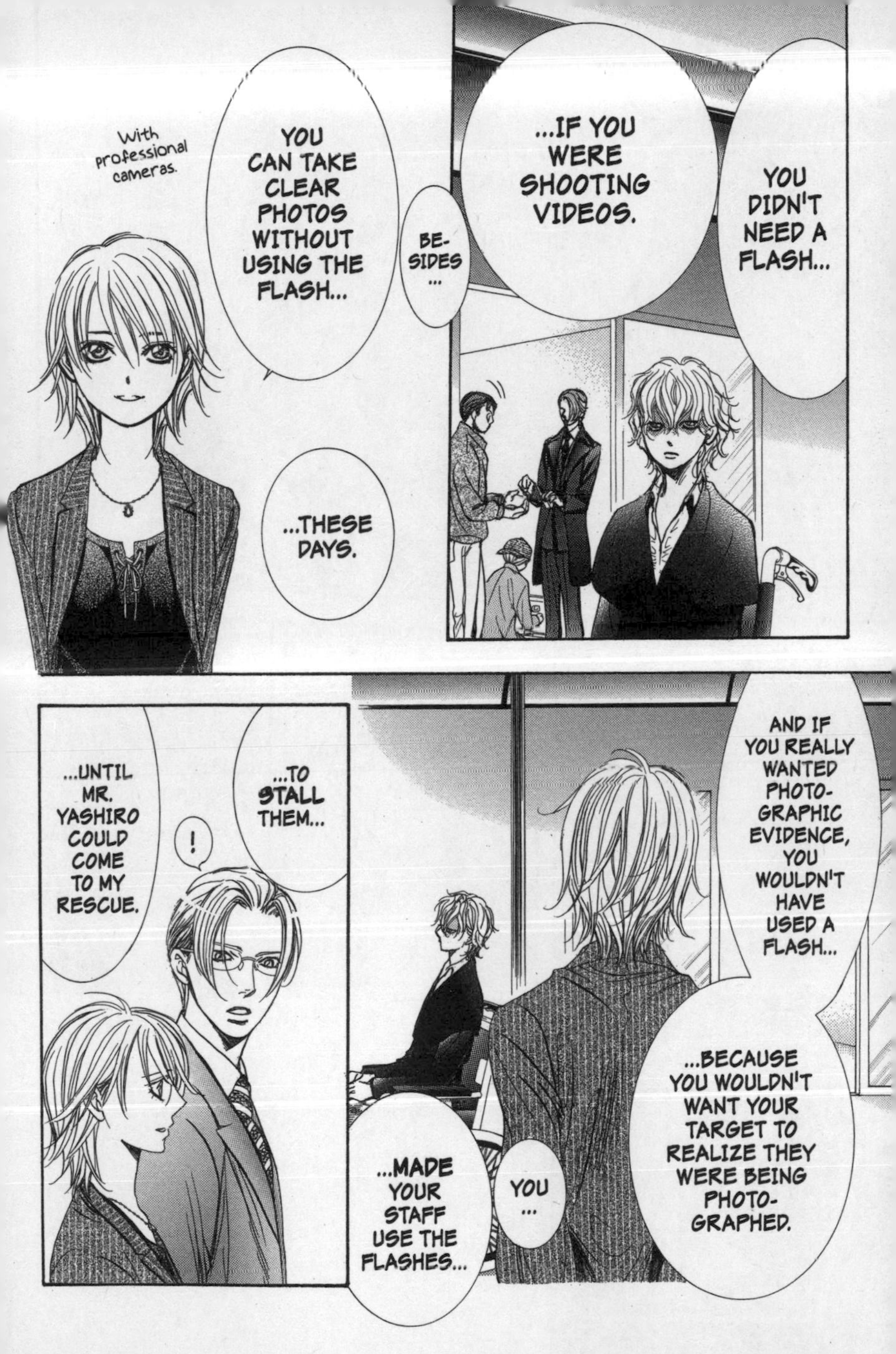
YOU DIDN'T NEED A FLASH...
...IF YOU WERE SHOOTING VIDEOS.
BE-SIDES...
YOU CAN TAKE CLEAR PHOTOS WITHOUT USING THE FLASH...
With professional cameras.
...THESE DAYS.
AND IF YOU REALLY WANTED PHOTO-GRAPHIC EVIDENCE, YOU WOULDN'T HAVE USED A FLASH...
...BECAUSE YOU WOULDN'T WANT YOUR TARGET TO REALIZE THEY WERE BEING PHOTO-GRAPHED.
YOU...
...MADE YOUR STAFF USE THE FLASHES...
...TO STALL THEM...
!
...UNTIL MR. YASHIRO COULD COME TO MY RESCUE.

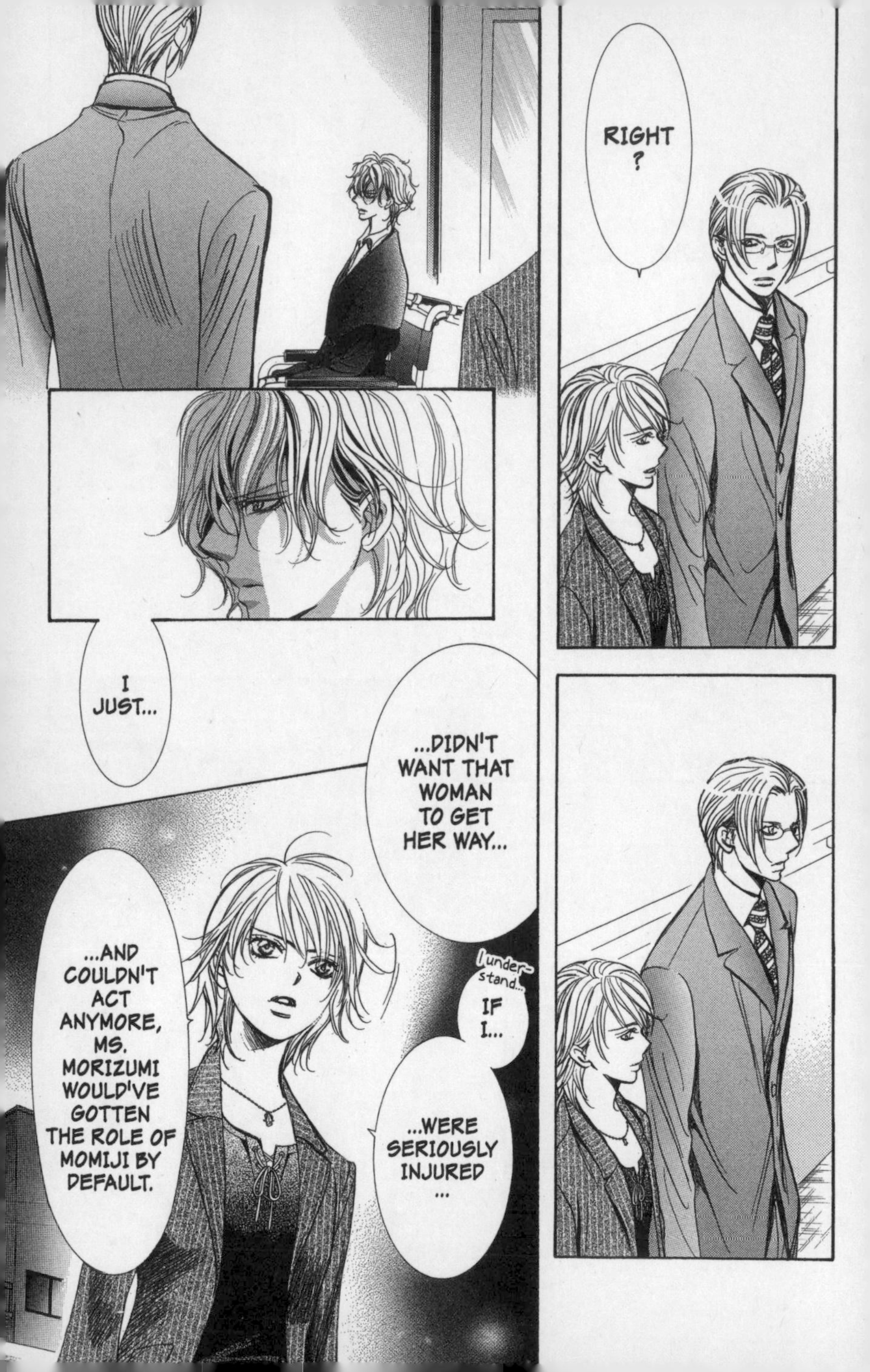

RIGHT?
I JUST...
...DIDN'T WANT THAT WOMAN TO GET HER WAY...
I under-stand...
IF I...
...WERE SERIOUSLY INJURED...
...AND COULDN'T ACT ANYMORE, MS. MORIZUMI WOULD'VE GOTTEN THE ROLE OF MOMIJI BY DEFAULT.

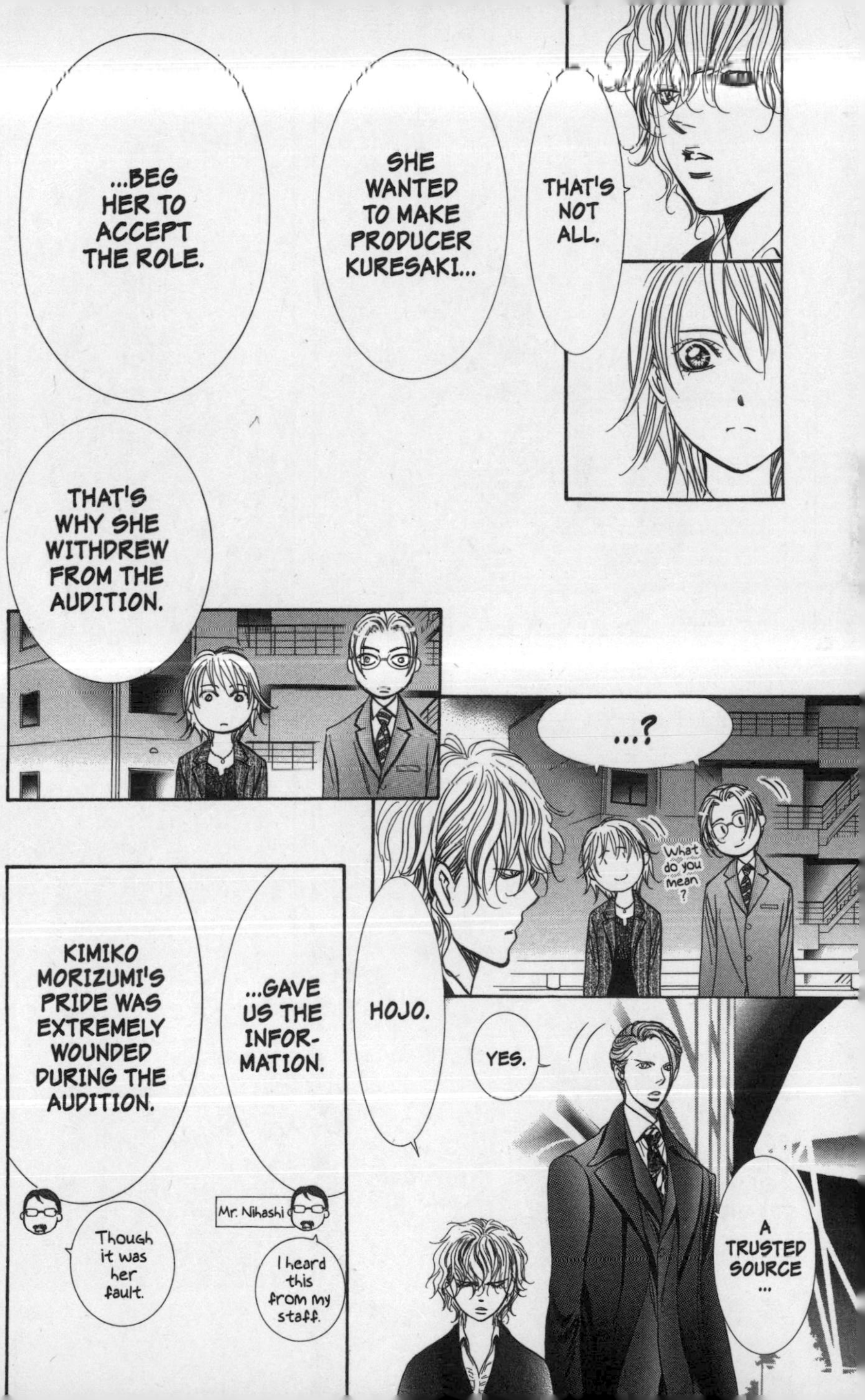
THAT'S NOT ALL.
SHE WANTED TO MAKE PRODUCER KURESAKI...
...BEG HER TO ACCEPT THE ROLE.
THAT'S WHY SHE WITHDREW FROM THE AUDITION.
...?
What do you mean?
HOJO.
YES.
A TRUSTED SOURCE ...
...GAVE US THE INFORMATION.
KIMIKO MORIZUMI'S PRIDE WAS EXTREMELY WOUNDED DURING THE AUDITION.
Mr. Nihashi
I heard this from my staff.
Though it was her fault.

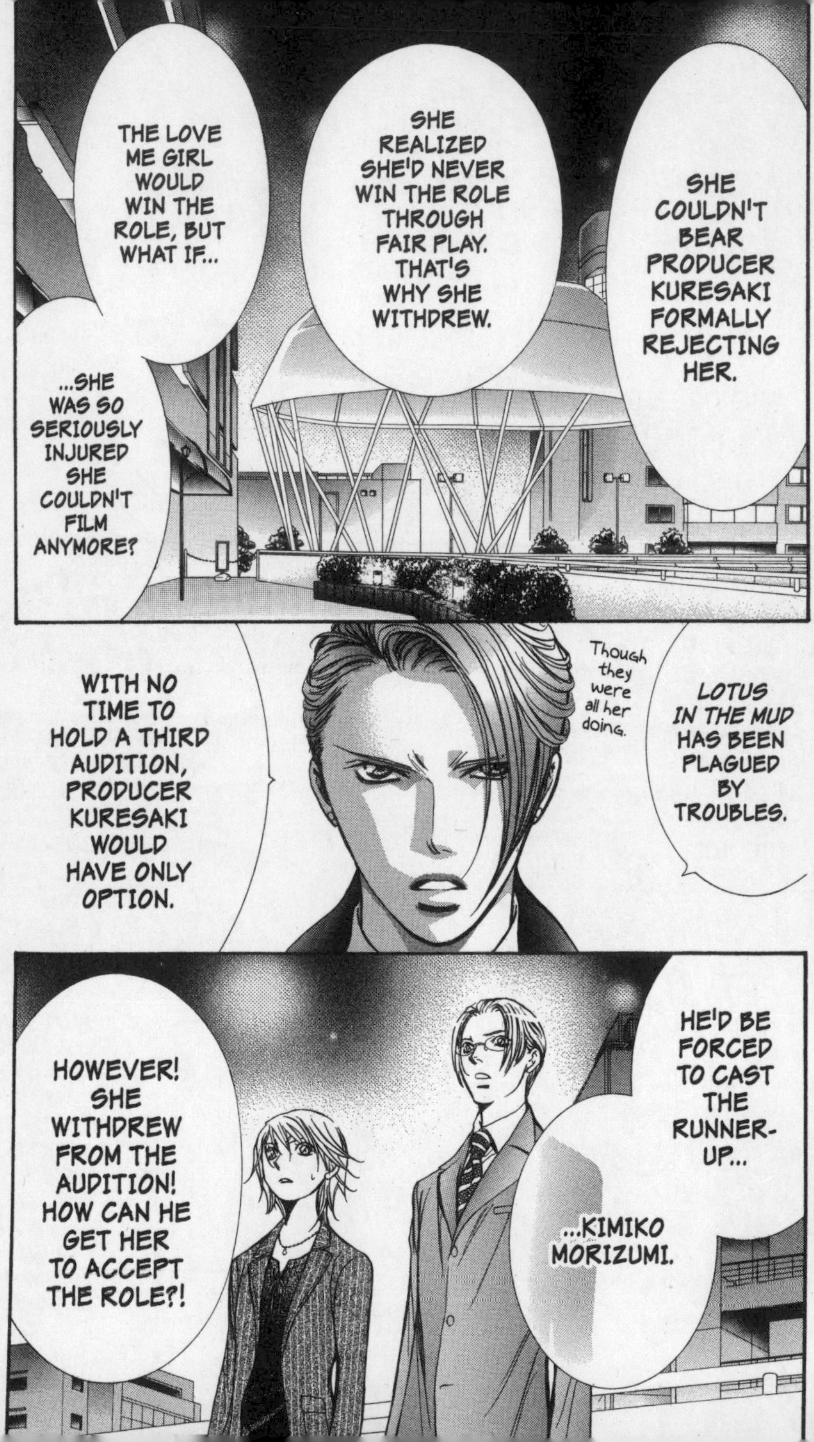
SHE COULDN'T BEAR PRODUCER KURESAKI FORMALLY REJECTING HER.
SHE REALIZED SHE'D NEVER WIN THE ROLE THROUGH FAIR PLAY. THAT'S WHY SHE WITHDREW.
THE LOVE ME GIRL WOULD WIN THE ROLE, BUT WHAT IF...
...SHE WAS SO SERIOUSLY INJURED SHE COULDN'T FILM ANYMORE?
LOTUS IN THE MUD HAS BEEN PLAGUED BY TROUBLES.
Though they were all her doing.
WITH NO TIME TO HOLD A THIRD AUDITION, PRODUCER KURESAKI WOULD HAVE ONLY OPTION.
HE'D BE FORCED TO CAST THE RUNNER-UP...
...KIMIKO MORIZUMI.
HOWEVER! SHE WITHDREW FROM THE AUDITION! HOW CAN HE GET HER TO ACCEPT THE ROLE?!

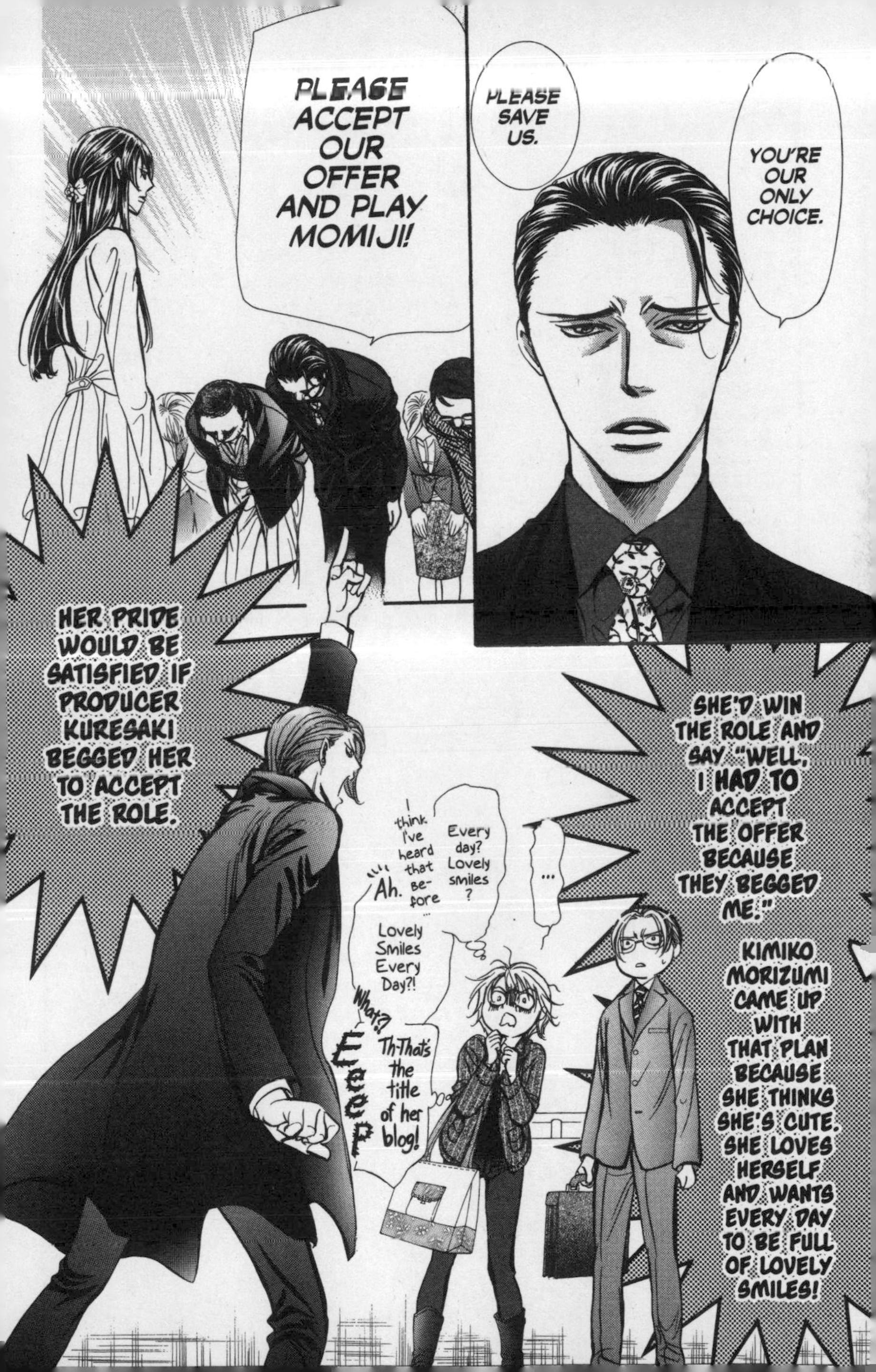
YOU'RE OUR ONLY CHOICE.
PLEASE SAVE US.
PLEASE ACCEPT OUR OFFER AND PLAY MOMIJI!
SHE'D WIN THE ROLE AND SAY "WELL, I HAD TO ACCEPT THE OFFER BECAUSE THEY BEGGED ME."
KIMIKO MORIZUMI CAME UP WITH THAT PLAN BECAUSE SHE THINKS SHE'S CUTE. SHE LOVES HERSELF AND WANTS EVERY DAY TO BE FULL OF LOVELY SMILES!
...
Every day? Lovely smiles?
I think I've heard that be-fore...
Ah.
Lovely Smiles Every Day?!
What?!
Th-That's the title of her blog!
Eeep
HER PRIDE WOULD BE SATISFIED IF PRODUCER KURESAKI BEGGED HER TO ACCEPT THE ROLE.

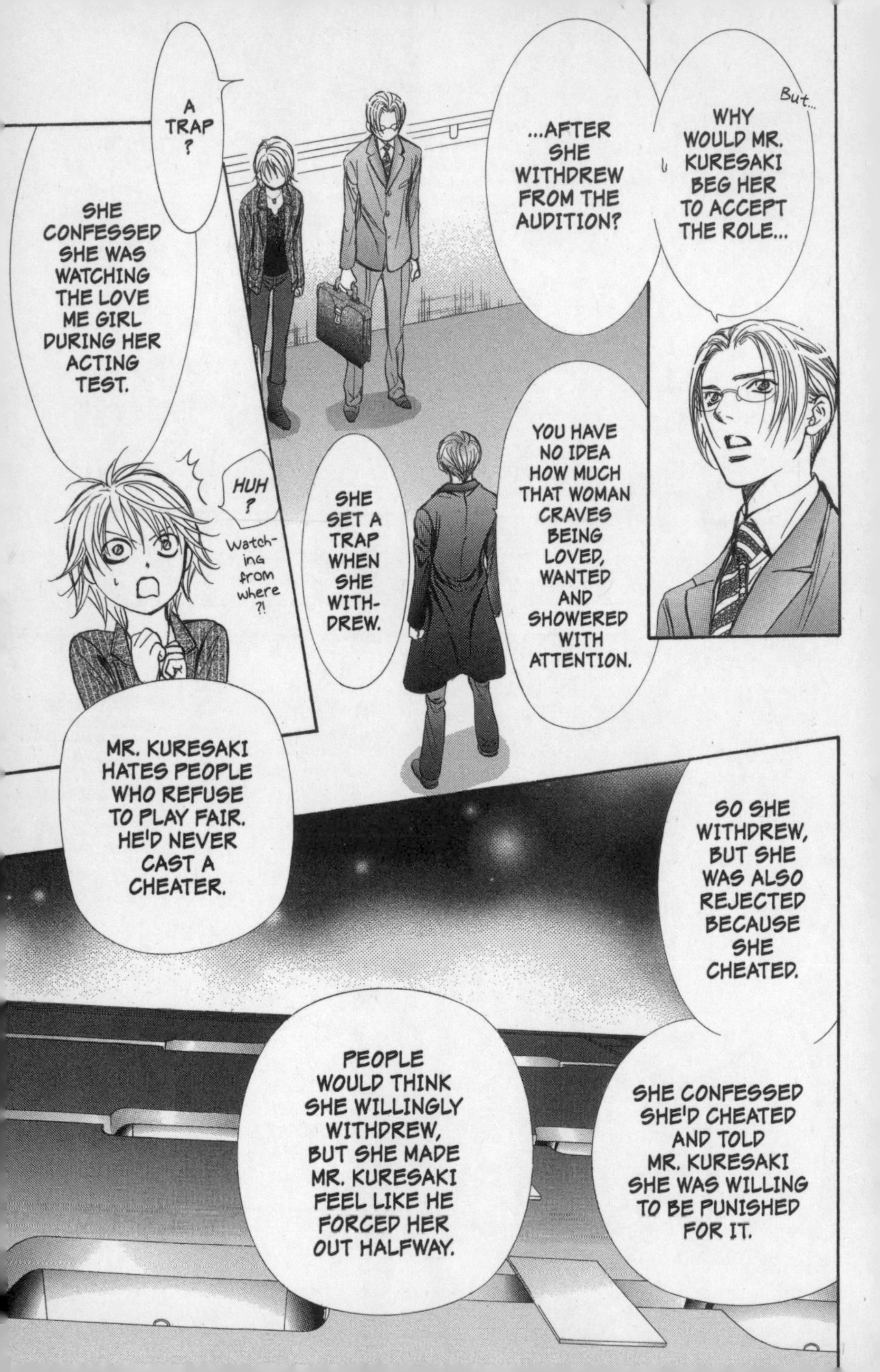
But...
WHY WOULD MR. KURESAKI BEG HER TO ACCEPT THE ROLE...
...AFTER SHE WITHDREW FROM THE AUDITION?
YOU HAVE NO IDEA HOW MUCH THAT WOMAN CRAVES BEING LOVED, WANTED AND SHOWERED WITH ATTENTION.
SHE SET A TRAP WHEN SHE WITH-DREW.
A TRAP?
SHE CONFESSED SHE WAS WATCHING THE LOVE ME GIRL DURING HER ACTING TEST.
HUH?
Watch-ing from where?!
MR. KURESAKI HATES PEOPLE WHO REFUSE TO PLAY FAIR. HE'D NEVER CAST A CHEATER.
SO SHE WITHDREW, BUT SHE WAS ALSO REJECTED BECAUSE SHE CHEATED.
SHE CONFESSED SHE'D CHEATED AND TOLD MR. KURESAKI SHE WAS WILLING TO BE PUNISHED FOR IT.
PEOPLE WOULD THINK SHE WILLINGLY WITHDREW, BUT SHE MADE MR. KURESAKI FEEL LIKE HE FORCED HER OUT HALFWAY.

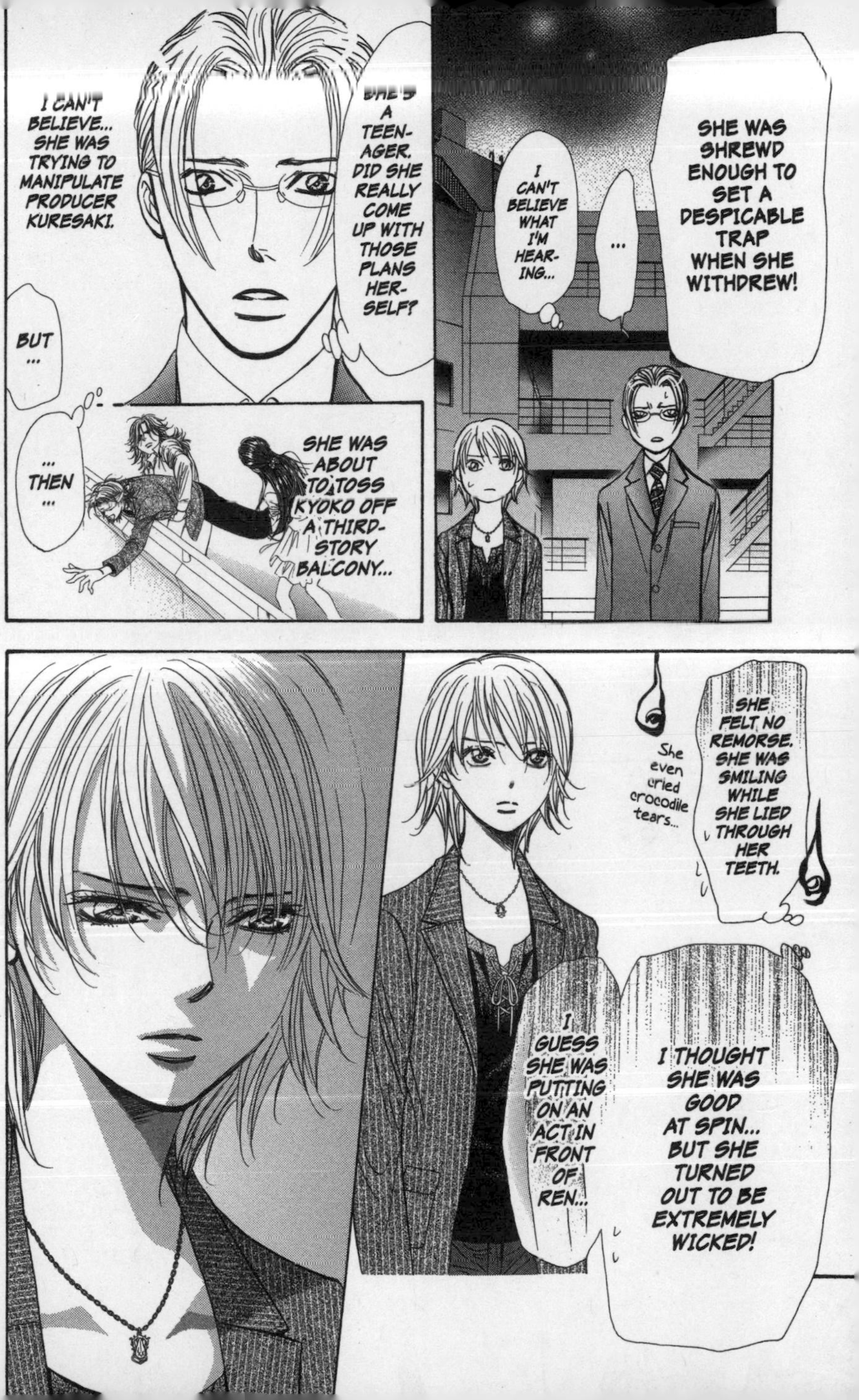

SHE WAS SHREWD ENOUGH TO SET A DESPICABLE TRAP WHEN SHE WITHDREW!
...
I CAN'T BELIEVE WHAT I'M HEARING...
SHE'S A TEEN-AGER. DID SHE REALLY COME UP WITH THOSE PLANS HERSELF?
I CAN'T BELIEVE... SHE WAS TRYING TO MANIPULATE PRODUCER KURESAKI.
BUT...
SHE WAS ABOUT TO TOSS KYOKO OFF A THIRD-STORY BALCONY...
...THEN...
SHE FELT NO REMORSE. SHE WAS SMILING WHILE SHE LIED THROUGH HER TEETH.
She even cried crocodile tears...
I THOUGHT SHE WAS GOOD AT SPIN... BUT SHE TURNED OUT TO BE EXTREMELY WICKED!
I GUESS SHE WAS PUTTING ON AN ACT IN FRONT OF REN...

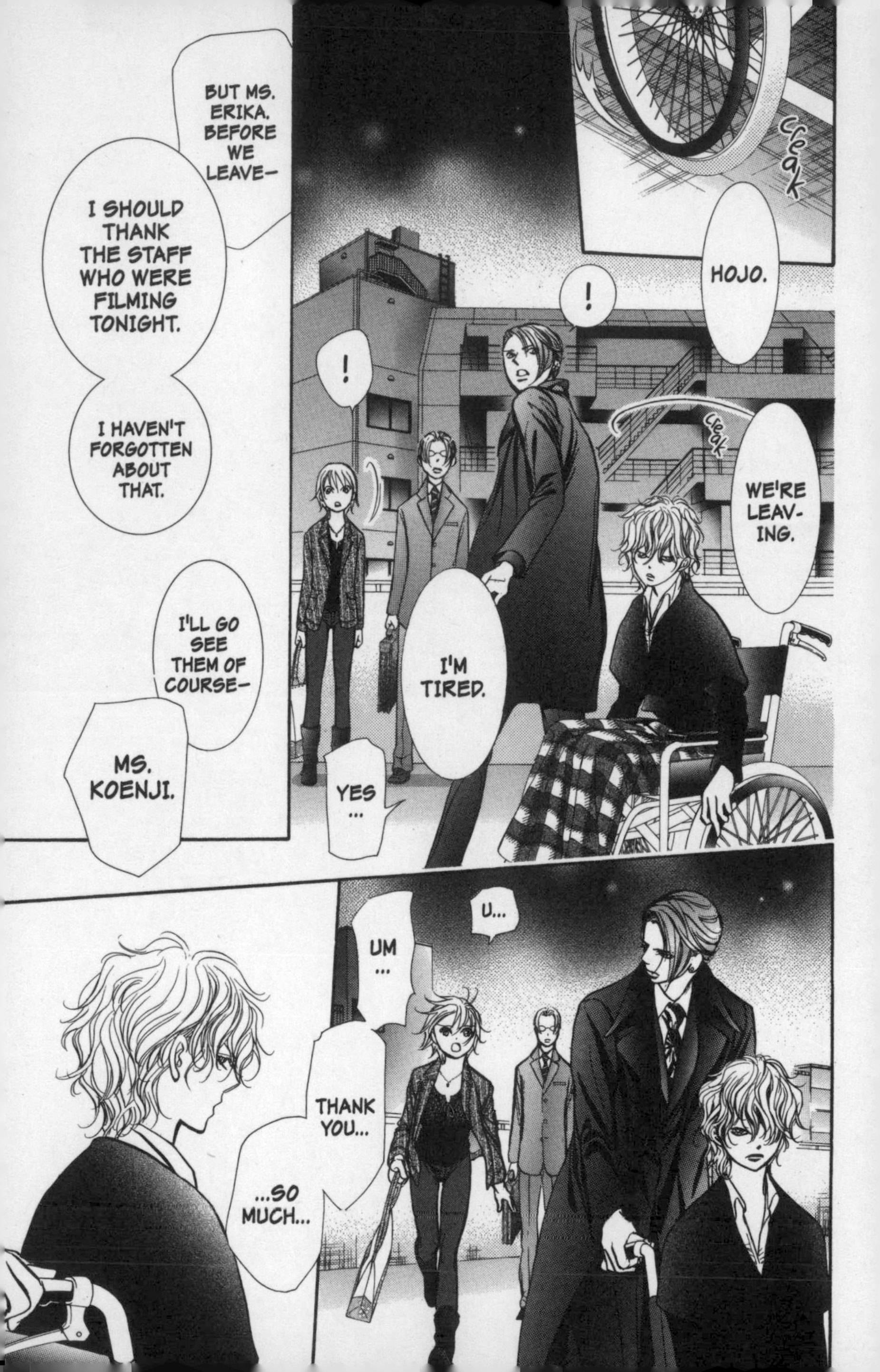
creak
HOJO.
WE'RE LEAV-ING.
creak
!
!
I'M TIRED.
YES ...
BUT MS. ERIKA. BEFORE WE LEAVE—
I SHOULD THANK THE STAFF WHO WERE FILMING TONIGHT.
I HAVEN'T FORGOTTEN ABOUT THAT.
I'LL GO SEE THEM OF COURSE—
MS. KOENJI.
U...
UM ...
THANK YOU...
...SO MUCH...

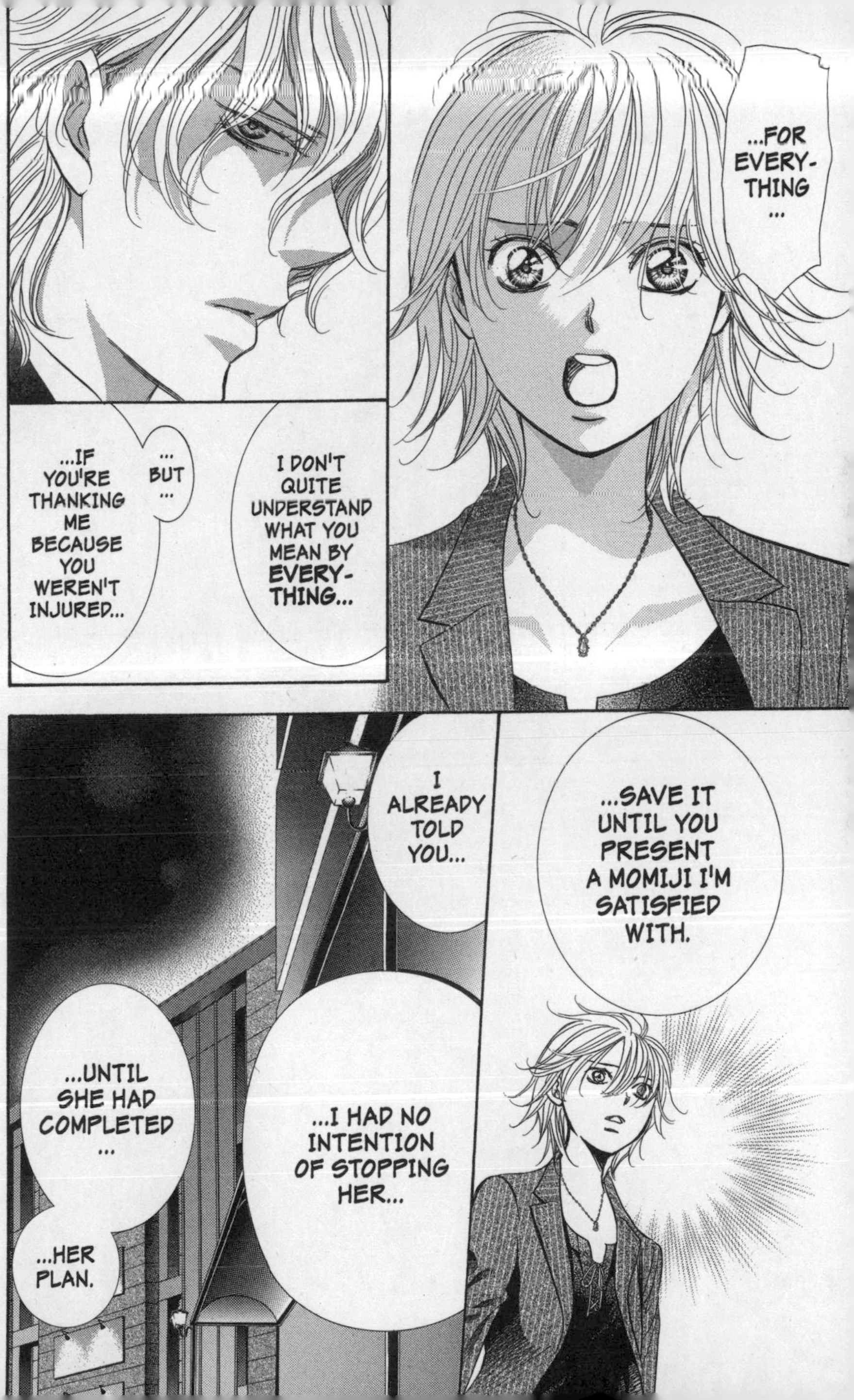
...FOR EVERYTHING...
I DON'T QUITE UNDERSTAND WHAT YOU MEAN BY EVERYTHING...
...BUT...
...IF YOU'RE THANKING ME BECAUSE YOU WEREN'T INJURED...
...SAVE IT UNTIL YOU PRESENT A MOMIJI I'M SATISFIED WITH.
I ALREADY TOLD YOU...
...I HAD NO INTENTION OF STOPPING HER...
...UNTIL SHE HAD COMPLETED...
...HER PLAN.

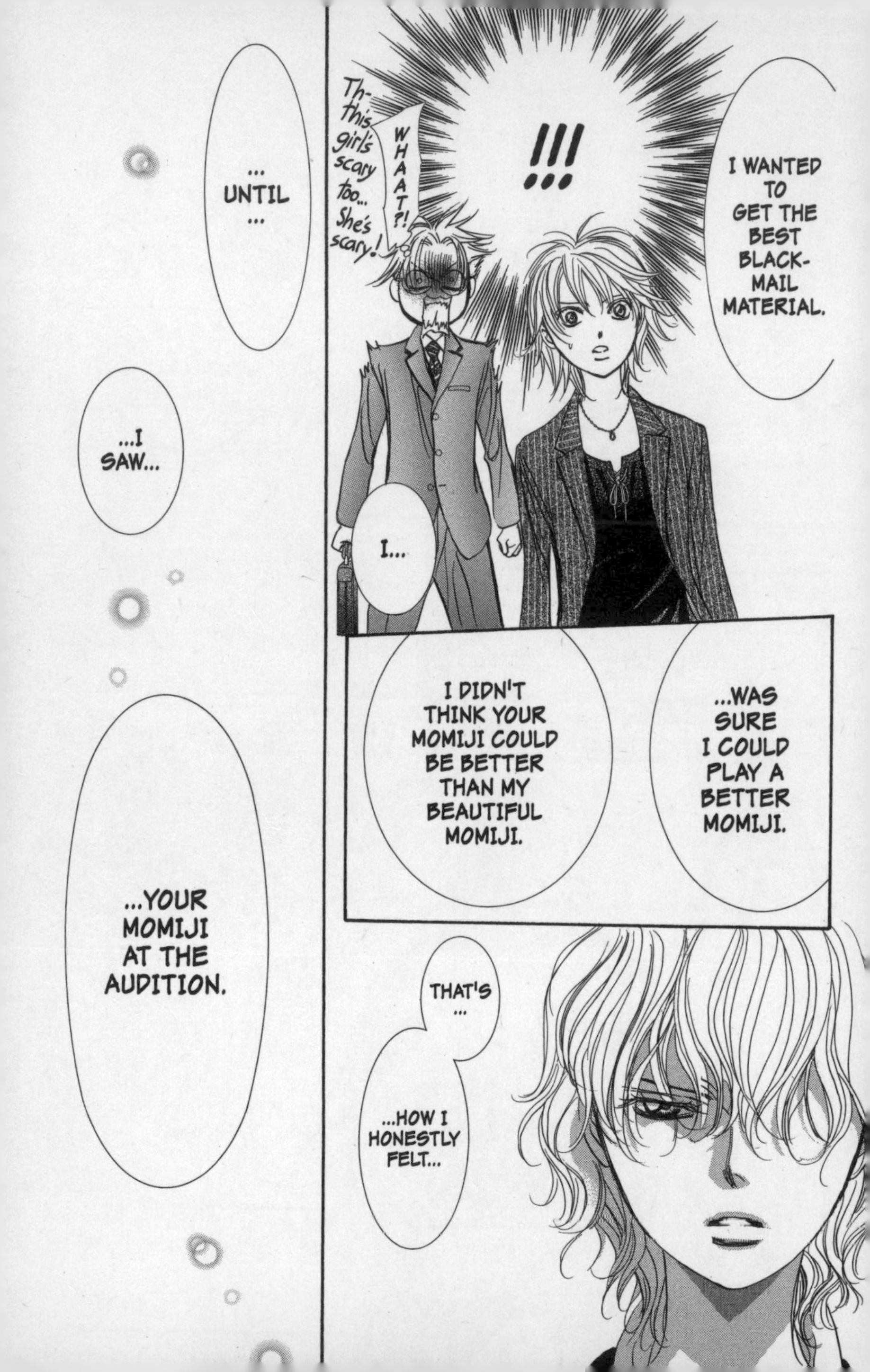
I WANTED TO GET THE BEST BLACK-MAIL MATERIAL.
!!!
WHAAAT?!
Th-this girl's scary too... She's scary!
I...
...WAS SURE I COULD PLAY A BETTER MOMIJI.
I DIDN'T THINK YOUR MOMIJI COULD BE BETTER THAN MY BEAUTIFUL MOMIJI.
THAT'S...
...HOW I HONESTLY FELT...
...UNTIL...
...I SAW...
...YOUR MOMIJI AT THE AUDITION.

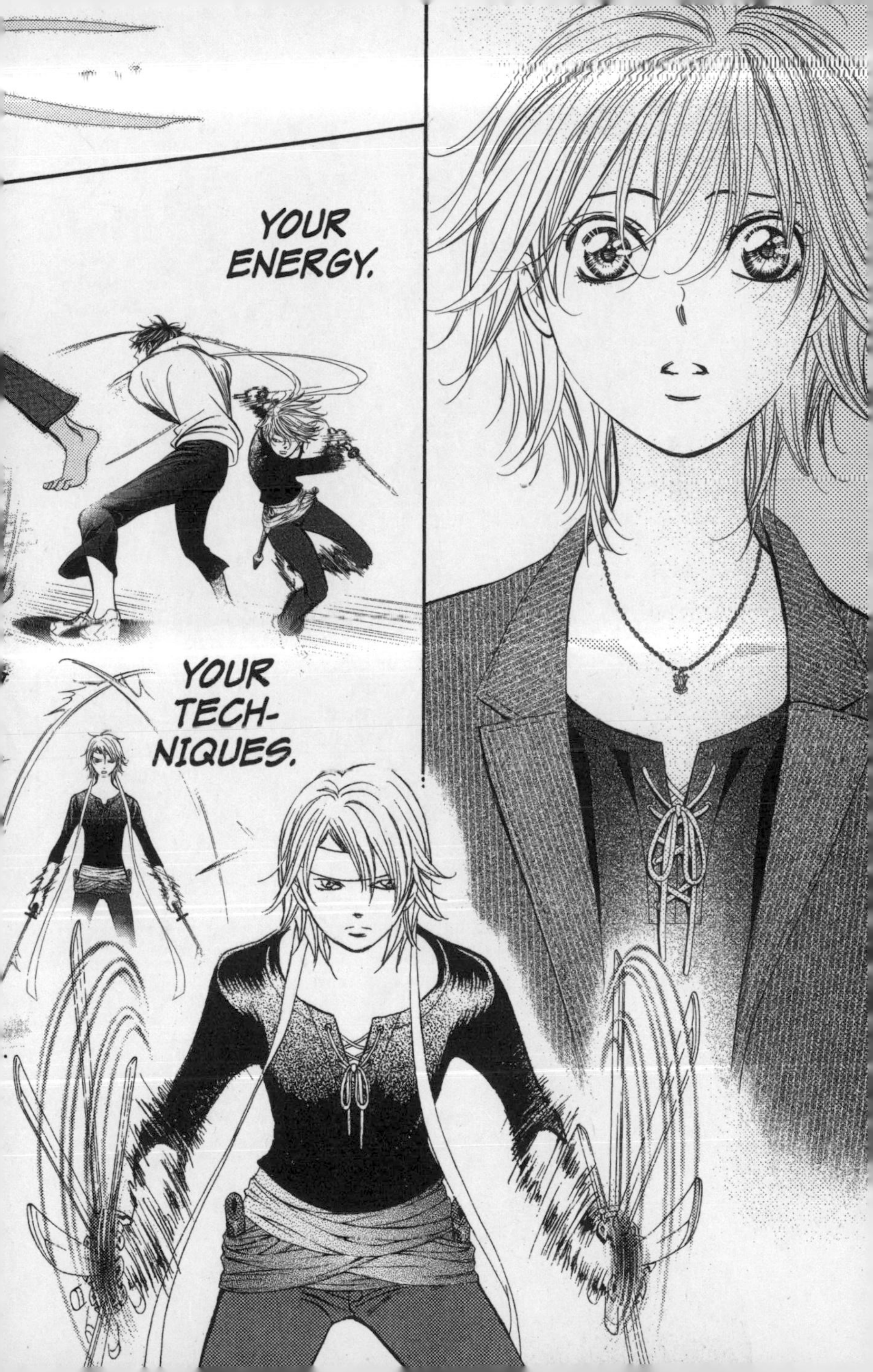
YOUR ENERGY.
YOUR TECH-
NIQUES.

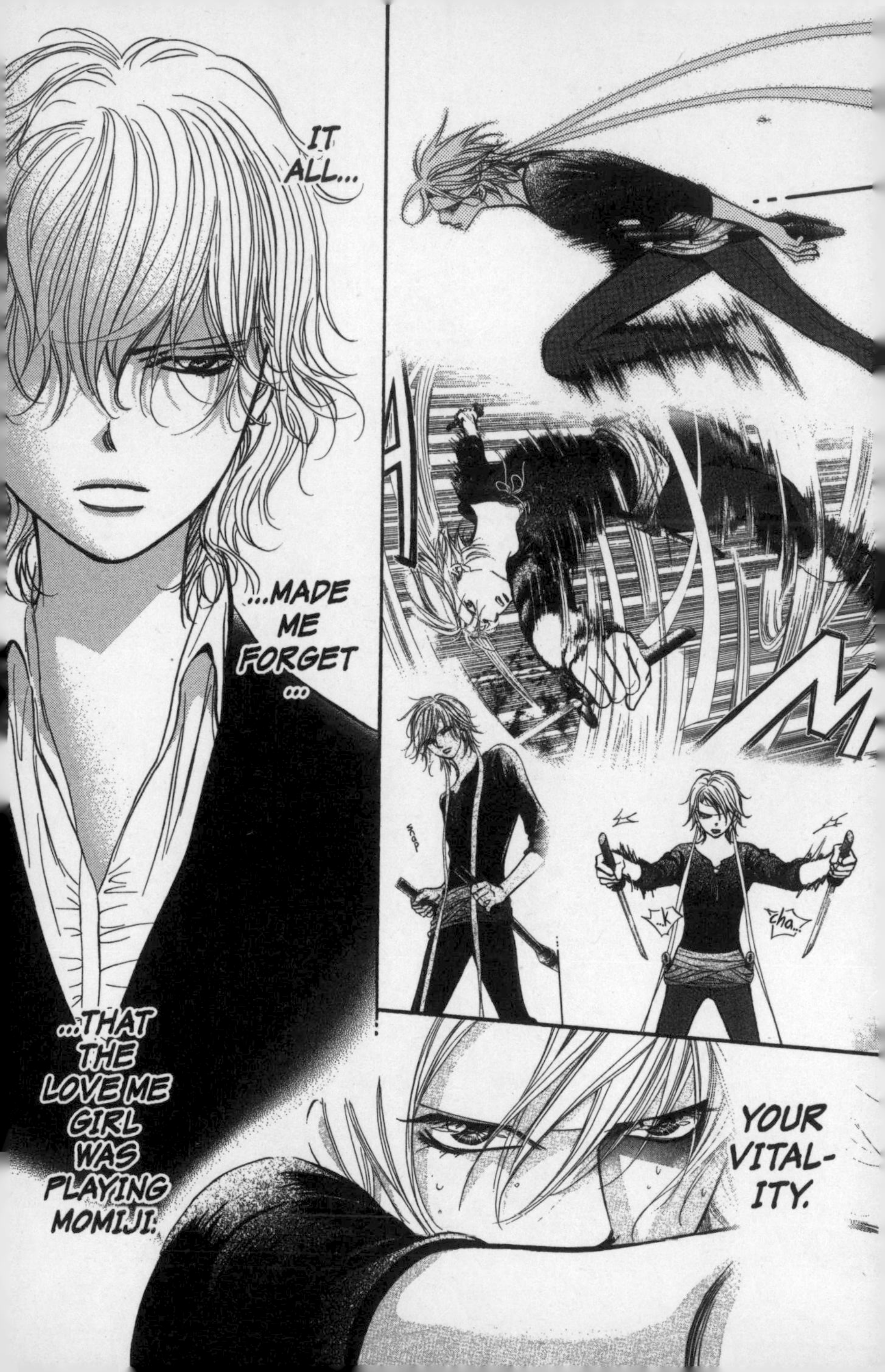
cha...
...k
YOUR VITAL-ITY.
IT ALL...
...MADE ME FORGET ...
...THAT THE LOVE ME GIRL WAS PLAYING MOMIJI.

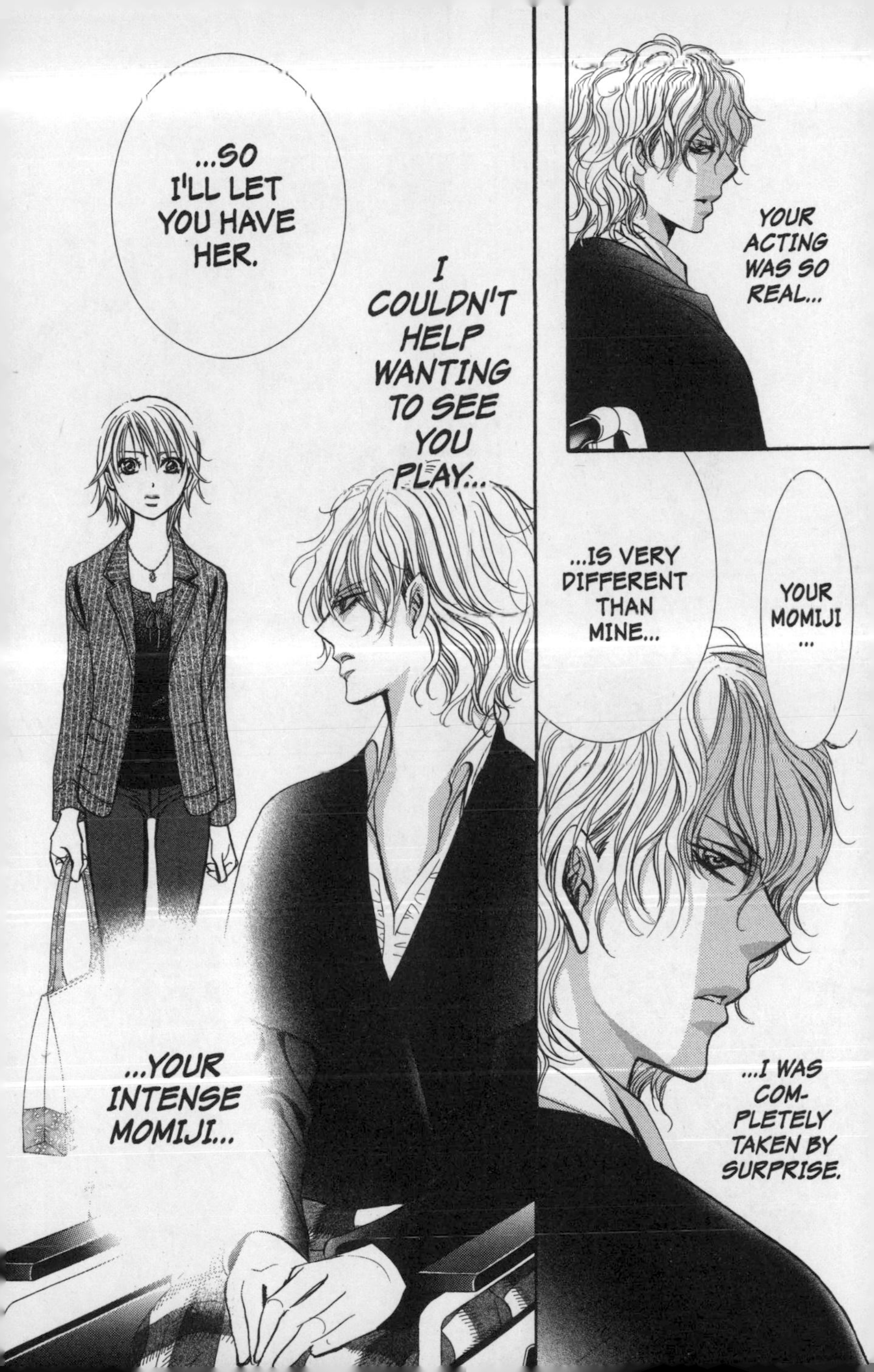
YOUR ACTING WAS SO REAL...
YOUR MOMIJI ...
...IS VERY DIFFERENT THAN MINE...
...I WAS COM-PLETELY TAKEN BY SURPRISE.
...YOUR INTENSE MOMIJI...
I COULDN'T HELP WANTING TO SEE YOU PLAY...
...SO I'LL LET YOU HAVE HER.

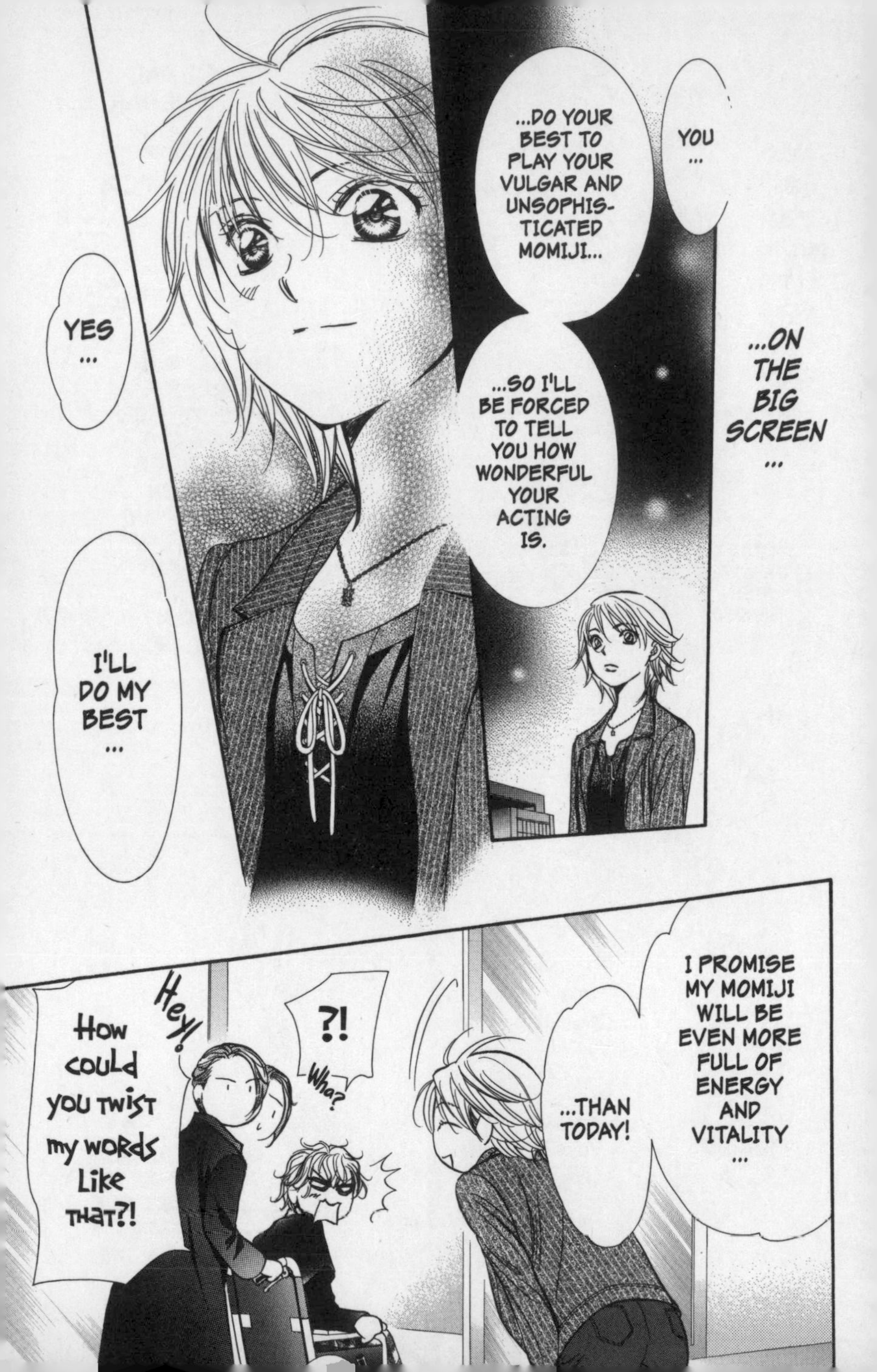
YOU ...
...DO YOUR BEST TO PLAY YOUR VULGAR AND UNSOPHISTICATED MOMIJI...
...ON THE BIG SCREEN ...
...SO I'LL BE FORCED TO TELL YOU HOW WONDERFUL YOUR ACTING IS.
YES ...
I'LL DO MY BEST ...
I PROMISE MY MOMIJI WILL BE EVEN MORE FULL OF ENERGY AND VITALITY ...
...THAN TODAY!
?!
Wha?
Hey!
How could you twist my words like that?!

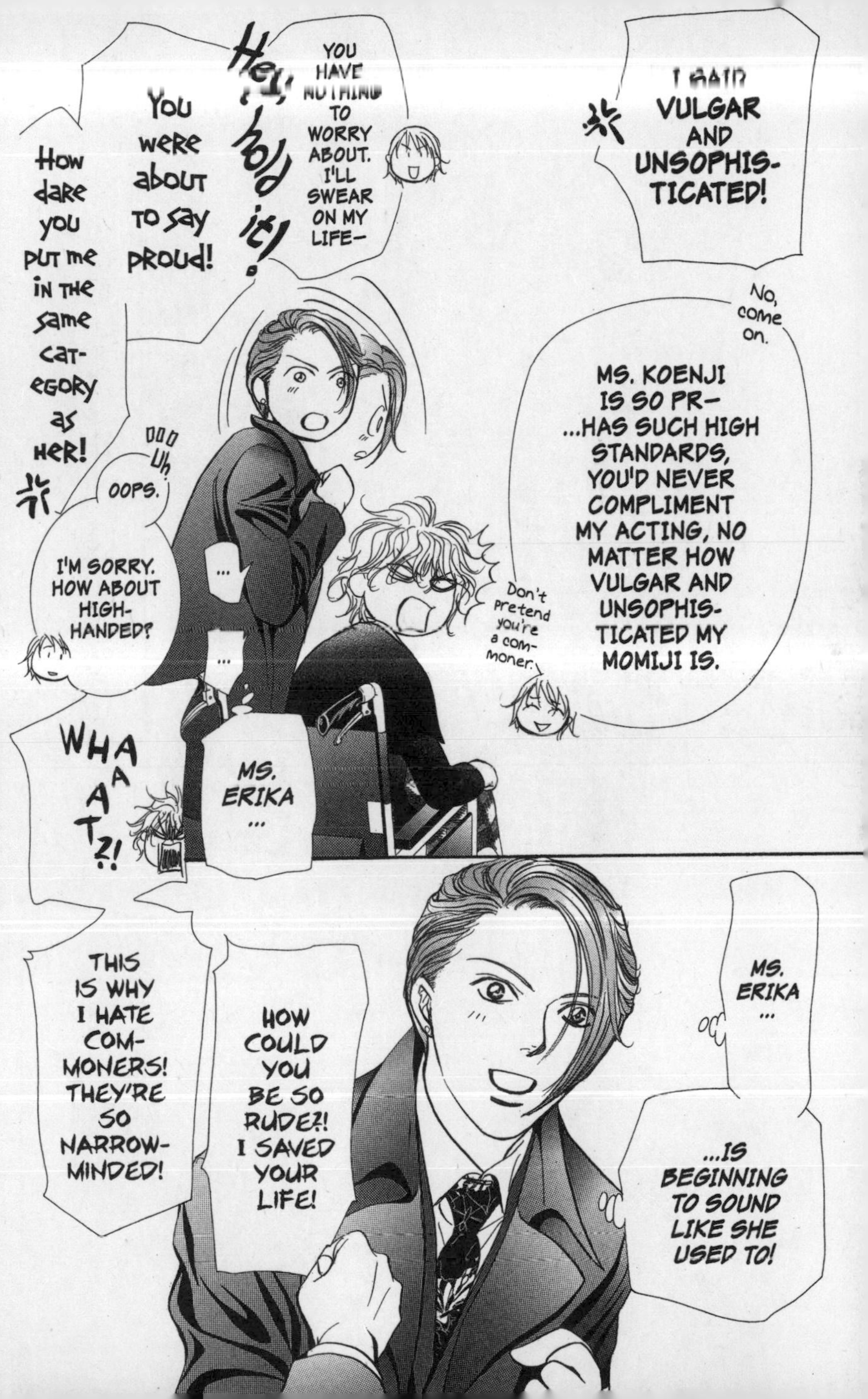
I SAID VULGAR AND UNSOPHISTICATED!
YOU HAVE NOTHING TO WORRY ABOUT. I'LL SWEAR ON MY LIFE—
Hey, hold it!
You were about to say proud!
How dare you put me in the same category as her!
No, come on.
MS. KOENJI IS SO PR— ...HAS SUCH HIGH STANDARDS, YOU'D NEVER COMPLIMENT MY ACTING, NO MATTER HOW VULGAR AND UNSOPHISTICATED MY MOMIJI IS.
Don't pretend you're a commoner.
...
...
Uh
OOPS.
I'M SORRY. HOW ABOUT HIGH-HANDED?
MS. ERIKA ...
WHAAAT?!
MS. ERIKA ...
...IS BEGINNING TO SOUND LIKE SHE USED TO!
HOW COULD YOU BE SO RUDE?! I SAVED YOUR LIFE!
THIS IS WHY I HATE COMMONERS! THEY'RE SO NARROW-MINDED!

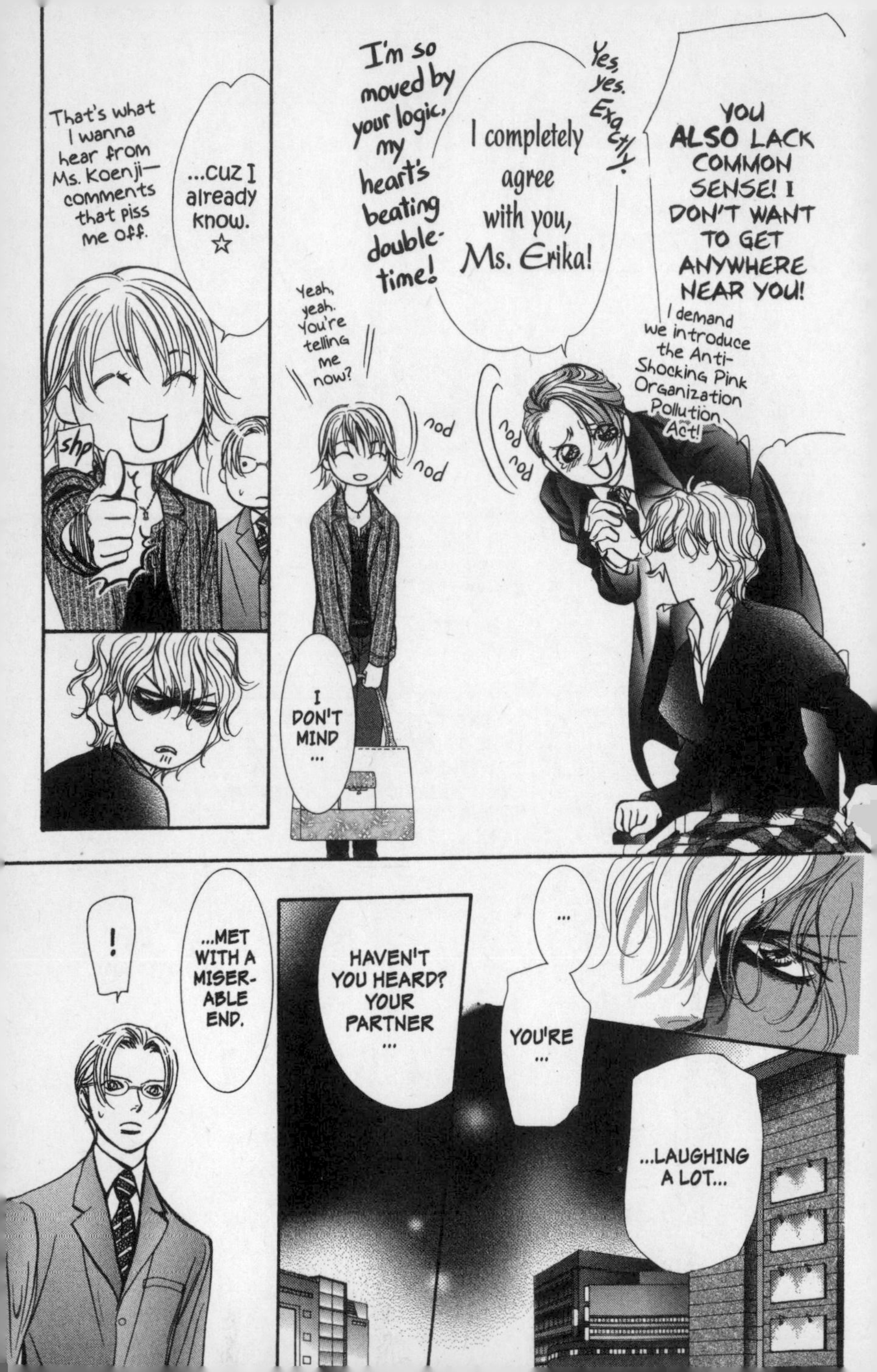
YOU ALSO LACK COMMON SENSE! I DON'T WANT TO GET ANYWHERE NEAR YOU!
I demand we introduce the Anti-Shocking Pink Organization Pollution Act!
Yes, yes. Exactly.
I completely agree with you, Ms. Erika!
I'm so moved by your logic, my heart's beating double-time!
nod nod
nod nod
Yeah, yeah. You're telling me now?
I DON'T MIND ...
...cuz I already know. ☆
That's what I wanna hear from Ms. Koenji—comments that piss me off.
shp
...
YOU'RE ...
...LAUGHING A LOT...
HAVEN'T YOU HEARD? YOUR PARTNER ...
...MET WITH A MISERABLE END.
!

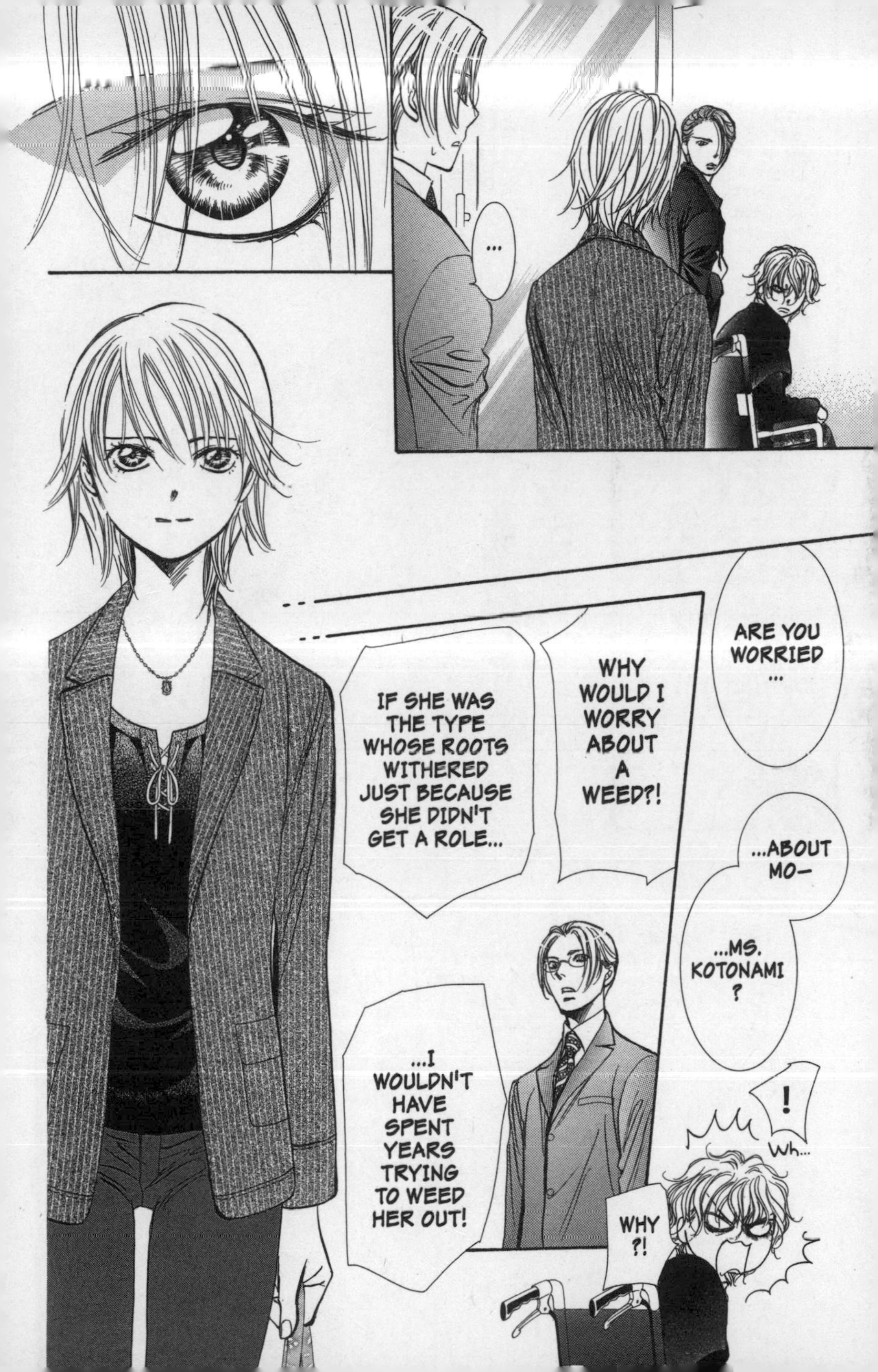
...
ARE YOU WORRIED ...
...ABOUT MO—
...MS. KOTONAMI ?
!
Wh...
WHY ?!
WHY WOULD I WORRY ABOUT A WEED?!
IF SHE WAS THE TYPE WHOSE ROOTS WITHERED JUST BECAUSE SHE DIDN'T GET A ROLE...
...I WOULDN'T HAVE SPENT YEARS TRYING TO WEED HER OUT!

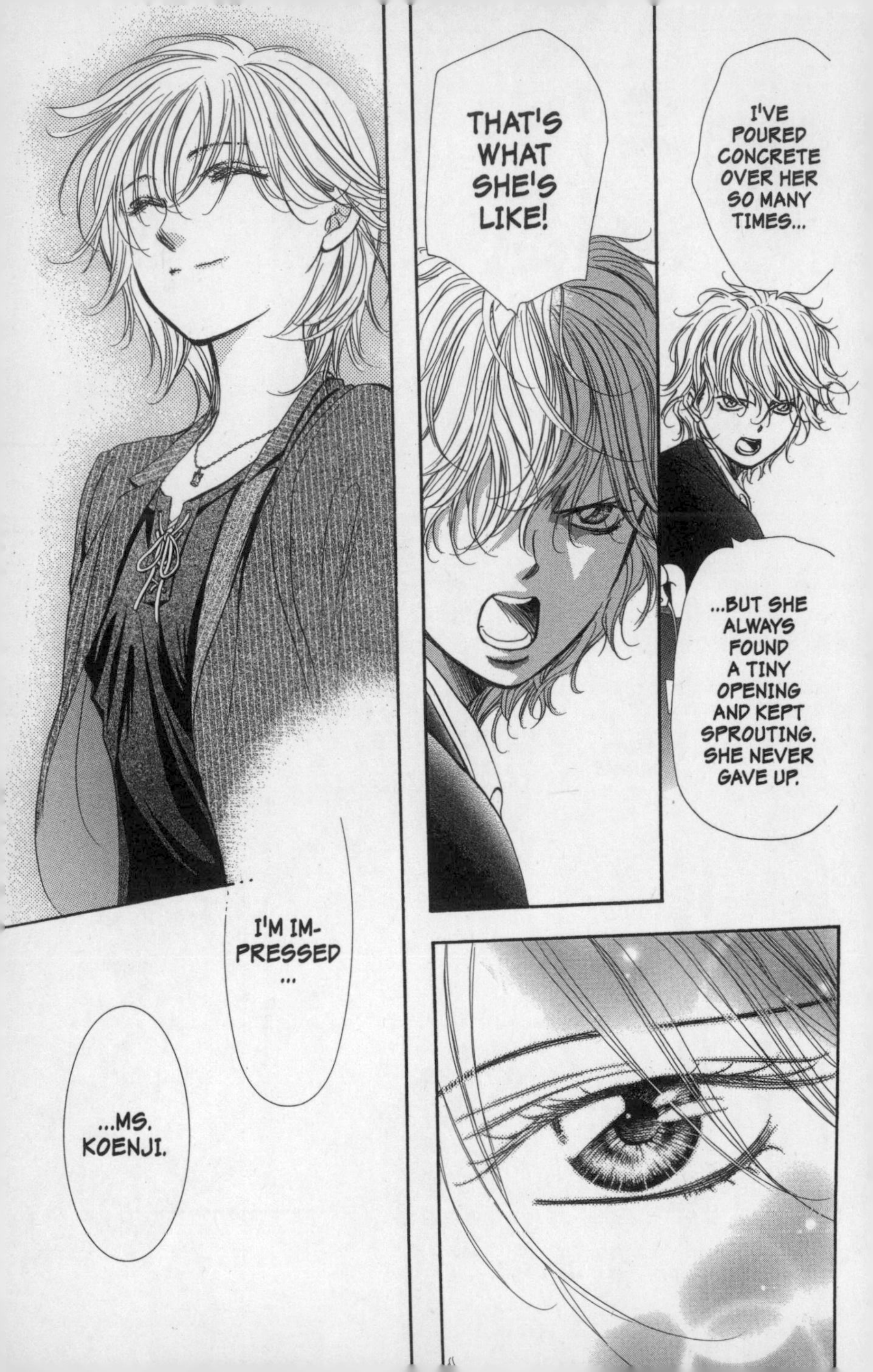
I'VE POURED CONCRETE OVER HER SO MANY TIMES...
...BUT SHE ALWAYS FOUND A TINY OPENING AND KEPT SPROUTING. SHE NEVER GAVE UP.
THAT'S WHAT SHE'S LIKE!
...
I'M IM-PRESSED...
...MS. KOENJI.

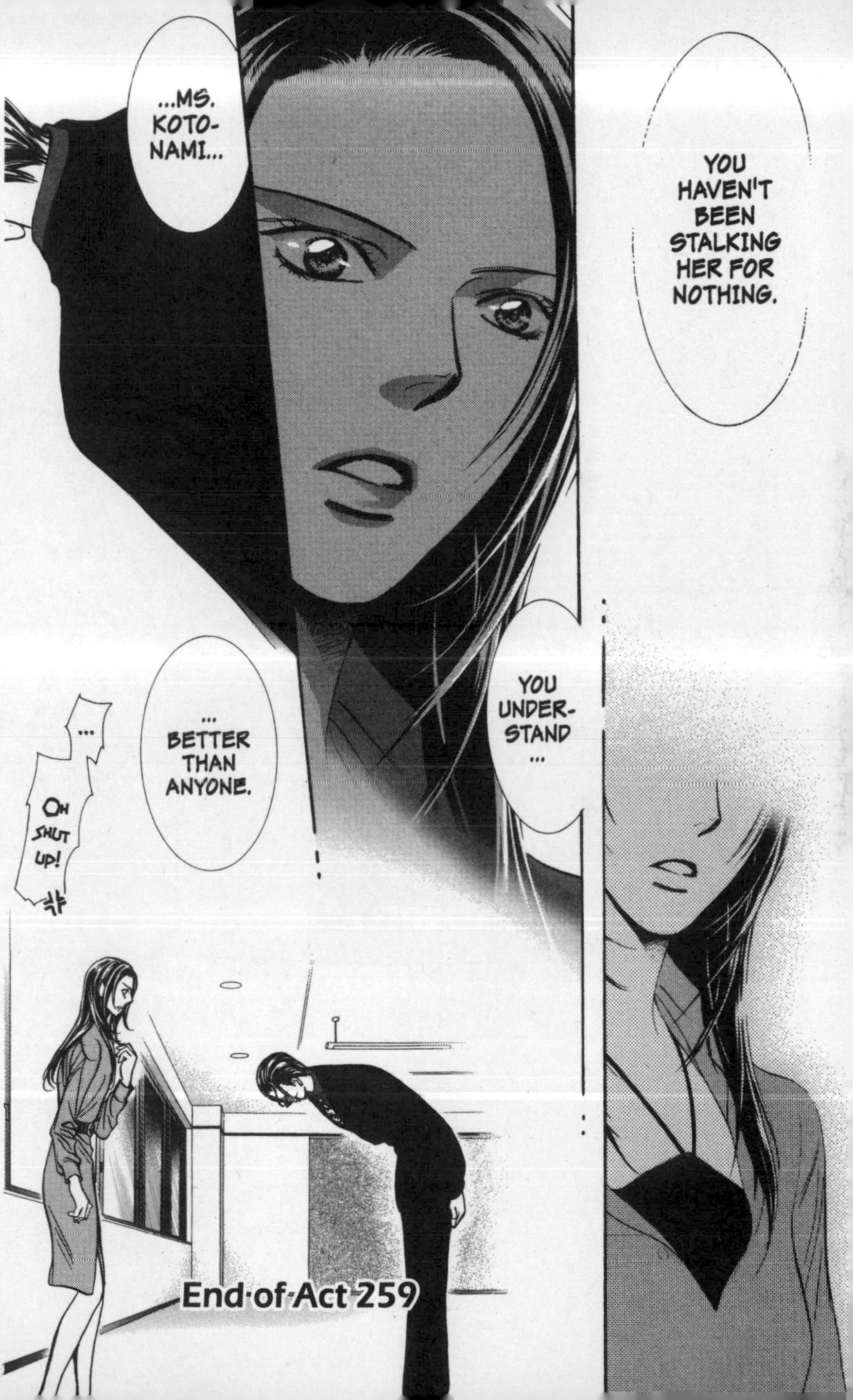
YOU HAVEN'T BEEN STALKING HER FOR NOTHING.
...MS. KOTO-NAMI...
YOU UNDER-STAND ...
... BETTER THAN ANYONE.
...
OH SHUT UP!
End of Act 259

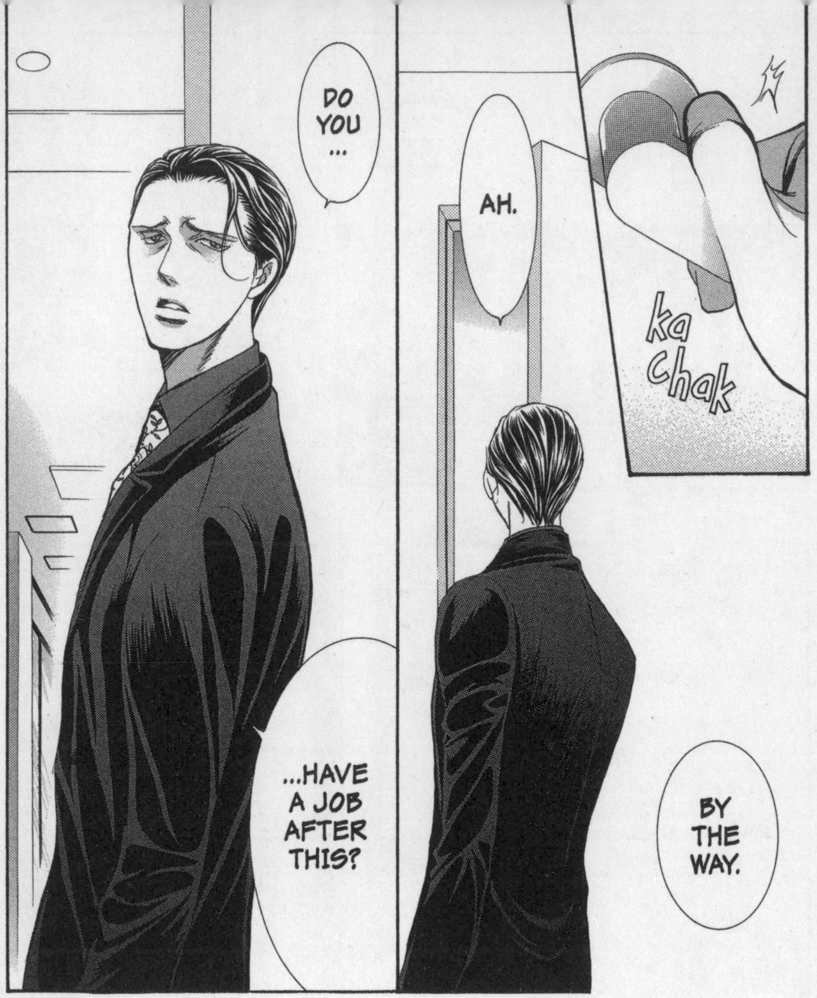
ka chak
AH.
BY THE WAY.
DO YOU ...
...HAVE A JOB AFTER THIS?

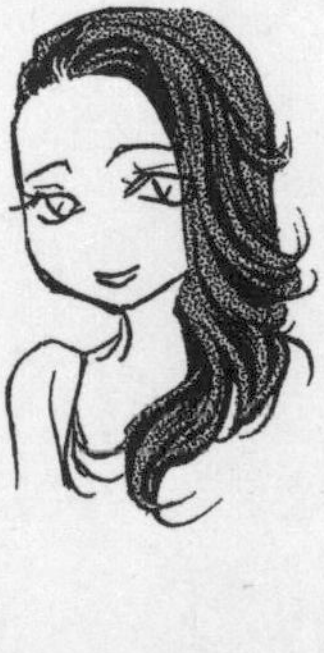

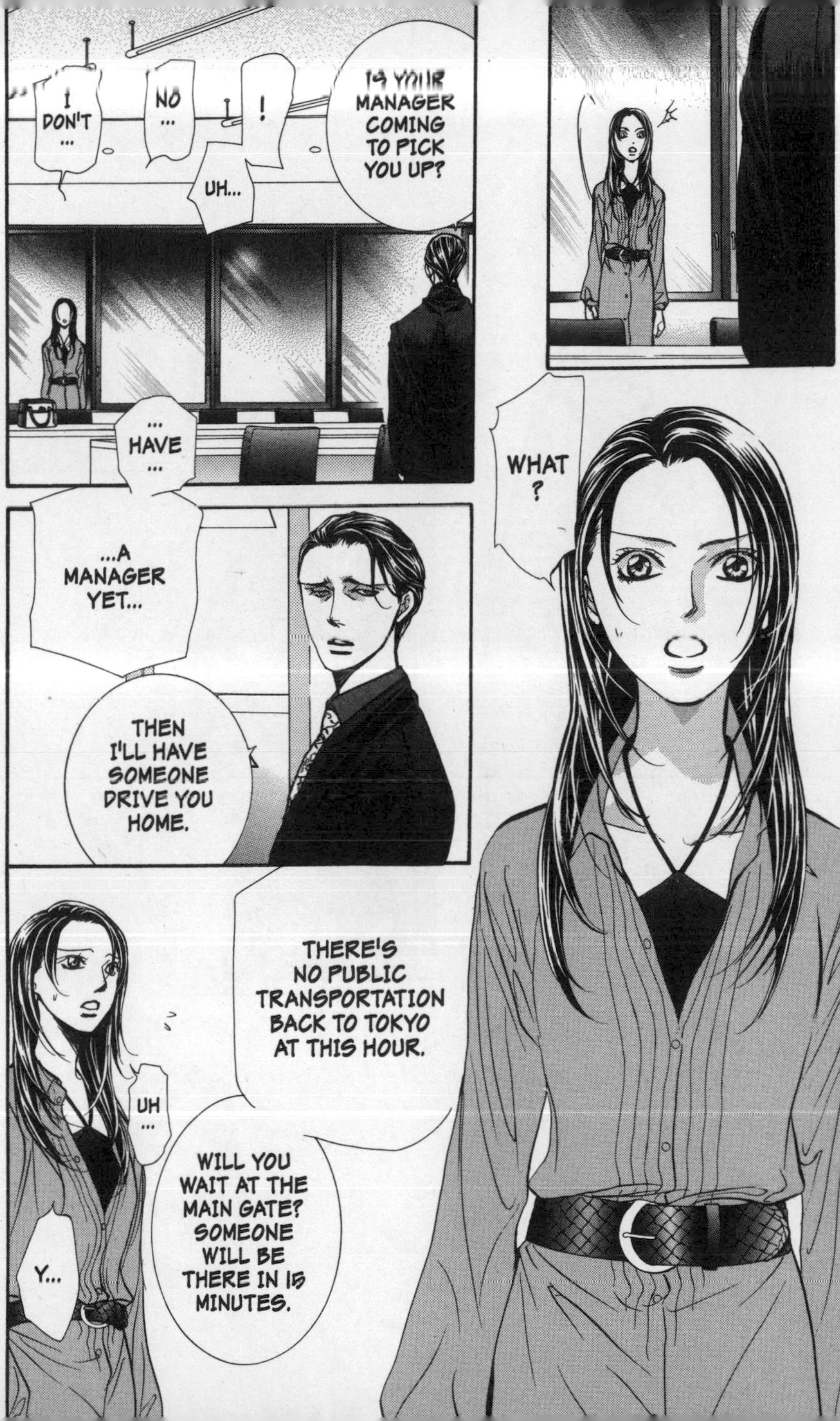
IS YOUR MANAGER COMING TO PICK YOU UP?
UH...
!
NO...
I DON'T...
...HAVE...
...A MANAGER YET...
THEN I'LL HAVE SOMEONE DRIVE YOU HOME.
WHAT?
THERE'S NO PUBLIC TRANSPORTATION BACK TO TOKYO AT THIS HOUR.
UH...
WILL YOU WAIT AT THE MAIN GATE? SOMEONE WILL BE THERE IN 15 MINUTES.
Y...

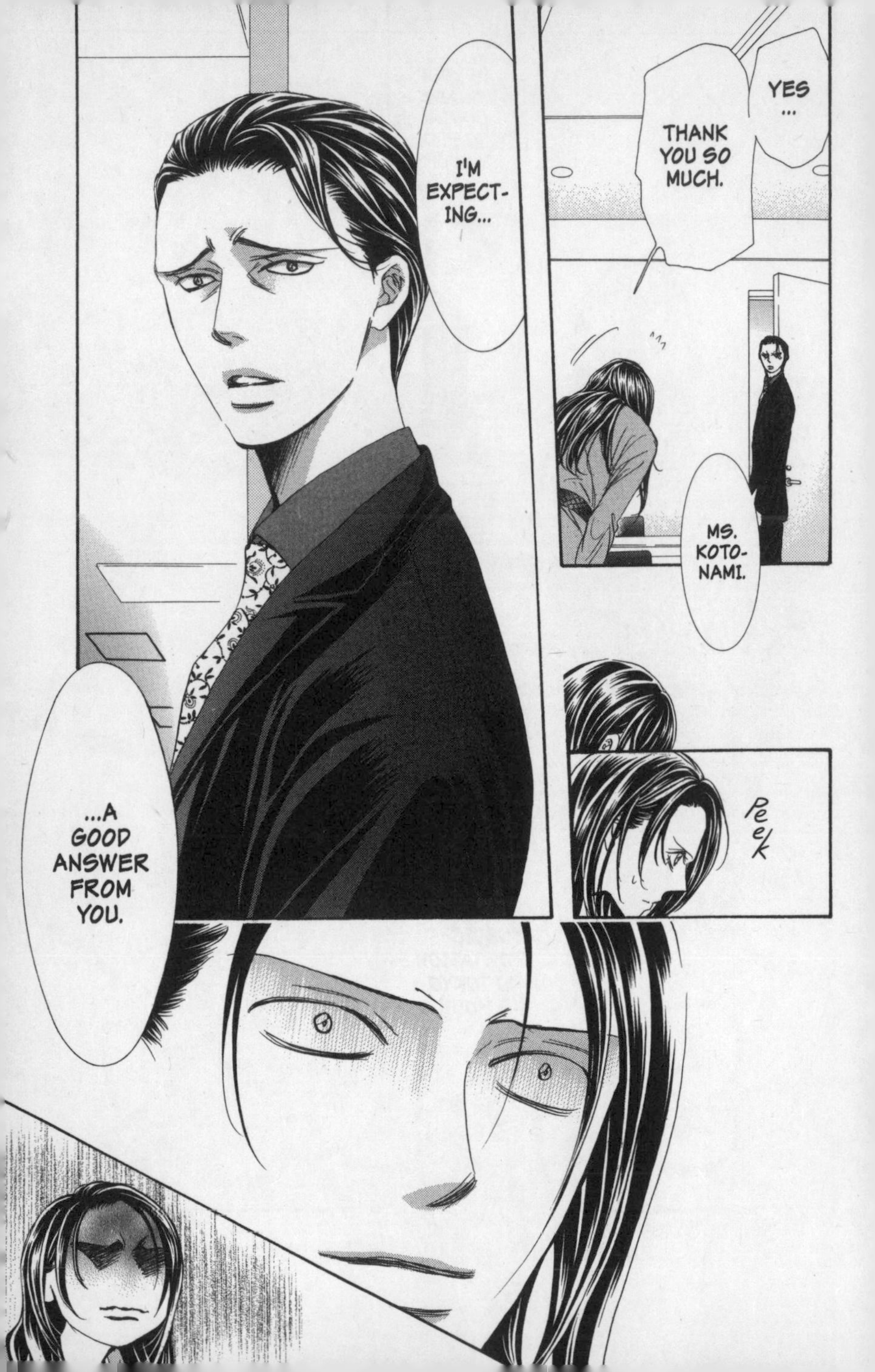
YES ...
THANK YOU SO MUCH.
MS. KOTO-NAMI.
Peek
I'M EXPECT-ING...
...A GOOD ANSWER FROM YOU.

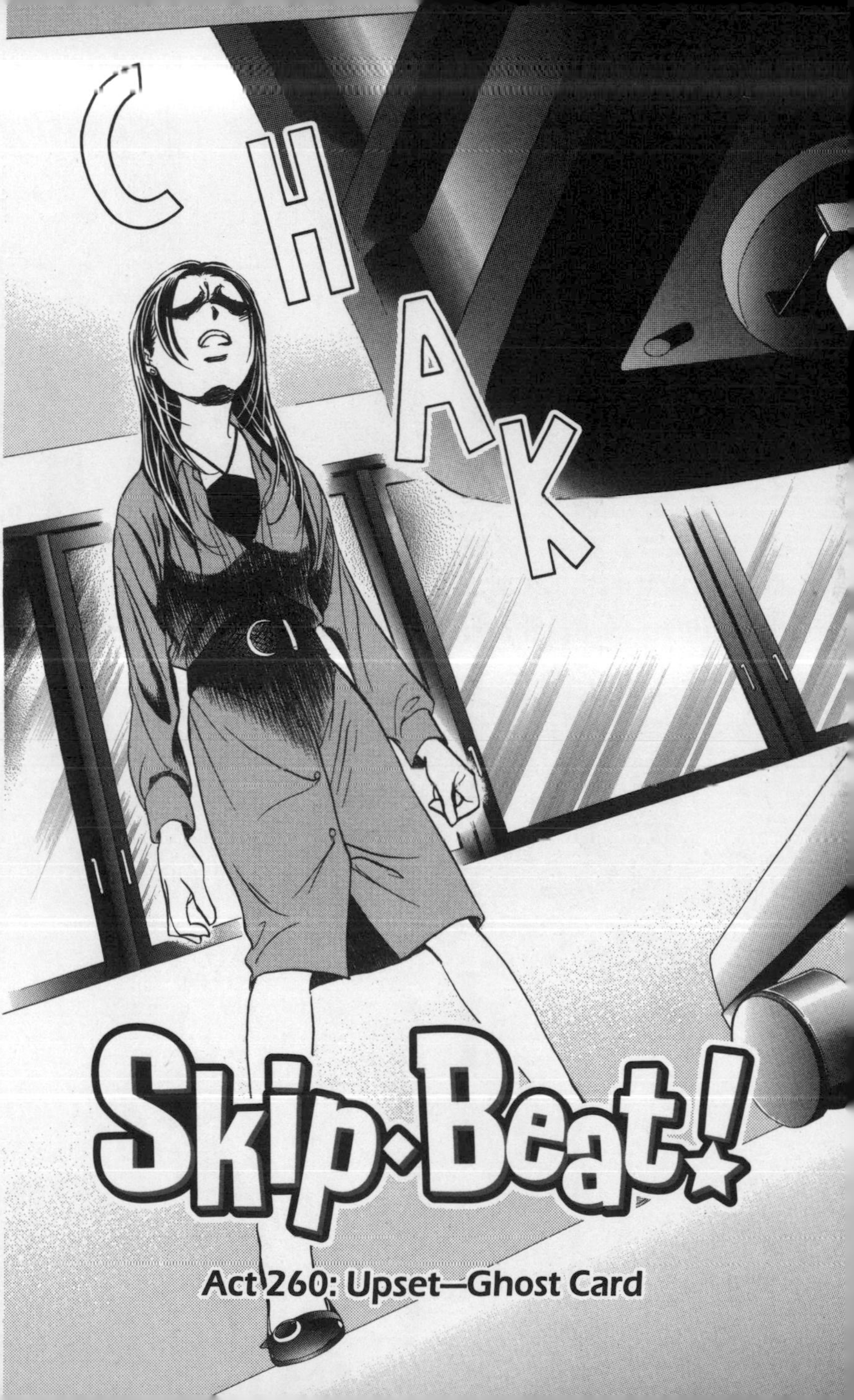
CHAK
Skip·Beat!
Act 260: Upset—Ghost Card

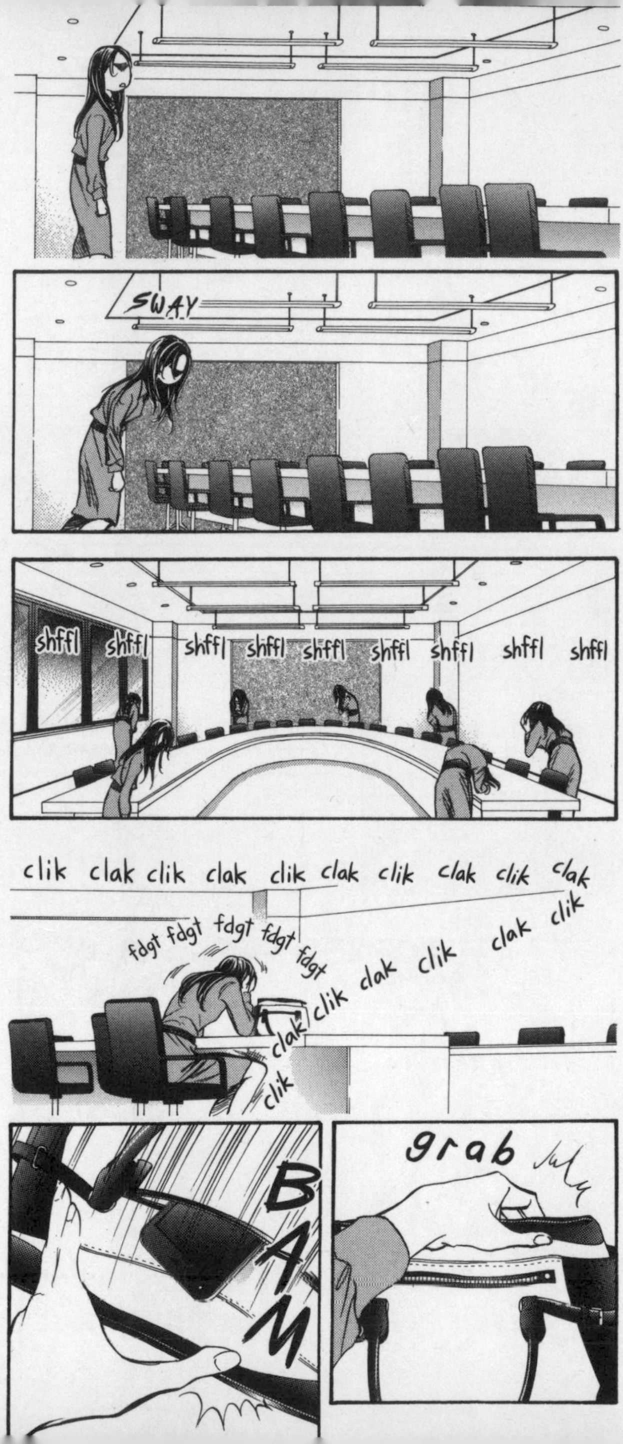
SWAY
shffl shffl shffl shffl shffl shffl shffl shffl shffl
clik clak clik clak clik clak clik clak clik clak
clik clak clik clak clik clak clik
fdgt fdgt fdgt fdgt fdgt
grab
BAM
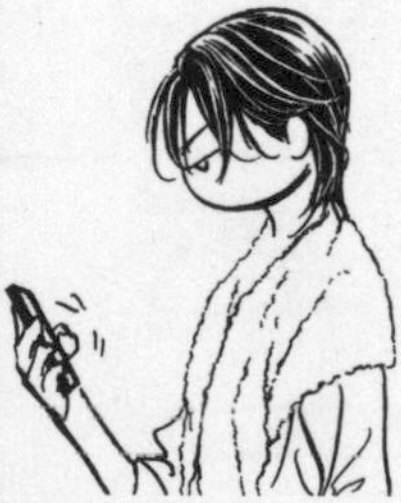

I SHOULD CALL SUPER-VISOR MATSU-SHIMA...

I....

SHP

tp tp tp
tp
tp

Unlocking her phone

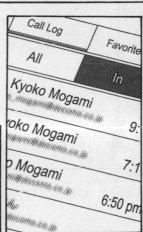

Call Log | Favorite
All | In
Kyoko Mogami
Koyo Mogami | 9:
p Mogami | 7:1
6:50 pm

SOME-ONE CALLED ME...

3

3

†P

HEH...

tmp

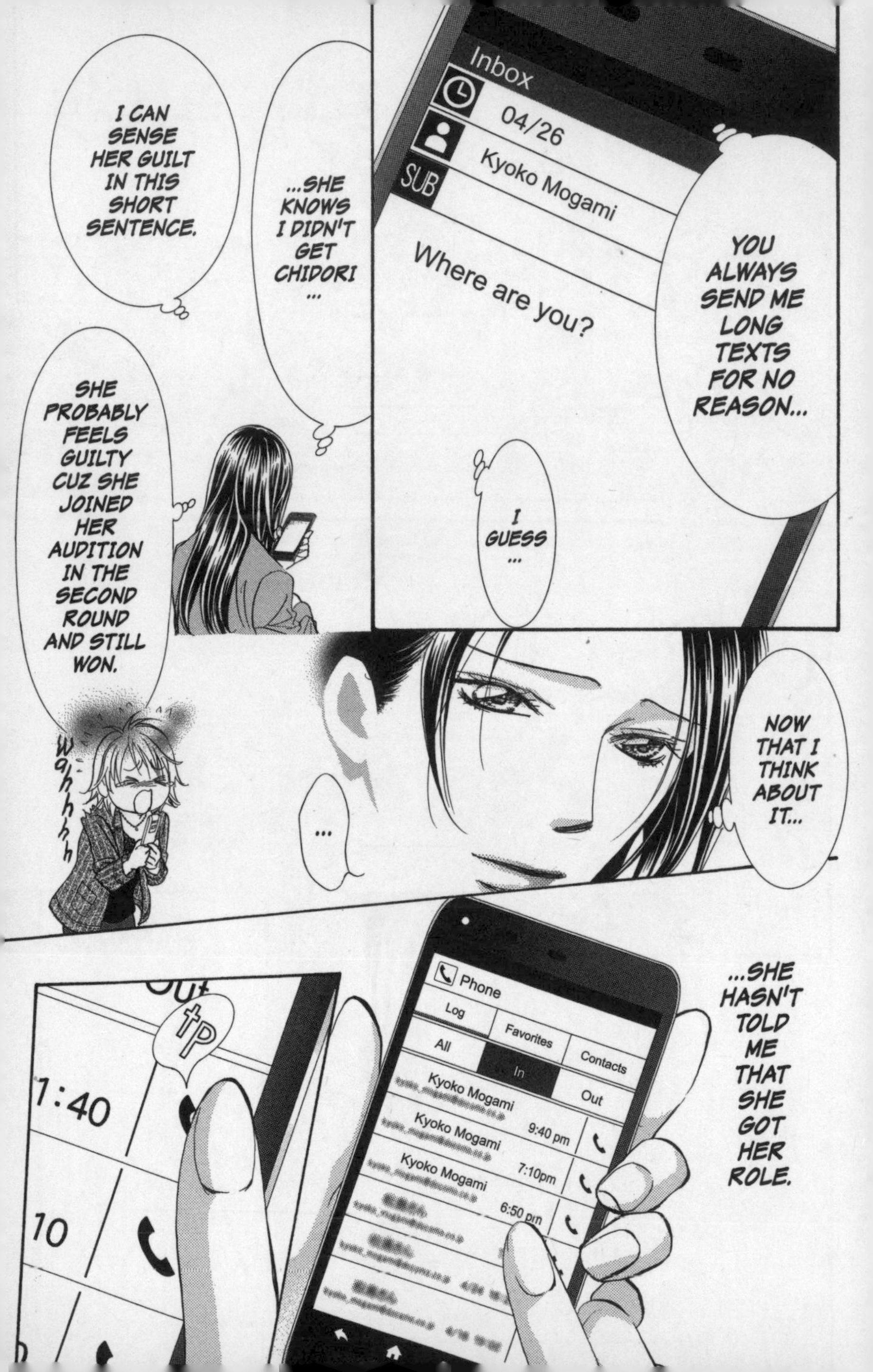
Inbox
04/26
Kyoko Mogami
SUB
Where are you?
YOU ALWAYS SEND ME LONG TEXTS FOR NO REASON...
I GUESS...
...SHE KNOWS I DIDN'T GET CHIDORI...
I CAN SENSE HER GUILT IN THIS SHORT SENTENCE.
SHE PROBABLY FEELS GUILTY CUZ SHE JOINED HER AUDITION IN THE SECOND ROUND AND STILL WON.
Wahhhhh
NOW THAT I THINK ABOUT IT...
...
...SHE HASN'T TOLD ME THAT SHE GOT HER ROLE.
Phone
Log
Favorites
All
In
Contacts
Out
Kyoko Mogami
9:40 pm
Kyoko Mogami
7:10pm
Kyoko Mogami
6:50 pm
tp
Out
1:40
10

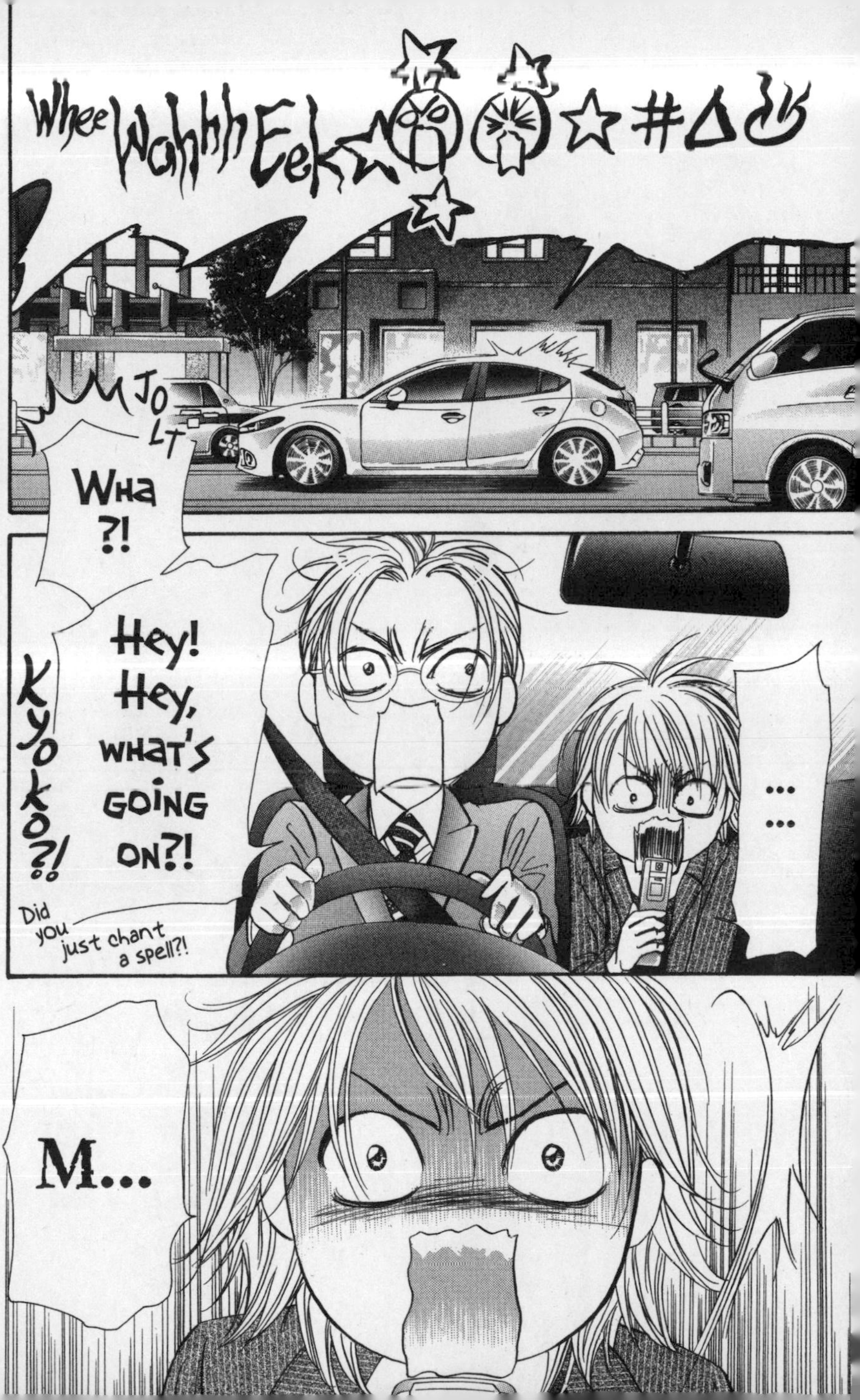
Whee Wahhh Eek ☆ # △
JOLT
WHA ?!
... ...
Hey! Hey, what's going on?!
Kyoko?!
Did you just chant a spell?!
M...

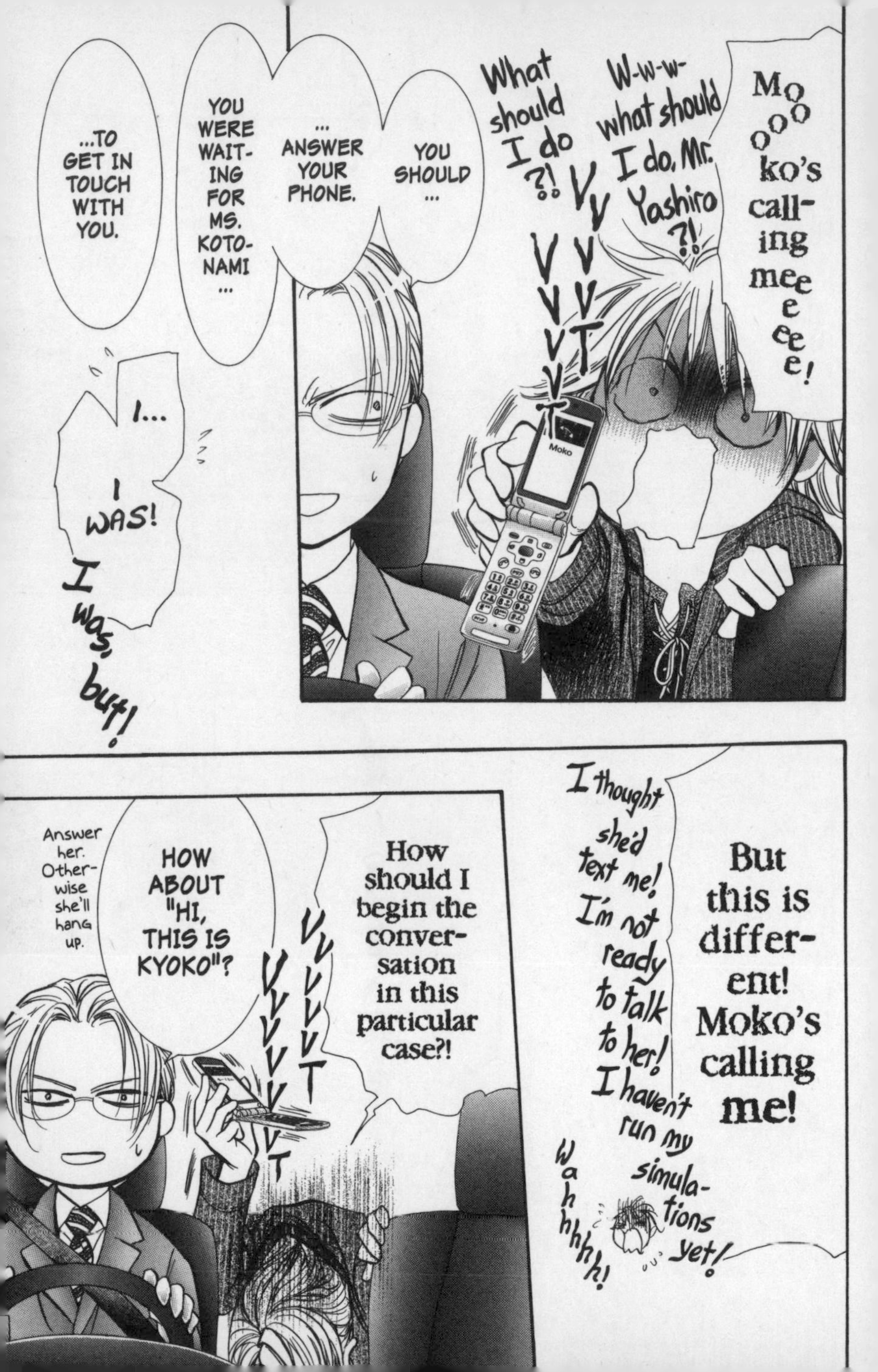
Mooooko's calling meeeeeee!
W-w-w-what should I do, Mr. Yashiro?!
What should I do?!
VVVVT
VVVVVT
Moko
YOU SHOULD ...
... ANSWER YOUR PHONE.
YOU WERE WAITING FOR MS. KOTONAMI ...
...TO GET IN TOUCH WITH YOU.
I... I WAS!
I was, but!
But this is different! Moko's calling me!
I thought she'd text me! I'm not ready to talk to her! I haven't run my simulations yet!
Wahhhhh!
How should I begin the conversation in this particular case?!
VVVVVVVT
VVVVT
HOW ABOUT "HI, THIS IS KYOKO"?
Answer her. Otherwise she'll hang up.

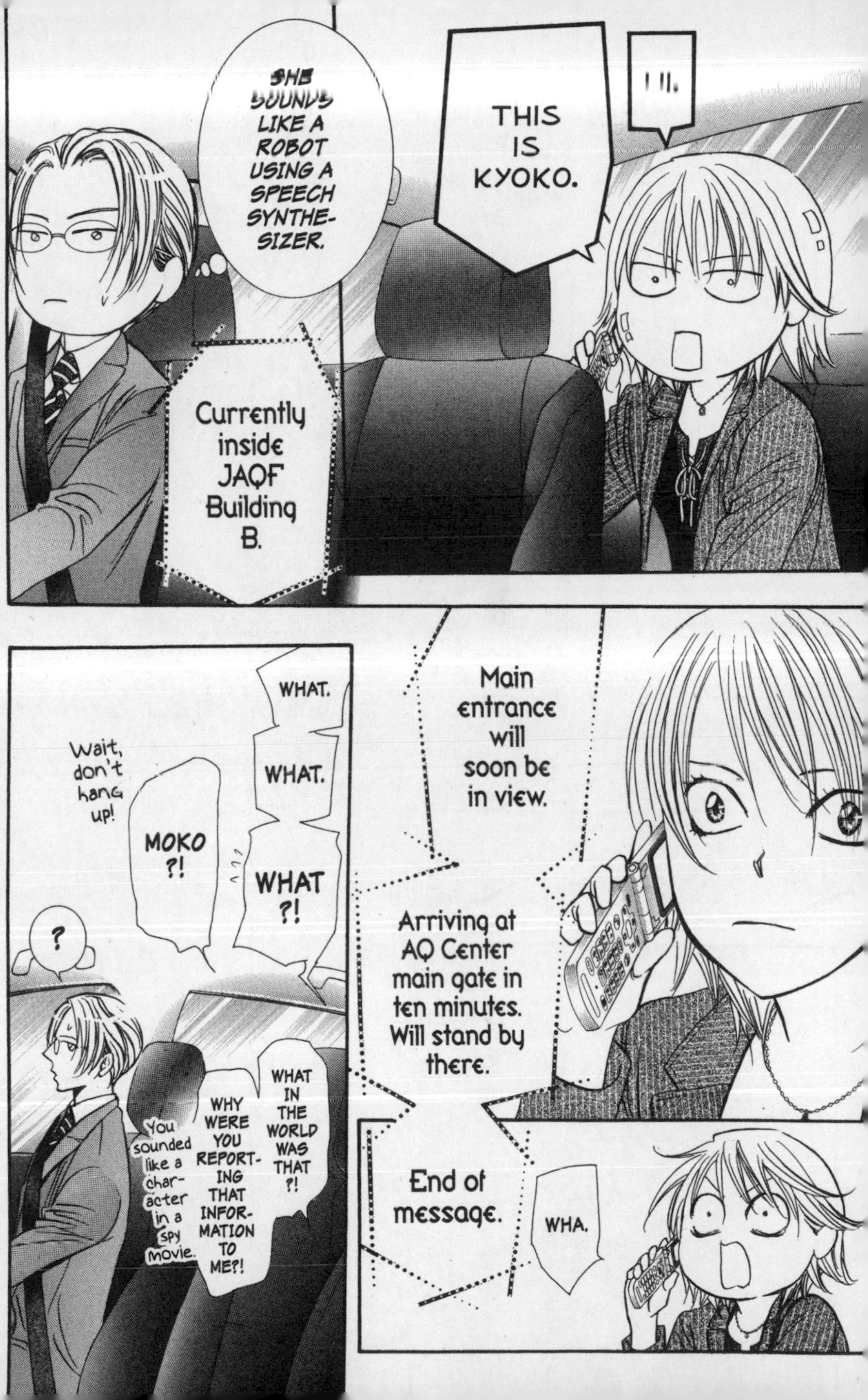

THIS IS KYOKO.
SHE SOUNDS LIKE A ROBOT USING A SPEECH SYNTHESIZER.
Currently inside JAQF Building B.
Main entrance will soon be in view.
Arriving at AQ Center main gate in ten minutes. Will stand by there.
End of message.
WHA.
WHAT.
WHAT.
WHAT?!
Wait, don't hang up!
MOKO?!
?
WHAT IN THE WORLD WAS THAT?!
WHY WERE YOU REPORTING THAT INFORMATION TO ME?!
You sounded like a character in a spy movie.

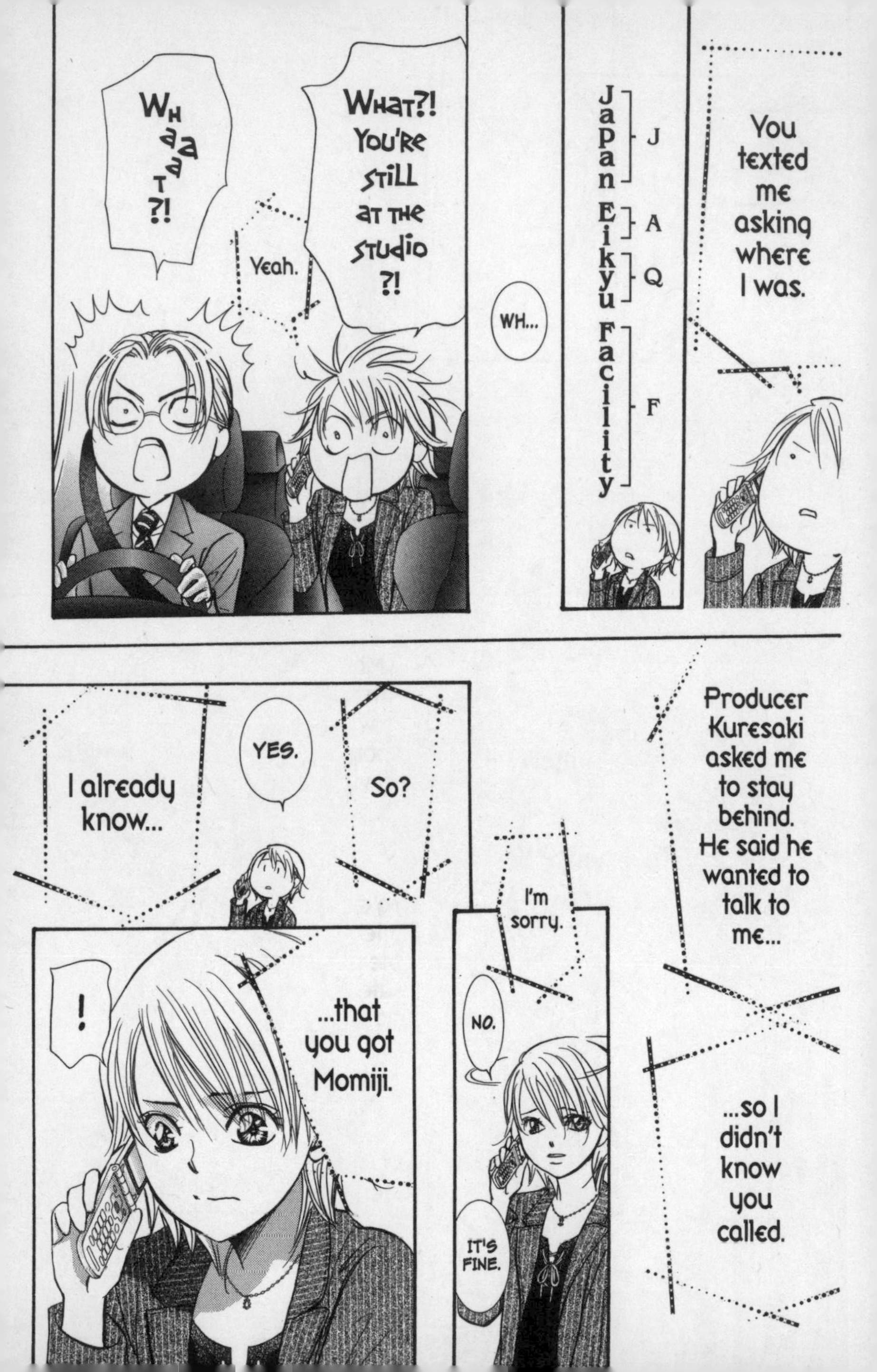
You texted me asking where I was.
WH...
Japan Eikyu Facility
J
A
Q
F
WHAT?! YOU'RE STILL AT THE STUDIO?!
Yeah.
WHaaaT?!
Producer Kuresaki asked me to stay behind. He said he wanted to talk to me...
...so I didn't know you called.
I'm sorry.
NO.
IT'S FINE.
So?
YES.
I already know...
...that you got Momiji.
!

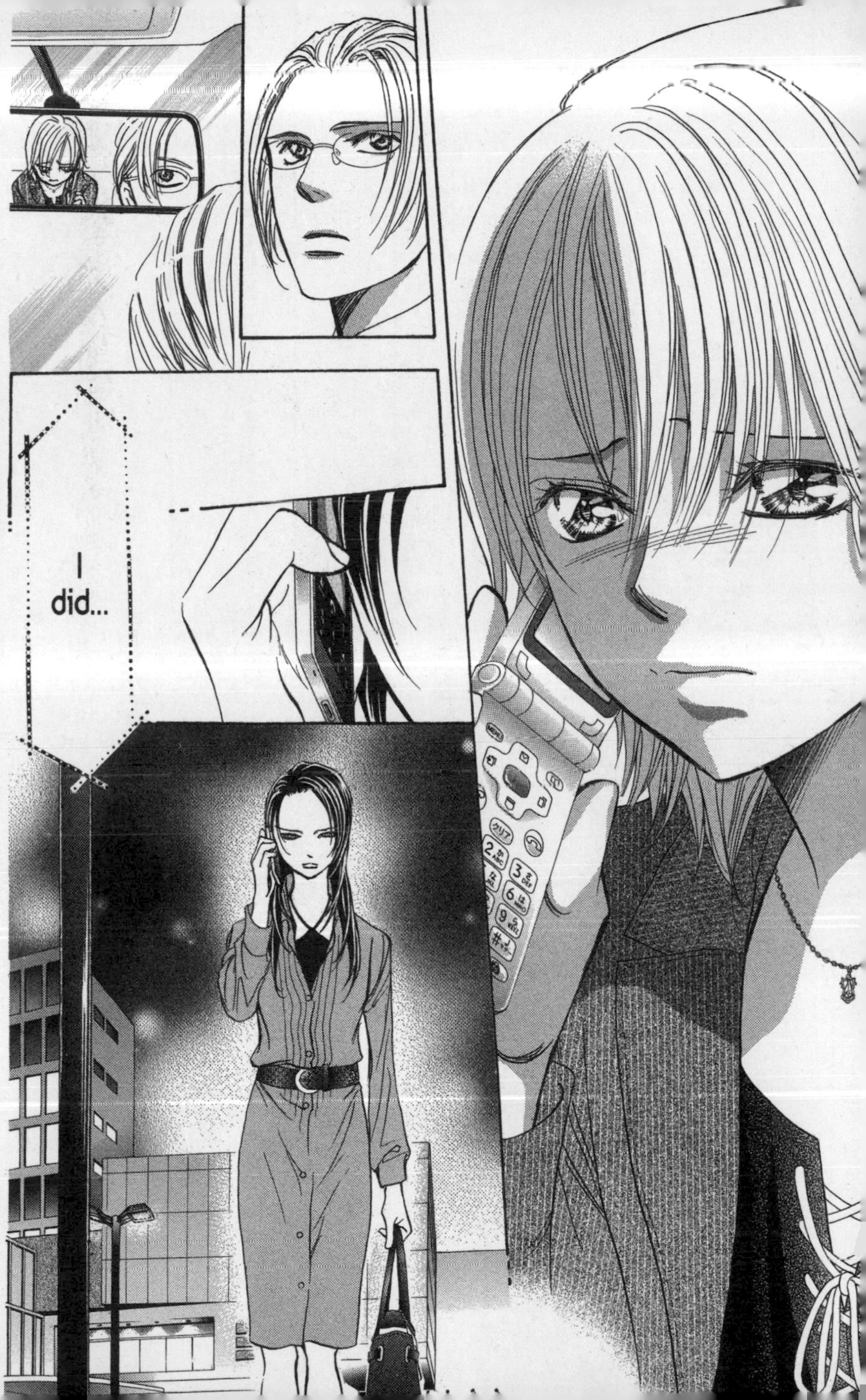
I did...

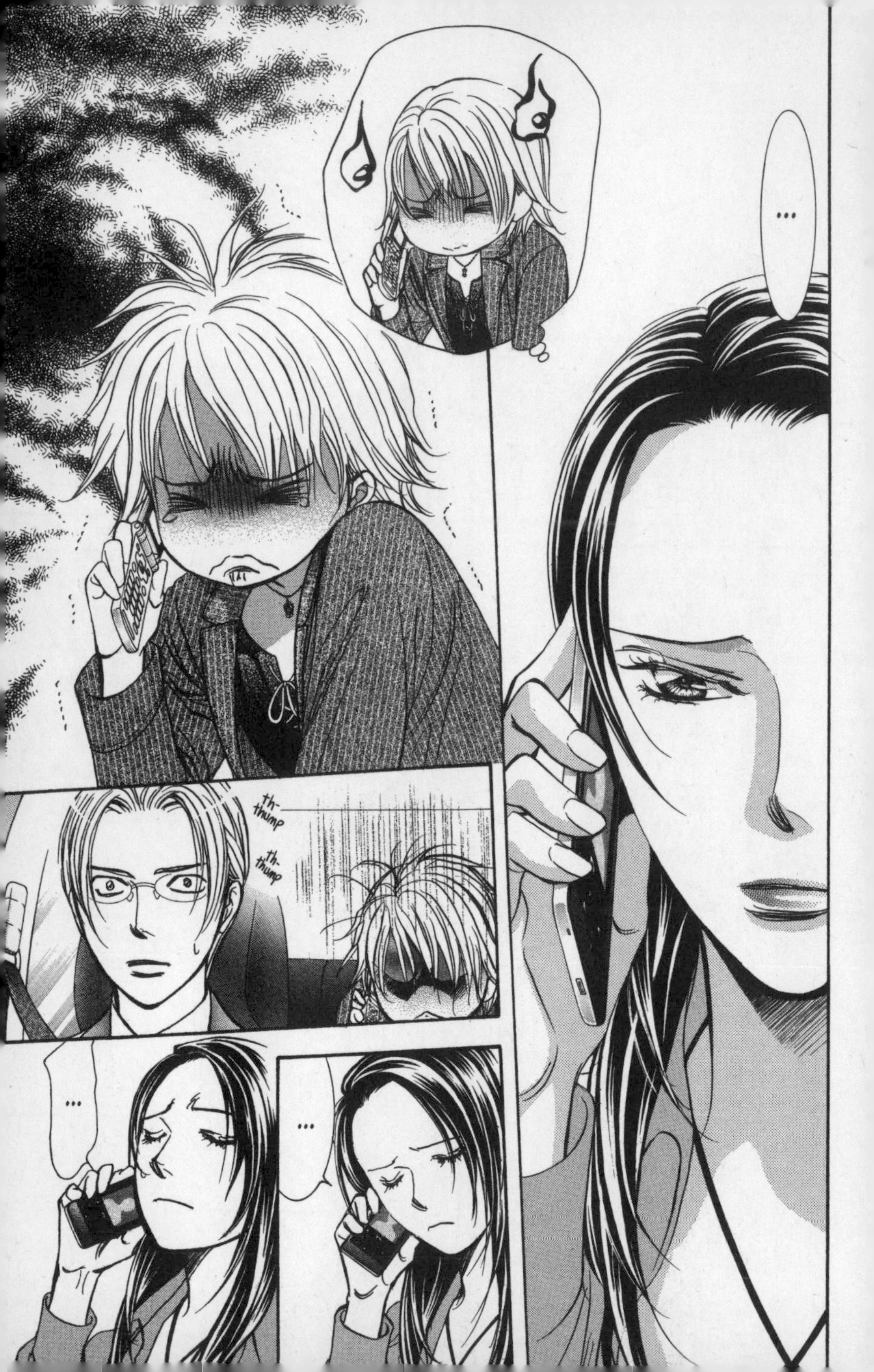
...
th-thump
th-thump
...
...

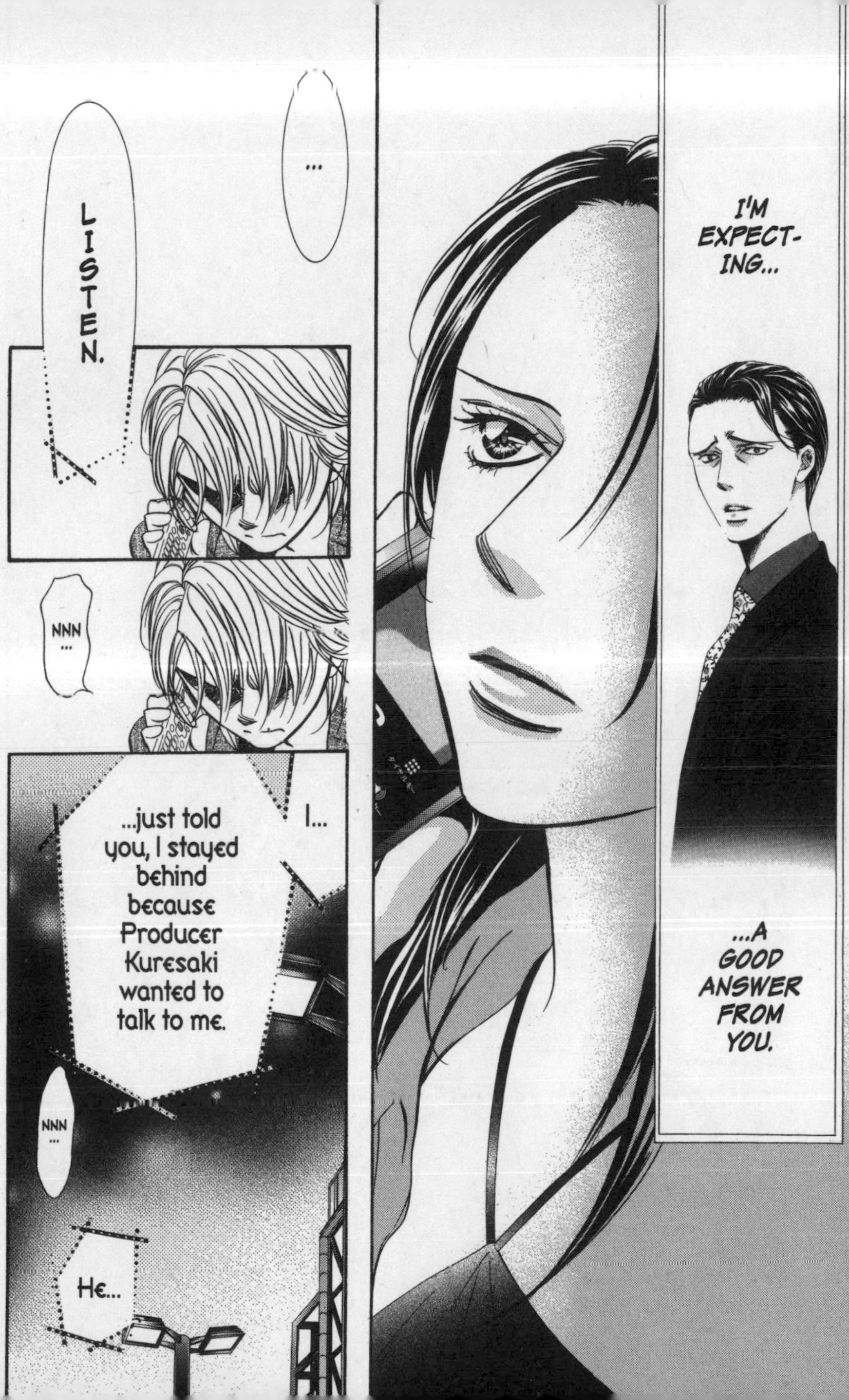
I'M EXPECTING...
...A GOOD ANSWER FROM YOU.
...
LISTEN.
NNN...
I...
...just told you, I stayed behind because Producer Kuresaki wanted to talk to me.
NNN...
He...

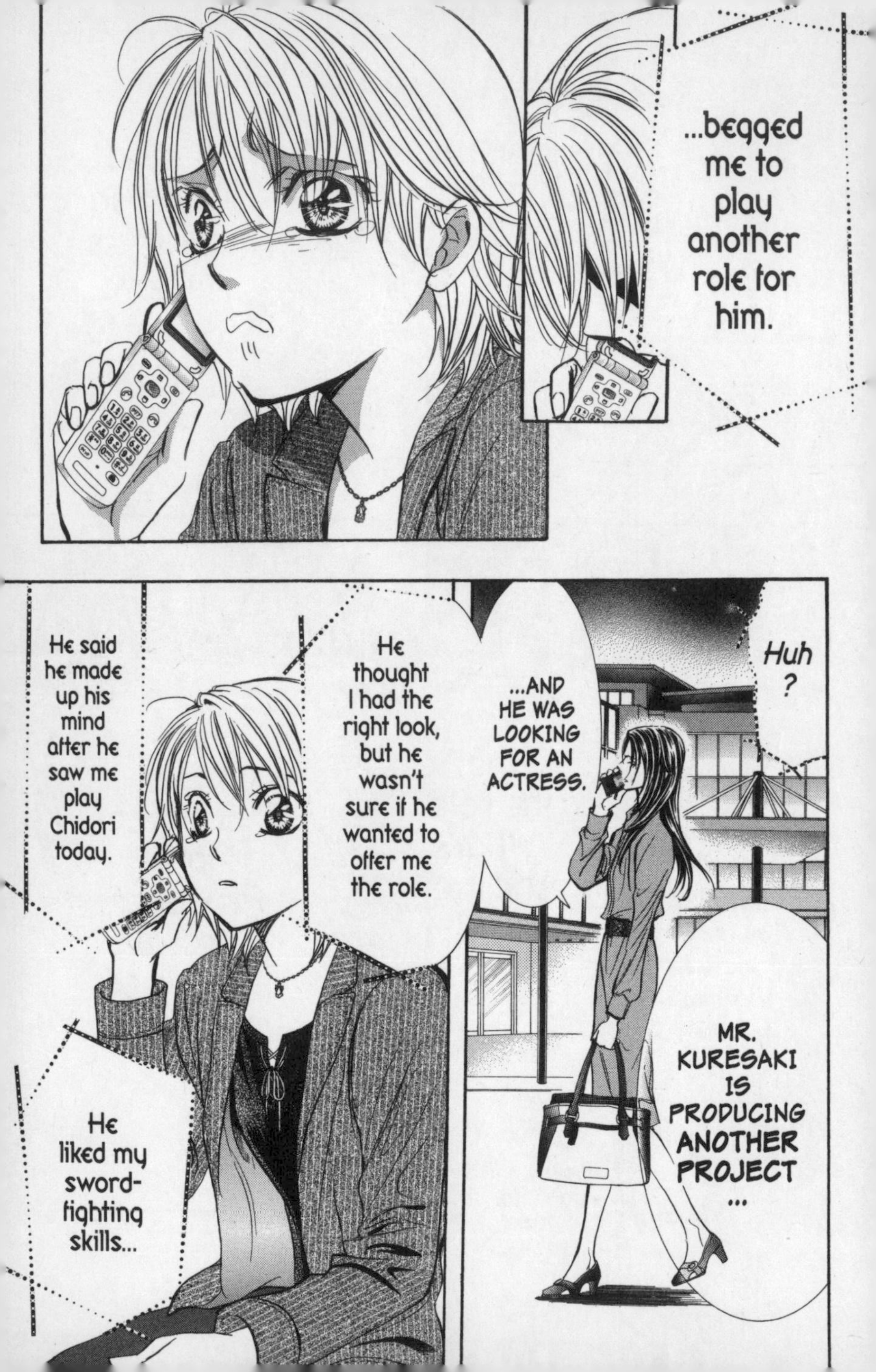
...begged me to play another role for him.
Huh?
MR. KURESAKI IS PRODUCING ANOTHER PROJECT ...
...AND HE WAS LOOKING FOR AN ACTRESS.
He thought I had the right look, but he wasn't sure if he wanted to offer me the role.
He said he made up his mind after he saw me play Chidori today.
He liked my sword-fighting skills...

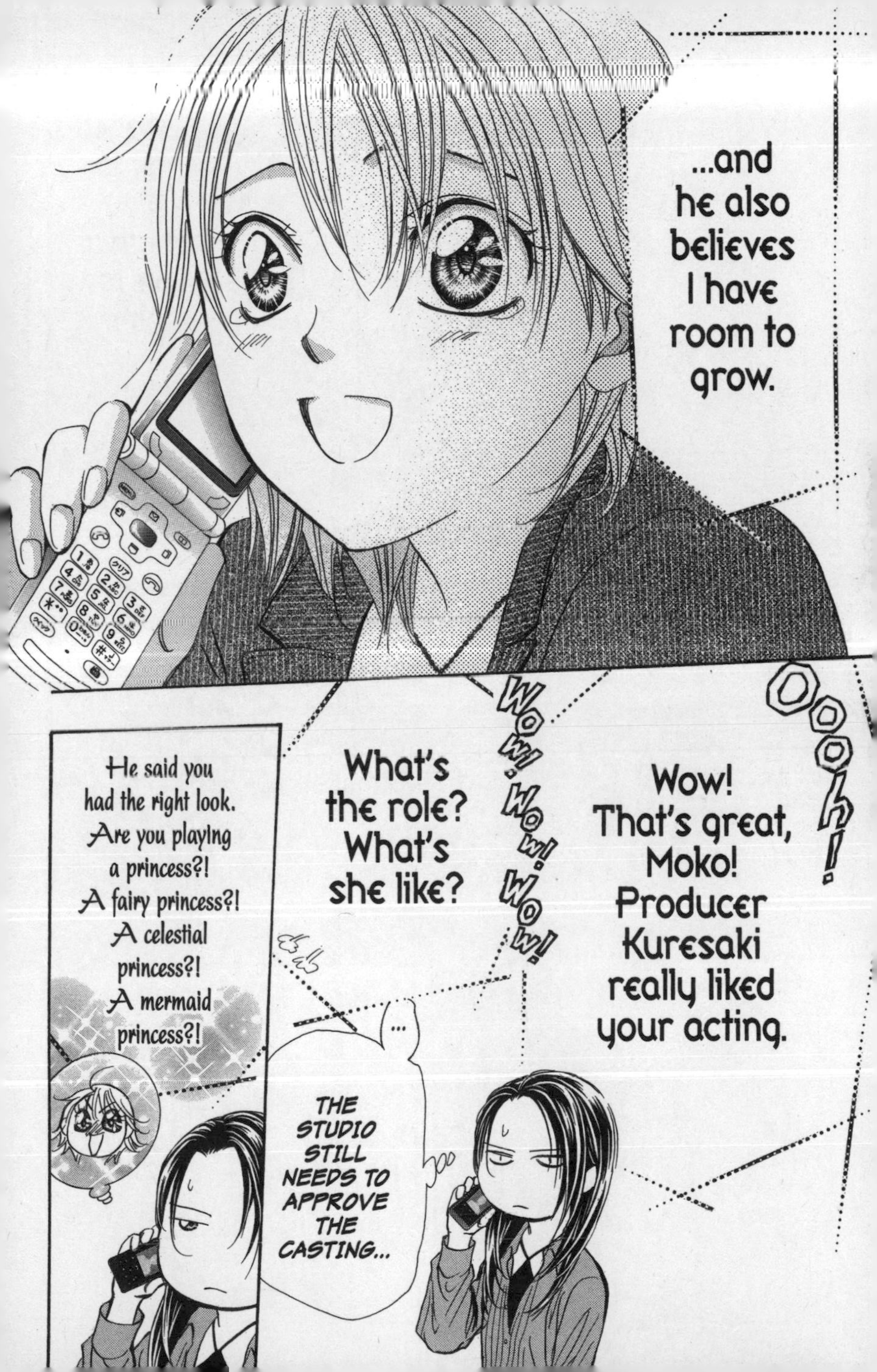
...and he also believes I have room to grow.
Oooh!
Wow! That's great, Moko! Producer Kuresaki really liked your acting.
Wow! Wow! Wow!
What's the role? What's she like?
...
He said you had the right look. Are you playing a princess?! A fairy princess?! A celestial princess?! A mermaid princess?!
THE STUDIO STILL NEEDS TO APPROVE THE CASTING...

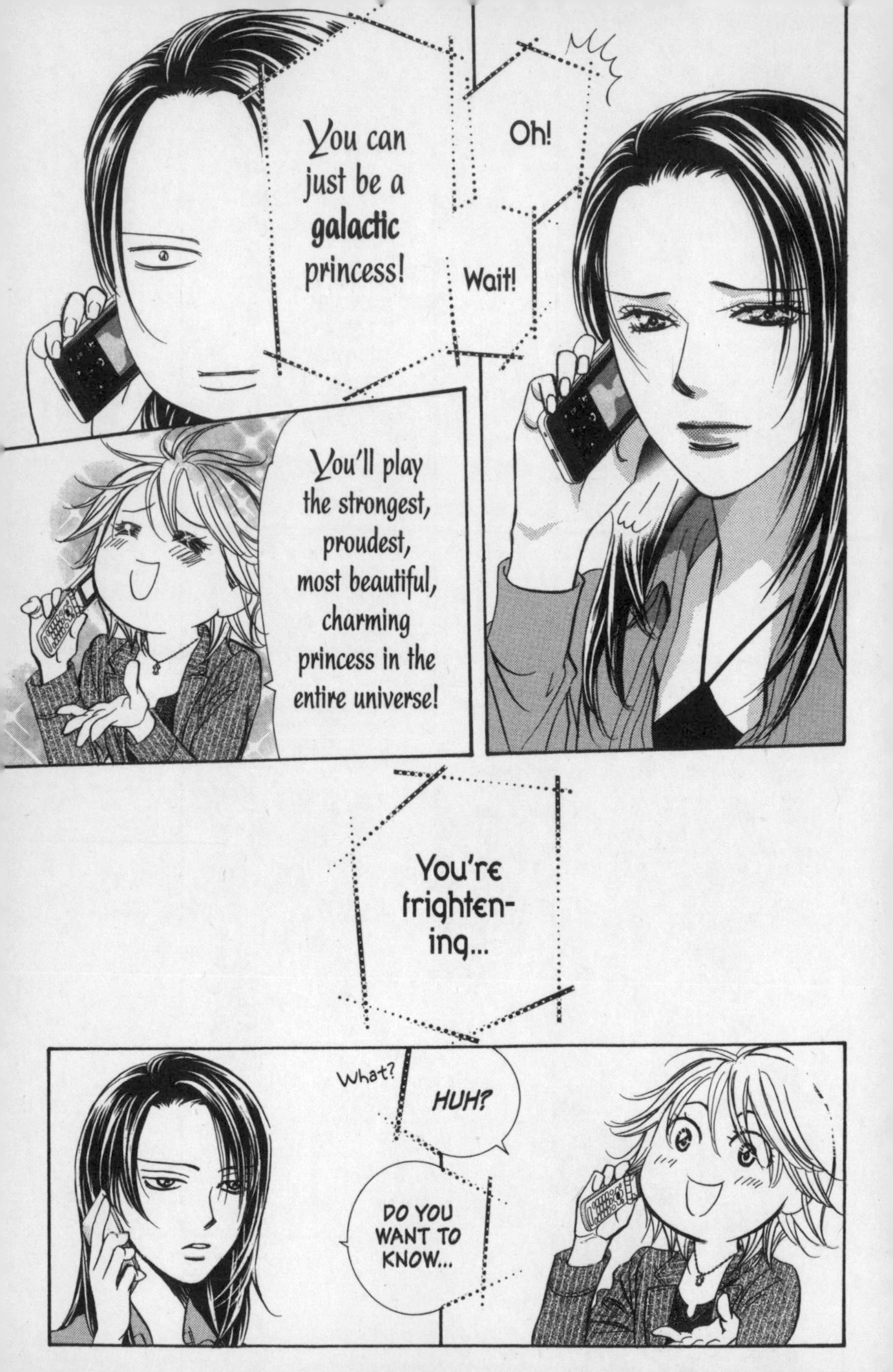
Oh!
Wait!
You can just be a galactic princess!
You'll play the strongest, proudest, most beautiful, charming princess in the entire universe!
You're frightening...
HUH?
What?
DO YOU WANT TO KNOW...

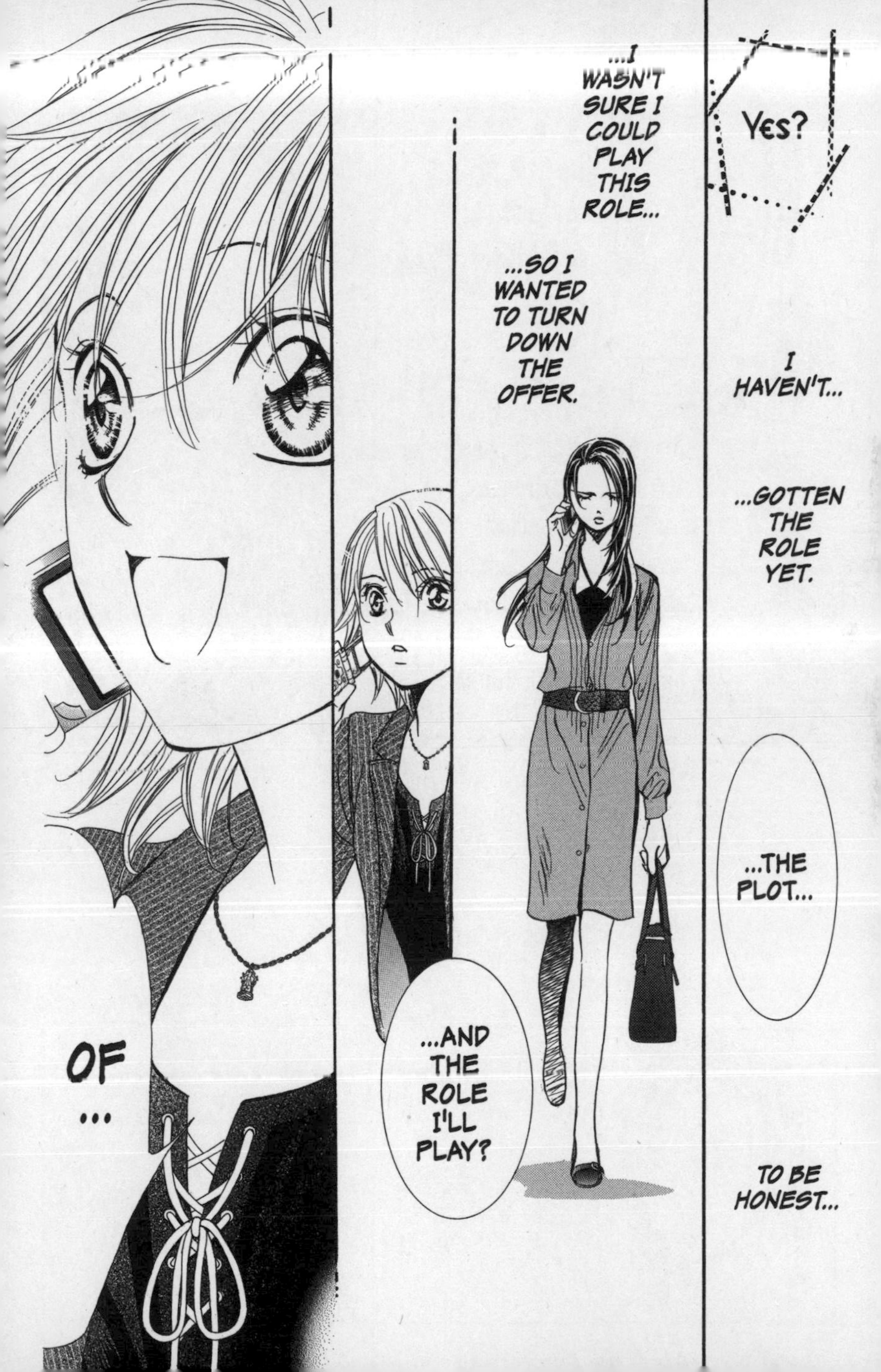
Yes?
I HAVEN'T...
...GOTTEN THE ROLE YET.
...THE PLOT...
TO BE HONEST...
...I WASN'T SURE I COULD PLAY THIS ROLE...
...SO I WANTED TO TURN DOWN THE OFFER.
...AND THE ROLE I'LL PLAY?
OF ...

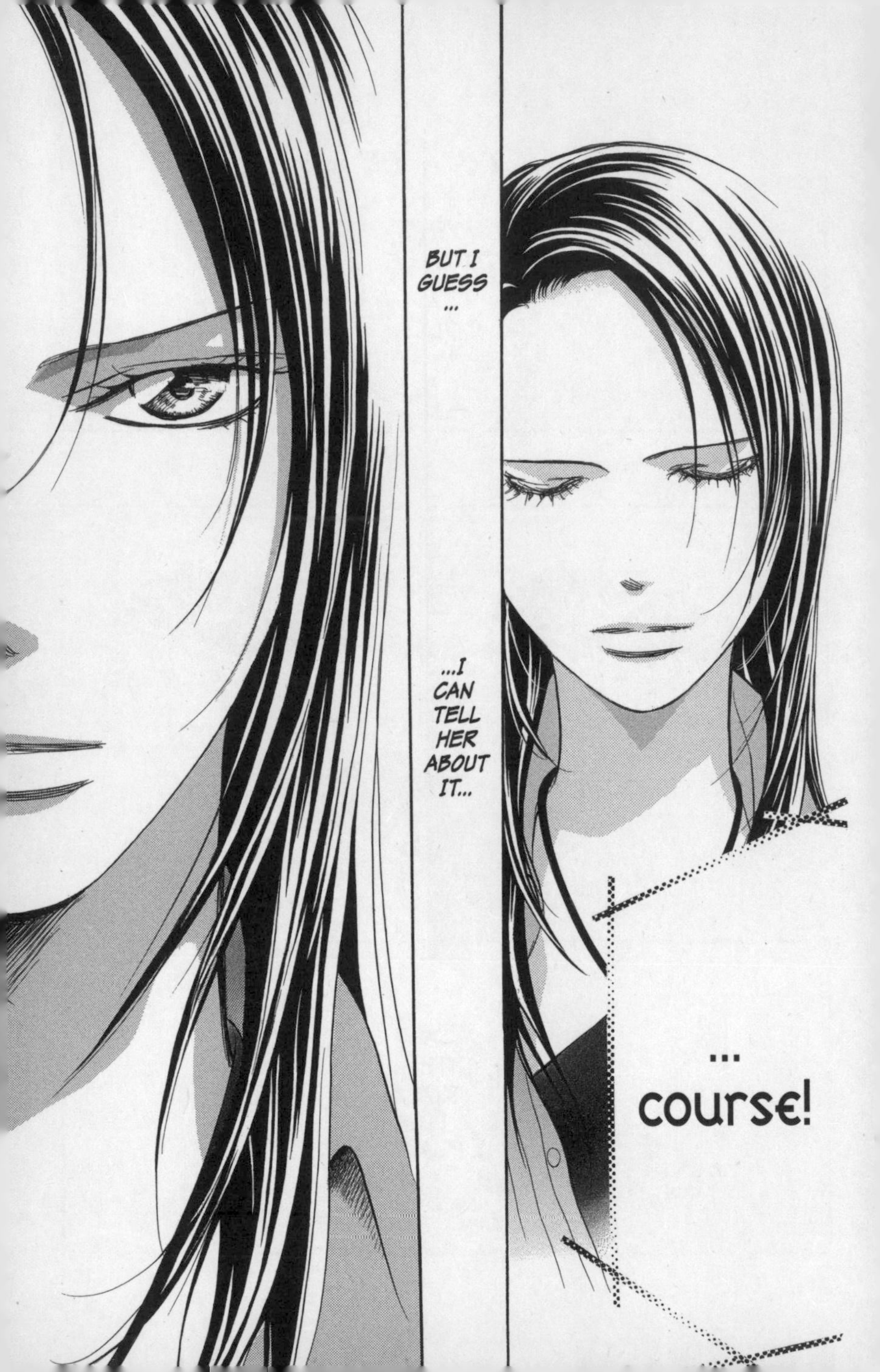
BUT I GUESS ...
...I CAN TELL HER ABOUT IT...
... course!

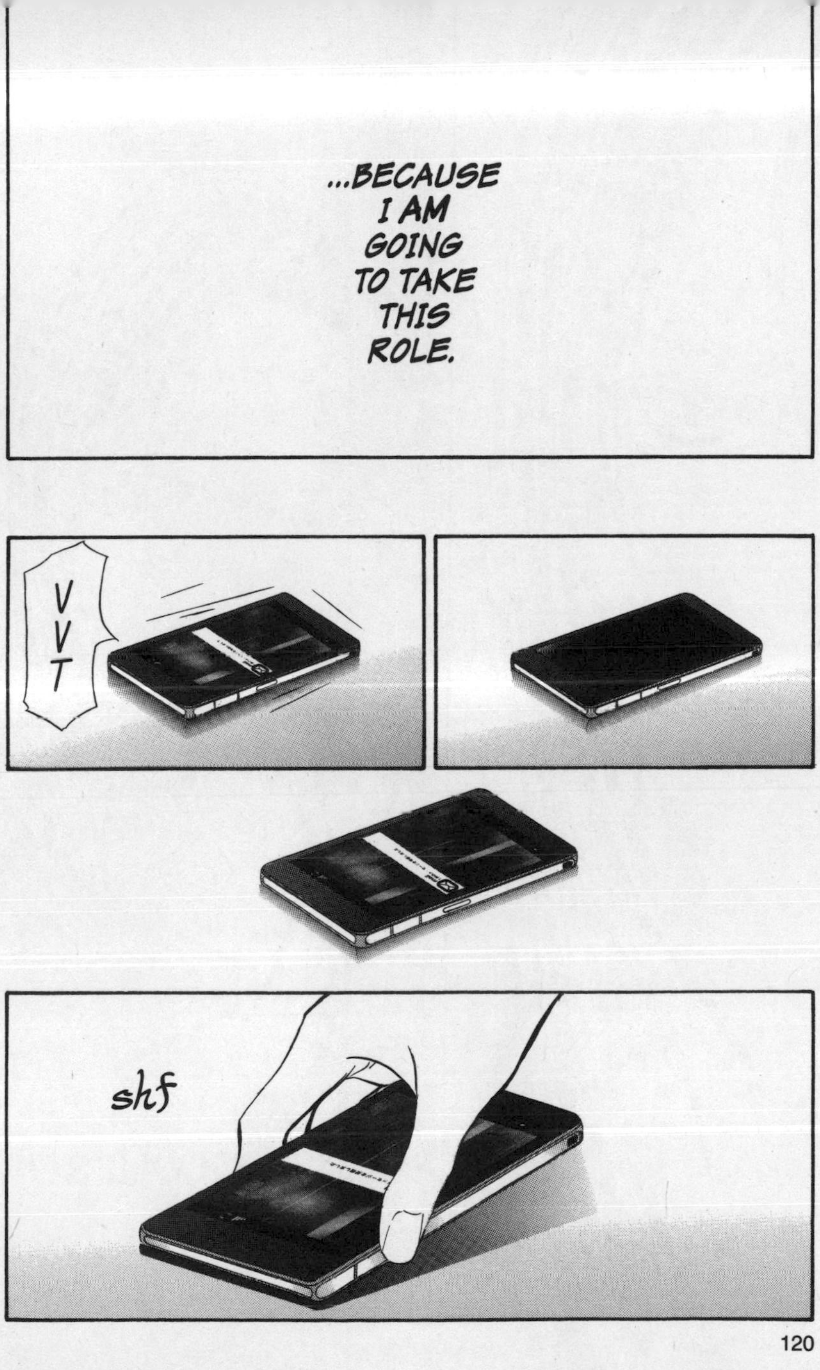
...BECAUSE I AM GOING TO TAKE THIS ROLE.
VVT
shf

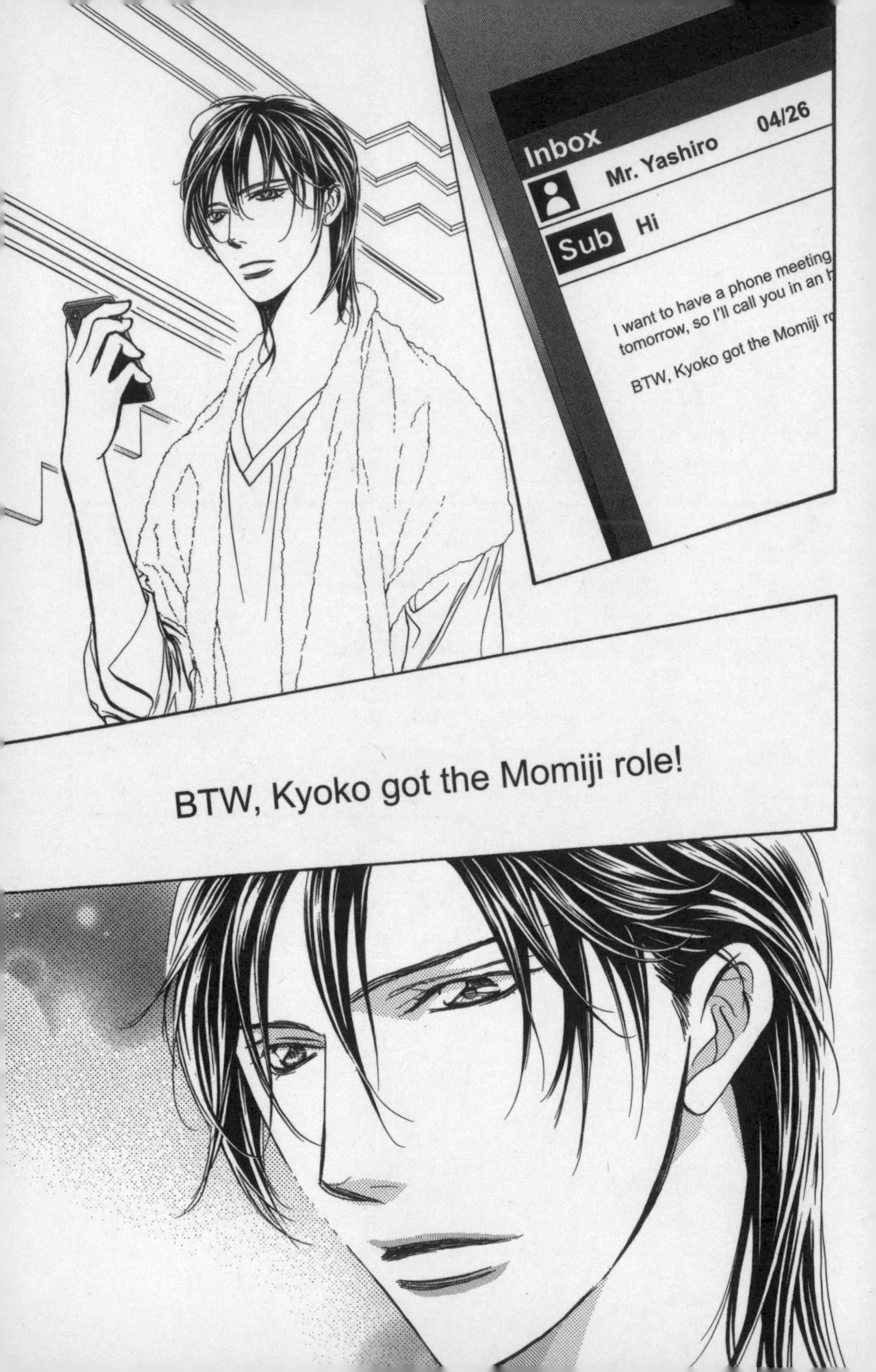
Inbox
04/26
Mr. Yashiro
Sub
Hi
I want to have a phone meeting
tomorrow, so I'll call you in an
BTW, Kyoko got the Momiji
BTW, Kyoko got the Momiji role!

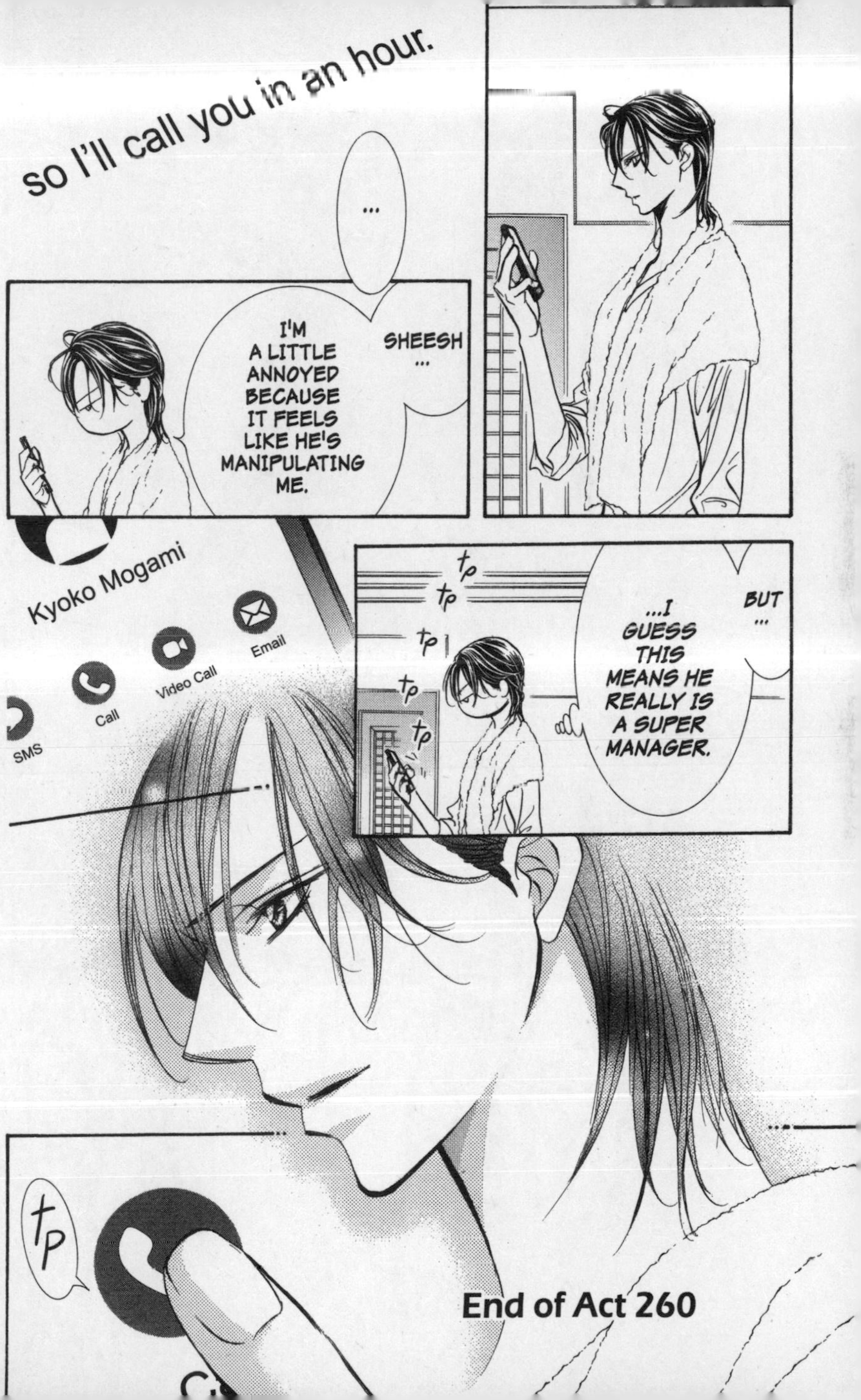
so I'll call you in an hour.
...
SHEESH ...
I'M A LITTLE ANNOYED BECAUSE IT FEELS LIKE HE'S MANIPULATING ME.
BUT ...
...I GUESS THIS MEANS HE REALLY IS A SUPER MANAGER.
tp tp tp tp tp
Kyoko Mogami
Email
Video Call
Call
SMS
tp
End of Act 260

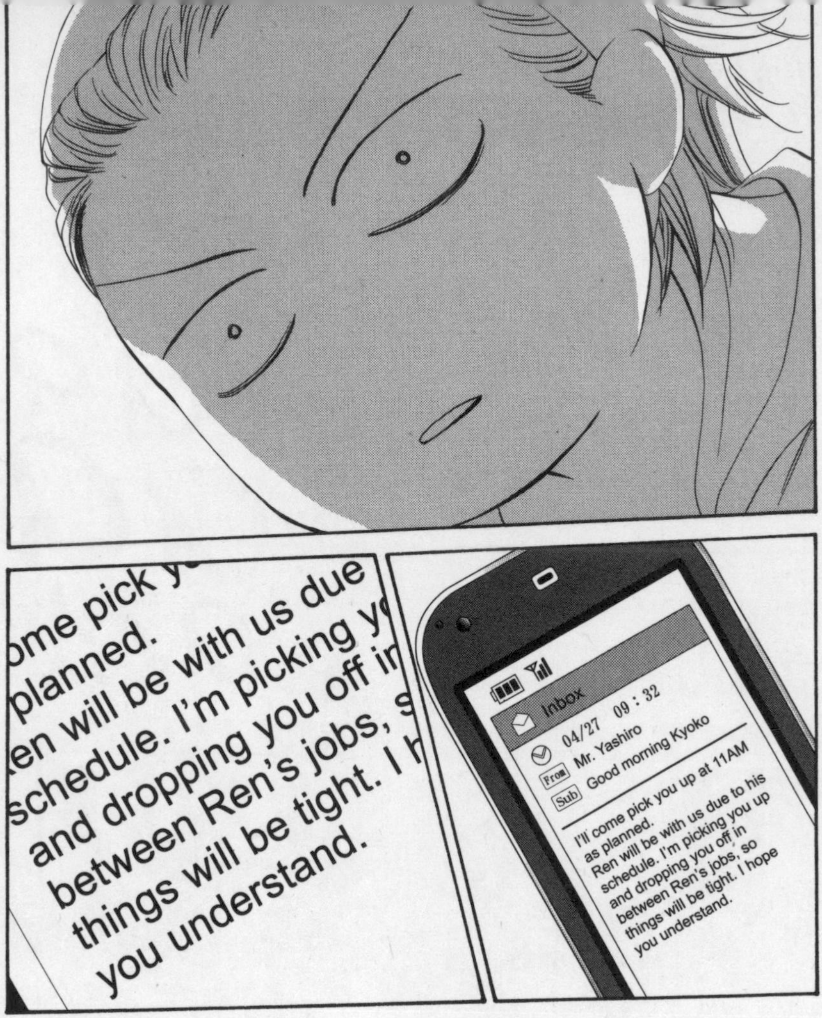
Inbox
04/27 09:32
From Mr. Yashiro
Sub Good morning Kyoko
I'll come pick you up at 11AM as planned. Ren will be with us due to his schedule. I'm picking you up and dropping you off in between Ren's jobs, so things will be tight. I hope you understand.
ome pick y
planned.
en will be with us due
schedule. I'm picking y
and dropping you off i
between Ren's jobs, s
things will be tight. I h
you understand.

Skip·Beat!

Act 261: Upset—Two Days to Go

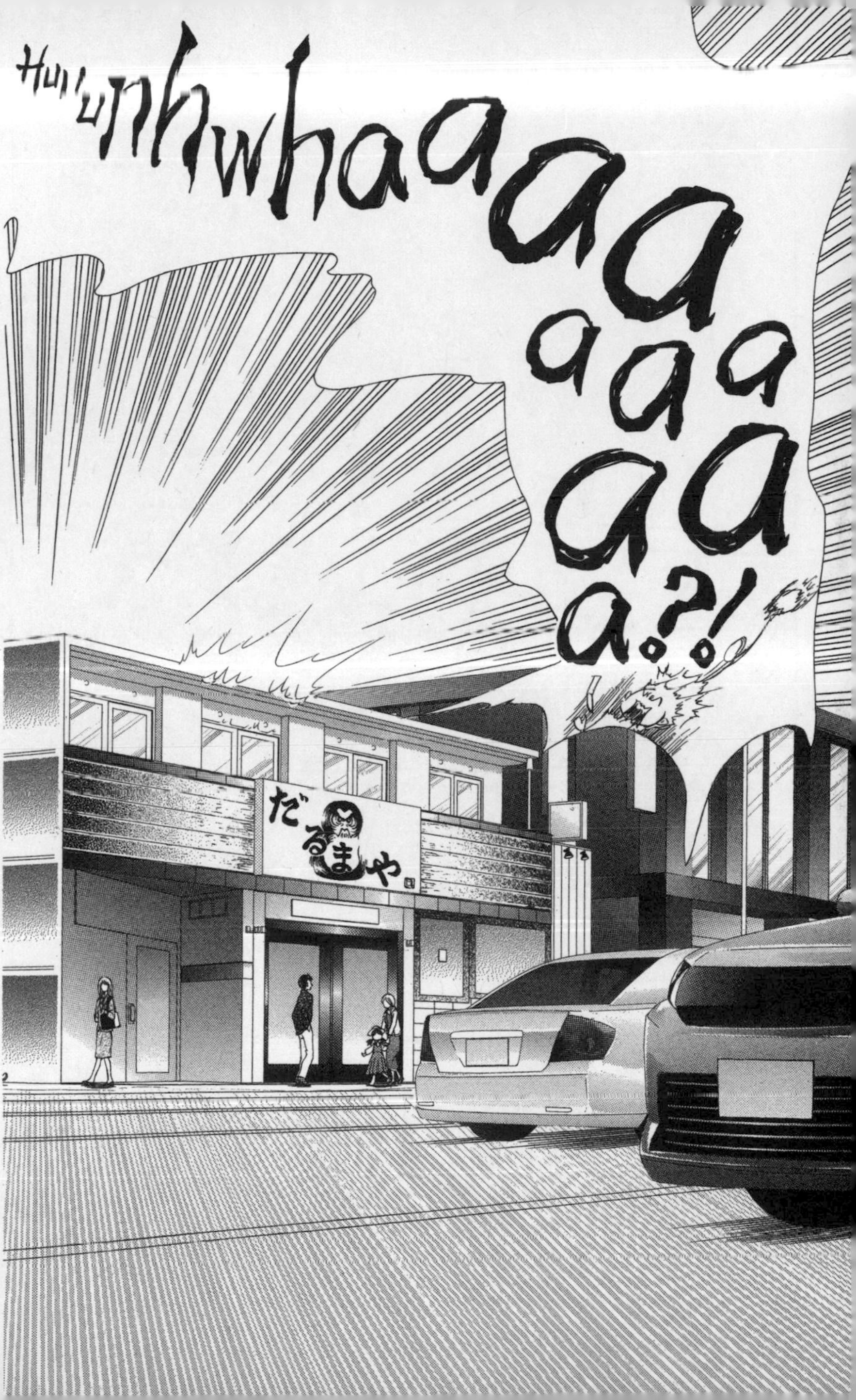
Huuunnhwhaaaaaaaaaaaa?!
だるまや

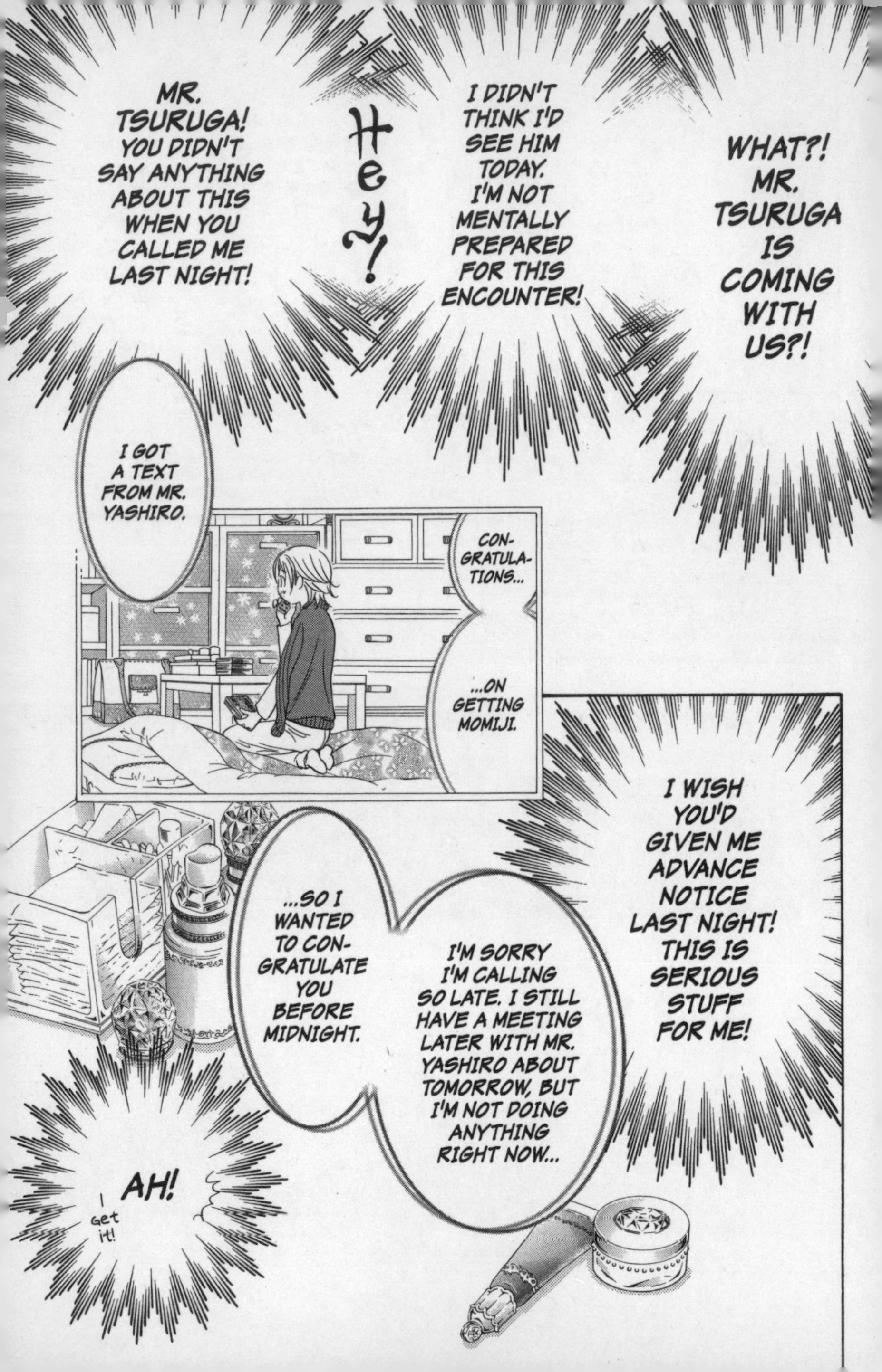
WHAT?! MR. TSURUGA IS COMING WITH US?!
I DIDN'T THINK I'D SEE HIM TODAY. I'M NOT MENTALLY PREPARED FOR THIS ENCOUNTER!
Hey!
MR. TSURUGA! YOU DIDN'T SAY ANYTHING ABOUT THIS WHEN YOU CALLED ME LAST NIGHT!
I WISH YOU'D GIVEN ME ADVANCE NOTICE LAST NIGHT! THIS IS SERIOUS STUFF FOR ME!
I GOT A TEXT FROM MR. YASHIRO.
CON-GRATULA-TIONS...
...ON GETTING MOMIJI.
I'M SORRY I'M CALLING SO LATE. I STILL HAVE A MEETING LATER WITH MR. YASHIRO ABOUT TOMORROW, BUT I'M NOT DOING ANYTHING RIGHT NOW...
...SO I WANTED TO CON-GRATULATE YOU BEFORE MIDNIGHT.
AH!
I get it!

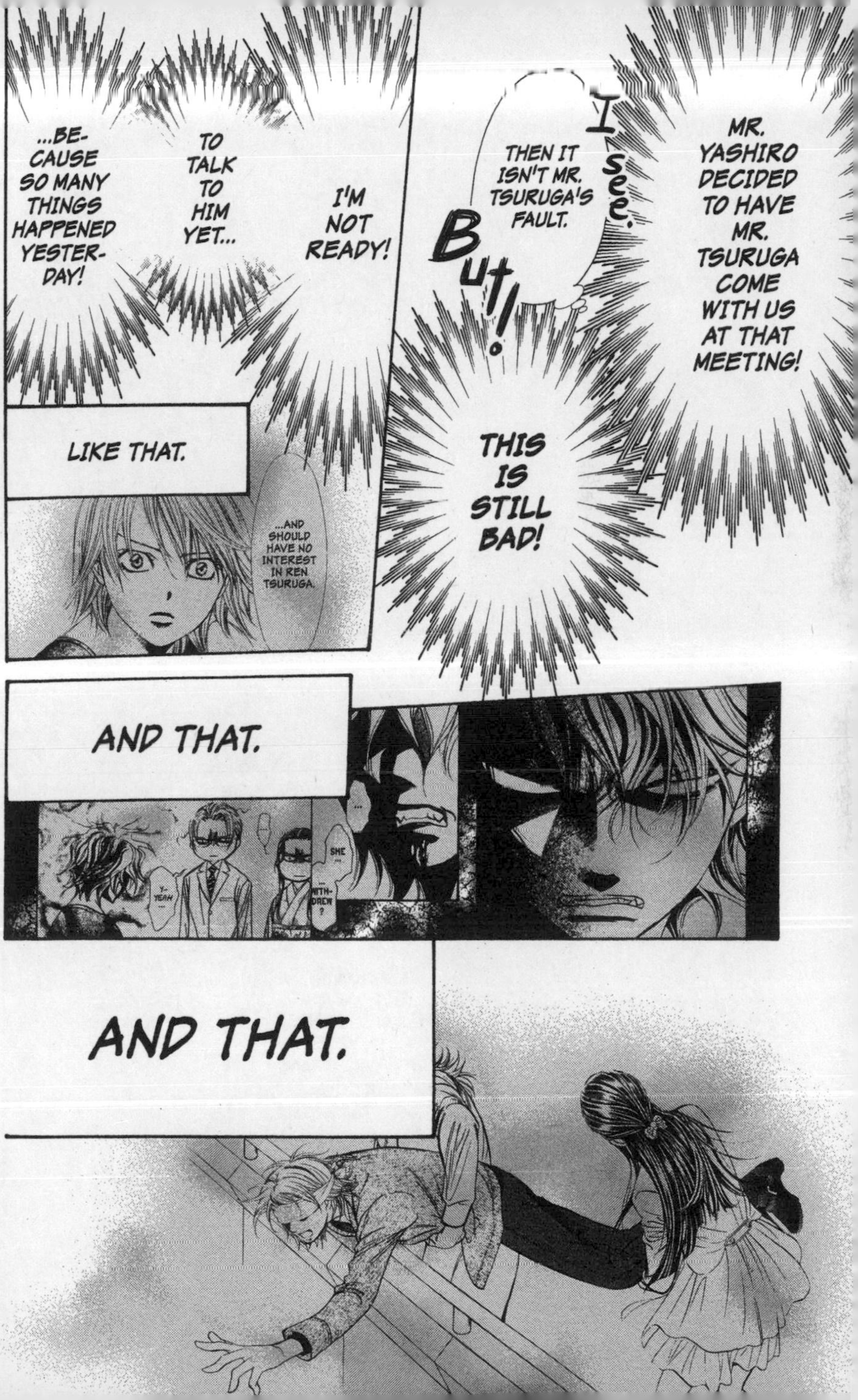
MR. YASHIRO DECIDED TO HAVE MR. TSURUGA COME WITH US AT THAT MEETING!
I see.
THEN IT ISN'T MR. TSURUGA'S FAULT.
But!
THIS IS STILL BAD!
I'M NOT READY!
TO TALK TO HIM YET...
...BE-CAUSE SO MANY THINGS HAPPENED YESTER-DAY!
LIKE THAT.
...AND SHOULD HAVE NO INTEREST IN REN TSURUGA.
AND THAT.
...
SHE ... WITH-DREW?
Y-YEAH ...
AND THAT.

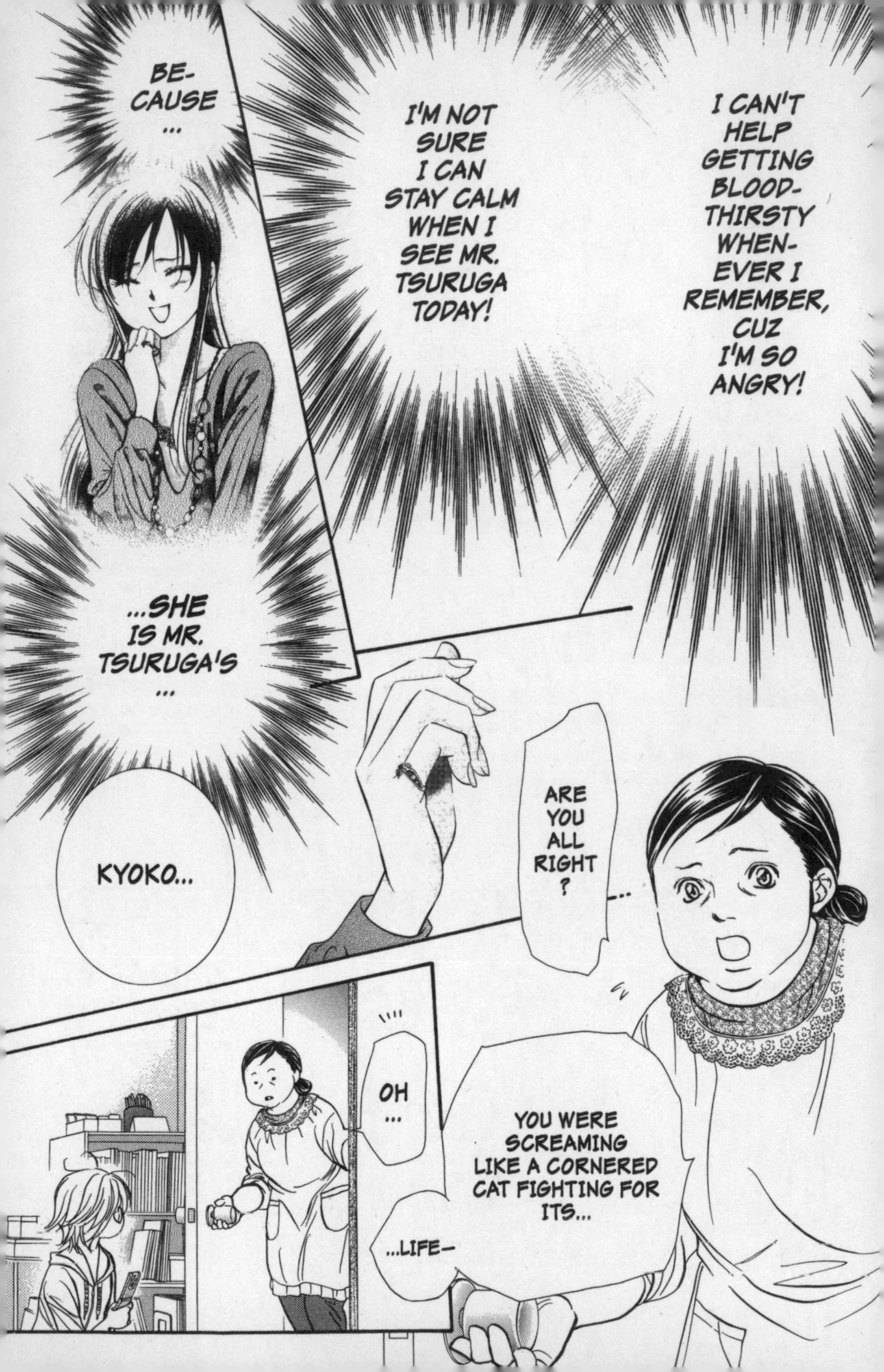
I CAN'T HELP GETTING BLOOD-THIRSTY WHEN-EVER I REMEMBER, CUZ I'M SO ANGRY!
I'M NOT SURE I CAN STAY CALM WHEN I SEE MR. TSURUGA TODAY!
BE-CAUSE ...
...SHE IS MR. TSURUGA'S ...
ARE YOU ALL RIGHT ?
...
KYOKO...
YOU WERE SCREAMING LIKE A CORNERED CAT FIGHTING FOR ITS...
...LIFE-
OH ...

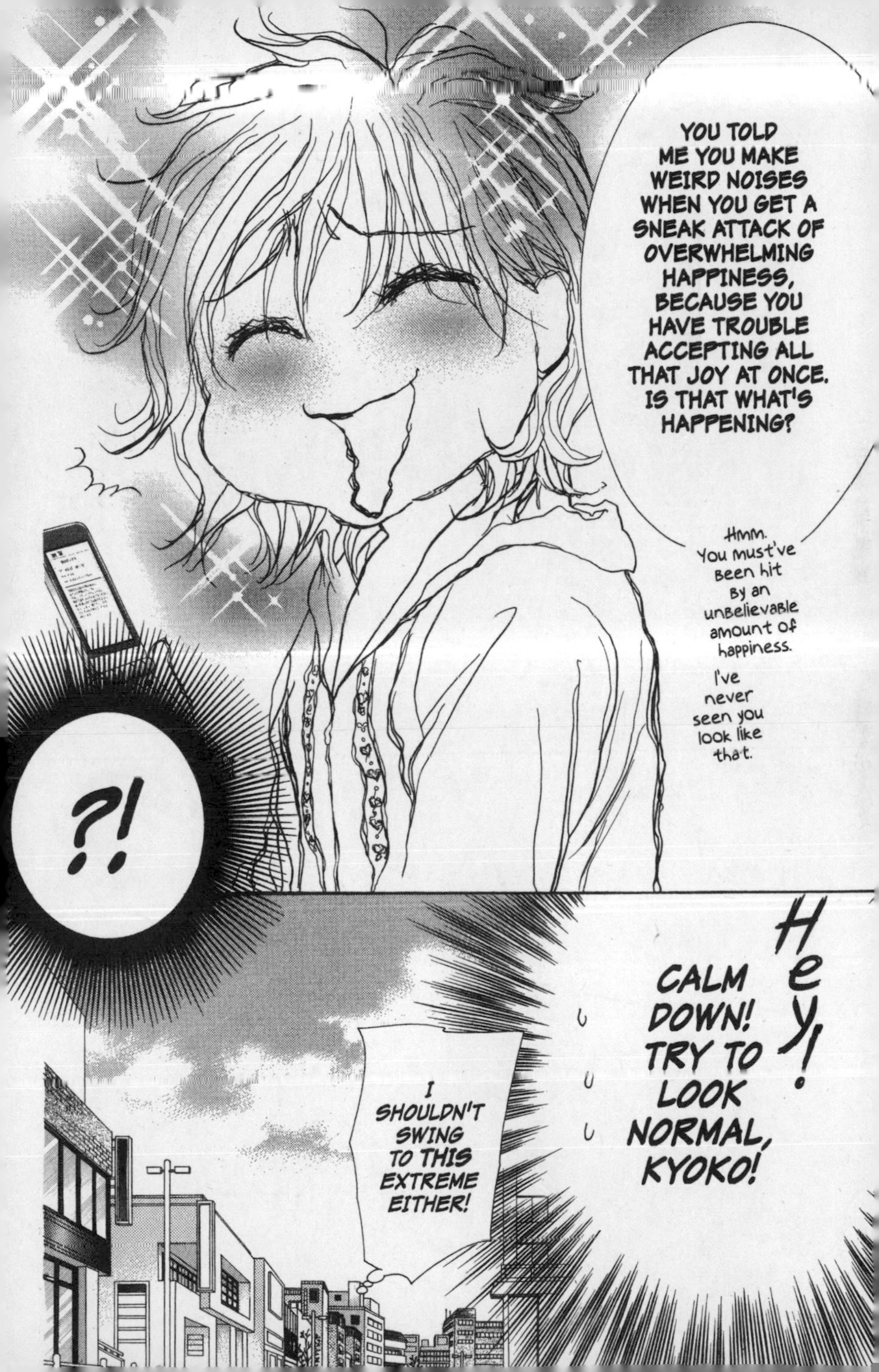
YOU TOLD ME YOU MAKE WEIRD NOISES WHEN YOU GET A SNEAK ATTACK OF OVERWHELMING HAPPINESS, BECAUSE YOU HAVE TROUBLE ACCEPTING ALL THAT JOY AT ONCE. IS THAT WHAT'S HAPPENING?
Hmm. You must've been hit by an unbelievable amount of happiness.
I've never seen you look like that.
?!
Hey!
CALM DOWN! TRY TO LOOK NORMAL, KYOKO!
I SHOULDN'T SWING TO THIS EXTREME EITHER!

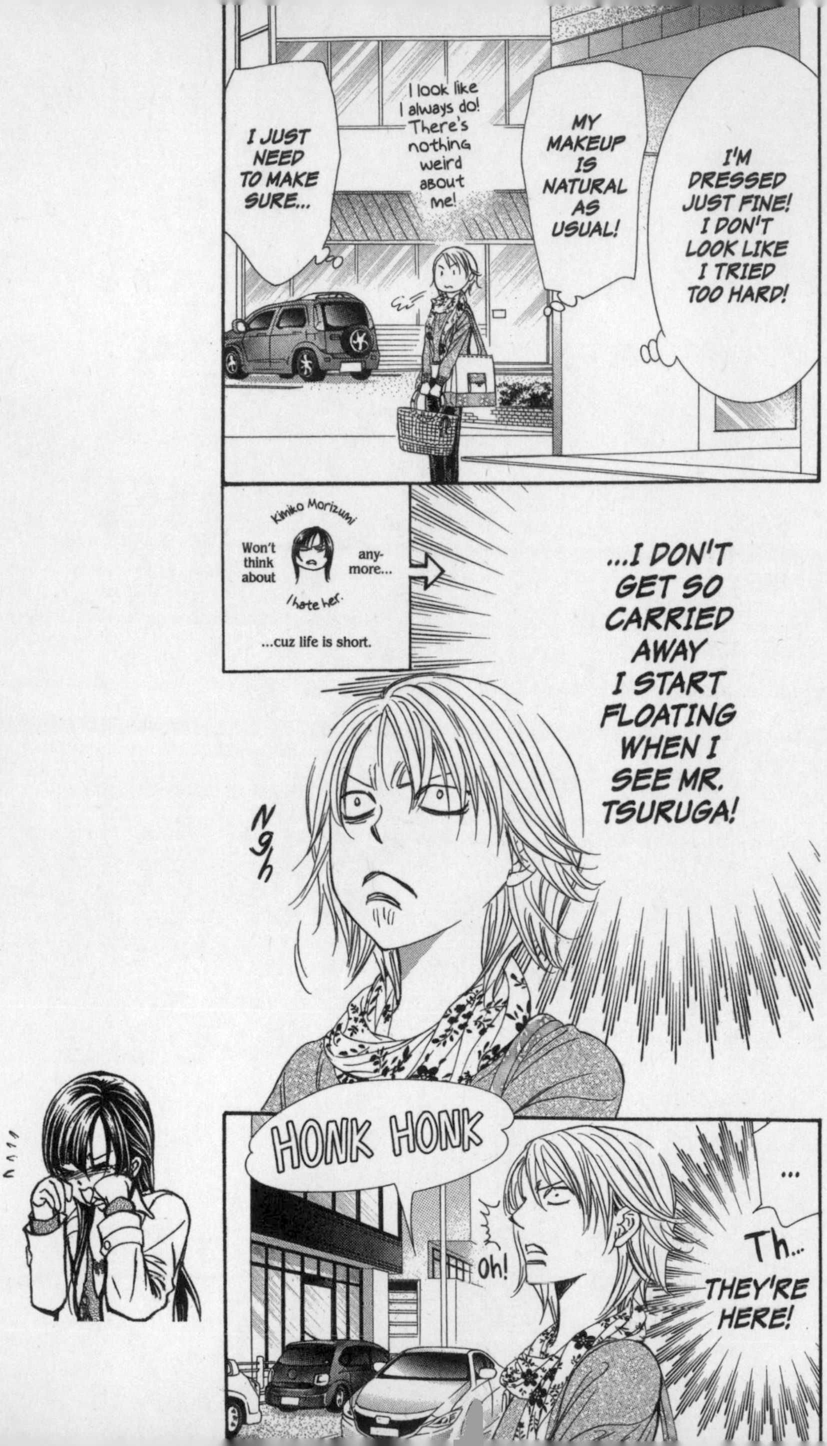
I'M DRESSED JUST FINE! I DON'T LOOK LIKE I TRIED TOO HARD!
MY MAKEUP IS NATURAL AS USUAL!
I look like I always do! There's nothing weird about me!
I JUST NEED TO MAKE SURE...
...I DON'T GET SO CARRIED AWAY I START FLOATING WHEN I SEE MR. TSURUGA!
Ngh
Kimiko Morizumi
Won't think about anymore...
I hate her.
...cuz life is short.
HONK HONK
Oh!
...
Th... THEY'RE HERE!

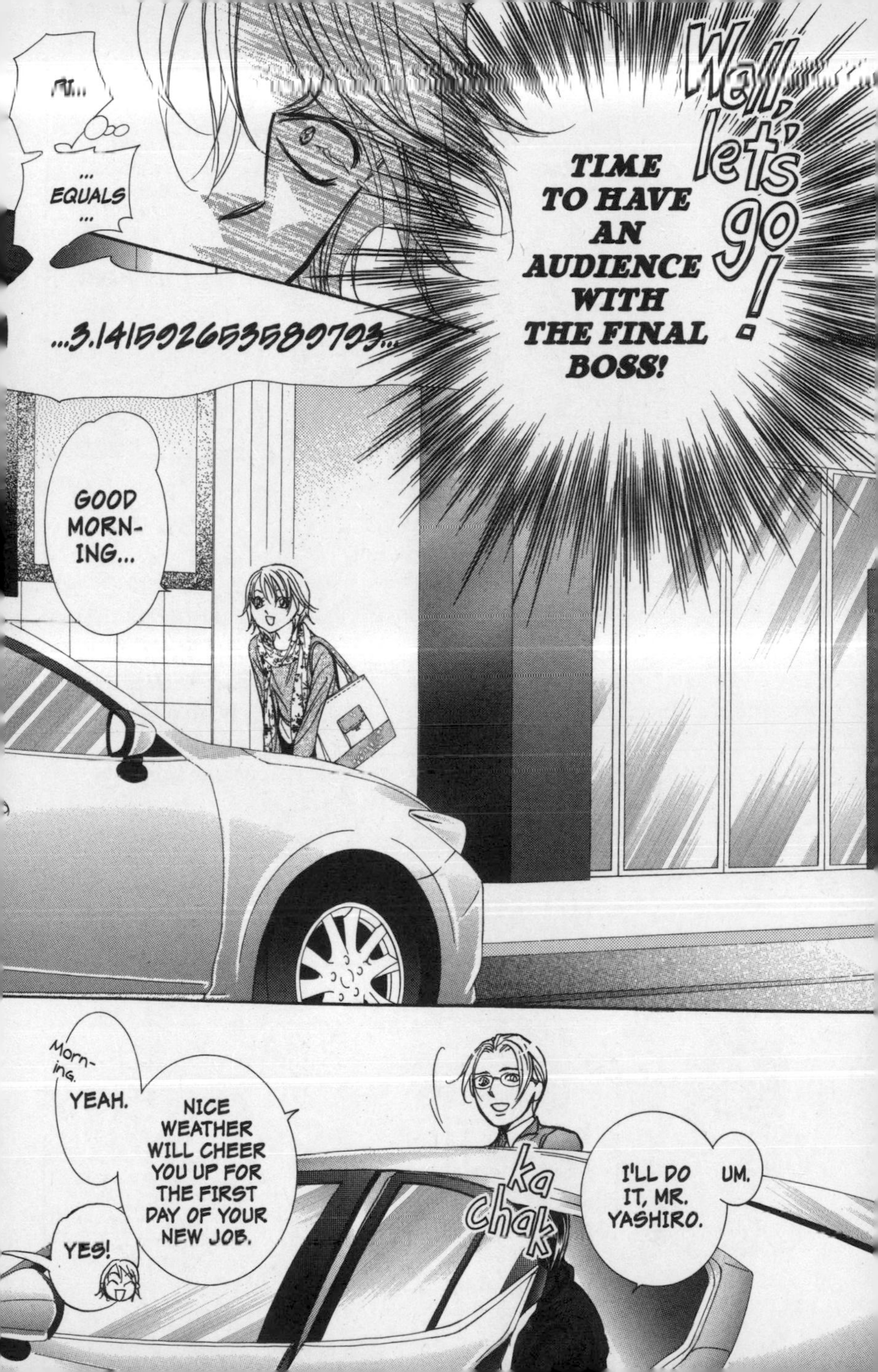
Well, let's go!
TIME TO HAVE AN AUDIENCE WITH THE FINAL BOSS!
π...
... EQUALS ...
...3.141592653589793...
GOOD MORN-ING...
UM.
I'LL DO IT, MR. YASHIRO.
ka chak
Morn-ing.
YEAH.
NICE WEATHER WILL CHEER YOU UP FOR THE FIRST DAY OF YOUR NEW JOB.
YES!

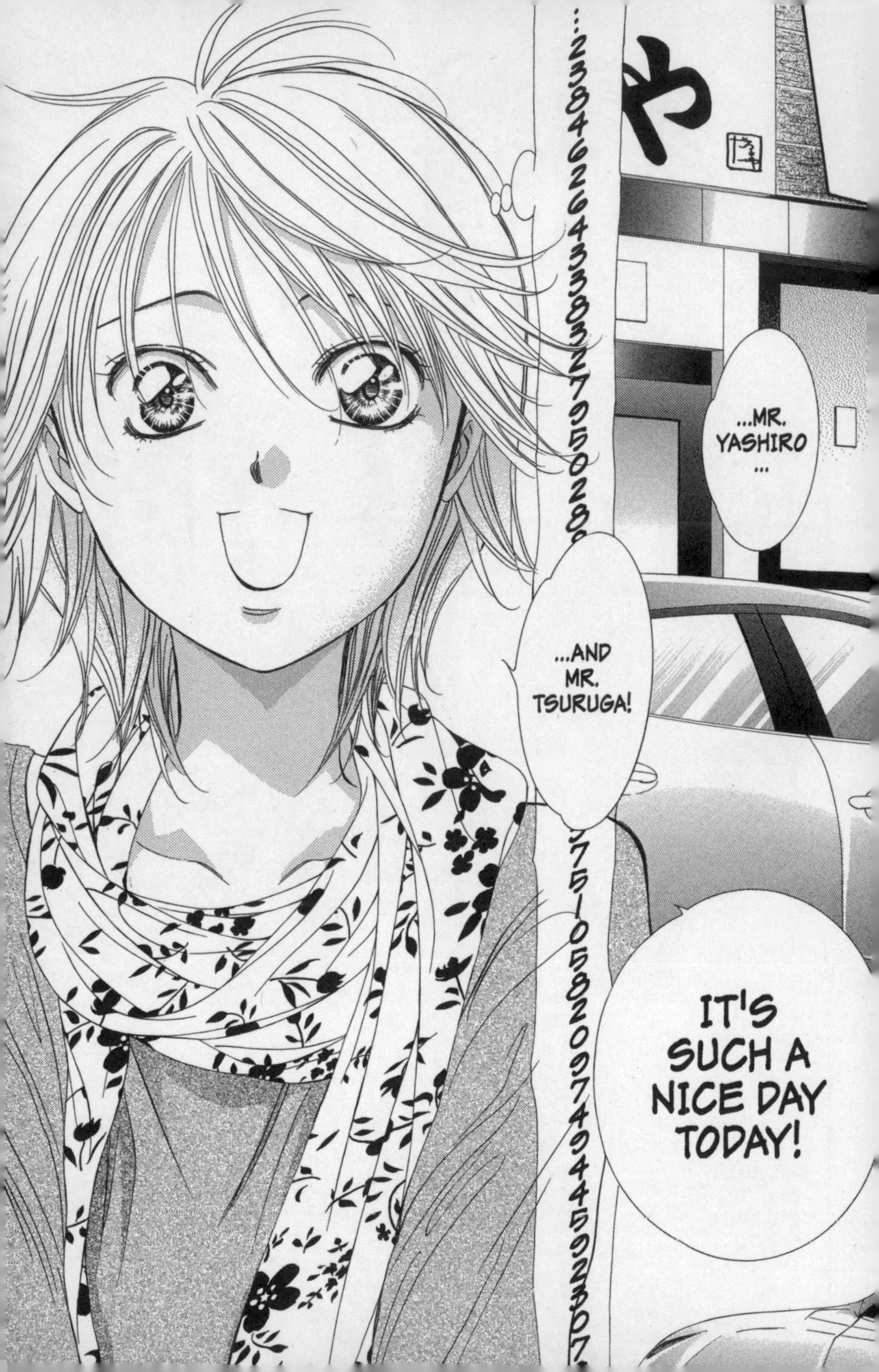

...2384626433832795028
...MR. YASHIRO ...
...AND MR. TSURUGA!
75105820974944592307
IT'S SUCH A NICE DAY TODAY!

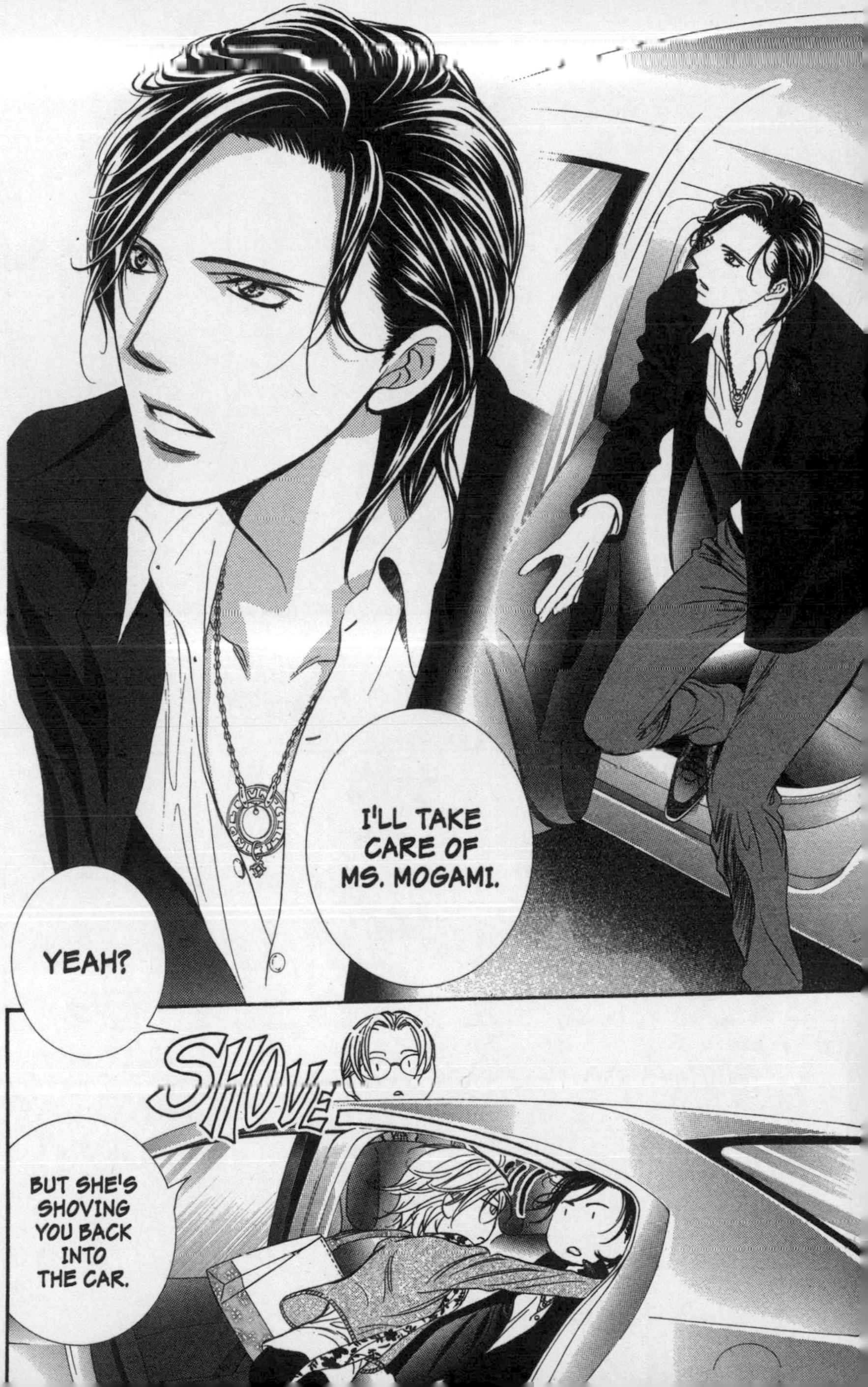
I'LL TAKE CARE OF MS. MOGAMI.
YEAH?
SHOVE
BUT SHE'S SHOVING YOU BACK INTO THE CAR.

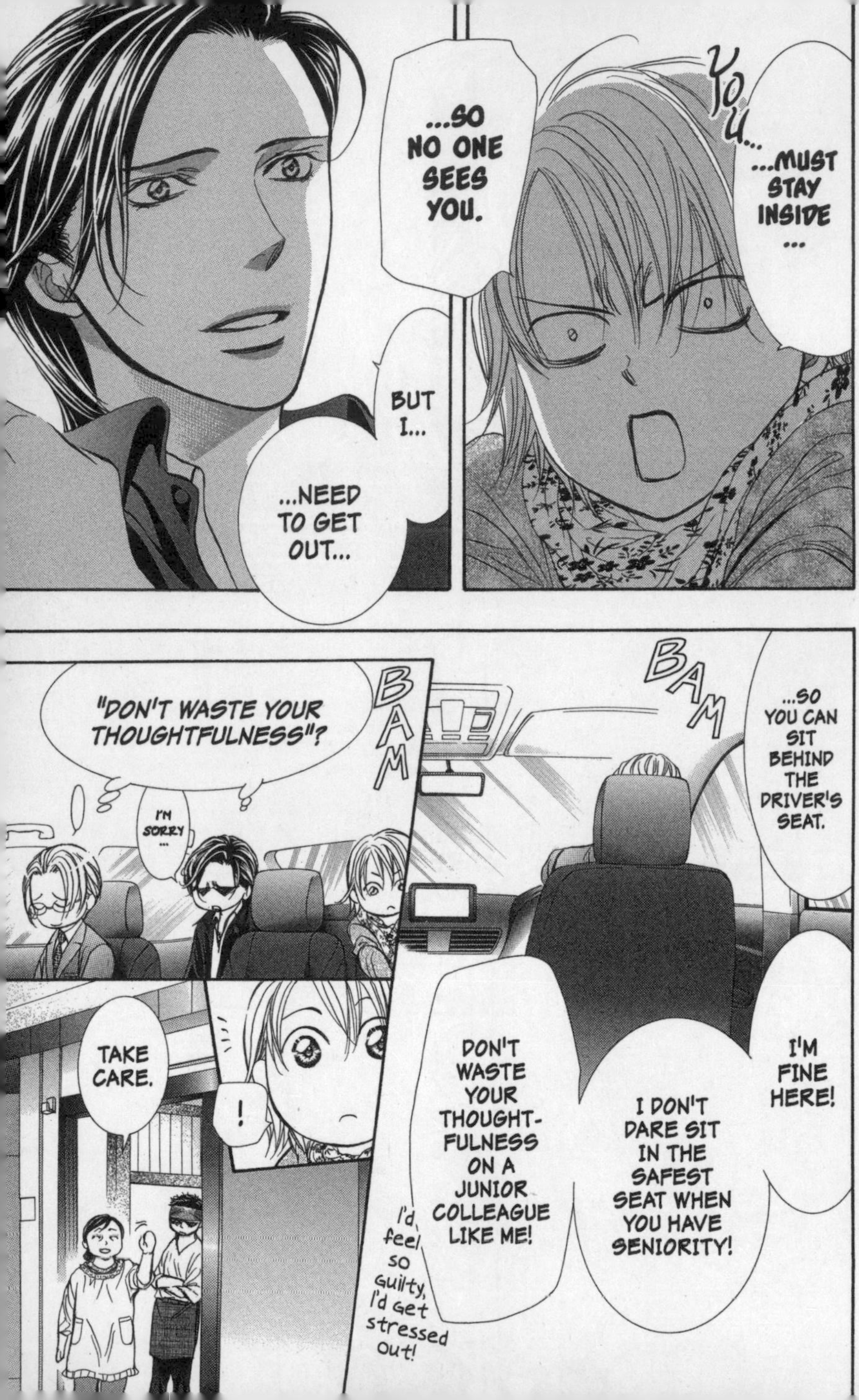
YOU...
...MUST STAY INSIDE ...
...SO NO ONE SEES YOU.
BUT I...
...NEED TO GET OUT...
BAM
...SO YOU CAN SIT BEHIND THE DRIVER'S SEAT.
I'M FINE HERE!
I DON'T DARE SIT IN THE SAFEST SEAT WHEN YOU HAVE SENIORITY!
DON'T WASTE YOUR THOUGHT-FULNESS ON A JUNIOR COLLEAGUE LIKE ME!
I'd feel so guilty, I'd get stressed out!
BAM
"DON'T WASTE YOUR THOUGHTFULNESS"?
I'M SORRY ...
!
TAKE CARE.

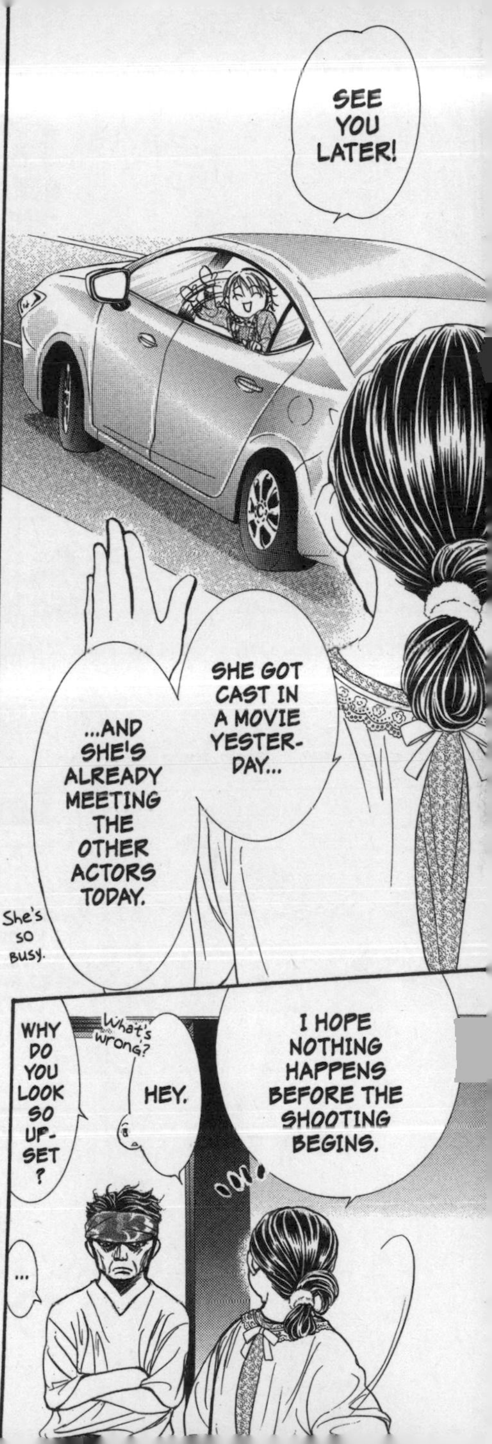
SEE YOU LATER!
SHE GOT CAST IN A MOVIE YESTER-DAY...
...AND SHE'S ALREADY MEETING THE OTHER ACTORS TODAY.
She's so busy.
I HOPE NOTHING HAPPENS BEFORE THE SHOOTING BEGINS.
HEY.
What's wrong?
WHY DO YOU LOOK SO UP-SET?
...
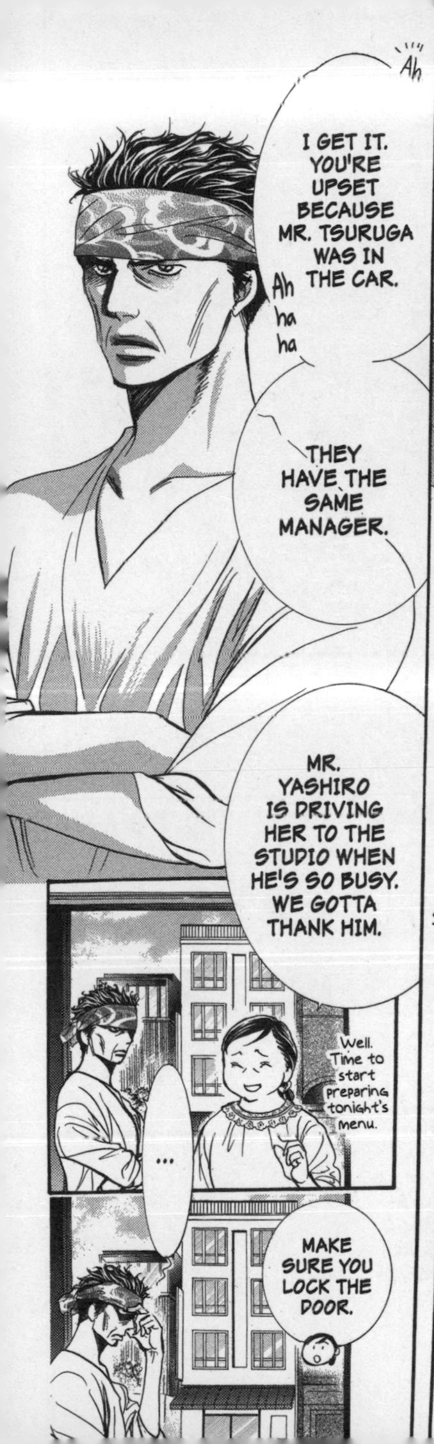
Ah
I GET IT. YOU'RE UPSET BECAUSE MR. TSURUGA WAS IN THE CAR.
Ah ha ha
THEY HAVE THE SAME MANAGER.
MR. YASHIRO IS DRIVING HER TO THE STUDIO WHEN HE'S SO BUSY. WE GOTTA THANK HIM.
Well. Time to start preparing tonight's menu.
...
MAKE SURE YOU LOCK THE DOOR.

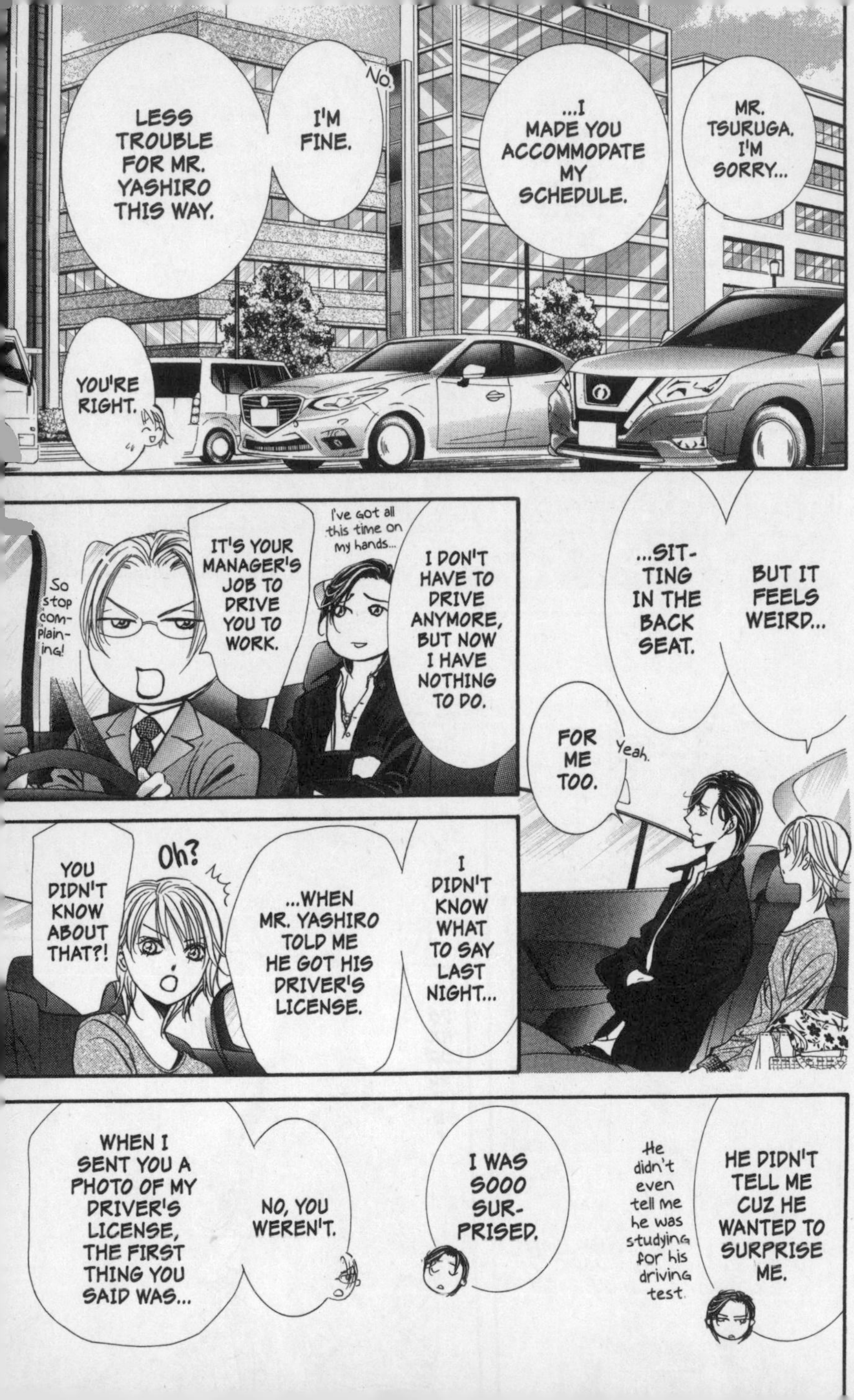
MR. TSURUGA. I'M SORRY...
...I MADE YOU ACCOMMODATE MY SCHEDULE.
No.
I'M FINE.
LESS TROUBLE FOR MR. YASHIRO THIS WAY.
YOU'RE RIGHT.
BUT IT FEELS WEIRD...
...SIT-TING IN THE BACK SEAT.
Yeah.
FOR ME TOO.
I DON'T HAVE TO DRIVE ANYMORE, BUT NOW I HAVE NOTHING TO DO.
I've got all this time on my hands...
IT'S YOUR MANAGER'S JOB TO DRIVE YOU TO WORK.
So stop com-plain-ing!
I DIDN'T KNOW WHAT TO SAY LAST NIGHT...
...WHEN MR. YASHIRO TOLD ME HE GOT HIS DRIVER'S LICENSE.
Oh?
YOU DIDN'T KNOW ABOUT THAT?!
HE DIDN'T TELL ME CUZ HE WANTED TO SURPRISE ME.
He didn't even tell me he was studying for his driving test.
I WAS SOOO SUR-PRISED.
NO, YOU WEREN'T.
WHEN I SENT YOU A PHOTO OF MY DRIVER'S LICENSE, THE FIRST THING YOU SAID WAS...

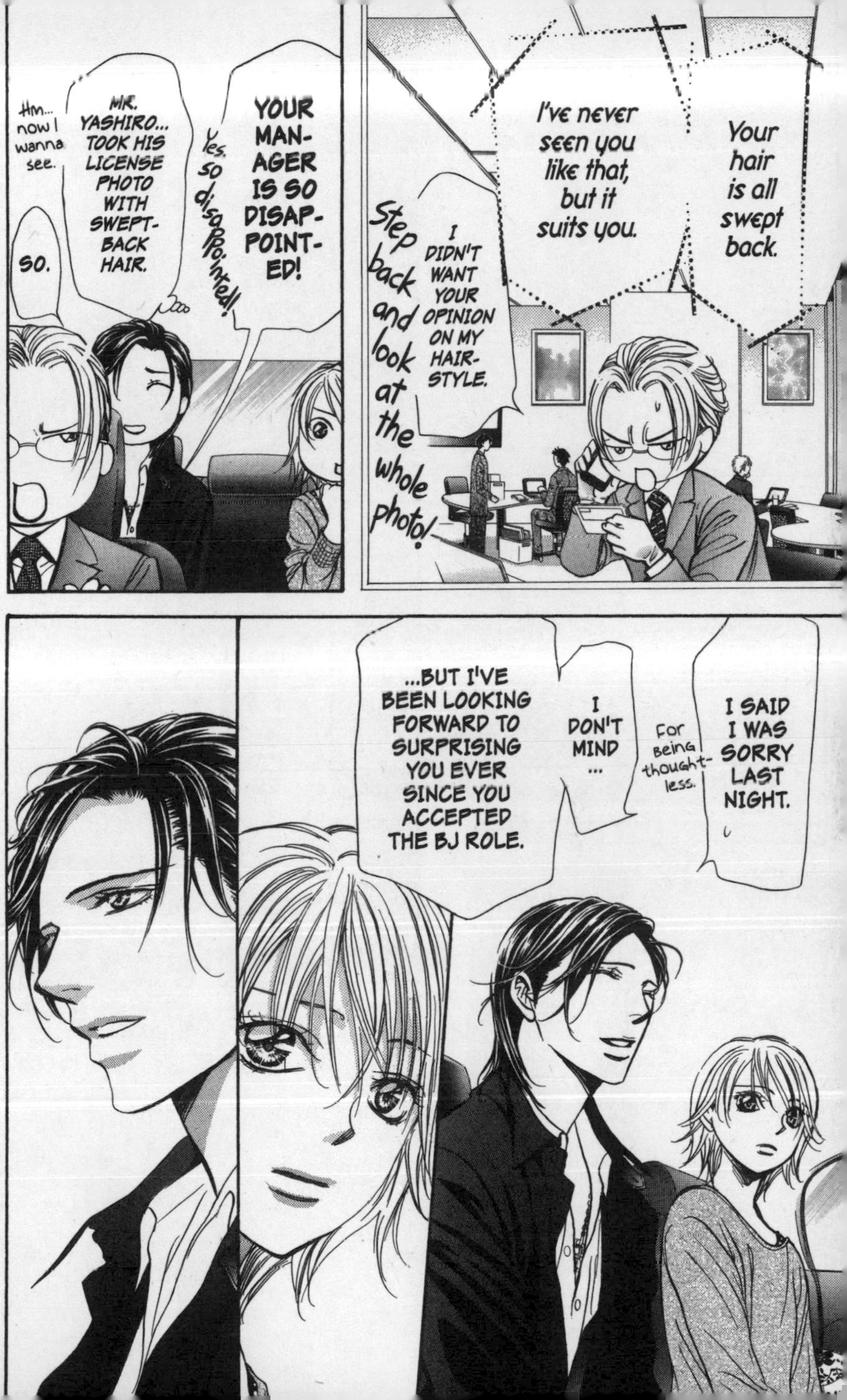
Your hair is all swept back.
I've never seen you like that, but it suits you.
I DIDN'T WANT YOUR OPINION ON MY HAIR-STYLE.
Step back and look at the whole photo!
YOUR MAN-AGER IS SO DISAP-POINT-ED!
Yes. so disappointed!
MR. YASHIRO... TOOK HIS LICENSE PHOTO WITH SWEPT-BACK HAIR.
Hm... now I wanna see.
SO.
I SAID I WAS SORRY LAST NIGHT.
For being thought-less.
I DON'T MIND...
...BUT I'VE BEEN LOOKING FORWARD TO SURPRISING YOU EVER SINCE YOU ACCEPTED THE BJ ROLE.

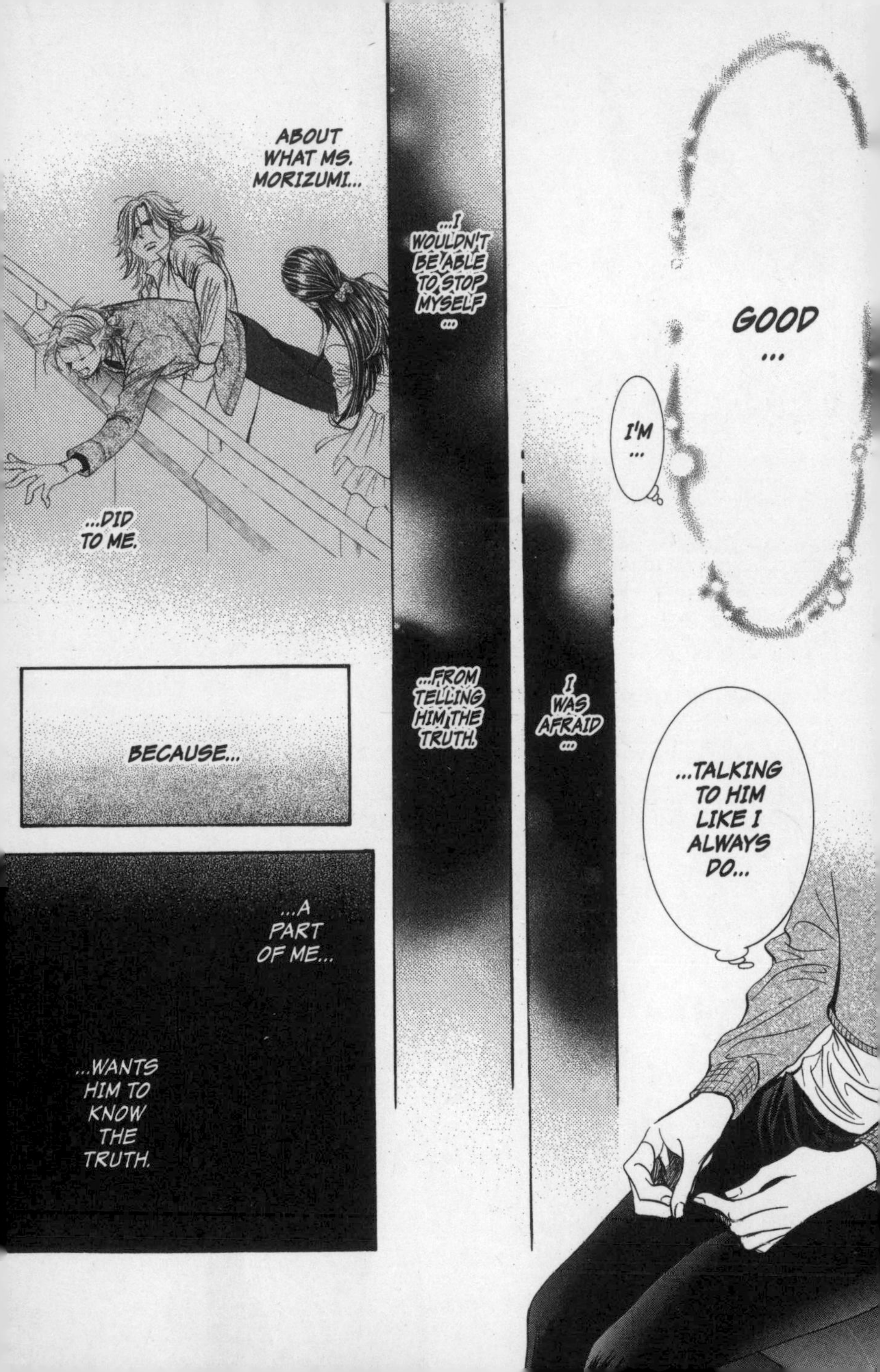
GOOD ...
I'M ...
...TALKING TO HIM LIKE I ALWAYS DO...
I WAS AFRAID ...
...I WOULDN'T BE ABLE TO STOP MYSELF ...
...FROM TELLING HIM THE TRUTH.
ABOUT WHAT MS. MORIZUMI...
...DID TO ME.
BECAUSE...
...A PART OF ME...
...WANTS HIM TO KNOW THE TRUTH.

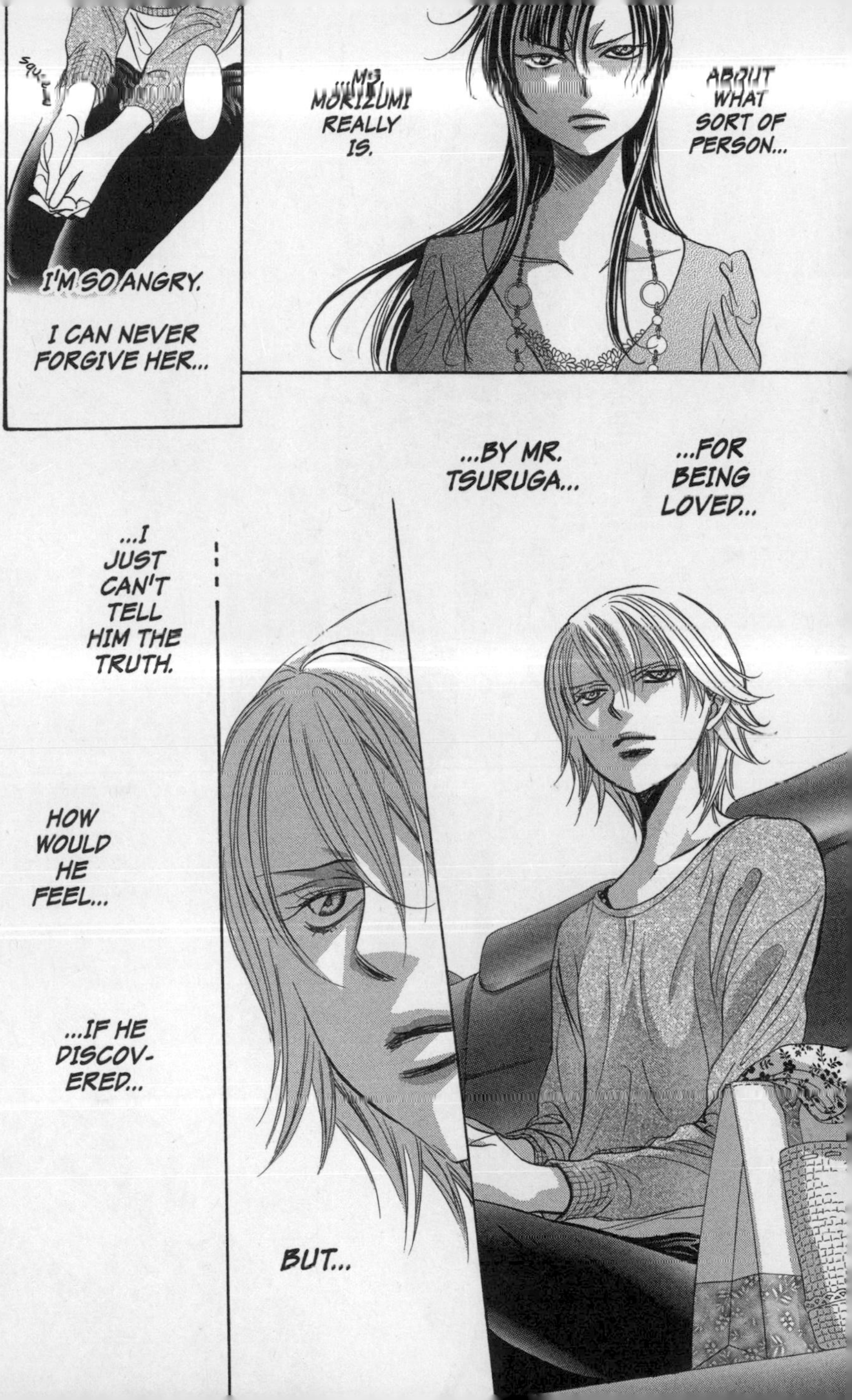
ABOUT WHAT SORT OF PERSON...
...MS. MORIZUMI REALLY IS.
I'M SO ANGRY.
I CAN NEVER FORGIVE HER...
...FOR BEING LOVED...
...BY MR. TSURUGA...
...I JUST CAN'T TELL HIM THE TRUTH.
HOW WOULD HE FEEL...
...IF HE DISCOVERED...
BUT...

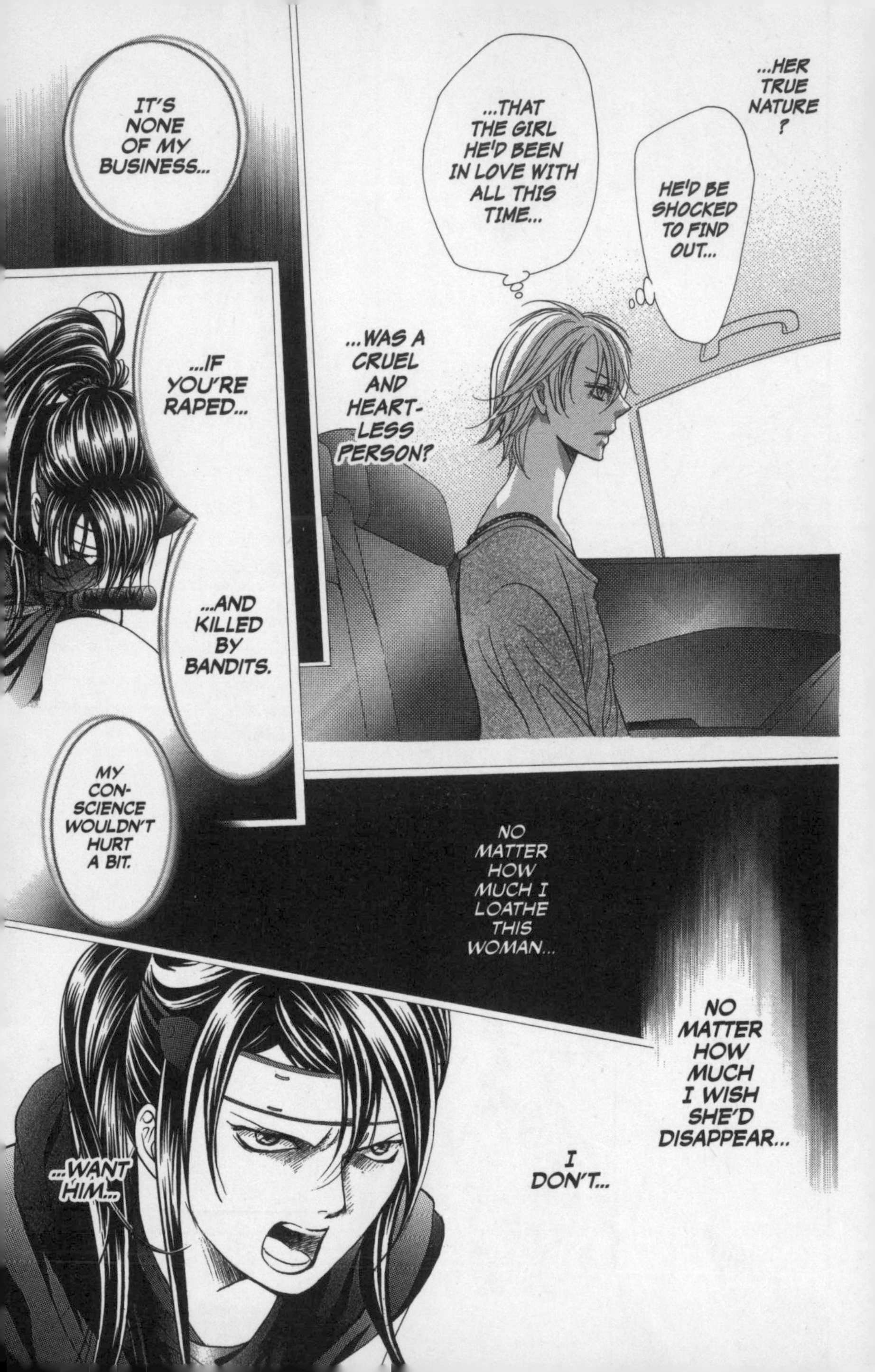
...HER TRUE NATURE?
HE'D BE SHOCKED TO FIND OUT...
...THAT THE GIRL HE'D BEEN IN LOVE WITH ALL THIS TIME...
...WAS A CRUEL AND HEART-LESS PERSON?
IT'S NONE OF MY BUSINESS...
...IF YOU'RE RAPED...
...AND KILLED BY BANDITS.
MY CON-SCIENCE WOULDN'T HURT A BIT.
NO MATTER HOW MUCH I LOATHE THIS WOMAN...
NO MATTER HOW MUCH I WISH SHE'D DISAPPEAR...
I DON'T...
...WANT HIM...

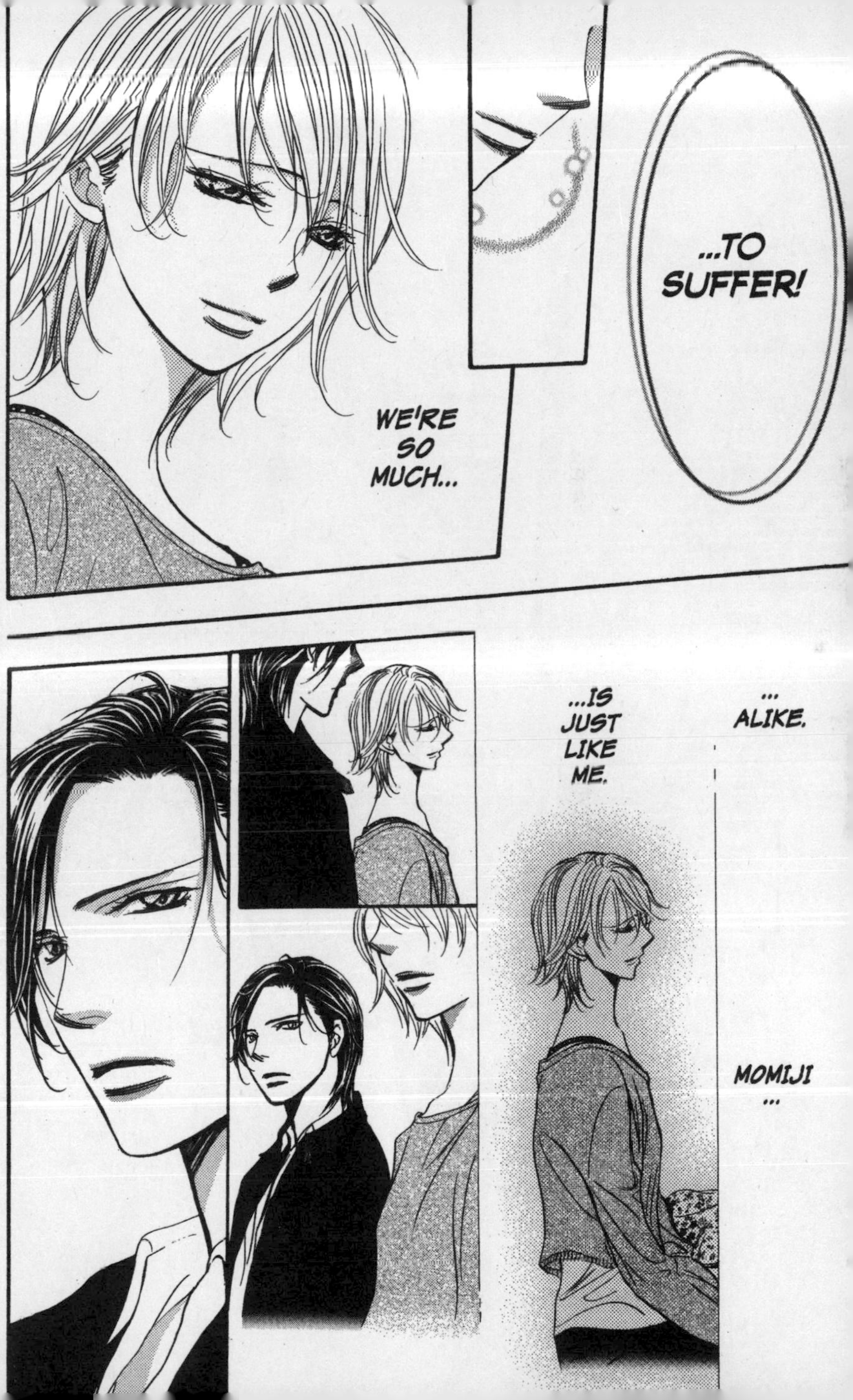
...TO SUFFER!
WE'RE SO MUCH...
... ALIKE.
MOMIJI ...
...IS JUST LIKE ME.

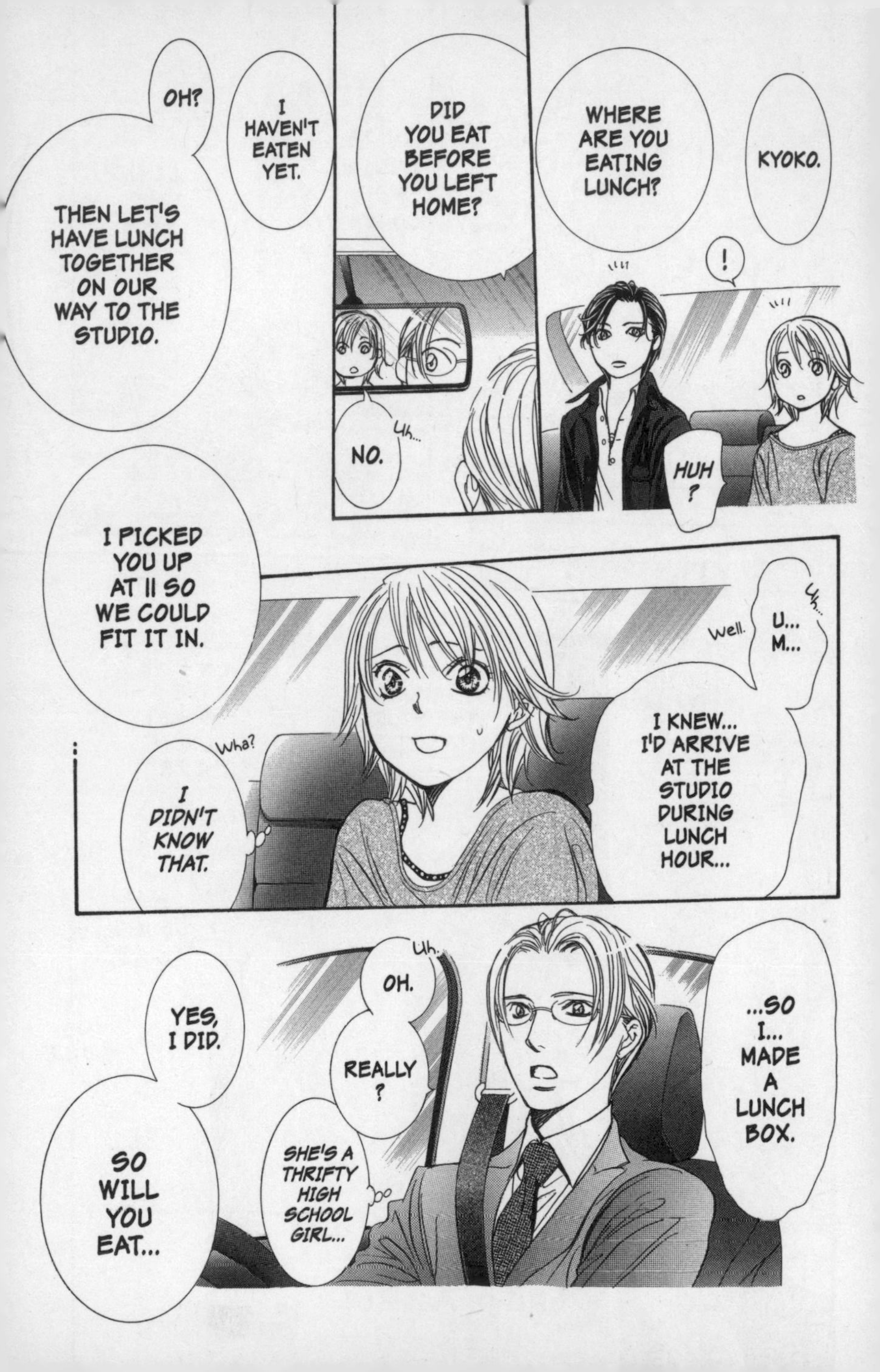
KYOKO.
WHERE ARE YOU EATING LUNCH?
!
HUH?
DID YOU EAT BEFORE YOU LEFT HOME?
Uh...
NO.
I HAVEN'T EATEN YET.
OH?
THEN LET'S HAVE LUNCH TOGETHER ON OUR WAY TO THE STUDIO.
Uh...
U... M...
Well.
I KNEW... I'D ARRIVE AT THE STUDIO DURING LUNCH HOUR...
Wha?
I DIDN'T KNOW THAT.
I PICKED YOU UP AT 11 SO WE COULD FIT IT IN.
...SO I... MADE A LUNCH BOX.
Uh.
OH.
REALLY?
SHE'S A THRIFTY HIGH SCHOOL GIRL...
YES, I DID.
SO WILL YOU EAT...

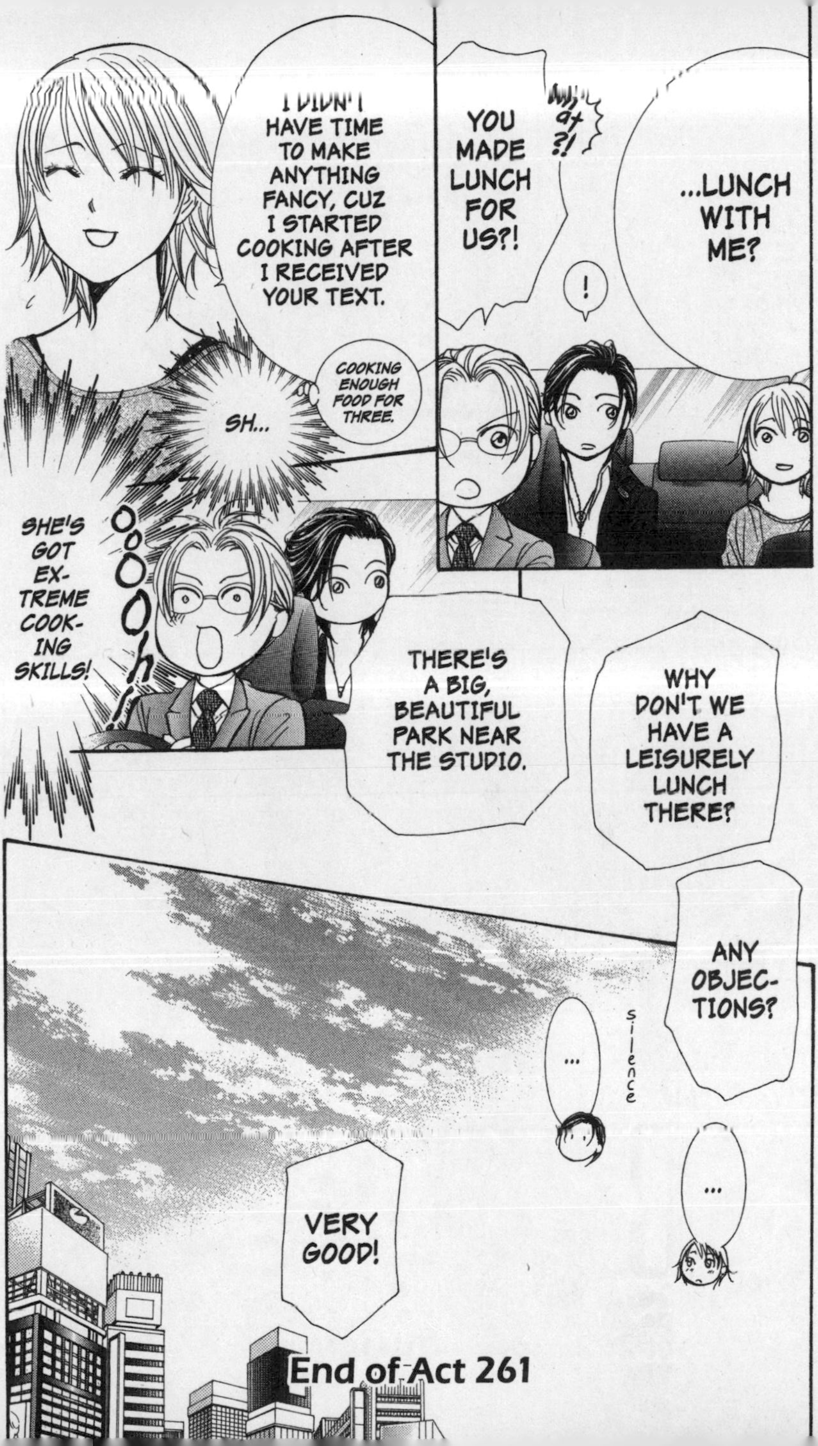
...LUNCH WITH ME?
What?!
YOU MADE LUNCH FOR US?!
!
I DIDN'T HAVE TIME TO MAKE ANYTHING FANCY, CUZ I STARTED COOKING AFTER I RECEIVED YOUR TEXT.
COOKING ENOUGH FOOD FOR THREE.
SH...
OOOOh!
SHE'S GOT EX-TREME COOK-ING SKILLS!
THERE'S A BIG, BEAUTIFUL PARK NEAR THE STUDIO.
WHY DON'T WE HAVE A LEISURELY LUNCH THERE?
ANY OBJEC-TIONS?
silence
...
...
VERY GOOD!
End of Act 261

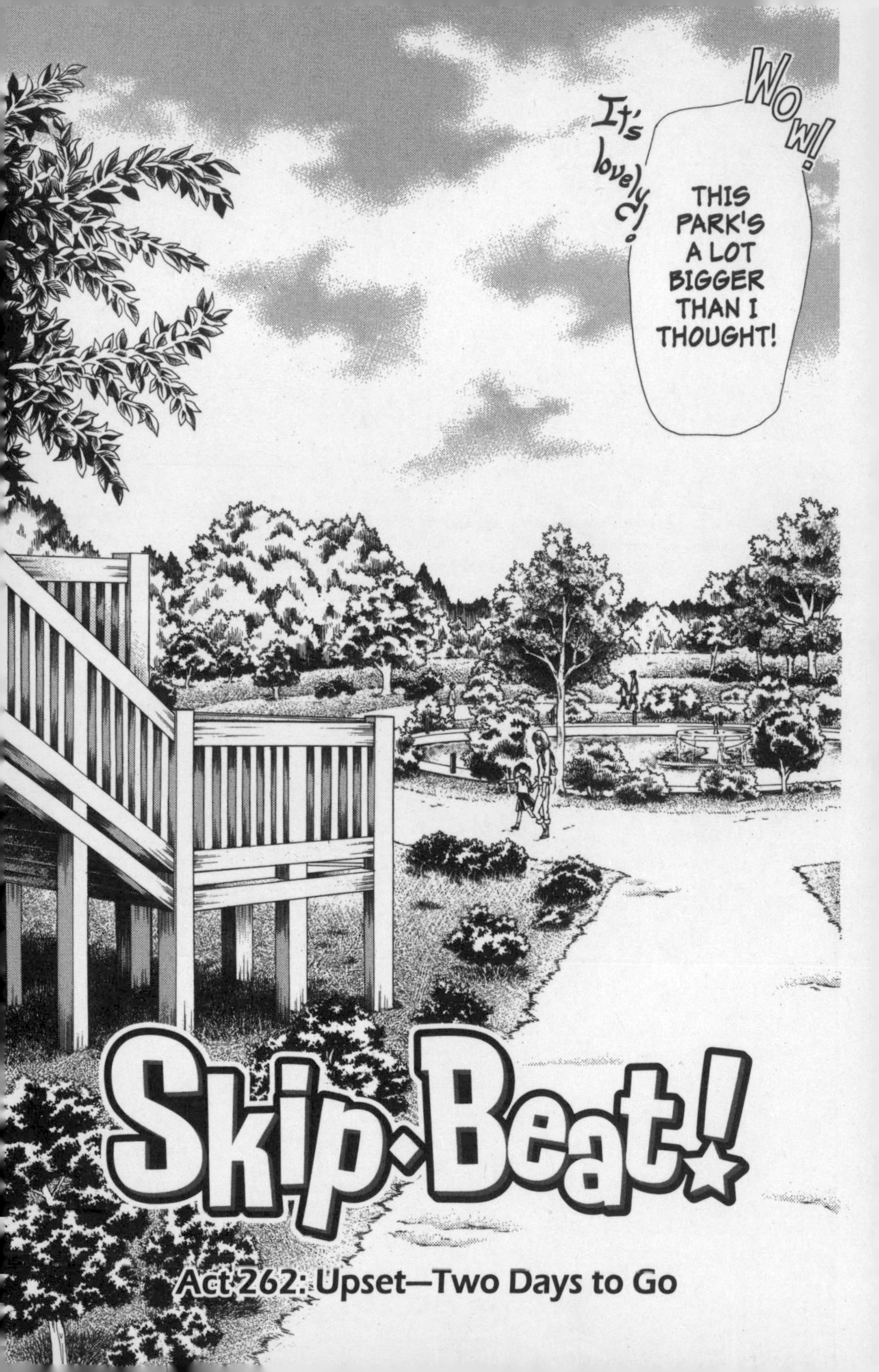
WOW!
THIS PARK'S A LOT BIGGER THAN I THOUGHT!
It's lovely♡!
Skip·Beat!
Act 262: Upset—Two Days to Go

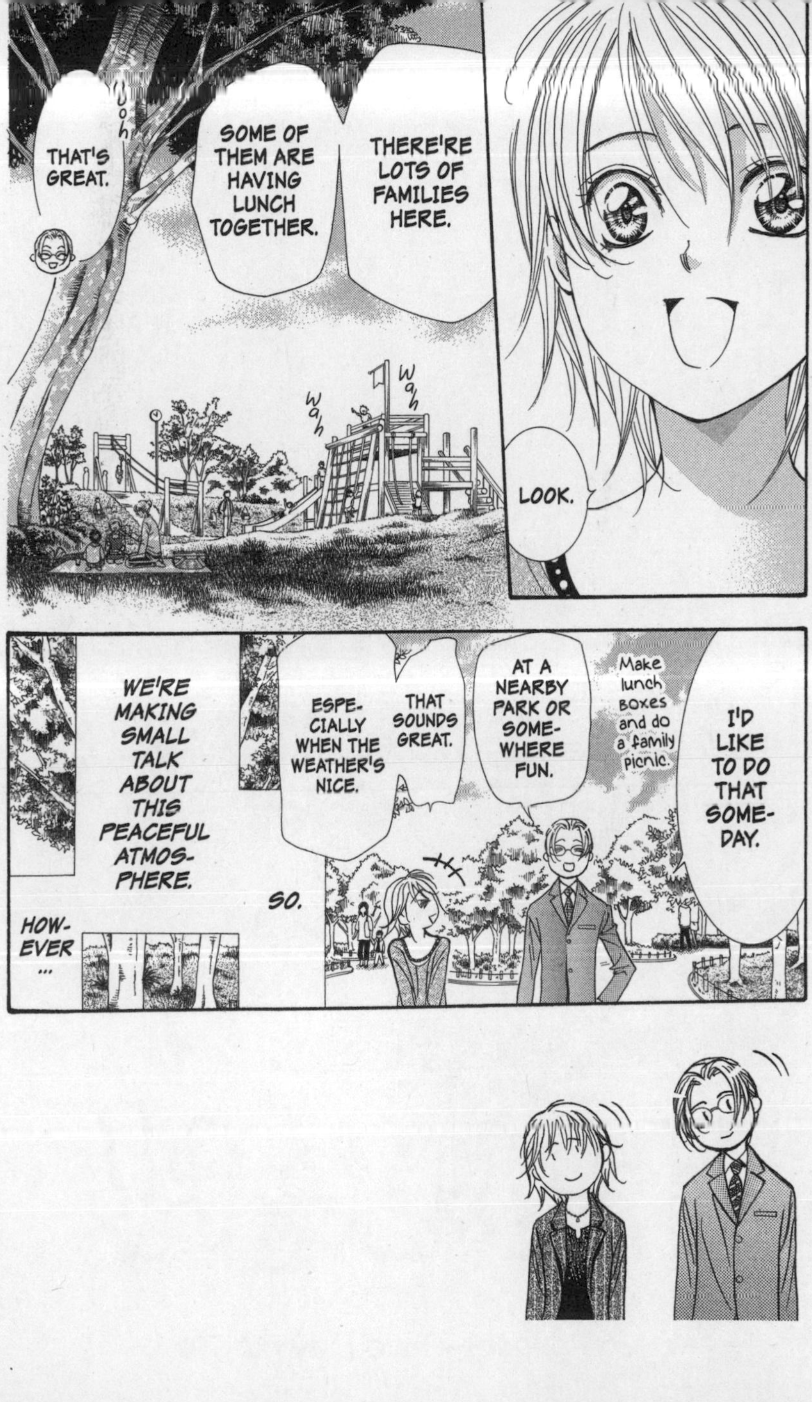
LOOK.
THERE'RE LOTS OF FAMILIES HERE.
SOME OF THEM ARE HAVING LUNCH TOGETHER.
THAT'S GREAT.
Wah
Wah
I'D LIKE TO DO THAT SOME-DAY.
Make lunch boxes and do a family picnic.
AT A NEARBY PARK OR SOME-WHERE FUN.
THAT SOUNDS GREAT.
ESPE-CIALLY WHEN THE WEATHER'S NICE.
SO.
WE'RE MAKING SMALL TALK ABOUT THIS PEACEFUL ATMOS-PHERE.
HOW-EVER ...

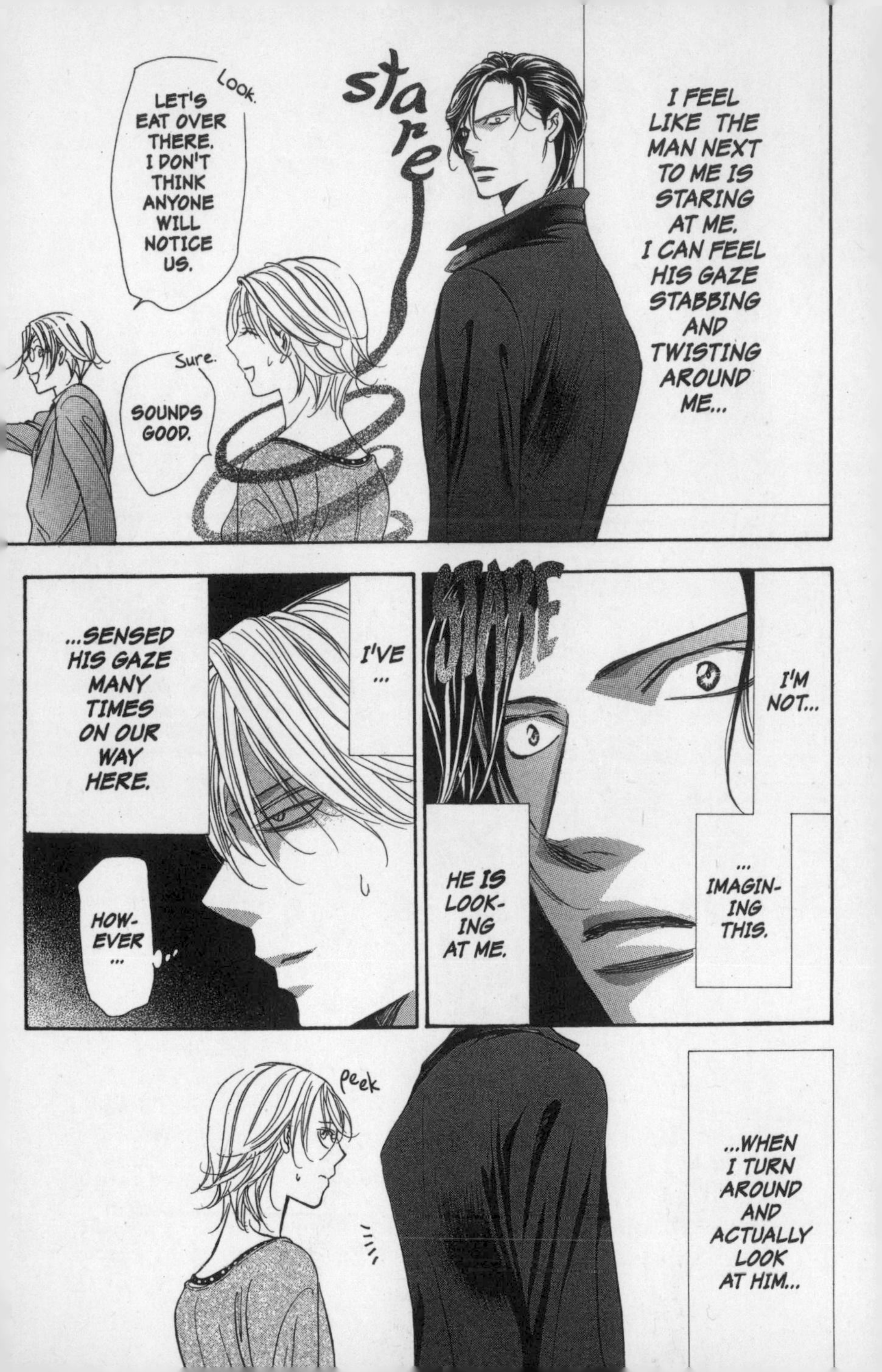
I FEEL LIKE THE MAN NEXT TO ME IS STARING AT ME. I CAN FEEL HIS GAZE STABBING AND TWISTING AROUND ME...
stare
Look.
LET'S EAT OVER THERE. I DON'T THINK ANYONE WILL NOTICE US.
Sure.
SOUNDS GOOD.
STARE
I'M NOT...
...IMAGINING THIS.
HE IS LOOK-ING AT ME.
I'VE...
...SENSED HIS GAZE MANY TIMES ON OUR WAY HERE.
HOW-EVER...
...WHEN I TURN AROUND AND ACTUALLY LOOK AT HIM...
peek

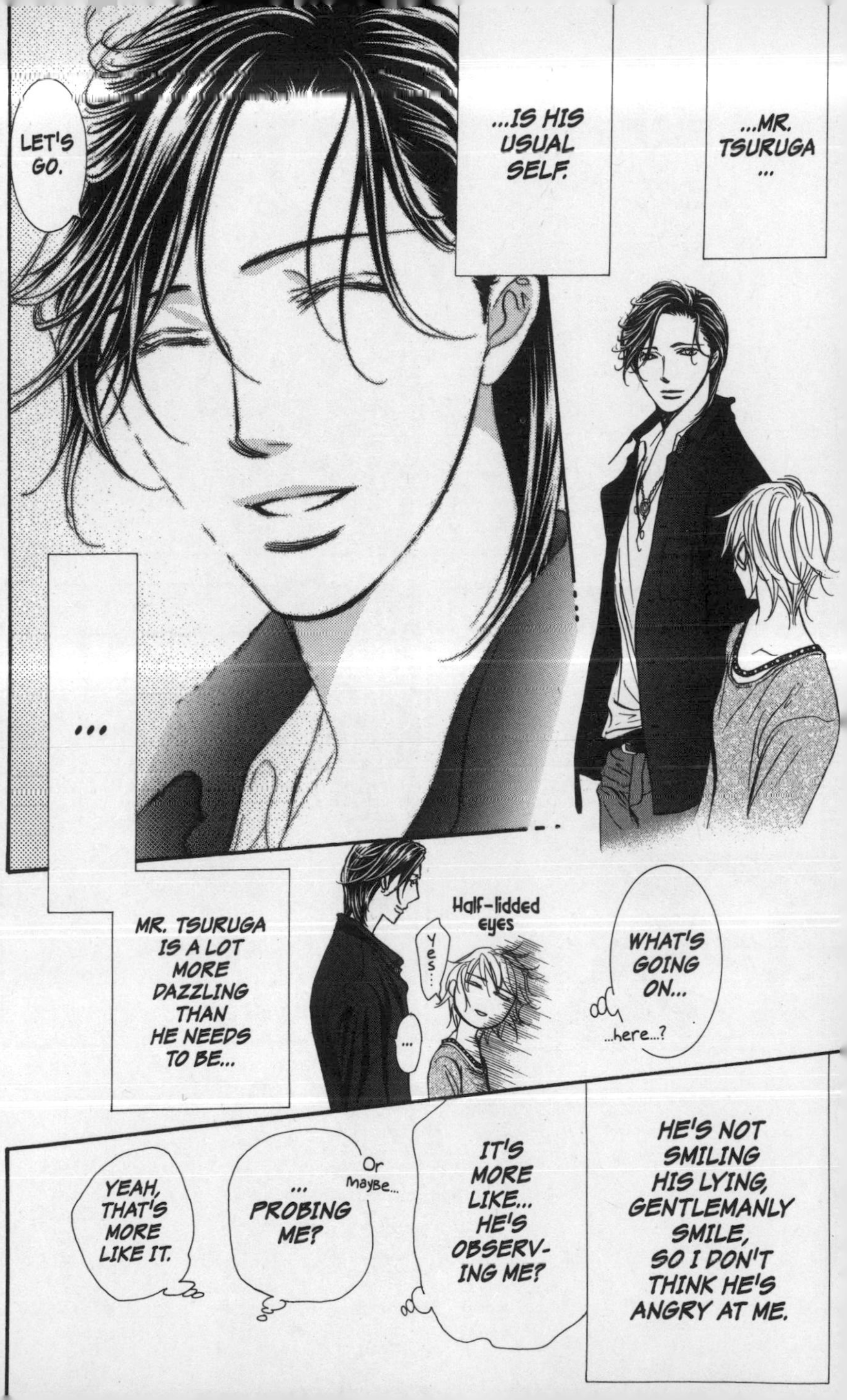
...MR. TSURUGA ...
...IS HIS USUAL SELF.
LET'S GO.
...
WHAT'S GOING ON...
...here...?
Half-lidded eyes
Yes...
...
MR. TSURUGA IS A LOT MORE DAZZLING THAN HE NEEDS TO BE...
HE'S NOT SMILING HIS LYING, GENTLEMANLY SMILE, SO I DON'T THINK HE'S ANGRY AT ME.
IT'S MORE LIKE... HE'S OBSERV-ING ME?
Or maybe...
...PROBING ME?
YEAH, THAT'S MORE LIKE IT.

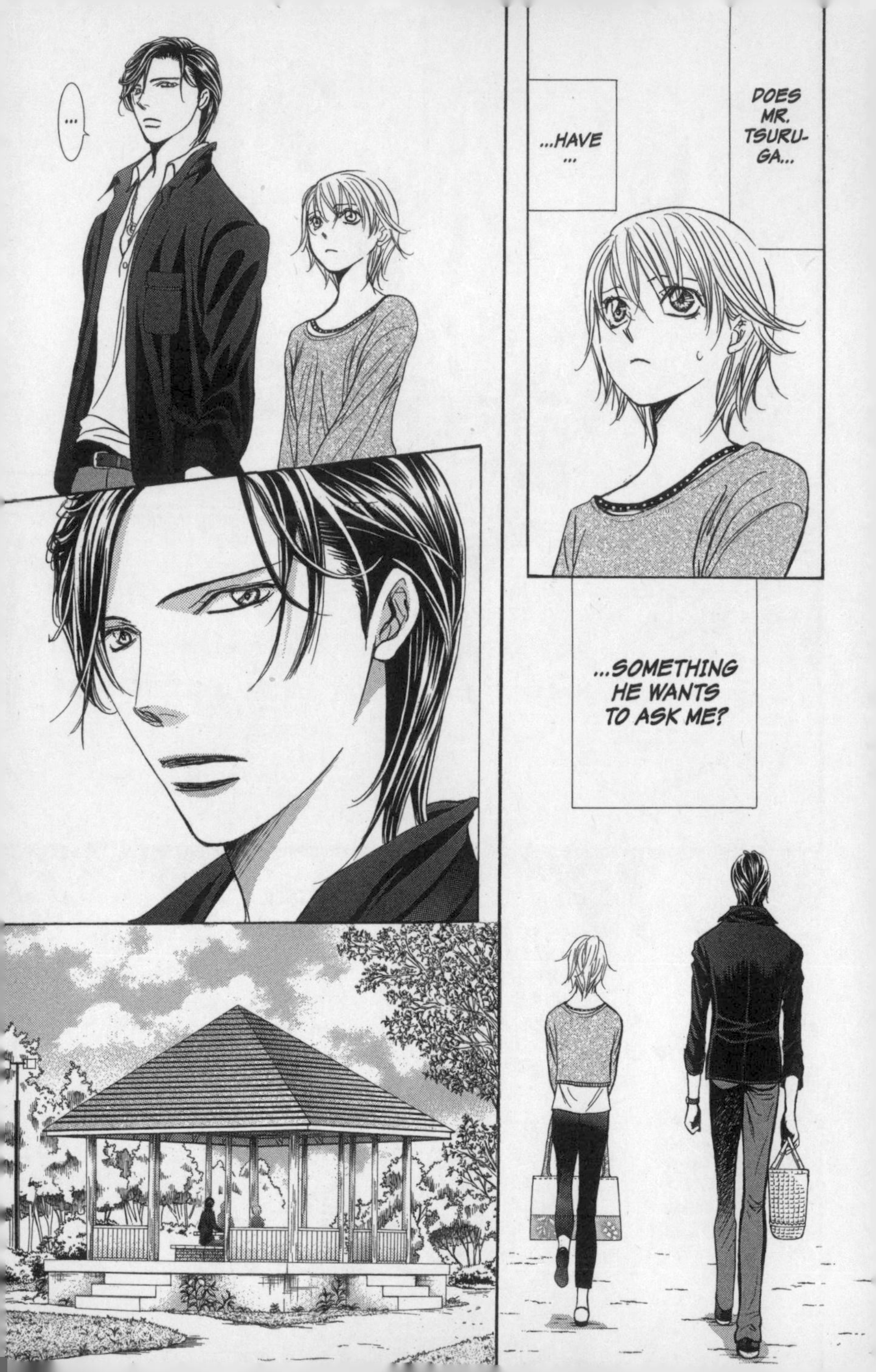
DOES MR. TSURUGA...
...HAVE ...
...SOMETHING HE WANTS TO ASK ME?
...

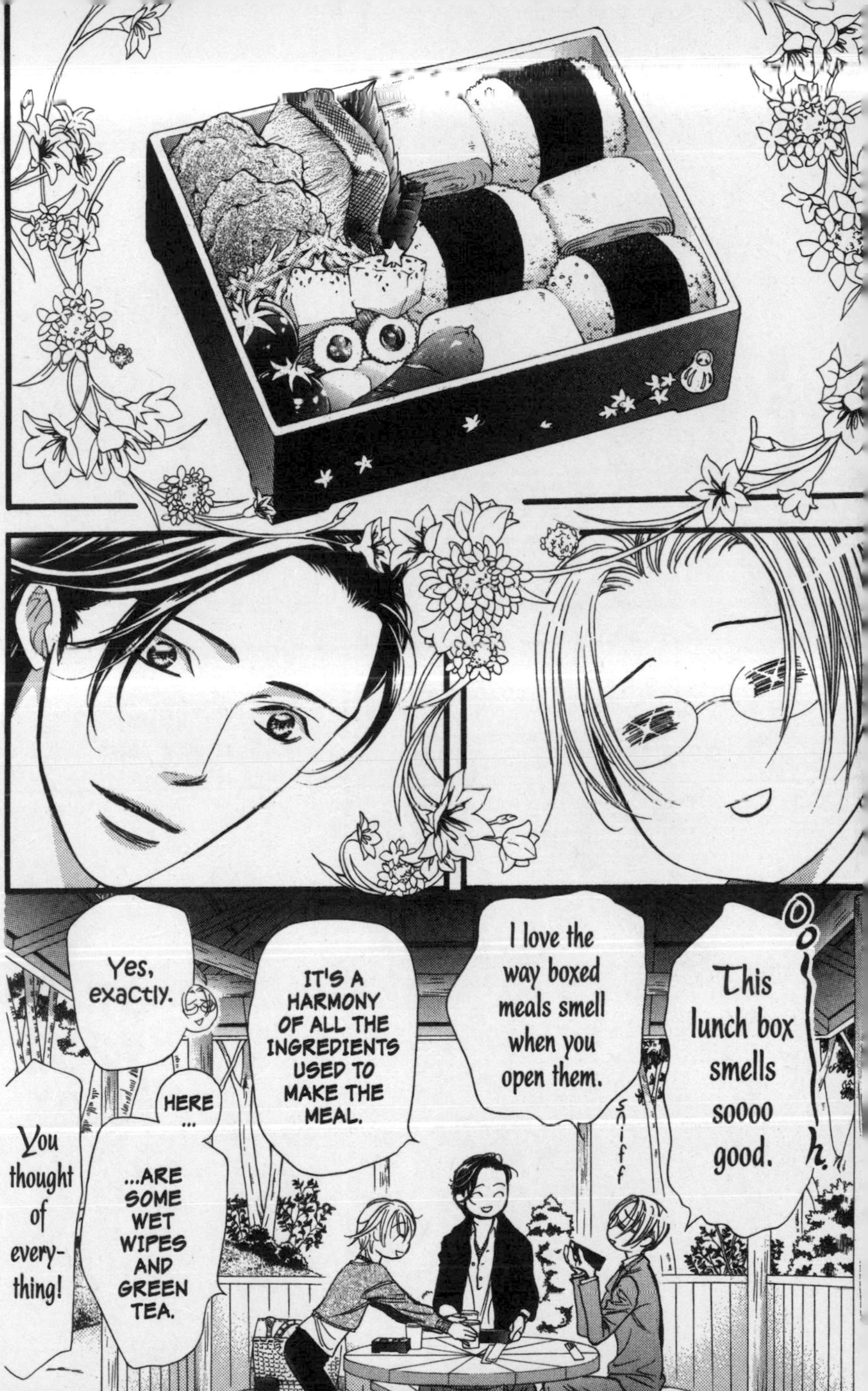
Oo—h.
This lunch box smells soooo good.
sniff
I love the way boxed meals smell when you open them.
IT'S A HARMONY OF ALL THE INGREDIENTS USED TO MAKE THE MEAL.
Yes, exactly.
HERE...
...ARE SOME WET WIPES AND GREEN TEA.
You thought of everything!

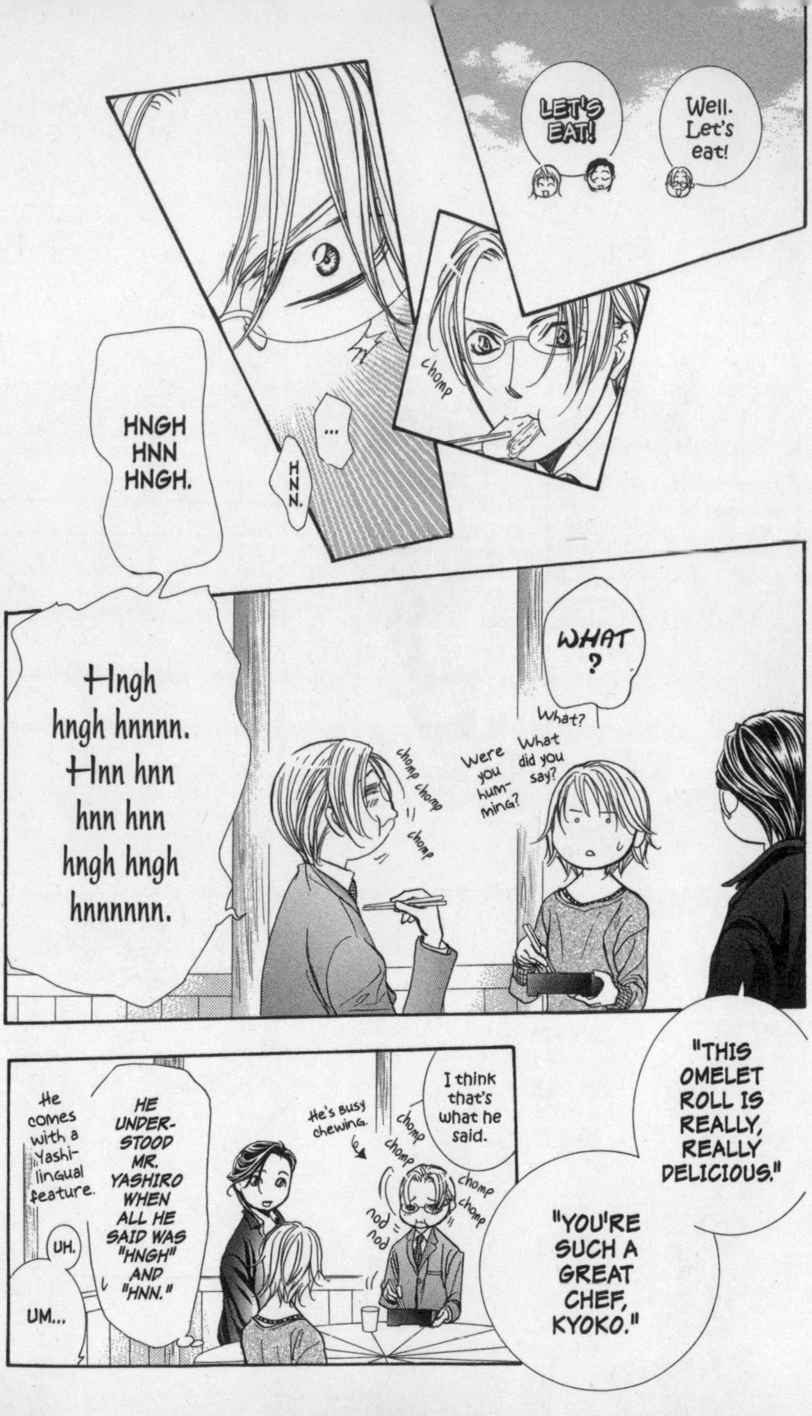
Well. Let's eat!
LET'S EAT!
chomp
...
HNN.
HNGH HNN HNGH.
WHAT?
What?
What did you say?
Were you humming?
chomp chomp
chomp
Hngh hngh hnnnn. Hnn hnn hnn hnn hngh hngh hnnnnnn.
"THIS OMELET ROLL IS REALLY, REALLY DELICIOUS."
"YOU'RE SUCH A GREAT CHEF, KYOKO."
I think that's what he said.
chomp chomp
chomp chomp
He's busy chewing.
nod nod
HE UNDERSTOOD MR. YASHIRO WHEN ALL HE SAID WAS "HNGH" AND "HNN."
He comes with a Yashi-lingual feature.
UH.
UM...

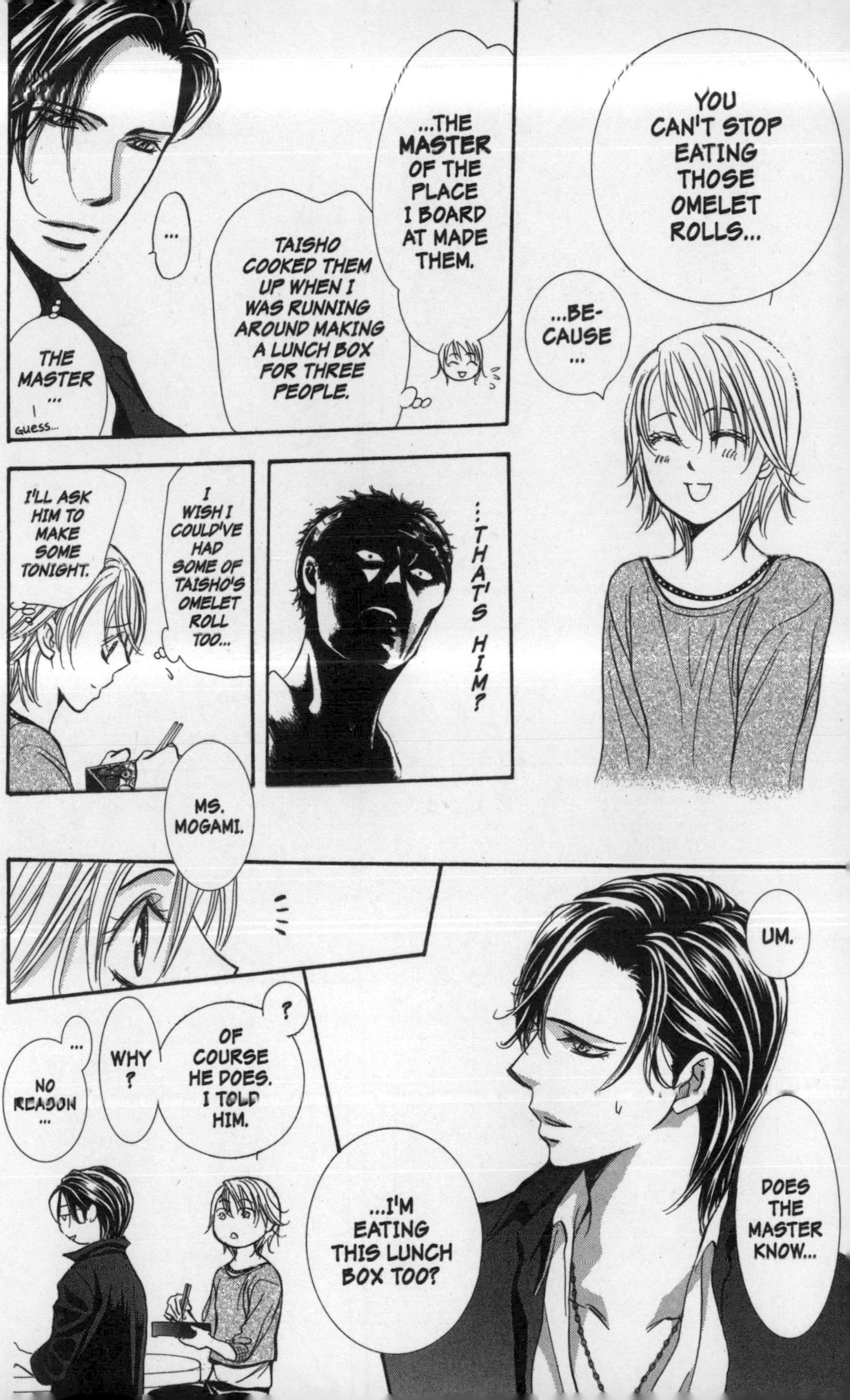
YOU CAN'T STOP EATING THOSE OMELET ROLLS...
...BE-CAUSE...
...THE MASTER OF THE PLACE I BOARD AT MADE THEM.
TAISHO COOKED THEM UP WHEN I WAS RUNNING AROUND MAKING A LUNCH BOX FOR THREE PEOPLE.
...
THE MASTER...
I GUESS...
...THAT'S HIM?
I WISH I COULD'VE HAD SOME OF TAISHO'S OMELET ROLL TOO...
I'LL ASK HIM TO MAKE SOME TONIGHT.
MS. MOGAMI.
UM.
DOES THE MASTER KNOW...
...I'M EATING THIS LUNCH BOX TOO?
?
OF COURSE HE DOES. I TOLD HIM.
WHY?
...
NO REASON...

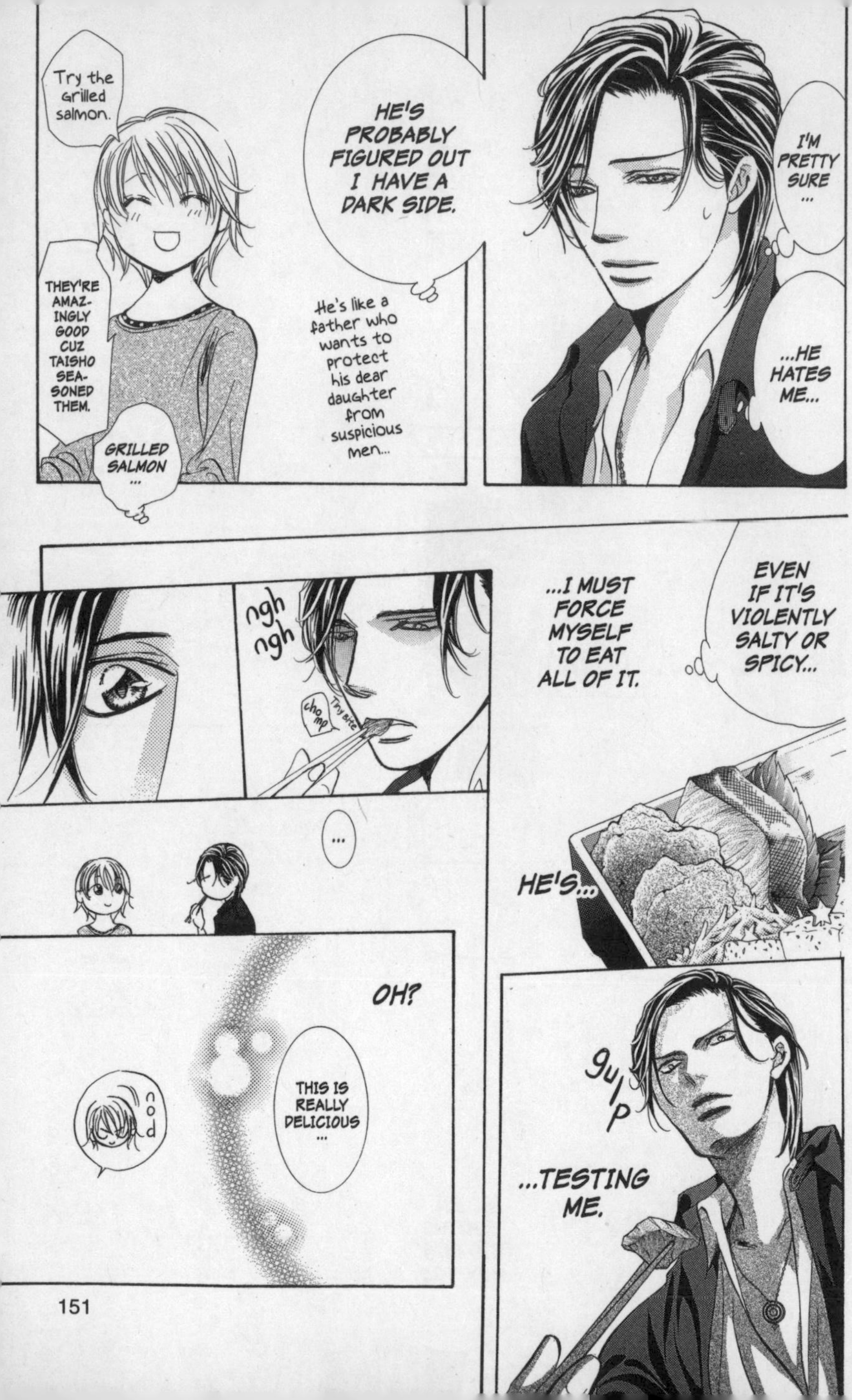
I'M PRETTY SURE ...
...HE HATES ME...
HE'S PROBABLY FIGURED OUT I HAVE A DARK SIDE.
He's like a father who wants to protect his dear daughter from suspicious men...
Try the grilled salmon.
THEY'RE AMAZINGLY GOOD CUZ TAISHO SEASONED THEM.
GRILLED SALMON ...
EVEN IF IT'S VIOLENTLY SALTY OR SPICY...
...I MUST FORCE MYSELF TO EAT ALL OF IT.
ngh ngh
Tiny bite
chomp
...
HE'S...
gulp
...TESTING ME.
OH?
THIS IS REALLY DELICIOUS ...
nod

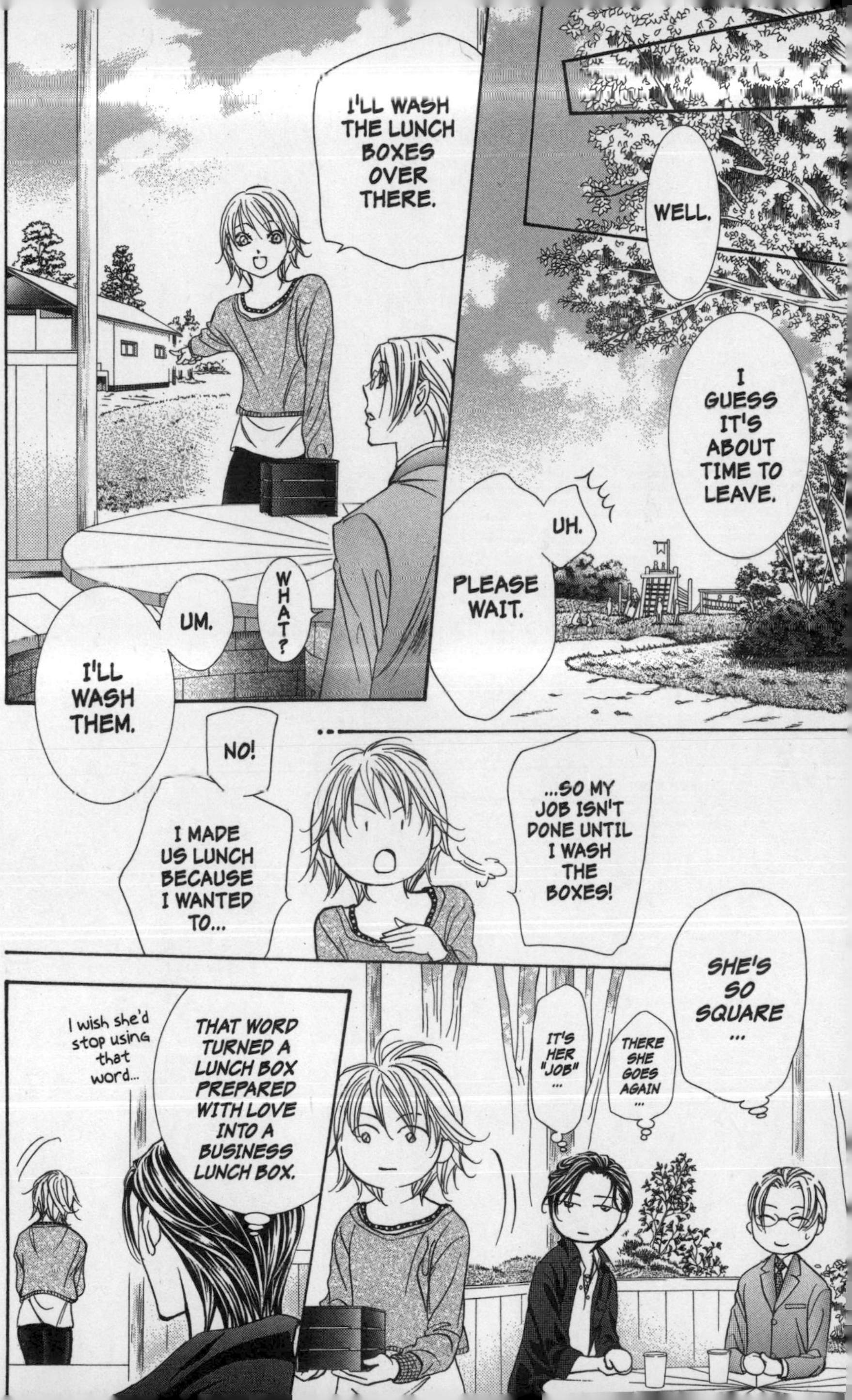
WELL.
I GUESS IT'S ABOUT TIME TO LEAVE.
UH.
PLEASE WAIT.
I'LL WASH THE LUNCH BOXES OVER THERE.
WHAT?
UM.
I'LL WASH THEM.
NO!
I MADE US LUNCH BECAUSE I WANTED TO...
...SO MY JOB ISN'T DONE UNTIL I WASH THE BOXES!
SHE'S SO SQUARE...
THERE SHE GOES AGAIN...
IT'S HER "JOB"...
THAT WORD TURNED A LUNCH BOX PREPARED WITH LOVE INTO A BUSINESS LUNCH BOX.
I wish she'd stop using that word...

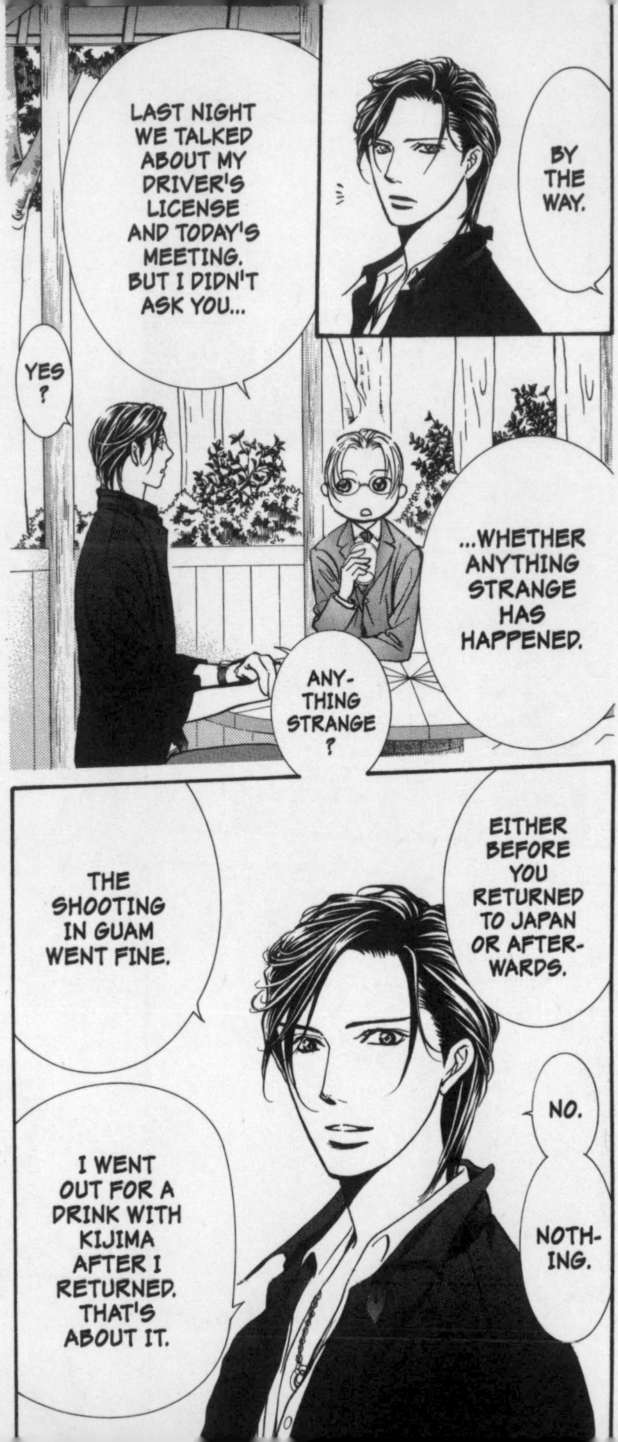
BY THE WAY.
LAST NIGHT WE TALKED ABOUT MY DRIVER'S LICENSE AND TODAY'S MEETING. BUT I DIDN'T ASK YOU...
YES?
...WHETHER ANYTHING STRANGE HAS HAPPENED.
ANY-THING STRANGE?
EITHER BEFORE YOU RETURNED TO JAPAN OR AFTER-WARDS.
NO.
NOTH-ING.
THE SHOOTING IN GUAM WENT FINE.
I WENT OUT FOR A DRINK WITH KIJIMA AFTER I RETURNED. THAT'S ABOUT IT.

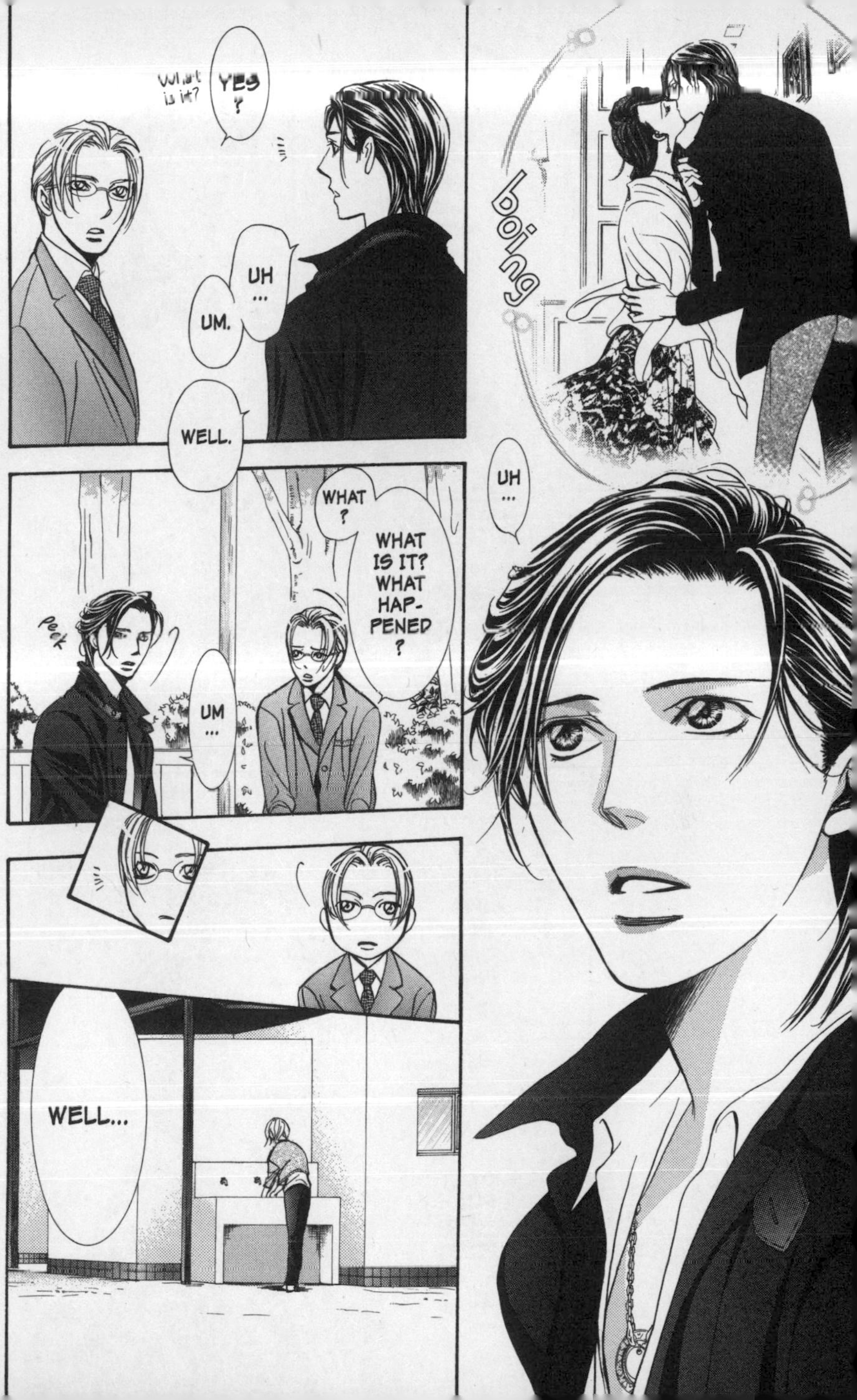
boing
UH ...
YES ?
What is it?
UH ...
UM.
WELL.
WHAT ?
WHAT IS IT? WHAT HAP-PENED ?
peck
UM ...
WELL...

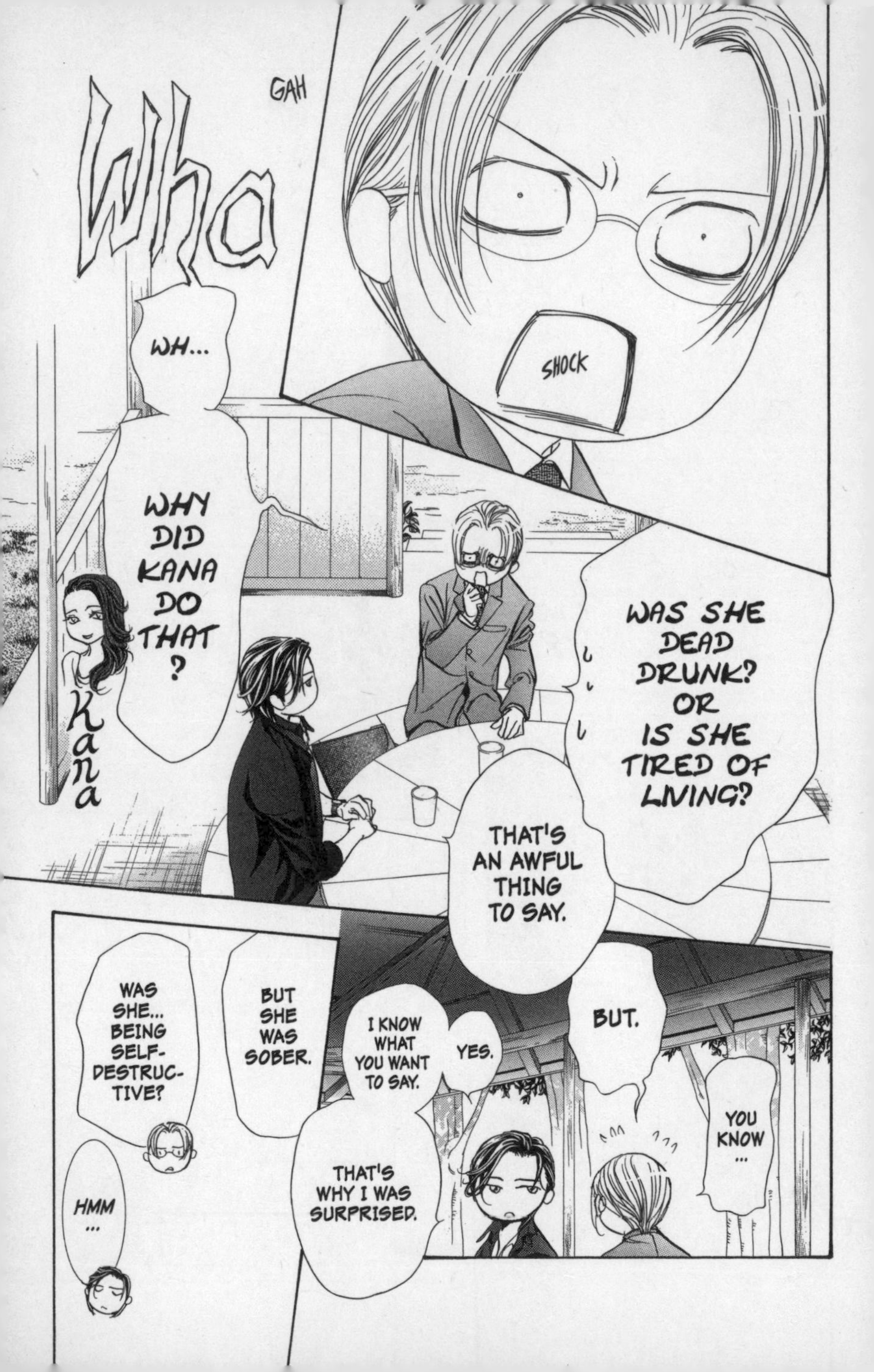
SHOCK
GAH
Wha
WH...
WHY DID KANA DO THAT?
Kana
WAS SHE DEAD DRUNK? OR IS SHE TIRED OF LIVING?
THAT'S AN AWFUL THING TO SAY.
YOU KNOW ...
BUT.
YES.
I KNOW WHAT YOU WANT TO SAY.
THAT'S WHY I WAS SURPRISED.
BUT SHE WAS SOBER.
WAS SHE... BEING SELF-DESTRUCTIVE?
HMM ...

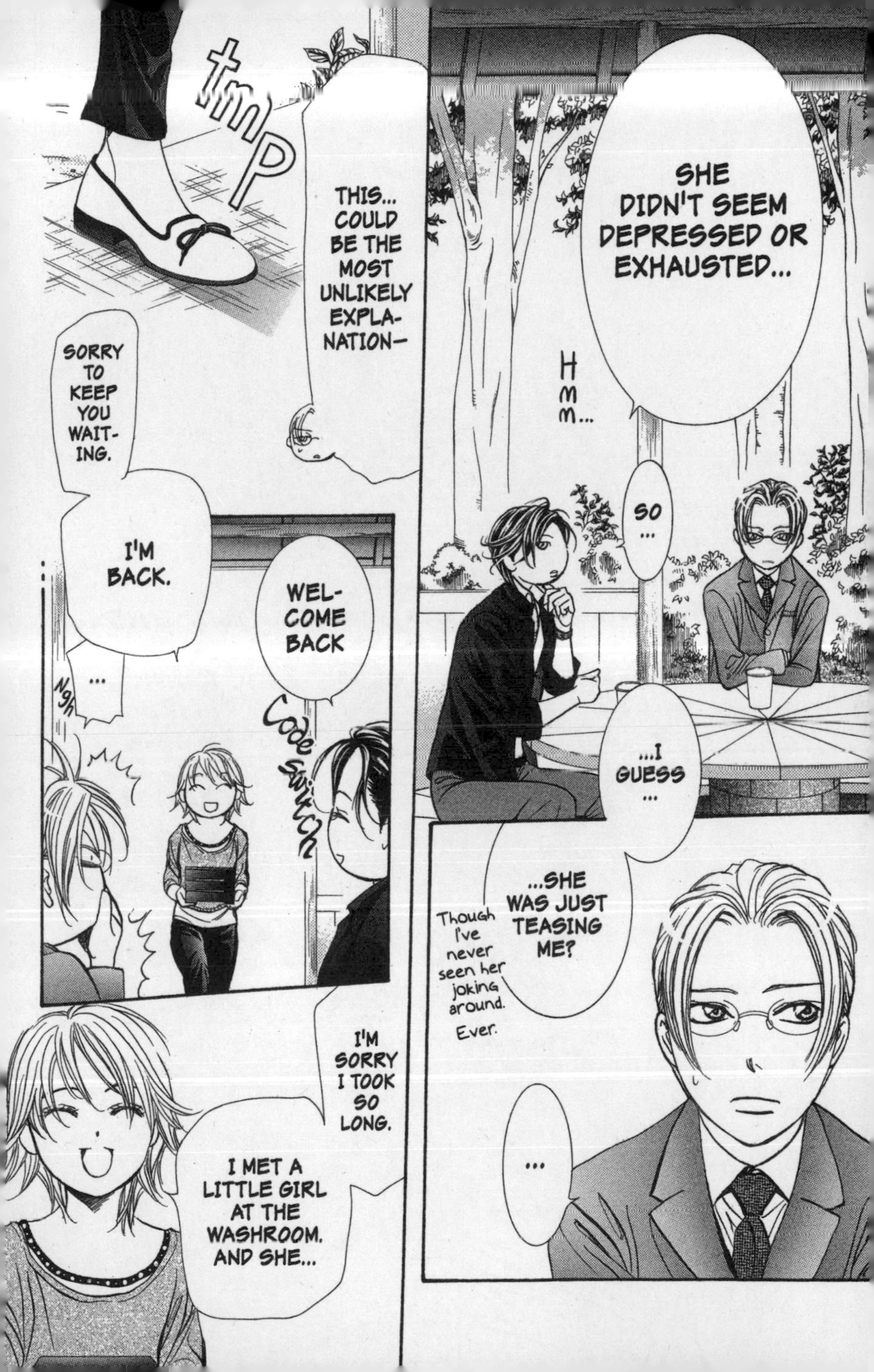
SHE DIDN'T SEEM DEPRESSED OR EXHAUSTED...
HMM...
SO...
...I GUESS...
...SHE WAS JUST TEASING ME?
Though I've never seen her joking around. Ever.
...
tmp
THIS... COULD BE THE MOST UNLIKELY EXPLA-NATION—
SORRY TO KEEP YOU WAIT-ING.
I'M BACK.
WEL-COME BACK
...
Ngh
Code switch
I'M SORRY I TOOK SO LONG.
I MET A LITTLE GIRL AT THE WASHROOM. AND SHE...

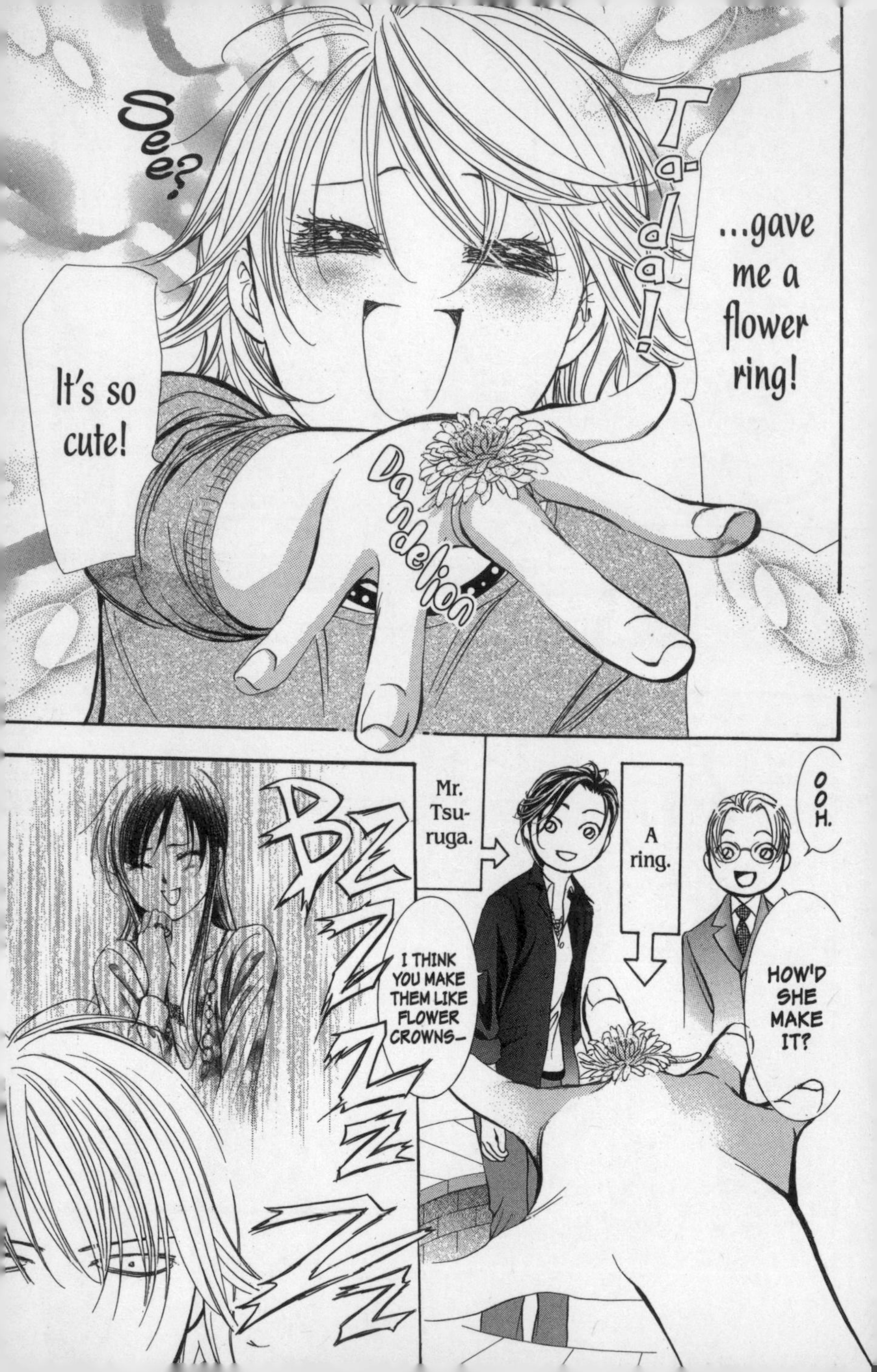

...gave me a flower ring!
Ta-da!
See?
Dandelion
It's so cute!
OOH.
HOW'D SHE MAKE IT?
A ring.
Mr. Tsuruga.
I THINK YOU MAKE THEM LIKE FLOWER CROWNS—

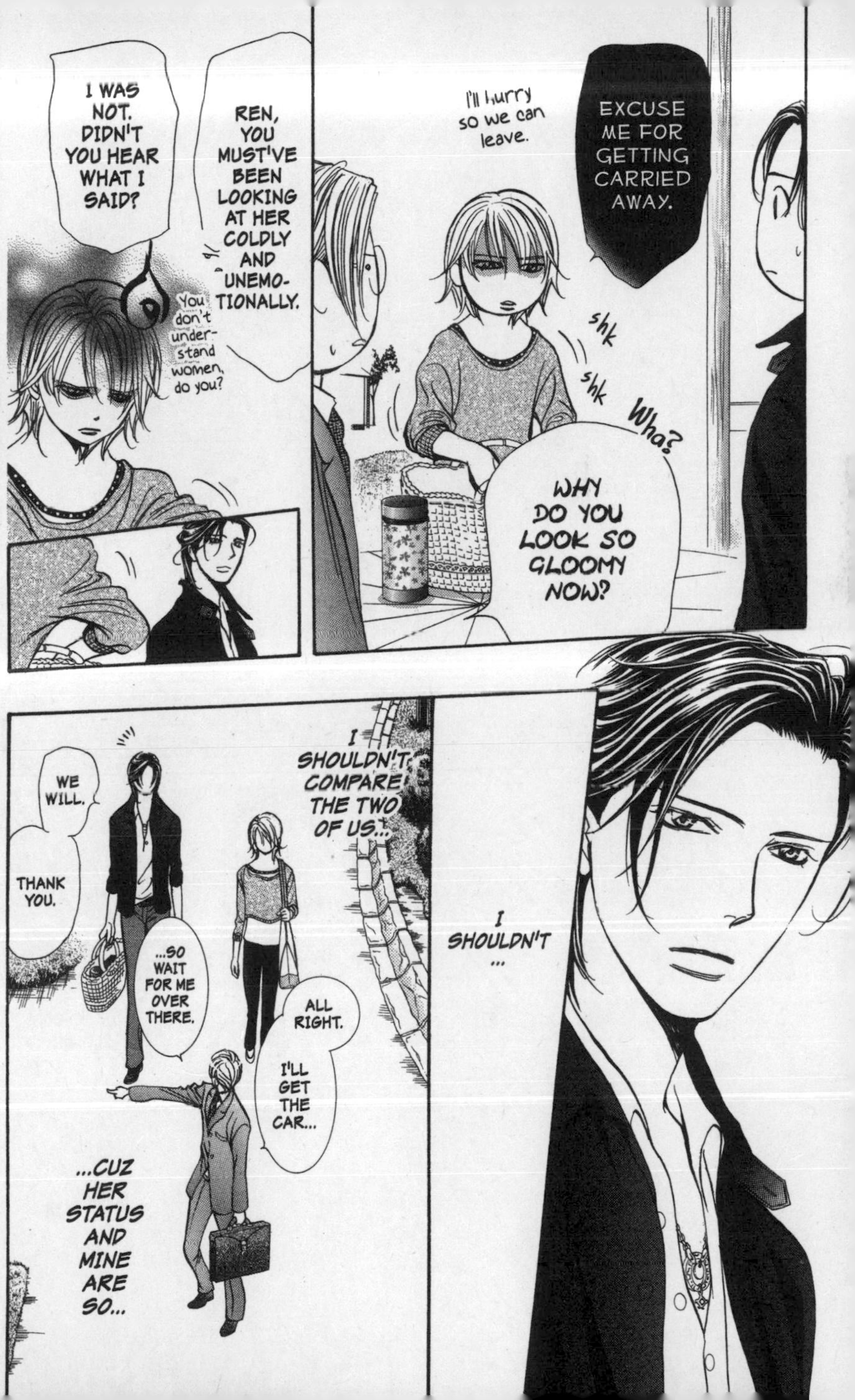
EXCUSE ME FOR GETTING CARRIED AWAY.
I'll hurry so we can leave.
shk
shk
Wha?
WHY DO YOU LOOK SO GLOOMY NOW?
REN, YOU MUST'VE BEEN LOOKING AT HER COLDLY AND UNEMOTIONALLY.
I WAS NOT. DIDN'T YOU HEAR WHAT I SAID?
You don't understand women, do you?
I SHOULDN'T...
I SHOULDN'T COMPARE THE TWO OF US...
ALL RIGHT. I'LL GET THE CAR...
...SO WAIT FOR ME OVER THERE.
WE WILL.
THANK YOU.
...CUZ HER STATUS AND MINE ARE SO...

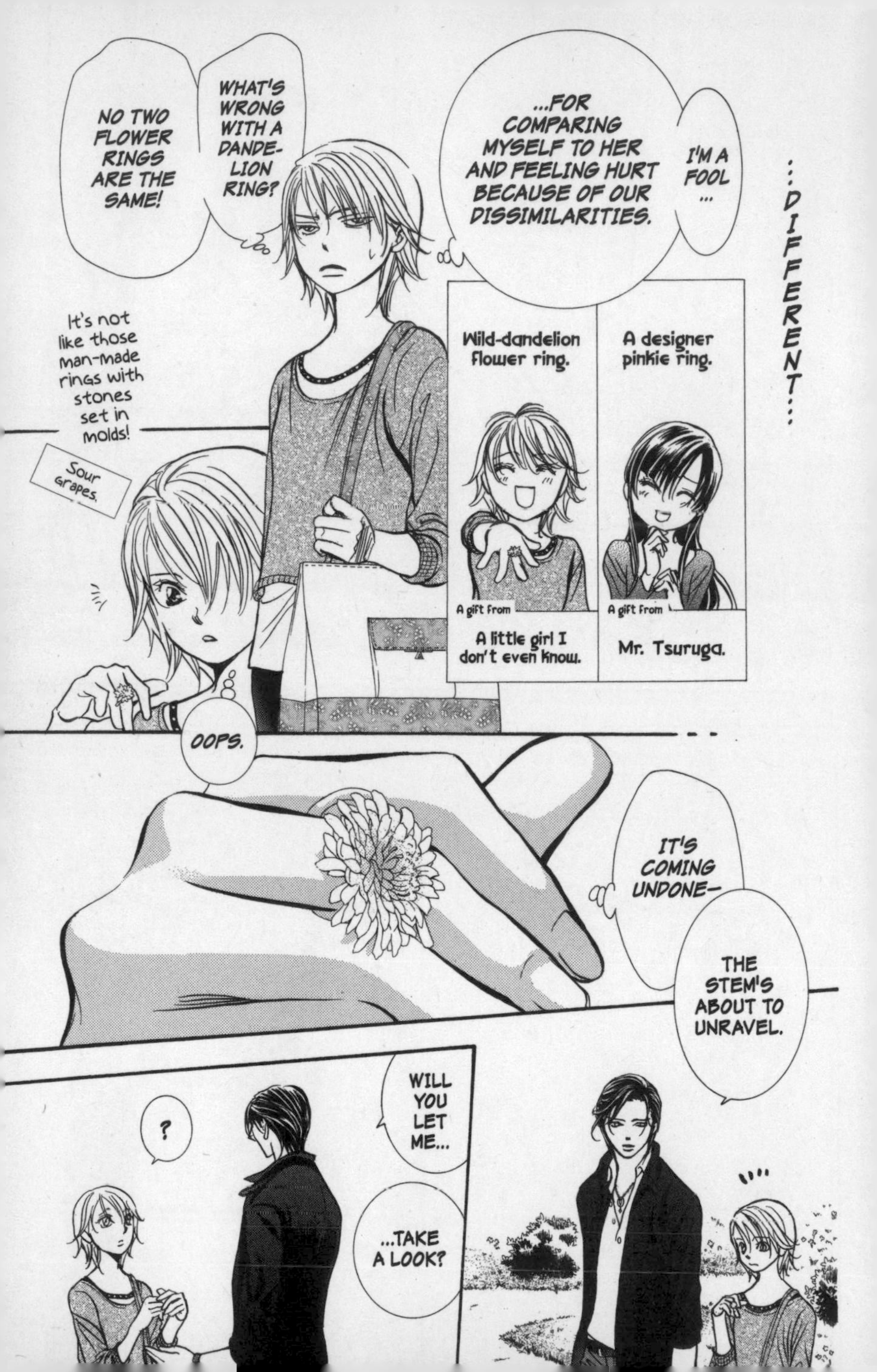

...DIFFERENT...
I'M A FOOL...
...FOR COMPARING MYSELF TO HER AND FEELING HURT BECAUSE OF OUR DISSIMILARITIES.
WHAT'S WRONG WITH A DANDELION RING?
NO TWO FLOWER RINGS ARE THE SAME!
A designer pinkie ring.
A gift from
Mr. Tsuruga.
Wild-dandelion flower ring.
A gift from
A little girl I don't even know.
It's not like those man-made rings with stones set in molds!
Sour Grapes.
OOPS.
IT'S COMING UNDONE—
THE STEM'S ABOUT TO UNRAVEL.
WILL YOU LET ME...
...TAKE A LOOK?
?

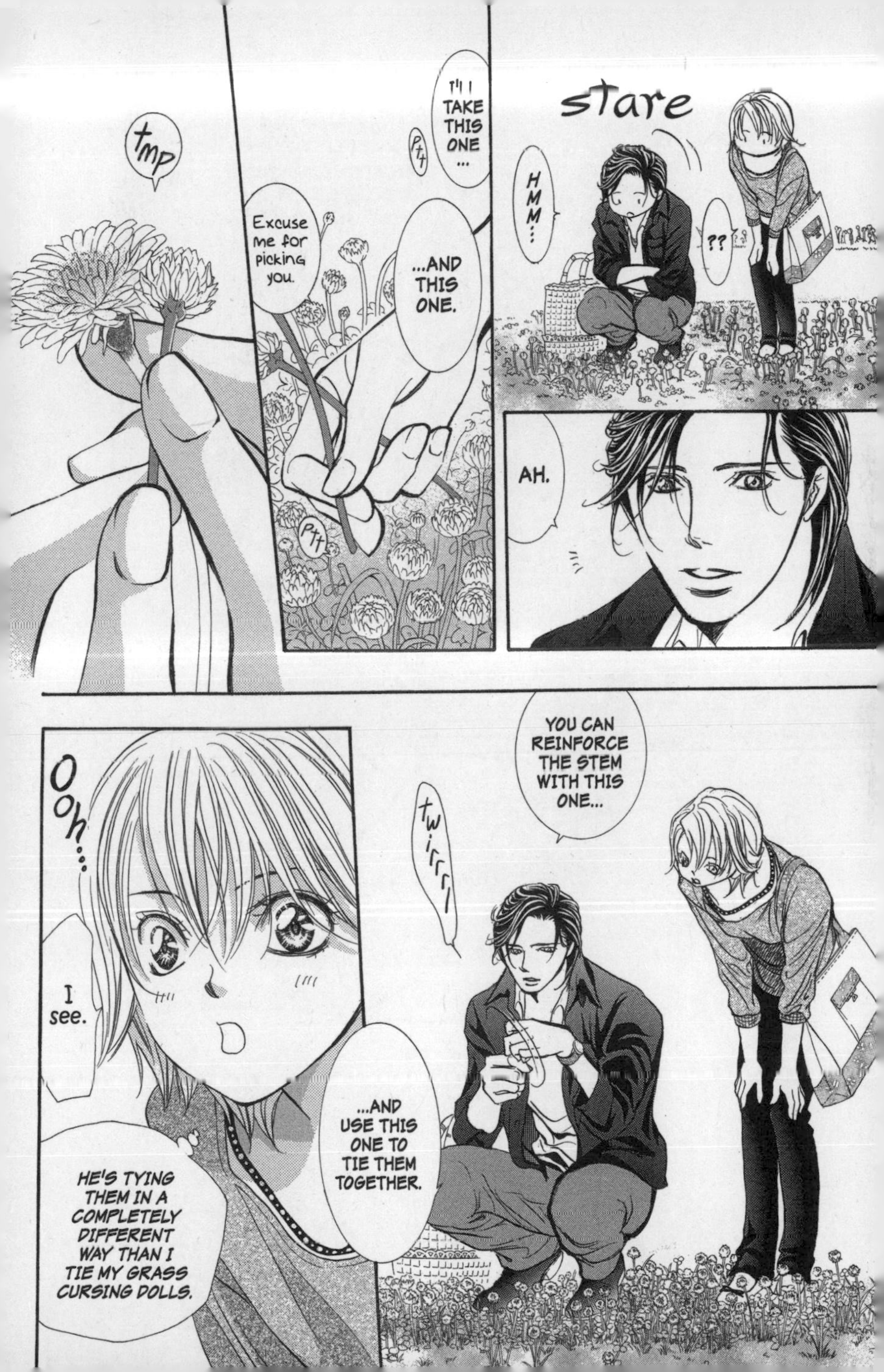
stare
HMM...
??
AH.
I'll TAKE THIS ONE...
Ptt
Excuse me for picking you.
...AND THIS ONE.
Ptt
tmp
YOU CAN REINFORCE THE STEM WITH THIS ONE...
twirrrl
...AND USE THIS ONE TO TIE THEM TOGETHER.
Oooh...
I see.
HE'S TYING THEM IN A COMPLETELY DIFFERENT WAY THAN I TIE MY GRASS CURSING DOLLS.

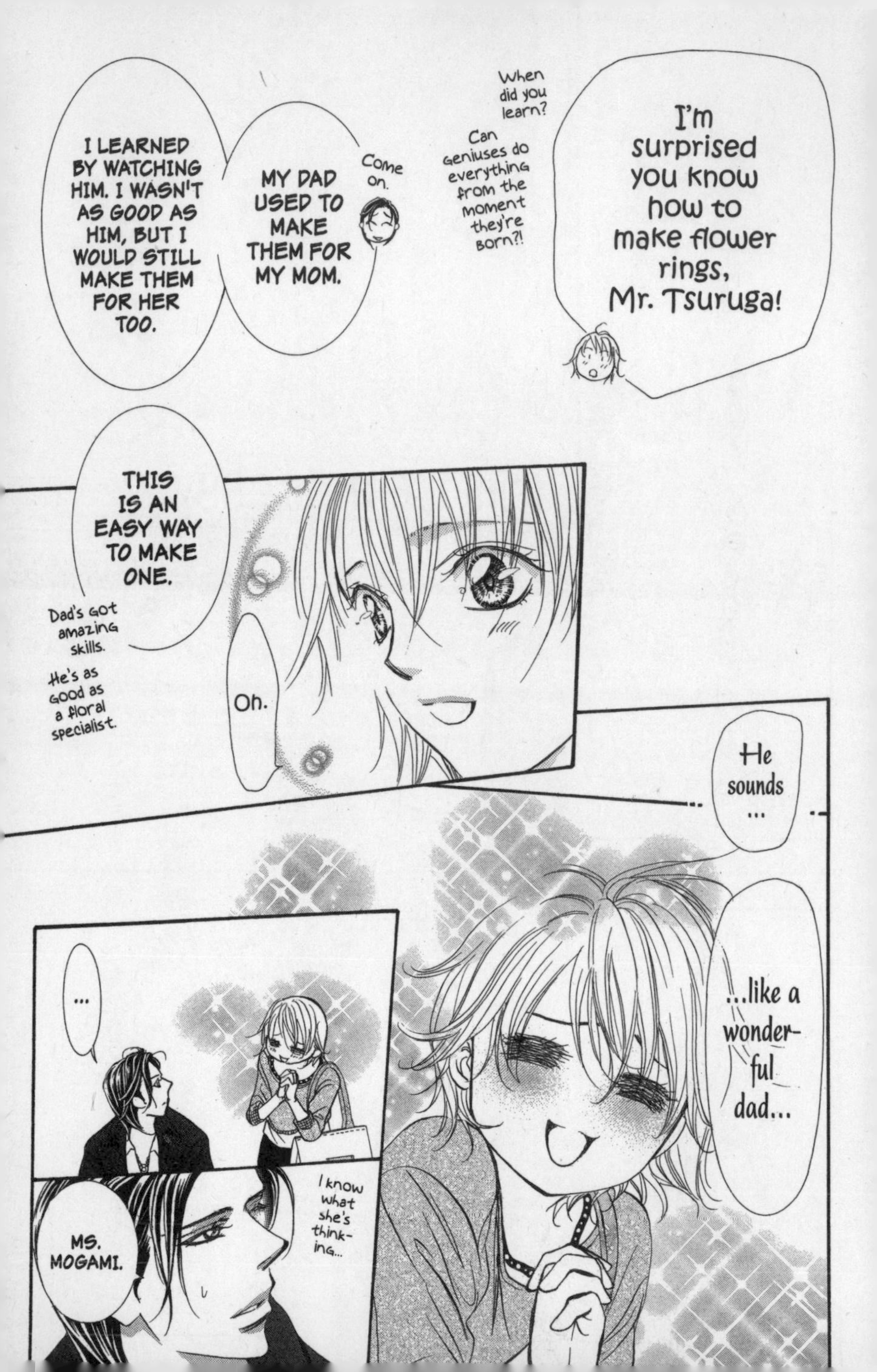

I'm surprised you know how to make flower rings, Mr. Tsuruga!
When did you learn?
Can geniuses do everything from the moment they're born?!
Come on.
MY DAD USED TO MAKE THEM FOR MY MOM.
I LEARNED BY WATCHING HIM. I WASN'T AS GOOD AS HIM, BUT I WOULD STILL MAKE THEM FOR HER TOO.
THIS IS AN EASY WAY TO MAKE ONE.
Dad's got amazing skills.
He's as good as a floral specialist.
Oh.
He sounds ...
...like a wonder-ful dad...
...
MS. MOGAMI.
I know what she's think-ing...

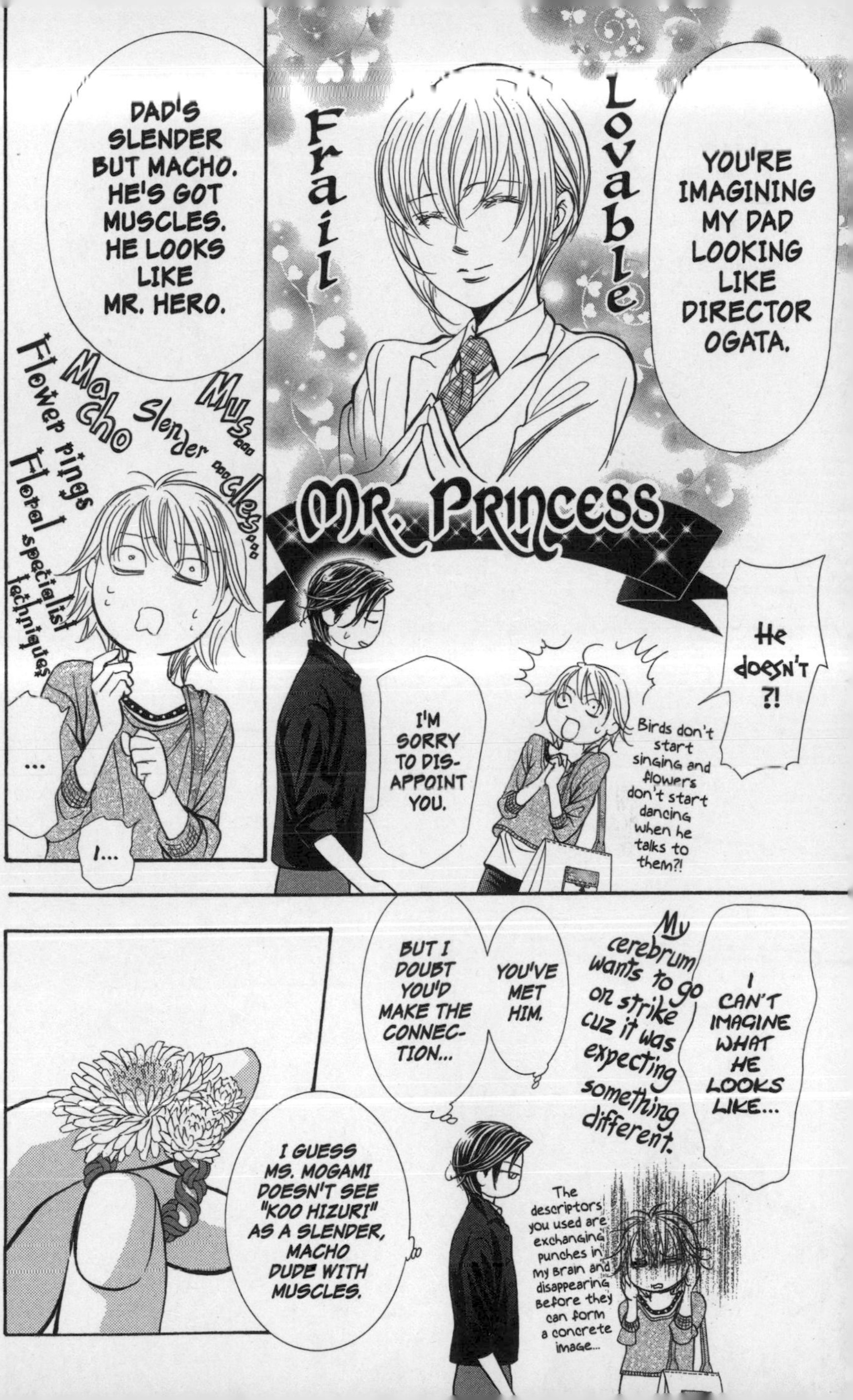

YOU'RE IMAGINING MY DAD LOOKING LIKE DIRECTOR OGATA.
Lovable
Frail
MR. PRINCESS
He doesn't ?!
Birds don't start singing and flowers don't start dancing when he talks to them?!
I'M SORRY TO DIS-APPOINT YOU.
DAD'S SLENDER BUT MACHO. HE'S GOT MUSCLES. HE LOOKS LIKE MR. HERO.
Mus... ...cles...
Slender
Macho
Flower rings
Floral specialist techniques
...
I...
I CAN'T IMAGINE WHAT HE LOOKS LIKE...
My cerebrum wants to go on strike cuz it was expecting something different.
The descriptors you used are exchanging punches in my brain and disappearing before they can form a concrete image...
YOU'VE MET HIM.
BUT I DOUBT YOU'D MAKE THE CONNEC-TION...
I GUESS MS. MOGAMI DOESN'T SEE "KOO HIZURI" AS A SLENDER, MACHO DUDE WITH MUSCLES.

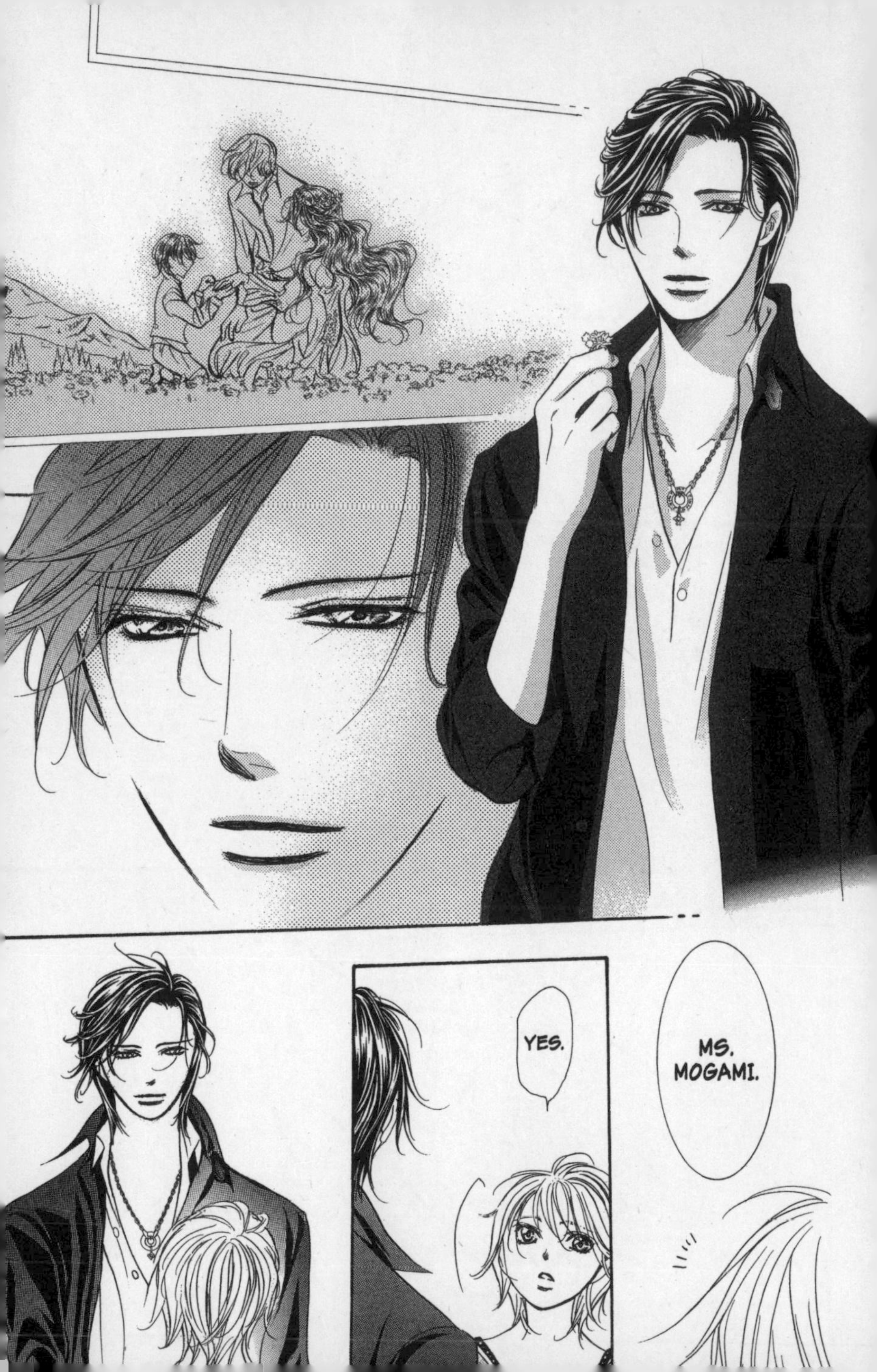
MS. MOGAMI.
YES.

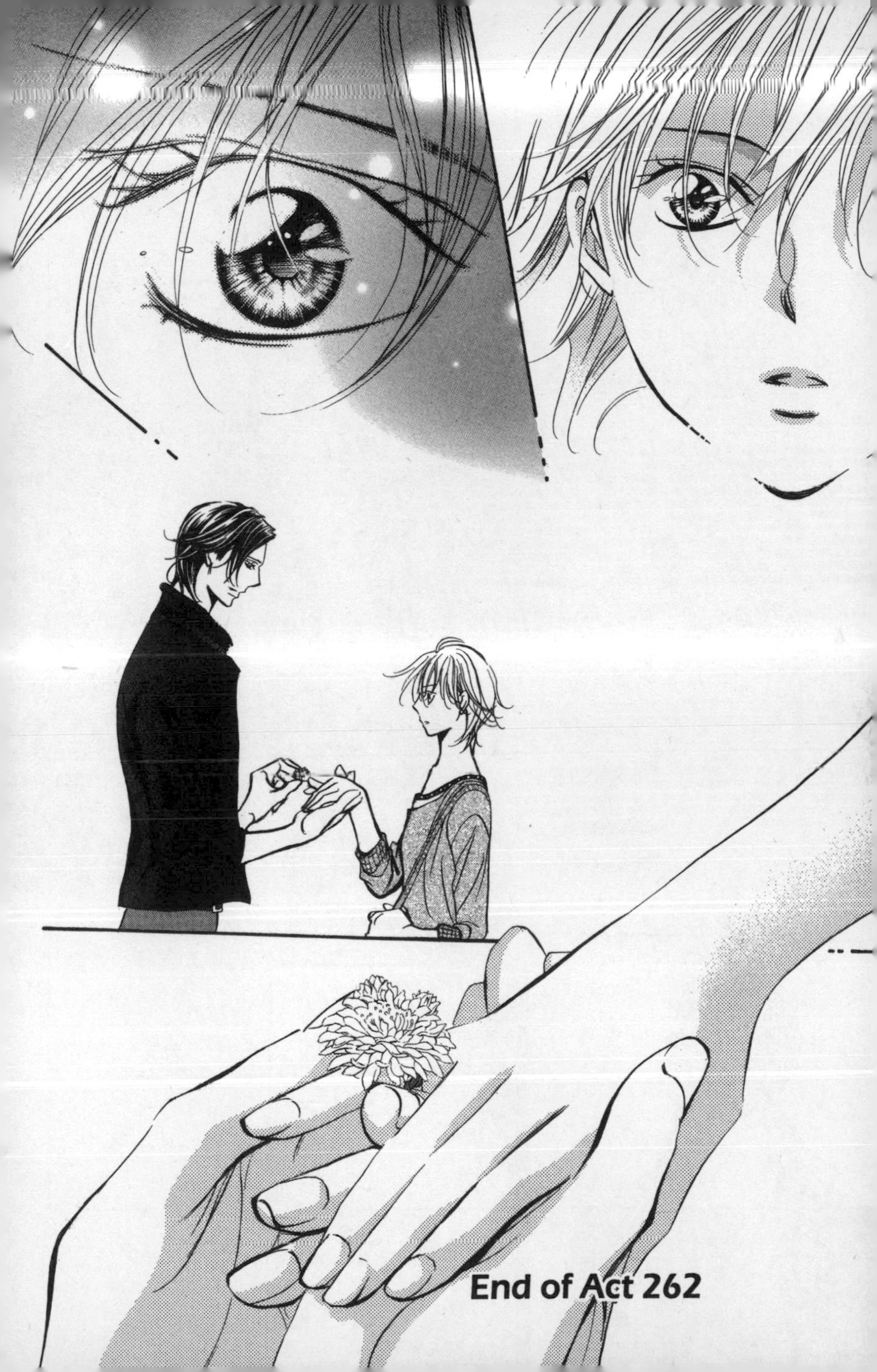
End of Act 262

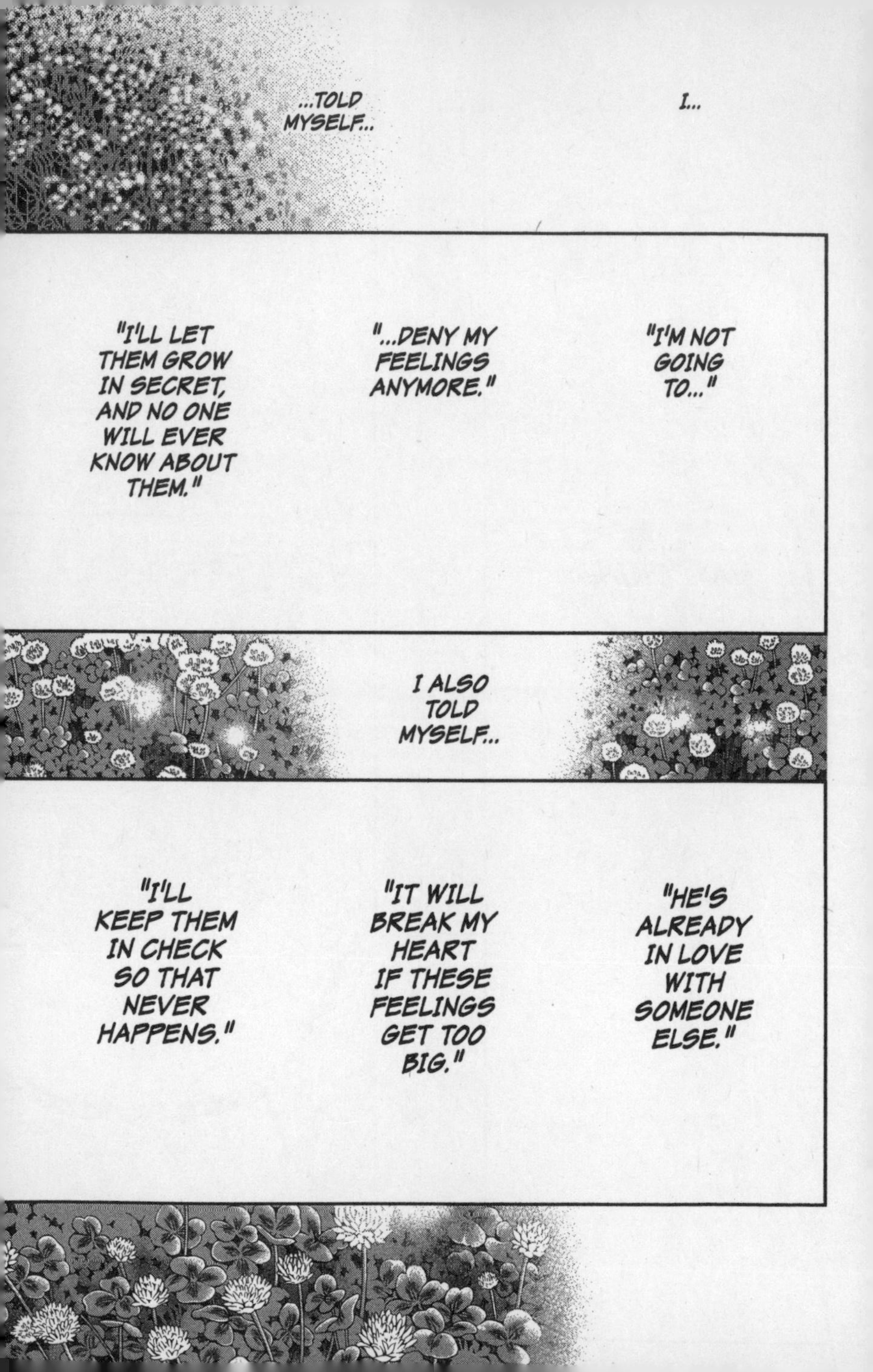
I...
...TOLD MYSELF...
"I'M NOT GOING TO..."
"...DENY MY FEELINGS ANYMORE."
"I'LL LET THEM GROW IN SECRET, AND NO ONE WILL EVER KNOW ABOUT THEM."
I ALSO TOLD MYSELF...
"HE'S ALREADY IN LOVE WITH SOMEONE ELSE."
"IT WILL BREAK MY HEART IF THESE FEELINGS GET TOO BIG."
"I'LL KEEP THEM IN CHECK SO THAT NEVER HAPPENS."

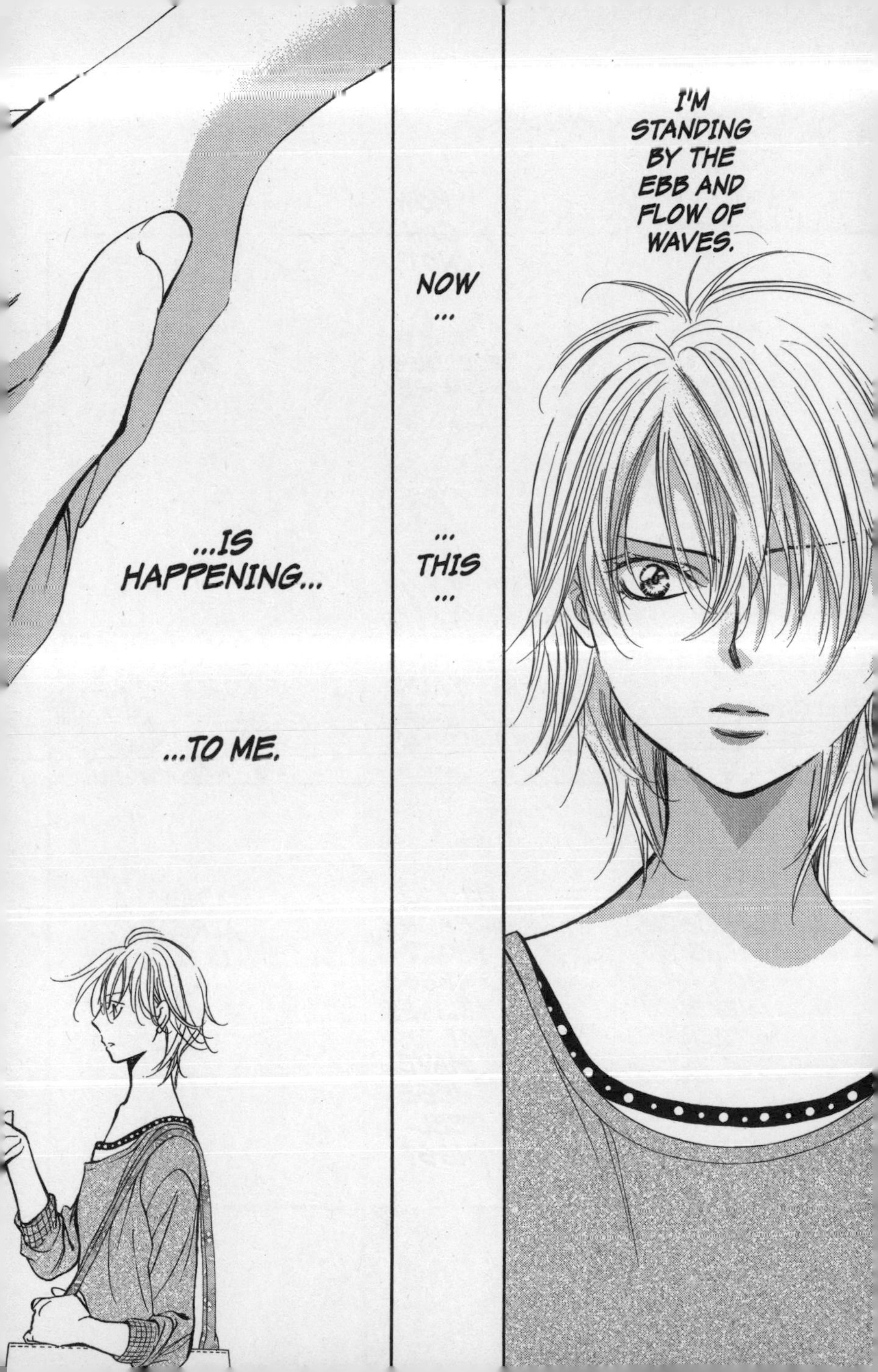
I'M STANDING BY THE EBB AND FLOW OF WAVES.
NOW ...
... THIS ...
...IS HAPPENING...
...TO ME.

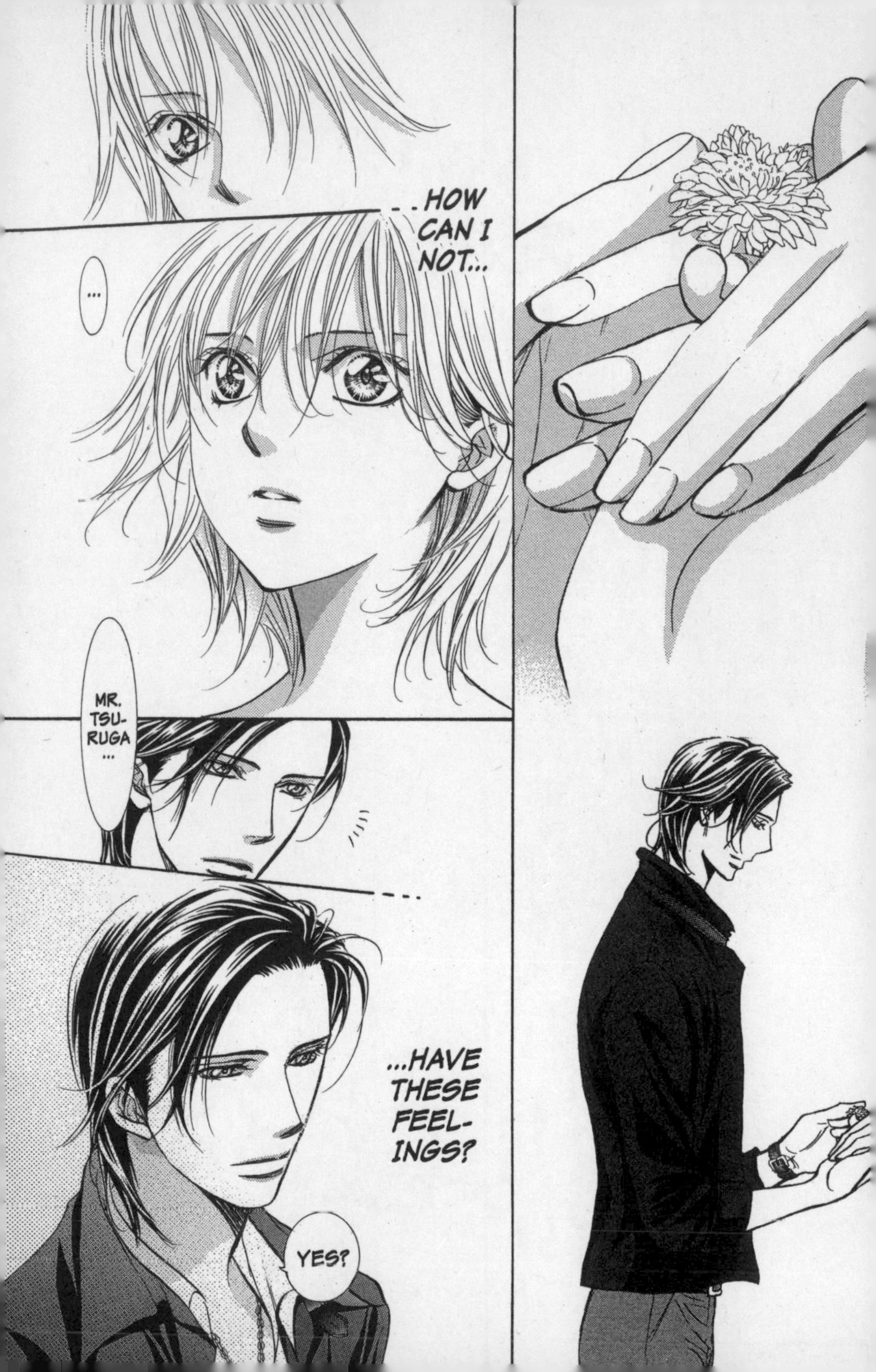

...HOW CAN I NOT...
...
MR. TSU-RUGA ...
...HAVE THESE FEEL-INGS?
YES?

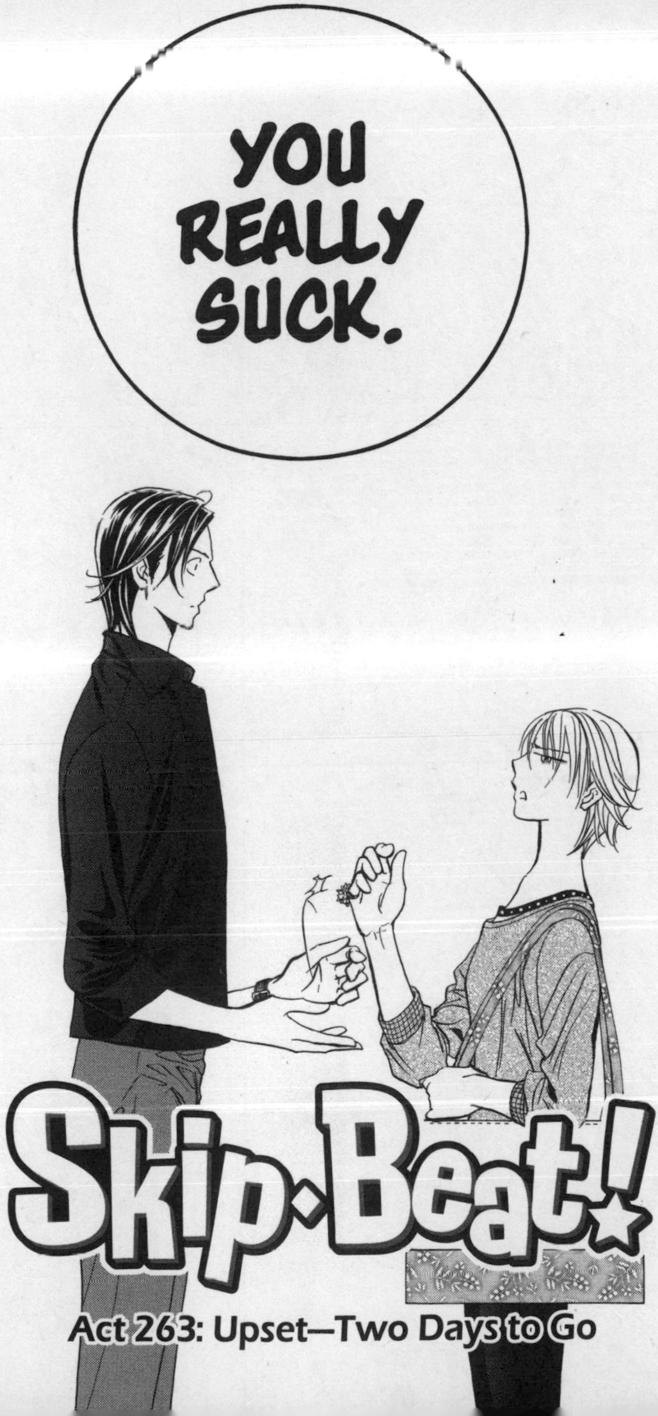
YOU REALLY SUCK.
Skip·Beat!
Act 263: Upset—Two Days to Go

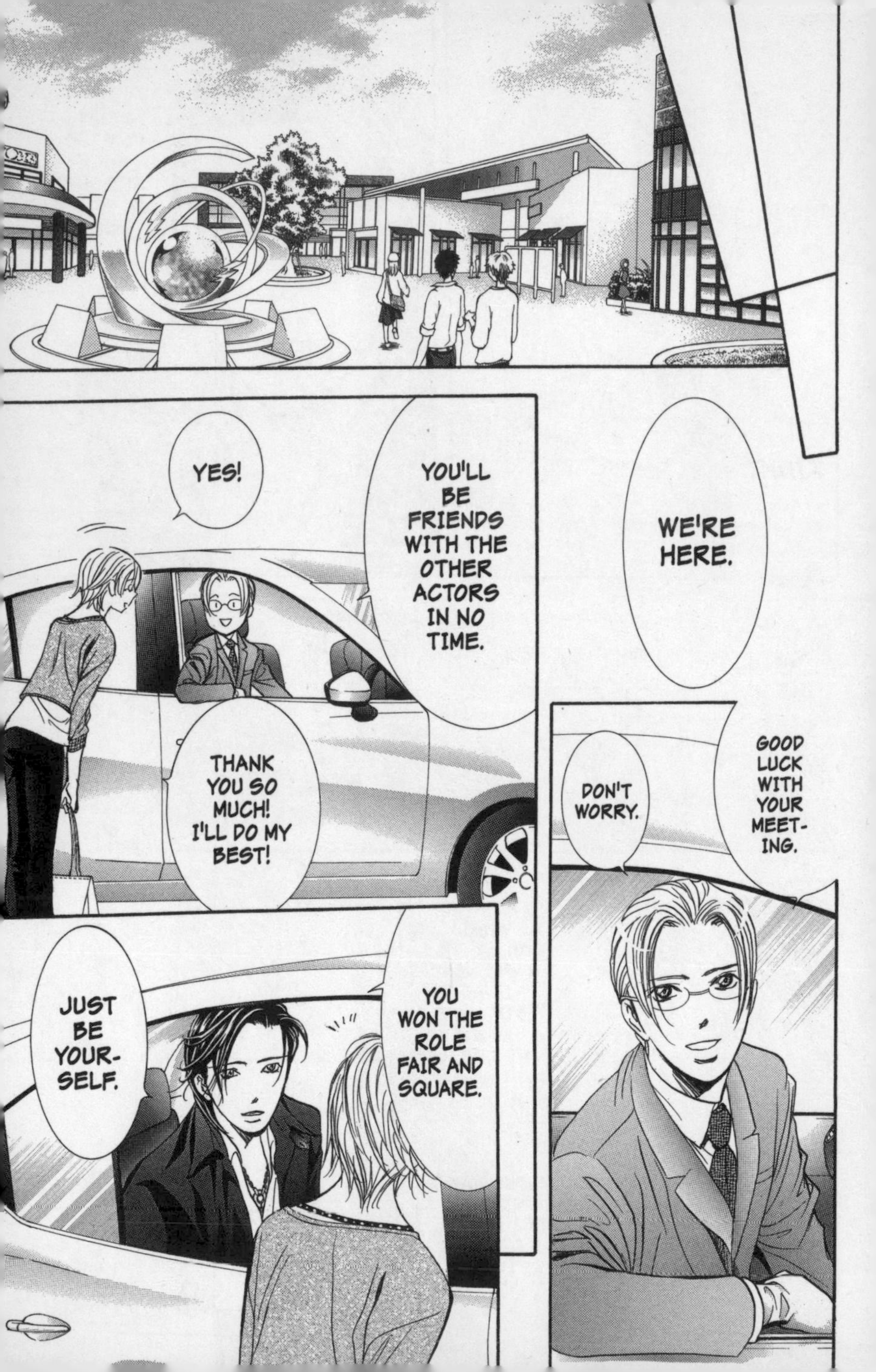
WE'RE HERE.
YOU'LL BE FRIENDS WITH THE OTHER ACTORS IN NO TIME.
YES!
THANK YOU SO MUCH! I'LL DO MY BEST!
GOOD LUCK WITH YOUR MEET-ING.
DON'T WORRY.
YOU WON THE ROLE FAIR AND SQUARE.
JUST BE YOUR-SELF.

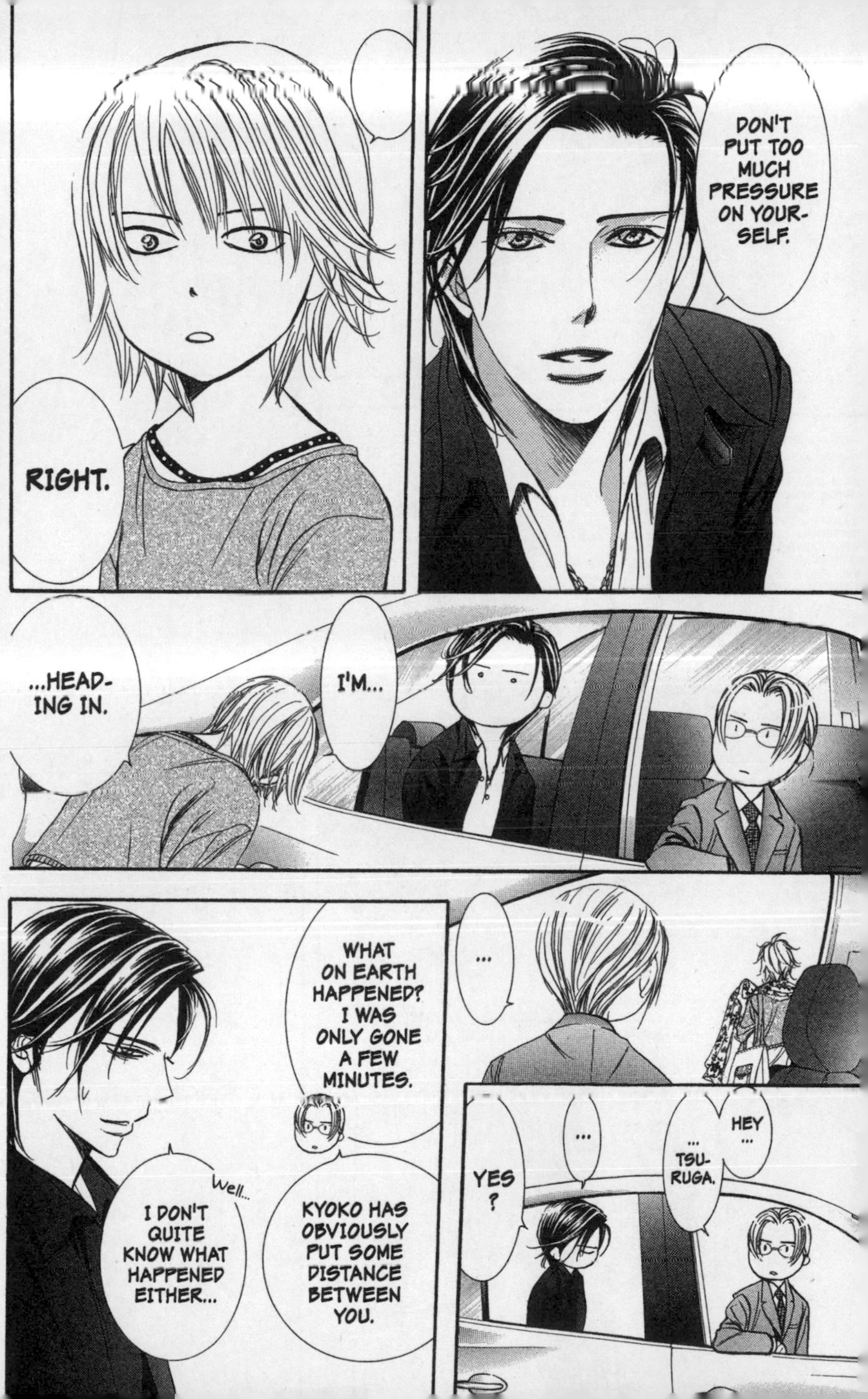
DON'T PUT TOO MUCH PRESSURE ON YOUR-SELF.
RIGHT.
I'M...
...HEAD-ING IN.
...
HEY ... TSU-RUGA.
...
YES ?
WHAT ON EARTH HAPPENED? I WAS ONLY GONE A FEW MINUTES.
KYOKO HAS OBVIOUSLY PUT SOME DISTANCE BETWEEN YOU.
Well...
I DON'T QUITE KNOW WHAT HAPPENED EITHER...

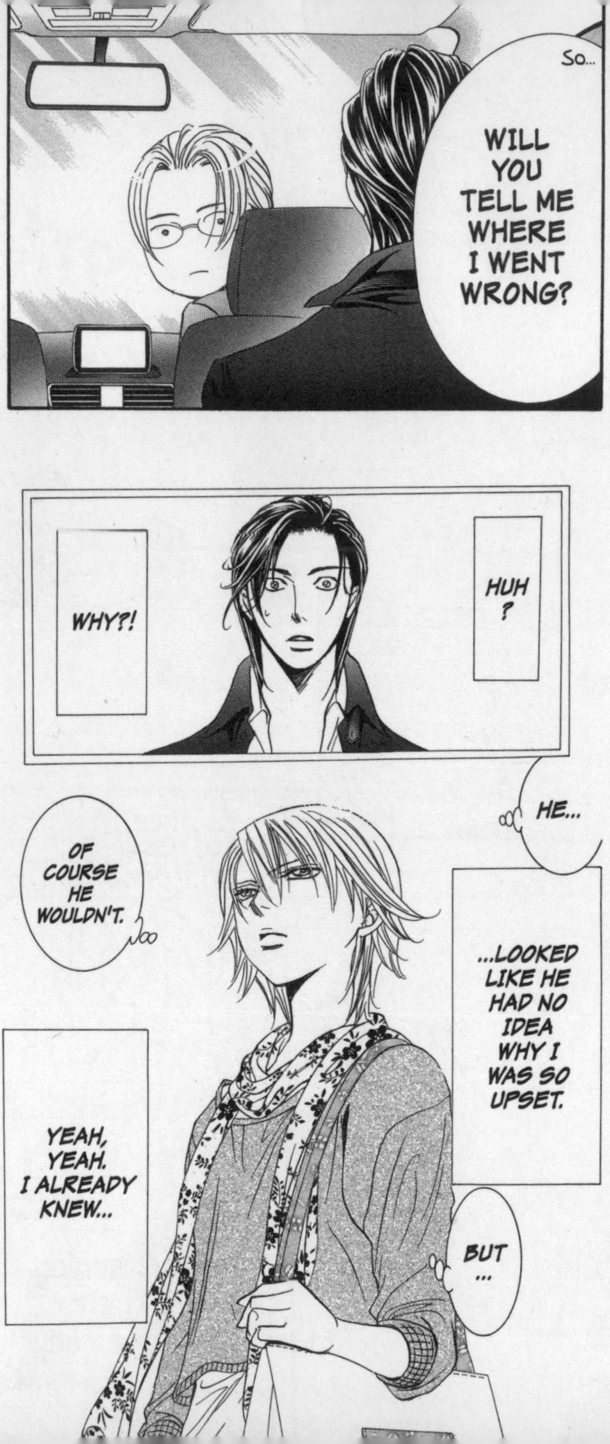
So...
WILL YOU TELL ME WHERE I WENT WRONG?
HUH?
WHY?!
HE...
...LOOKED LIKE HE HAD NO IDEA WHY I WAS SO UPSET.
OF COURSE HE WOULDN'T.
YEAH, YEAH. I ALREADY KNEW...
BUT ...

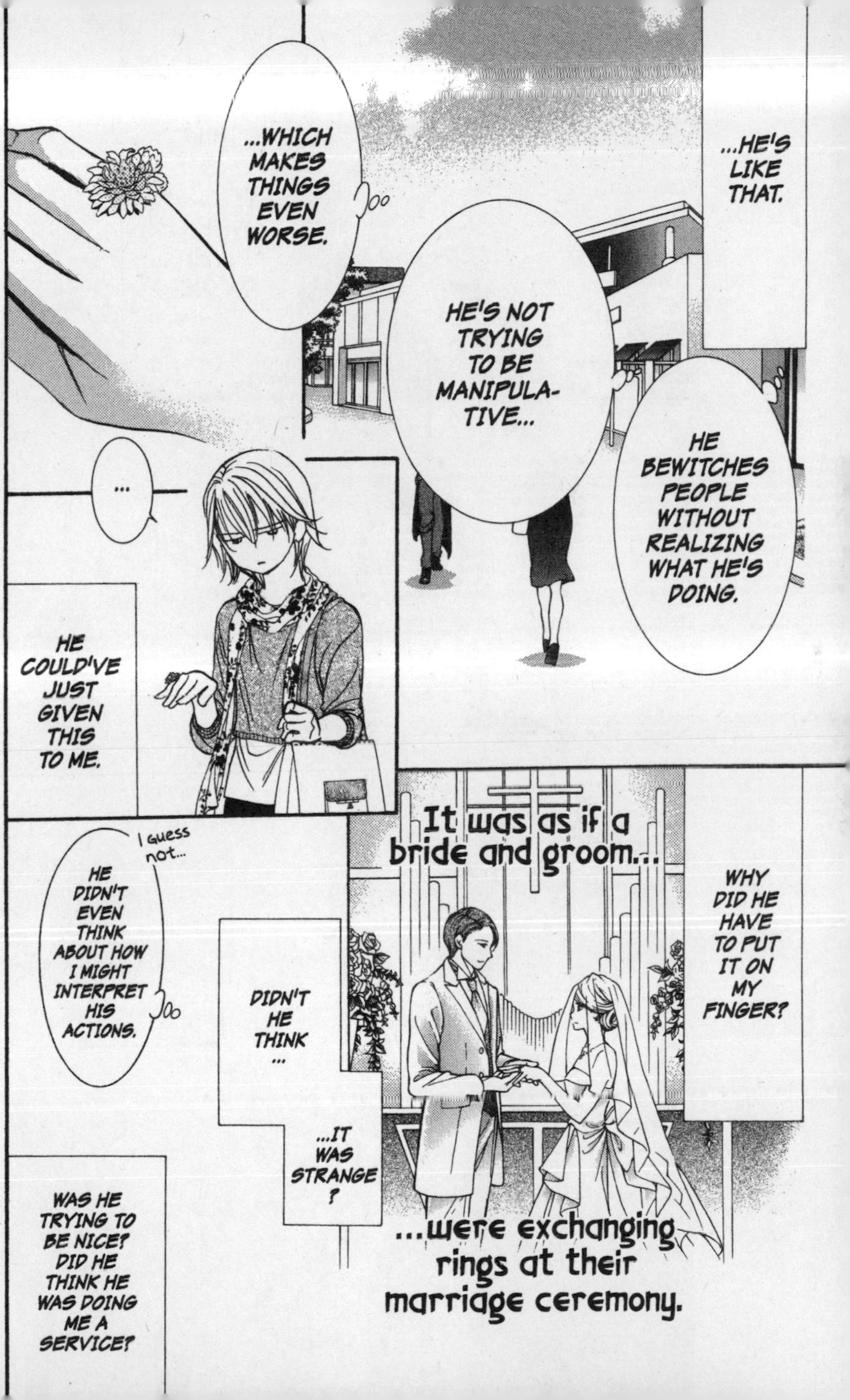
...HE'S LIKE THAT.
HE'S NOT TRYING TO BE MANIPULATIVE...
HE BEWITCHES PEOPLE WITHOUT REALIZING WHAT HE'S DOING.
...WHICH MAKES THINGS EVEN WORSE.
...
HE COULD'VE JUST GIVEN THIS TO ME.
WHY DID HE HAVE TO PUT IT ON MY FINGER?
It was as if a bride and groom...
...were exchanging rings at their marriage ceremony.
DIDN'T HE THINK...
...IT WAS STRANGE?
HE DIDN'T EVEN THINK ABOUT HOW I MIGHT INTERPRET HIS ACTIONS.
I guess not...
WAS HE TRYING TO BE NICE? DID HE THINK HE WAS DOING ME A SERVICE?

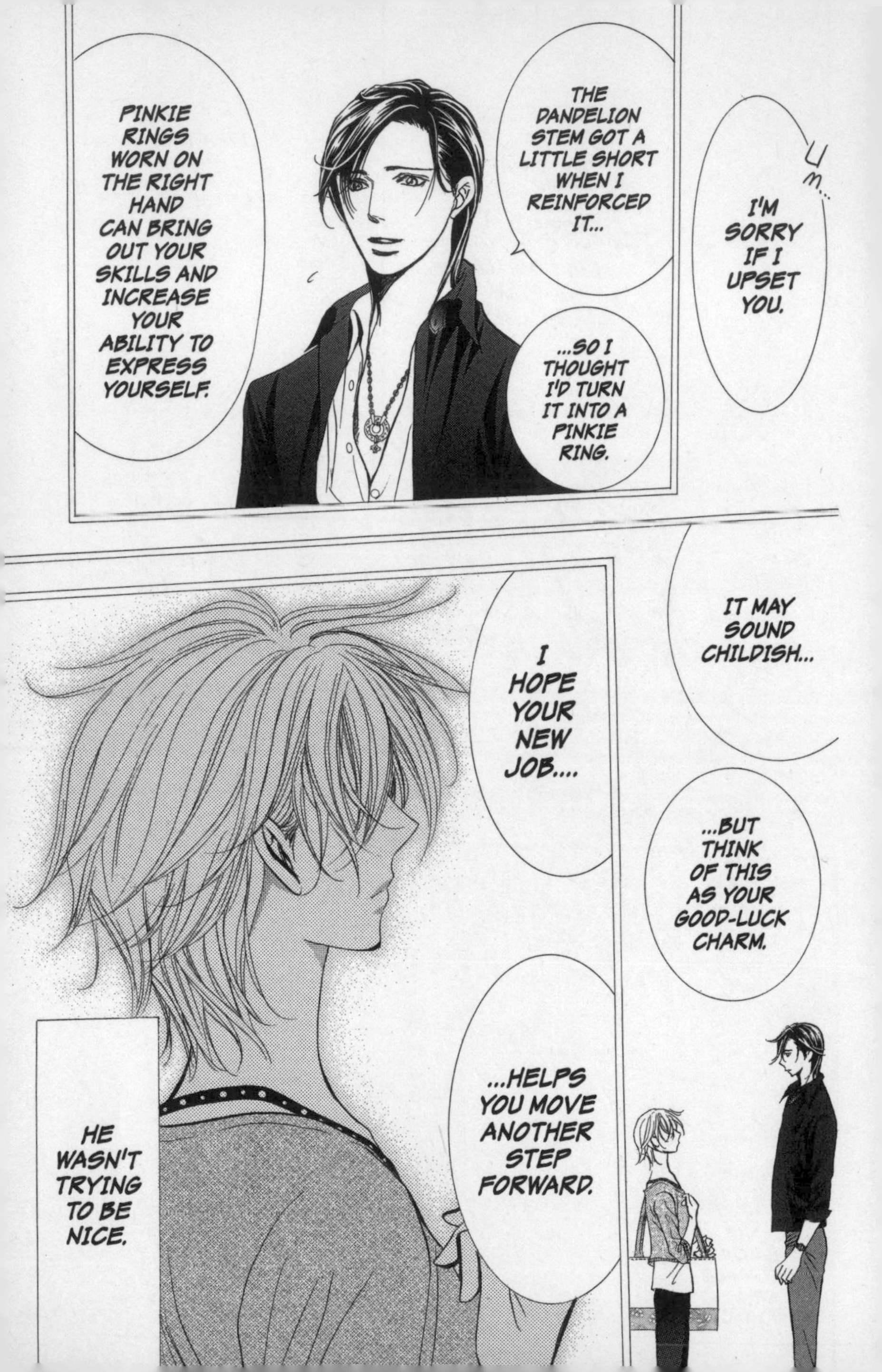
Um...
I'M SORRY IF I UPSET YOU.
THE DANDELION STEM GOT A LITTLE SHORT WHEN I REINFORCED IT...
...SO I THOUGHT I'D TURN IT INTO A PINKIE RING.
PINKIE RINGS WORN ON THE RIGHT HAND CAN BRING OUT YOUR SKILLS AND INCREASE YOUR ABILITY TO EXPRESS YOURSELF.
IT MAY SOUND CHILDISH...
...BUT THINK OF THIS AS YOUR GOOD-LUCK CHARM.
I HOPE YOUR NEW JOB....
...HELPS YOU MOVE ANOTHER STEP FORWARD.
HE WASN'T TRYING TO BE NICE.

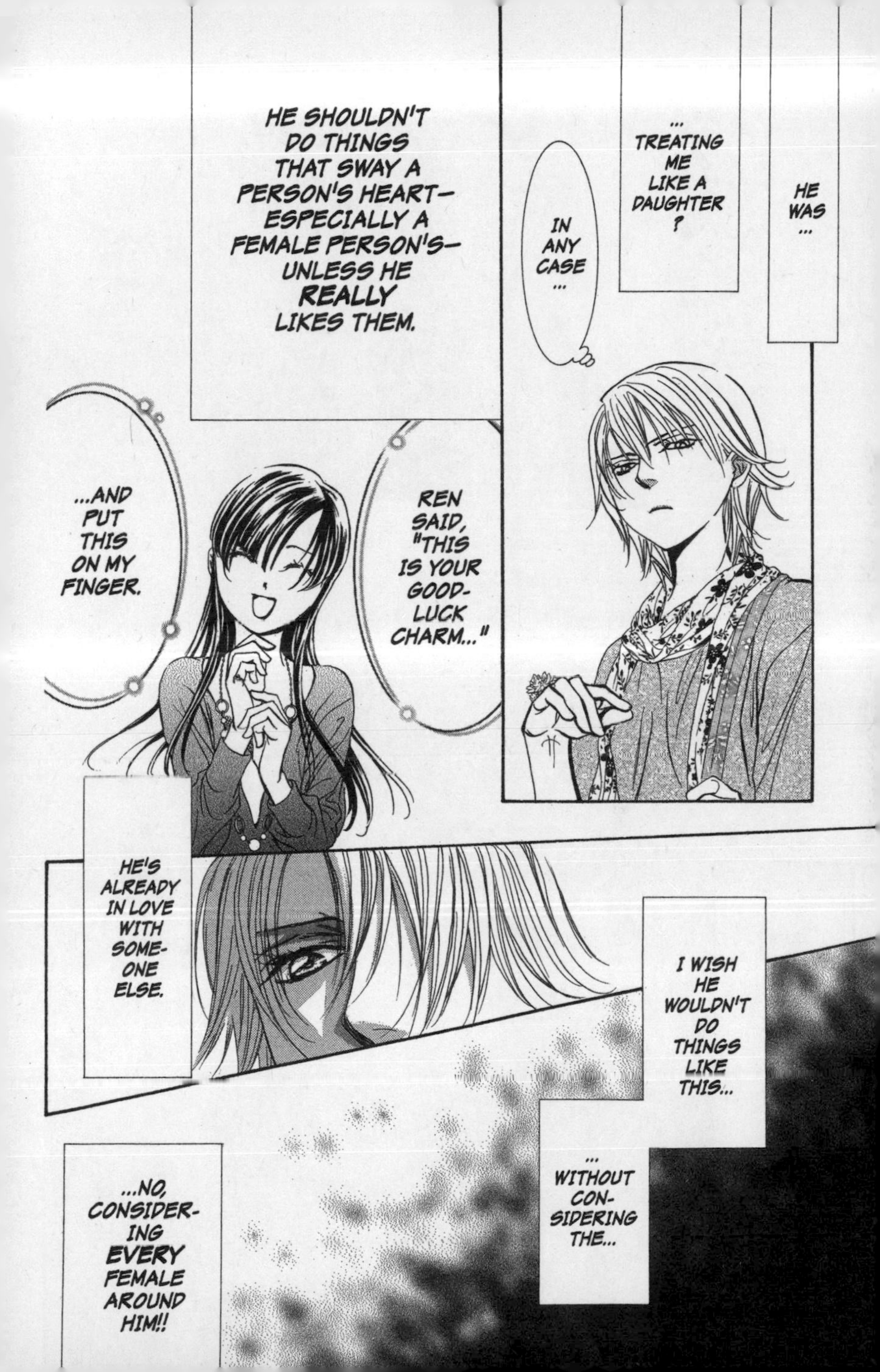
HE WAS...
...TREATING ME LIKE A DAUGHTER?
IN ANY CASE...
HE SHOULDN'T DO THINGS THAT SWAY A PERSON'S HEART—ESPECIALLY A FEMALE PERSON'S—UNLESS HE REALLY LIKES THEM.
REN SAID, "THIS IS YOUR GOOD-LUCK CHARM..."
...AND PUT THIS ON MY FINGER.
HE'S ALREADY IN LOVE WITH SOME-ONE ELSE.
I WISH HE WOULDN'T DO THINGS LIKE THIS...
...WITHOUT CON-SIDERING THE...
...NO, CONSIDER-ING EVERY FEMALE AROUND HIM!!

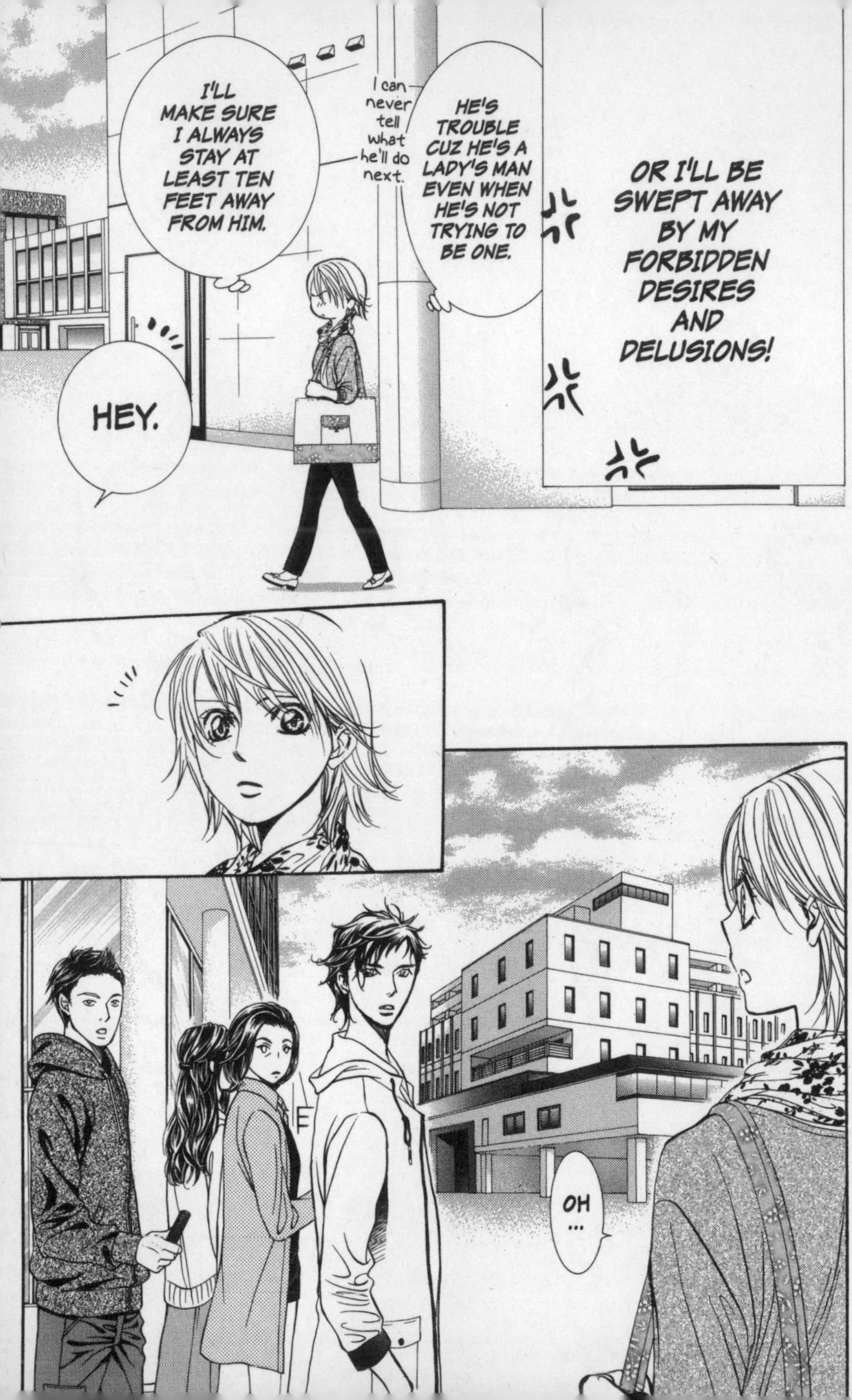
OR I'LL BE SWEPT AWAY BY MY FORBIDDEN DESIRES AND DELUSIONS!
HE'S TROUBLE CUZ HE'S A LADY'S MAN EVEN WHEN HE'S NOT TRYING TO BE ONE.
I can never tell what he'll do next.
I'LL MAKE SURE I ALWAYS STAY AT LEAST TEN FEET AWAY FROM HIM.
HEY.
OH ...

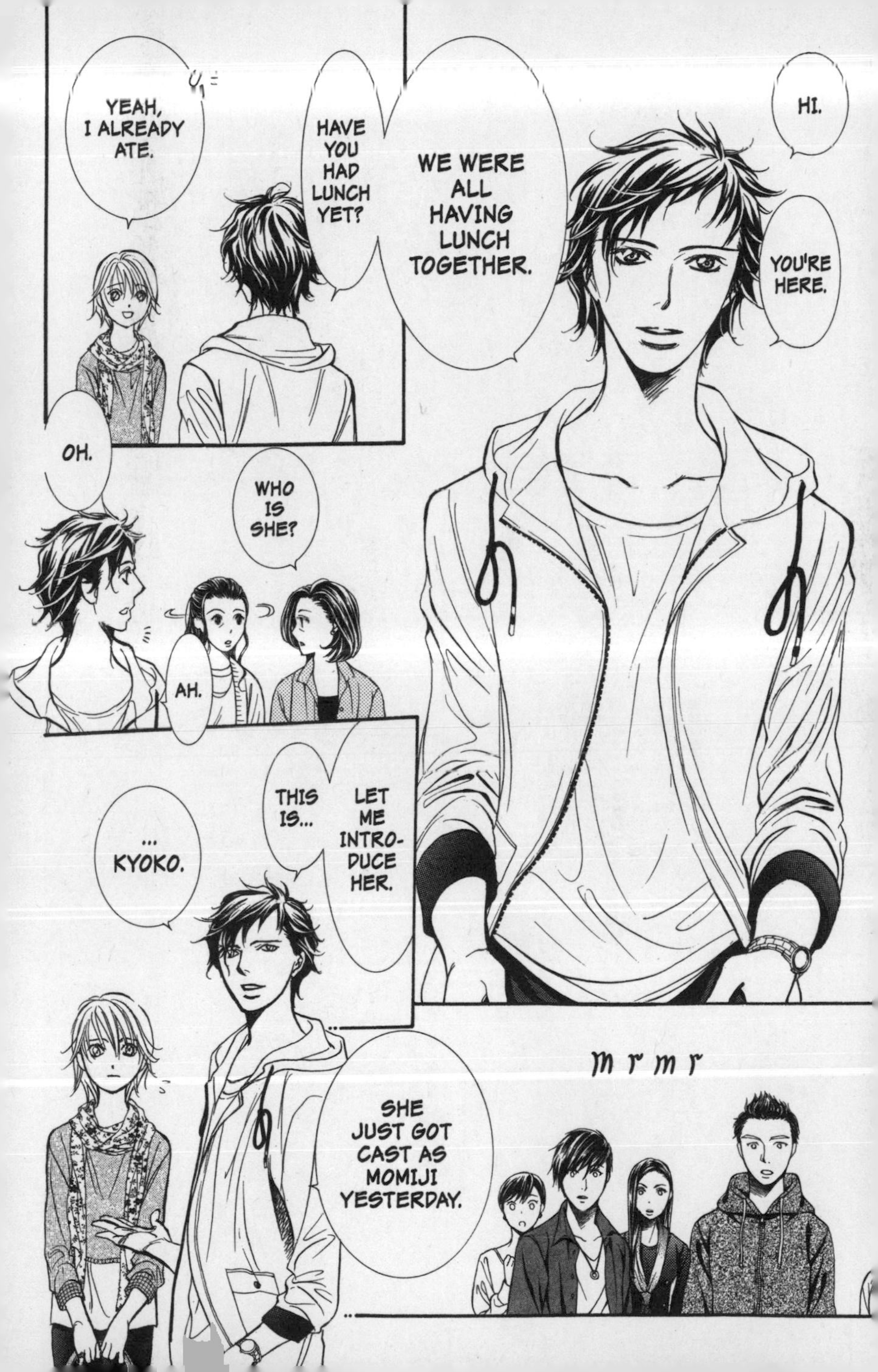
HI.
YOU'RE HERE.
WE WERE ALL HAVING LUNCH TOGETHER.
HAVE YOU HAD LUNCH YET?
YEAH, I ALREADY ATE.
OH.
WHO IS SHE?
AH.
LET ME INTRODUCE HER.
THIS IS...
...KYOKO.
mrmr
SHE JUST GOT CAST AS MOMIJI YESTERDAY.

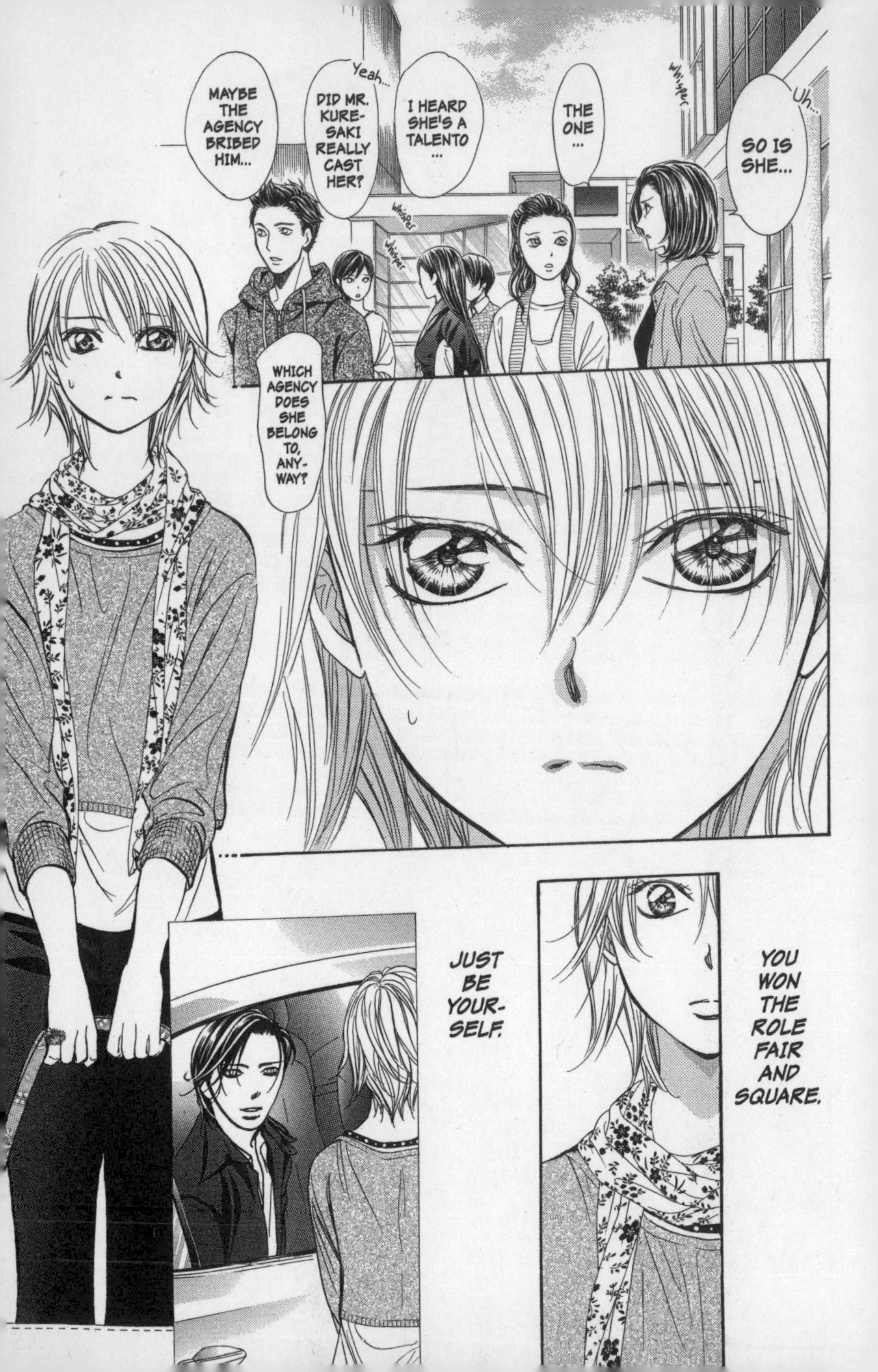
whisper
Uh...
SO IS SHE...
THE ONE ...
I HEARD SHE'S A TALENTO ...
Yeah...
DID MR. KURE-SAKI REALLY CAST HER?
MAYBE THE AGENCY BRIBED HIM...
whisper
whisper
WHICH AGENCY DOES SHE BELONG TO, ANYWAY?
YOU WON THE ROLE FAIR AND SQUARE.
JUST BE YOURSELF.

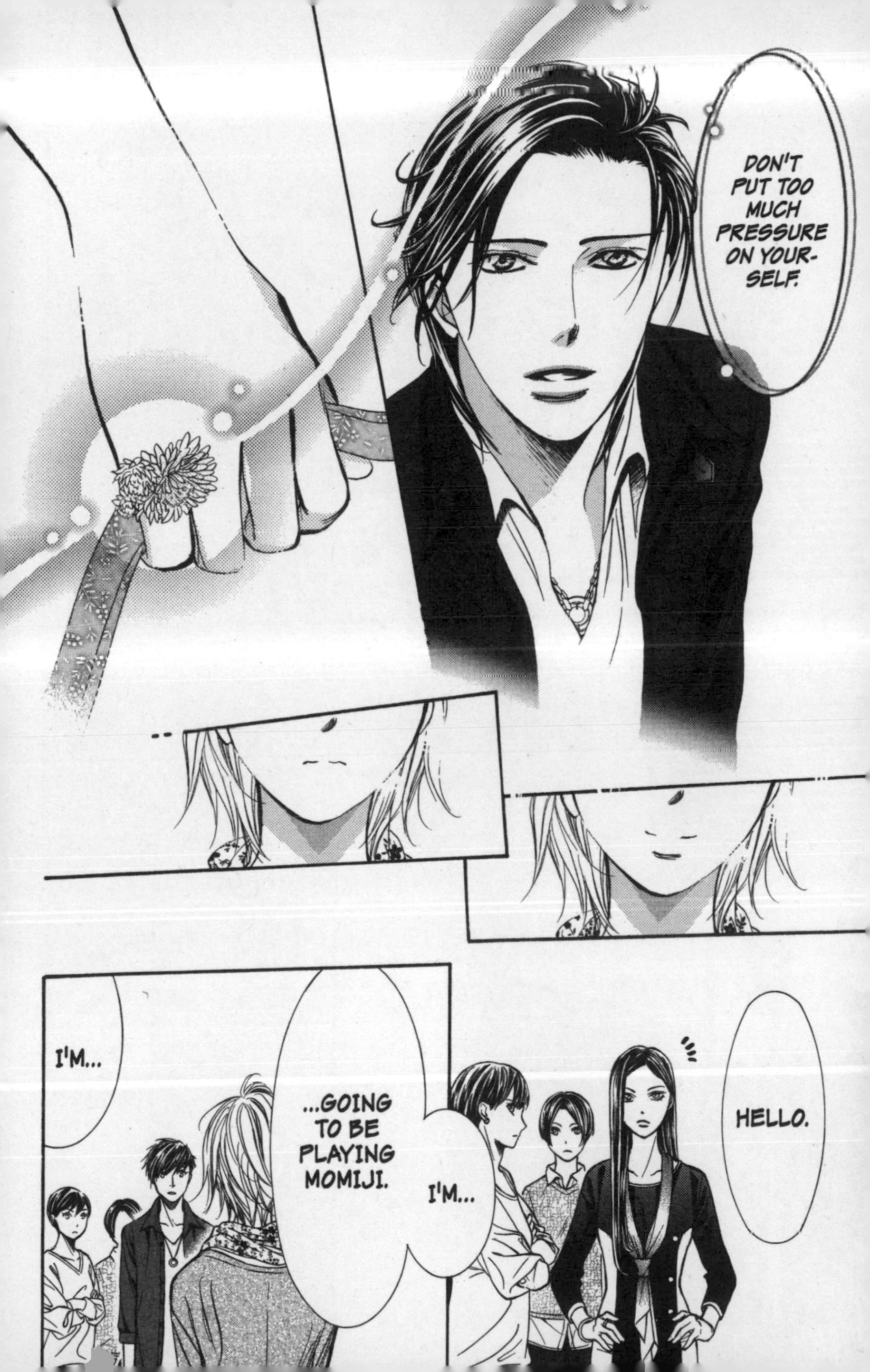
DON'T PUT TOO MUCH PRESSURE ON YOURSELF.
HELLO.
I'M...
...GOING TO BE PLAYING MOMIJI.
I'M...

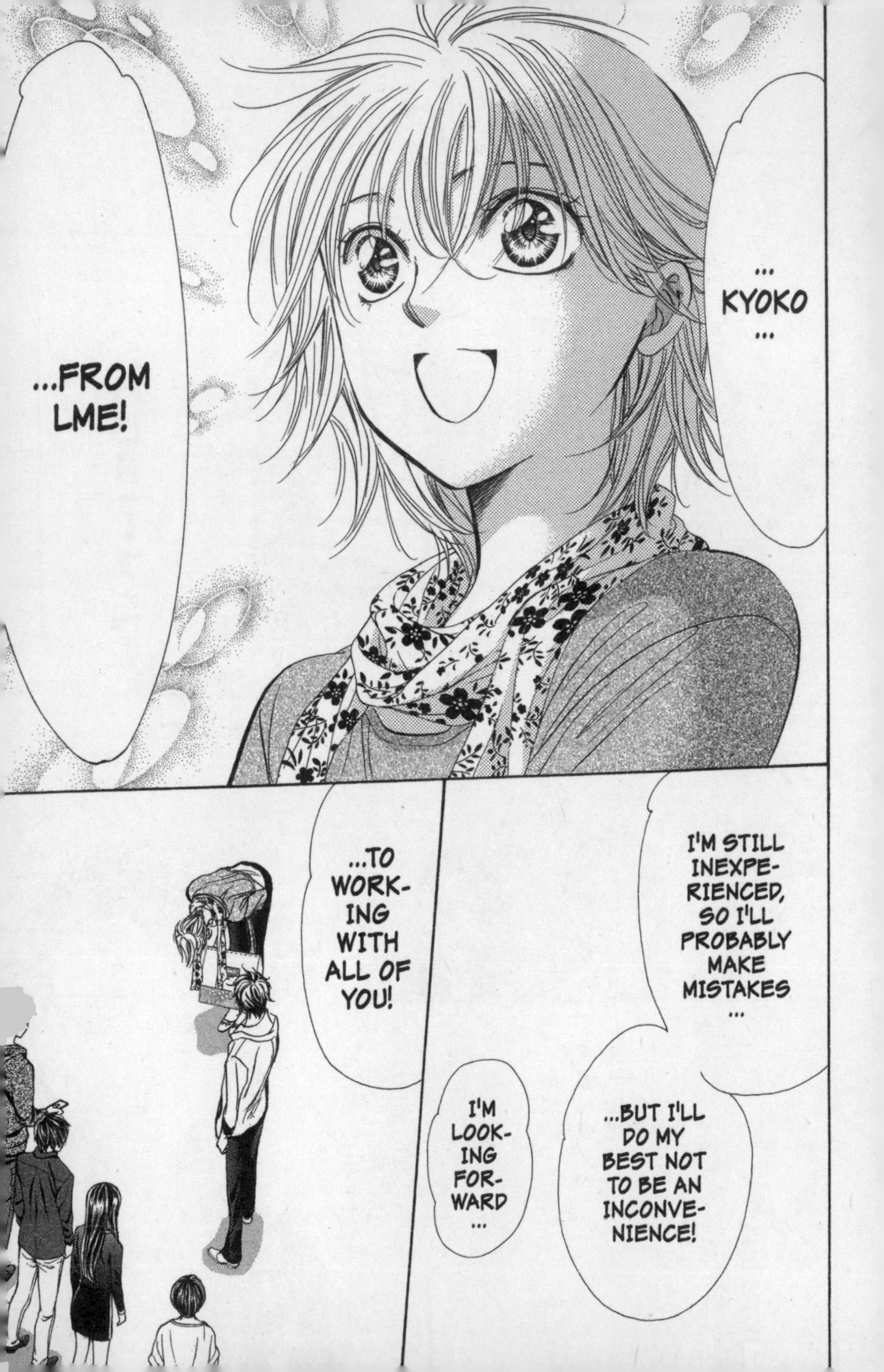
...KYOKO...
...FROM LME!
I'M STILL INEXPERIENCED, SO I'LL PROBABLY MAKE MISTAKES...
...BUT I'LL DO MY BEST NOT TO BE AN INCONVENIENCE!
I'M LOOKING FORWARD...
...TO WORKING WITH ALL OF YOU!

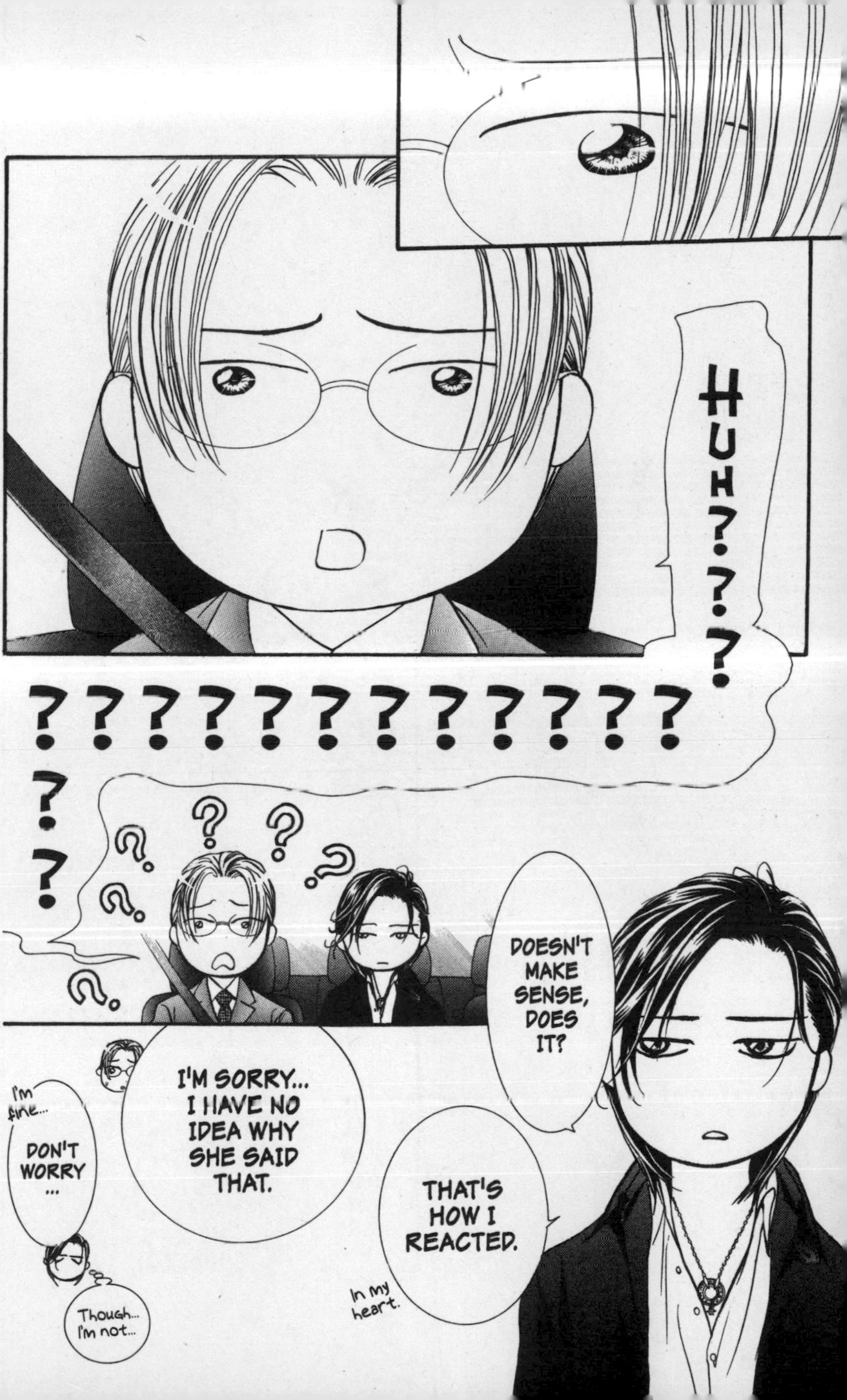
HUH????
??????????????
DOESN'T MAKE SENSE, DOES IT?
THAT'S HOW I REACTED.
In my heart.
I'M SORRY... I HAVE NO IDEA WHY SHE SAID THAT.
I'm fine...
DON'T WORRY...
Though... I'm not...

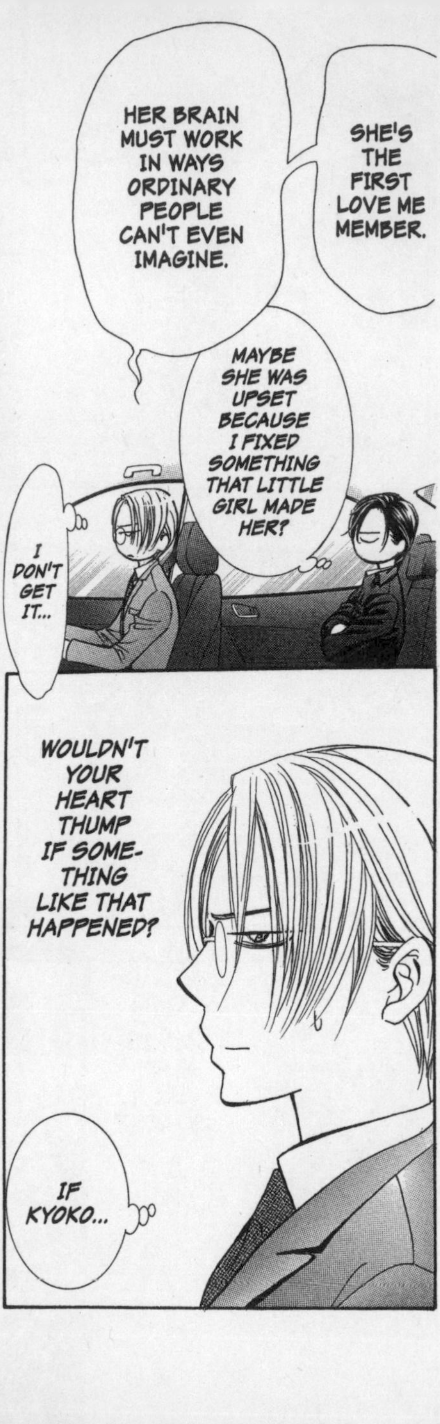
SHE'S THE FIRST LOVE ME MEMBER.
HER BRAIN MUST WORK IN WAYS ORDINARY PEOPLE CAN'T EVEN IMAGINE.
MAYBE SHE WAS UPSET BECAUSE I FIXED SOMETHING THAT LITTLE GIRL MADE HER?
I DON'T GET IT...
WOULDN'T YOUR HEART THUMP IF SOME-THING LIKE THAT HAPPENED?
IF KYOKO...

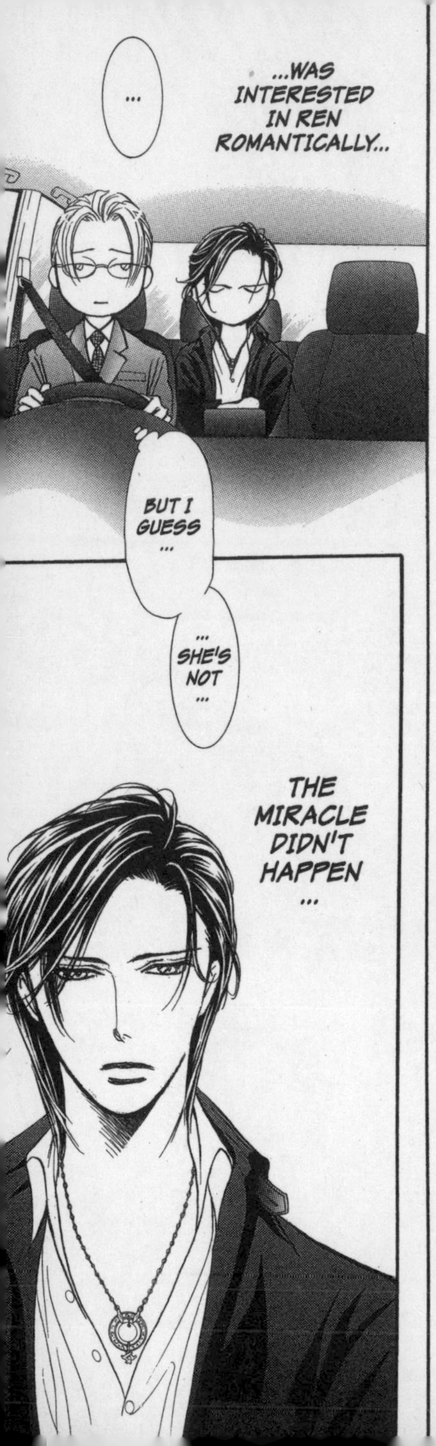
...WAS INTERESTED IN REN ROMANTICALLY...
...
BUT I GUESS...
...SHE'S NOT...
THE MIRACLE DIDN'T HAPPEN...

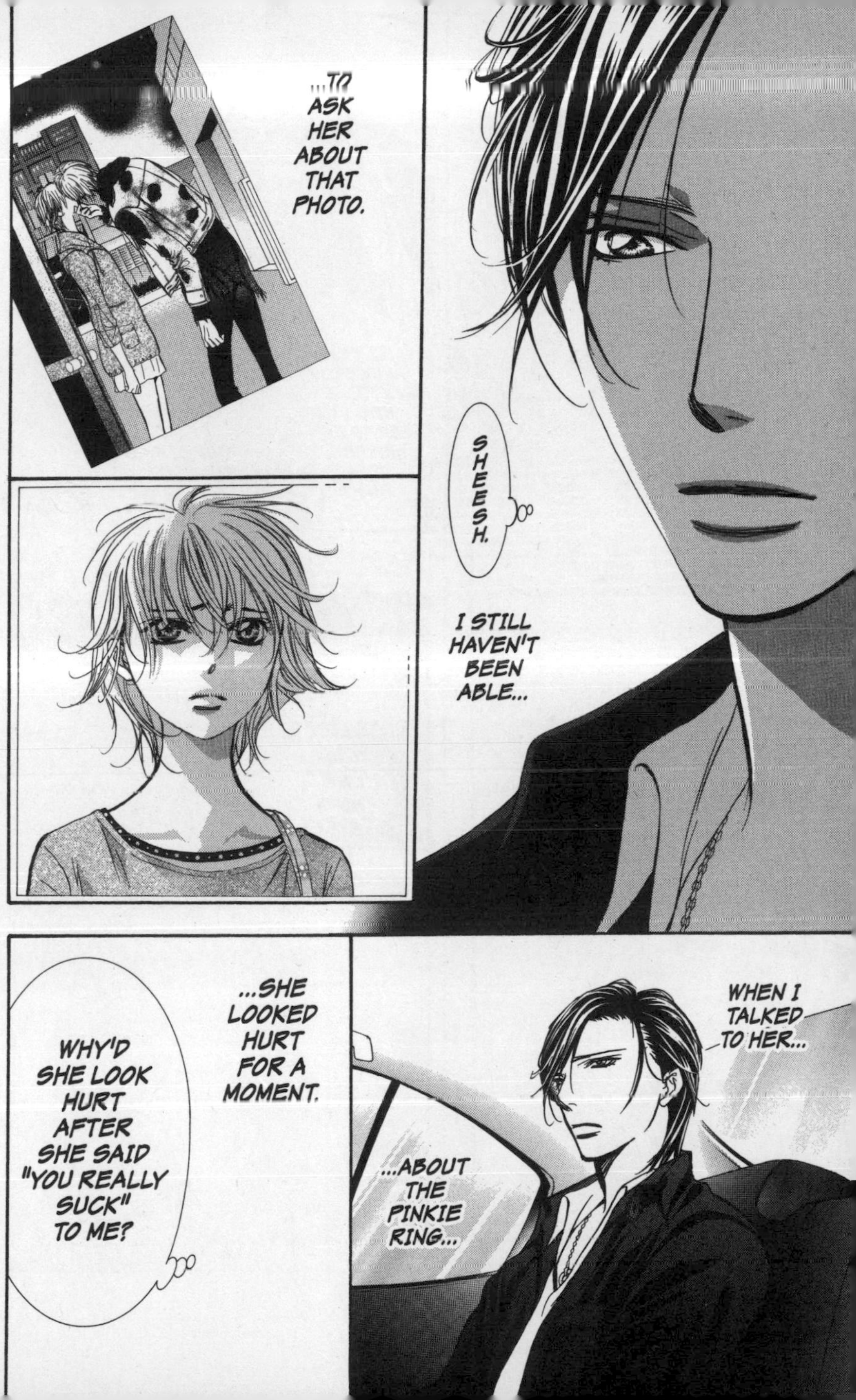
SHEESH.
I STILL HAVEN'T BEEN ABLE...
...TO ASK HER ABOUT THAT PHOTO.
WHEN I TALKED TO HER...
...ABOUT THE PINKIE RING...
...SHE LOOKED HURT FOR A MOMENT.
WHY'D SHE LOOK HURT AFTER SHE SAID "YOU REALLY SUCK" TO ME?

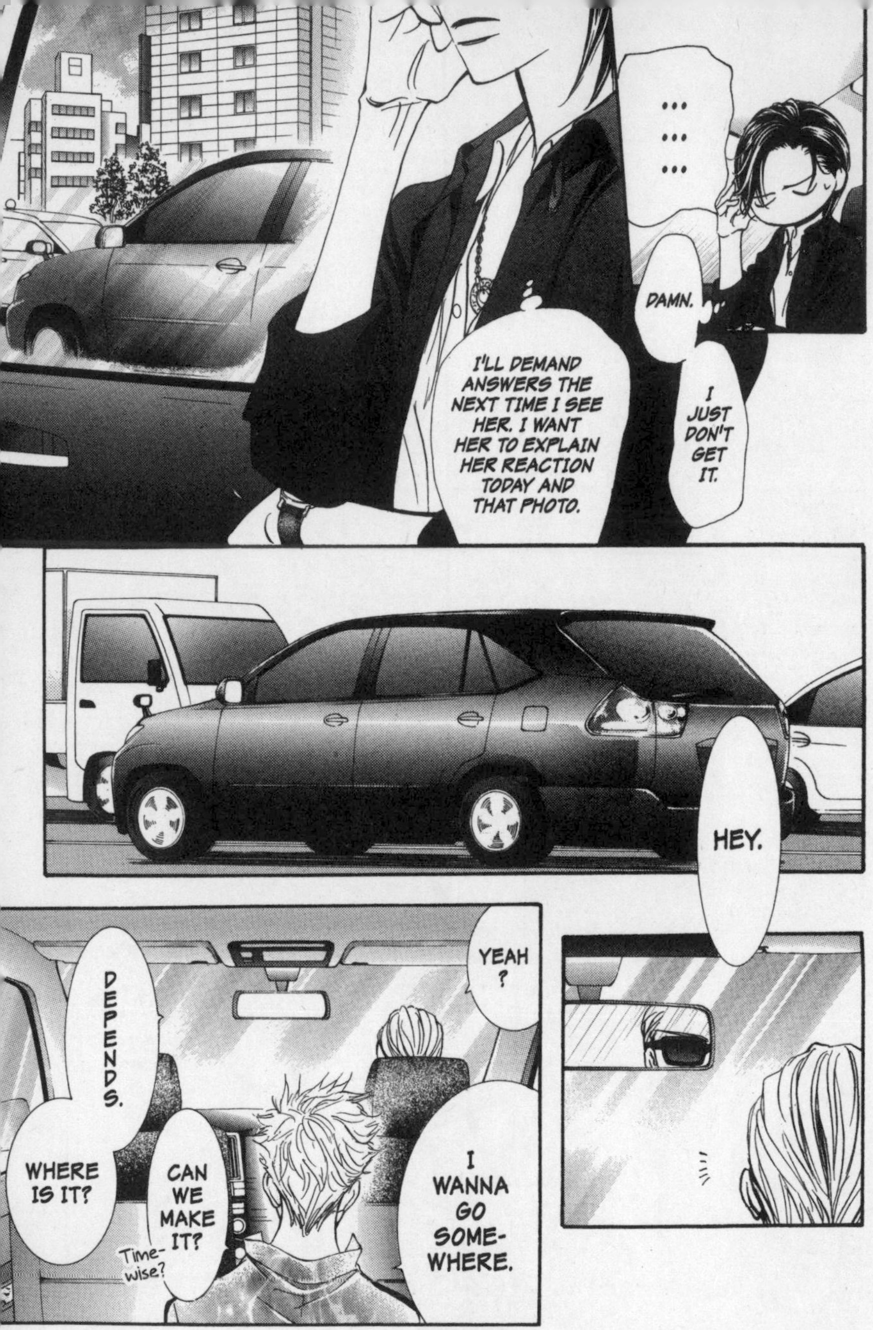
...
...
...
DAMN.
I JUST DON'T GET IT.
I'LL DEMAND ANSWERS THE NEXT TIME I SEE HER. I WANT HER TO EXPLAIN HER REACTION TODAY AND THAT PHOTO.
HEY.
YEAH?
I WANNA GO SOME-WHERE.
CAN WE MAKE IT?
Time-wise?
DEPENDS.
WHERE IS IT?

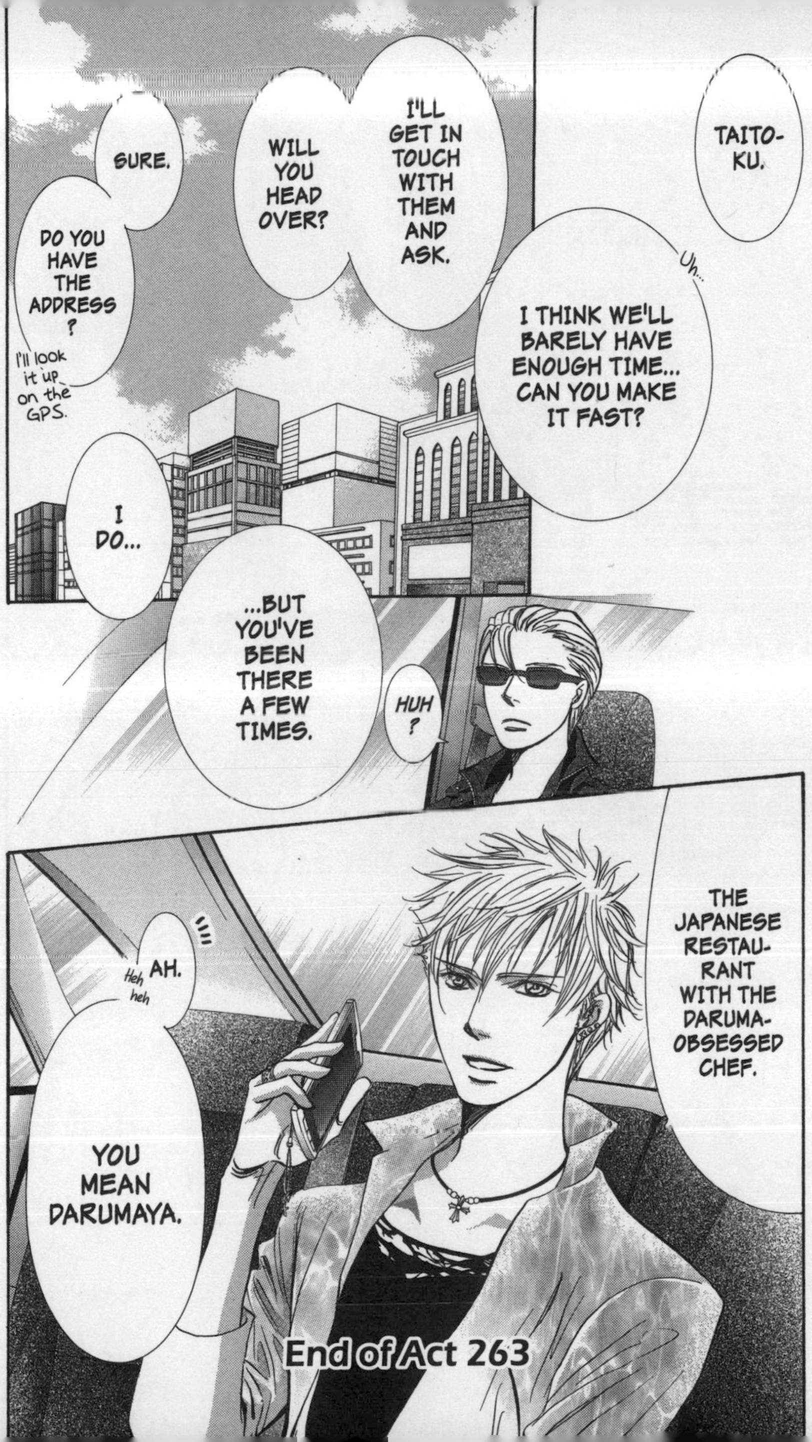
TAITO-KU.
Uh...
I THINK WE'LL BARELY HAVE ENOUGH TIME... CAN YOU MAKE IT FAST?
I'LL GET IN TOUCH WITH THEM AND ASK.
WILL YOU HEAD OVER?
SURE.
DO YOU HAVE THE ADDRESS?
I'll look it up on the GPS.
I DO...
HUH?
...BUT YOU'VE BEEN THERE A FEW TIMES.
THE JAPANESE RESTAURANT WITH THE DARUMA-OBSESSED CHEF.
!!
AH.
Heh heh
YOU MEAN DARUMAYA.
End of Act 263

Skip-Beat! End Notes

Everyone knows how to be a fan, but sometimes cool things from other cultures need a little help crossing the language barrier.

Page 39, panel 1: Tofu hamburger steak
A lower-calorie version of the classic hamburger steak that mixes tofu in with the ground meat, bread crumbs, egg and sauteed onions. Some versions might even omit the meat completely.

Page 39, panel 1: Konjac
A firm, gelatin-like substance made from the corm of the konjac plant. It has a similar firm texture to agar-agar gelatin.

Page 72, panel 5: White Day
The day when boys and men give small presents to the girls and women who gave them something on Valentine's.

Page 124, panel 1: Restaurant sign
Darumaya is named for Daruma, egg-shaped dolls modeled after Bodhidharma, the founder of Zen.

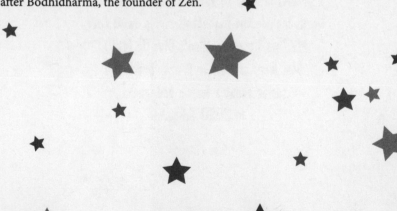

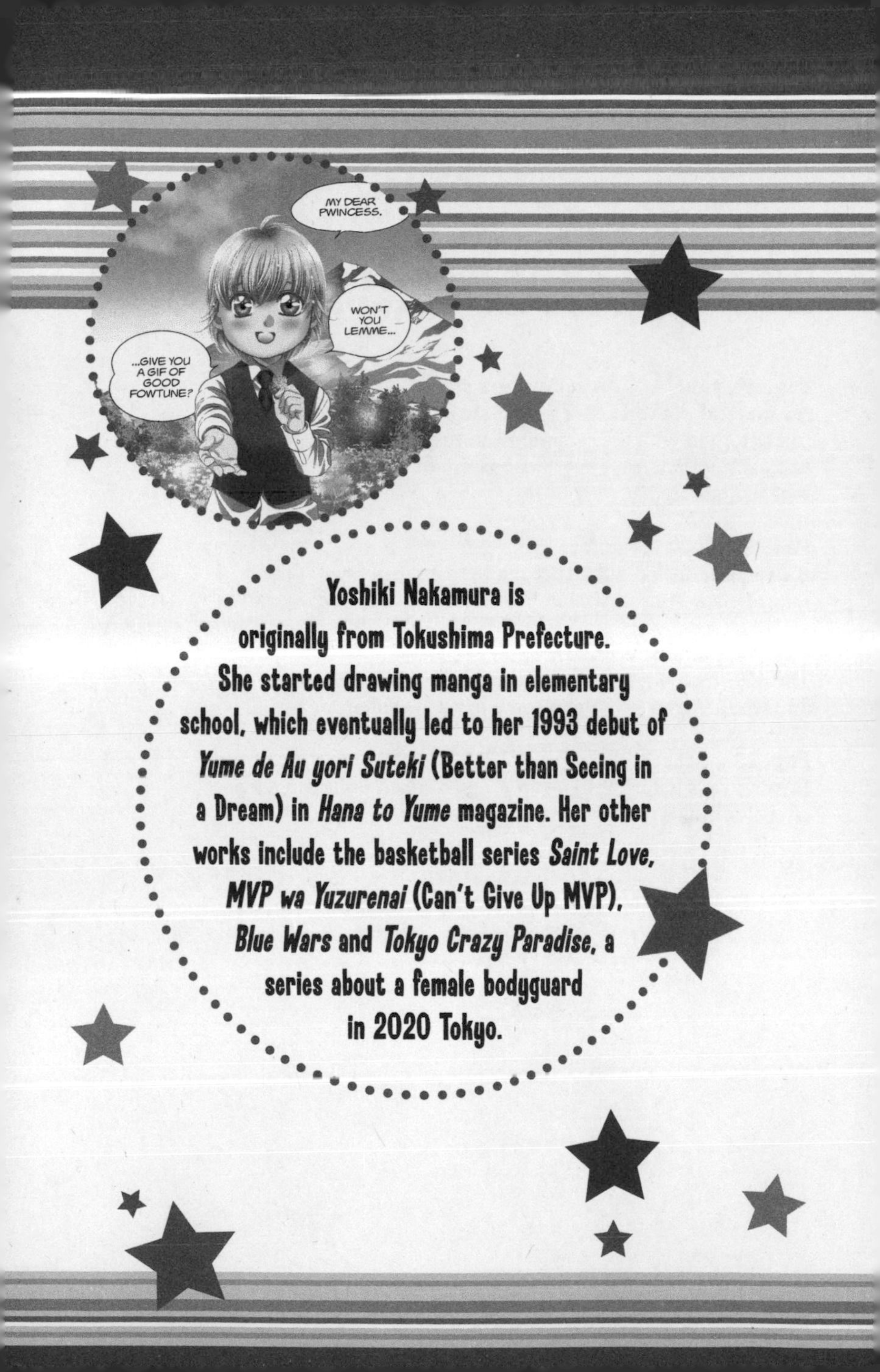
MY DEAR PWINCESS.
WON'T YOU LEMME...
...GIVE YOU A GIF OF GOOD FOWTUNE?

Yoshiki Nakamura is originally from Tokushima Prefecture. She started drawing manga in elementary school, which eventually led to her 1993 debut of *Yume de Au yori Suteki* (Better than Seeing in a Dream) in *Hana to Yume* magazine. Her other works include the basketball series *Saint Love*, *MVP wa Yuzurenai* (Can't Give Up MVP), *Blue Wars* and *Tokyo Crazy Paradise*, a series about a female bodyguard in 2020 Tokyo.

SKIP·BEAT!
Vol. 43
Shojo Beat Edition

STORY AND ART BY YOSHIKI NAKAMURA

English Translation & Adaptation/Tomo Kimura
Touch-up Art & Lettering/Sabrina Heep
Design/Veronica Casson
Editor/Pancha Diaz

Skip·Beat! by Yoshiki Nakamura © Yoshiki Nakamura 2019
All rights reserved. First published in Japan in 2019 by HAKUSENSHA, Inc., Tokyo.
English language translation rights arranged with HAKUSENSHA, Inc., Tokyo.

The stories, characters and incidents mentioned in this publication are entirely fictional.

No portion of this book may be reproduced or transmitted in any form or by any means without written permission from the copyright holders.

Printed in the U.S.A.

Published by VIZ Media, LLC
P.O. Box 77010
San Francisco, CA 94107

10 9 8 7 6 5 4 3 2 1
First printing, November 2019

PARENTAL ADVISORY
SKIP•BEAT! is rated T for Teen and is recommended for ages 13 and up. This volume contains a grudge.

Snow White
with the Red Hair

Inspired
the anime!

STORY & ART BY
SORATA AKIDUKI

Shirayuki is an herbalist famous for her naturally bright-red hair, and the prince of Tanbarun wants her all to himself! Unwilling to become the prince's possession, she seeks shelter in the woods of the neighboring kingdom, where she gains an unlikely ally—the prince of that kingdom! He rescues her from her plight, and thus begins the love story between a lovestruck prince and an unusual herbalist.

Akagami no Shirayukihime © Sorata Akiduki 2007/HAKUSENSHA, Inc.

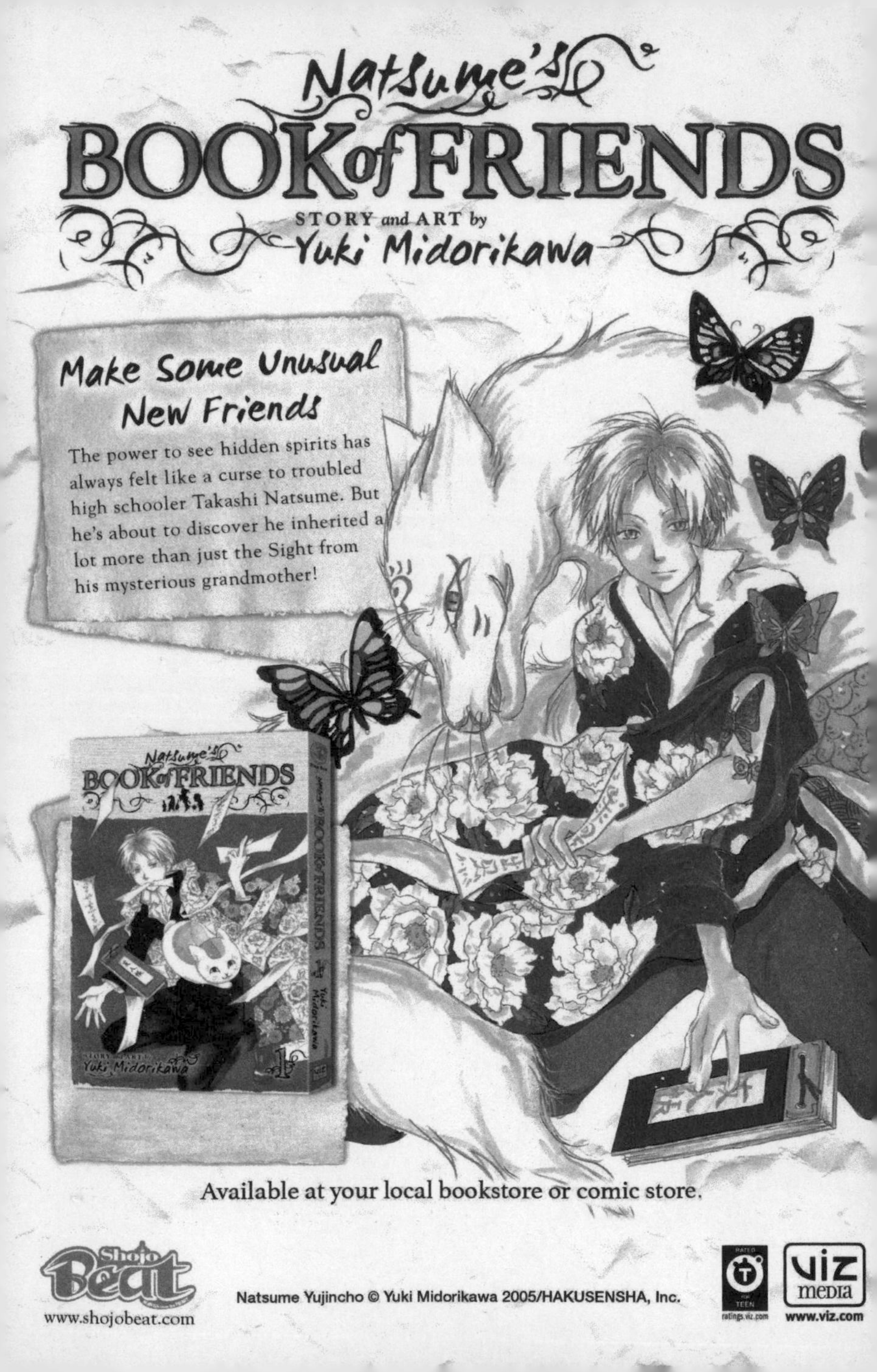
Natsume's
BOOK of FRIENDS
STORY and ART by
Yuki Midorikawa
Make Some Unusual New Friends
The power to see hidden spirits has always felt like a curse to troubled high schooler Takashi Natsume. But he's about to discover he inherited a lot more than just the Sight from his mysterious grandmother!
Natsume's BOOK of FRIENDS
STORY and ART by Yuki Midorikawa
Available at your local bookstore or comic store.
Shojo Beat
www.shojobeat.com
Natsume Yujincho © Yuki Midorikawa 2005/HAKUSENSHA, Inc.
RATED T FOR TEEN
ratings.viz.com
VIZ media
www.viz.com

Beautiful boy rebels using their fists to fall in love!

KENKA BANCHO
Otome
LOVE'S BATTLE ROYALE

STORY & ART BY **CHIE SHIMADA**

Based on the game created by Spike Chunsoft

Hinako thought she didn't have any family, but on the day she starts high school, her twin brother Hikaru suddenly appears and tricks her into taking his place. But the new school Hinako attends in his stead is beyond unusual. Now she must fight her way to the top of Shishiku Academy, an all-boys school of delinquents!

Kenka Bancho Otome: Koi no Battle Royale © Chie Shimada / HAKUSENSHA, INC. © Spike Chunsoft

Behind the Scenes!!

STORY AND ART BY **BISCO HATORI**

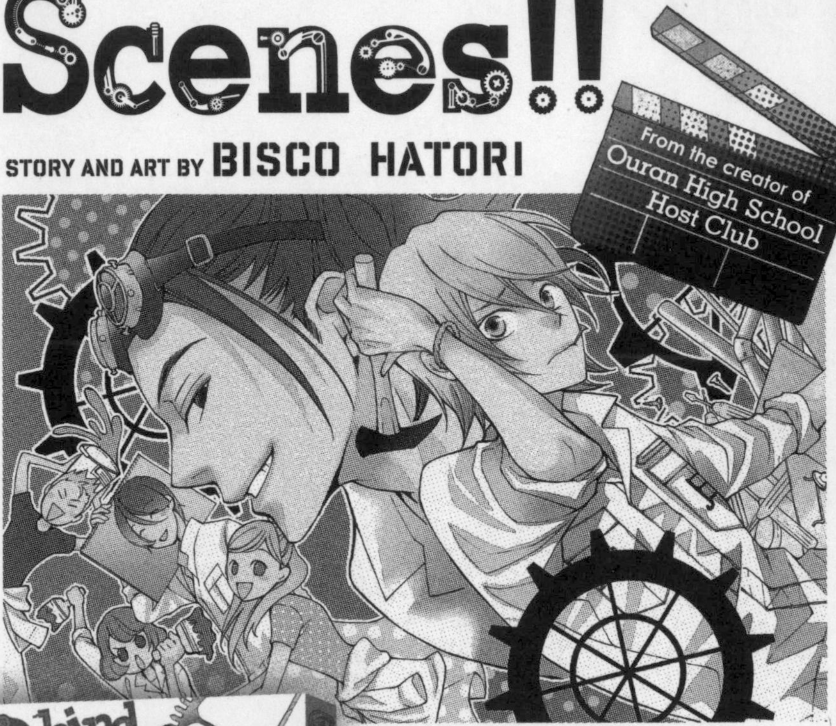
From the creator of
Ouran High School
Host Club

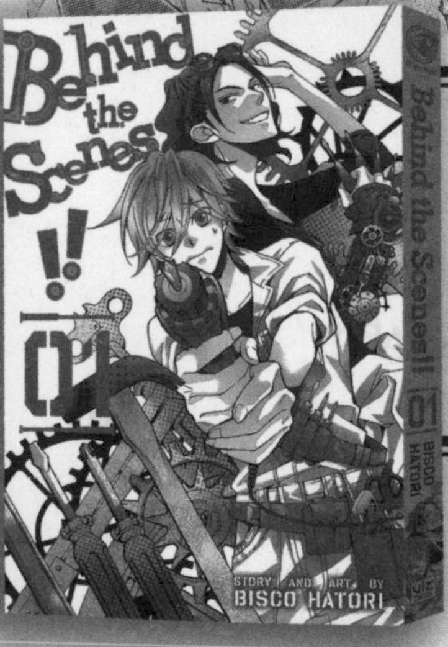
Behind the Scenes!!
01
Behind the Scenes!! 01
BISCO HATORI
STORY AND ART BY
BISCO HATORI

Ranmaru Kurisu comes from a family of hardy, rough-and-tumble fisherfolk and he sticks out at home like a delicate, artistic sore thumb. It's given him a raging inferiority complex and a permanently pessimistic outlook. Now that he's in college, he's hoping to find a sense of belonging. But after a whole life of being left out, does he even know how to fit in?!

SURPRISE!

You may be reading the wrong way!

It's true: In keeping with the original Japanese comic format, this book reads from right to left—so action, sound effects, and word balloons are completely reversed. This preserves the orientation of the original artwork—plus, it's fun! Check out the diagram shown here to get the hang of things, and then turn to the other side of the book to get started!

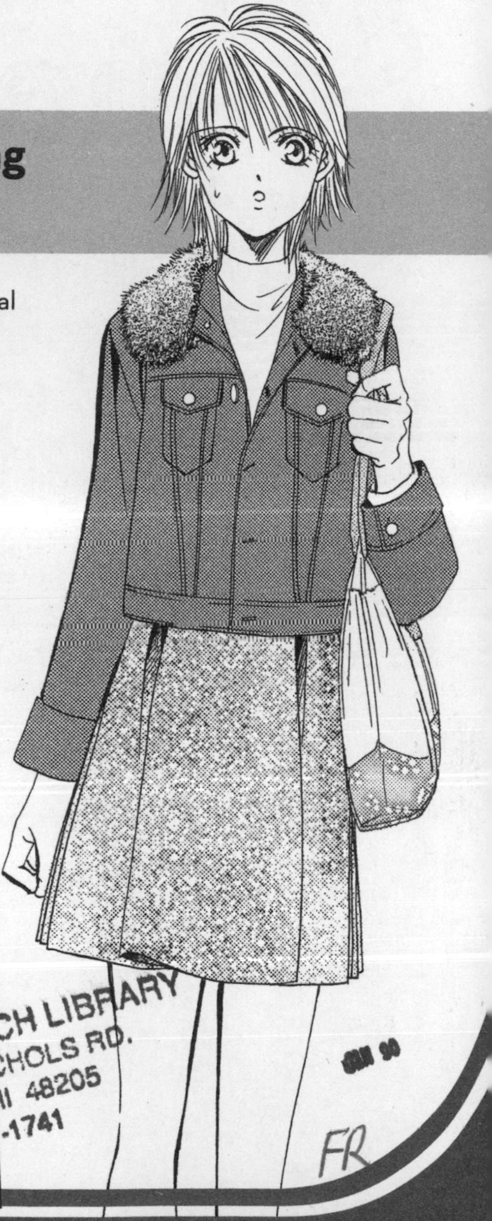

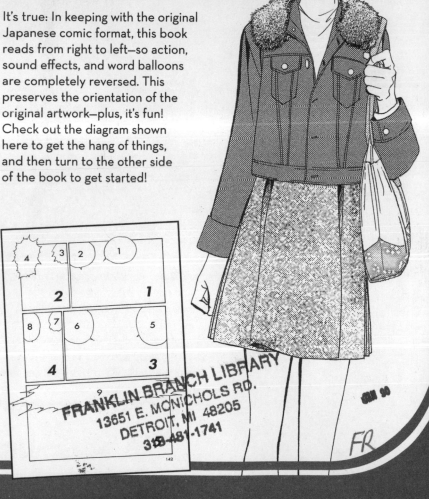

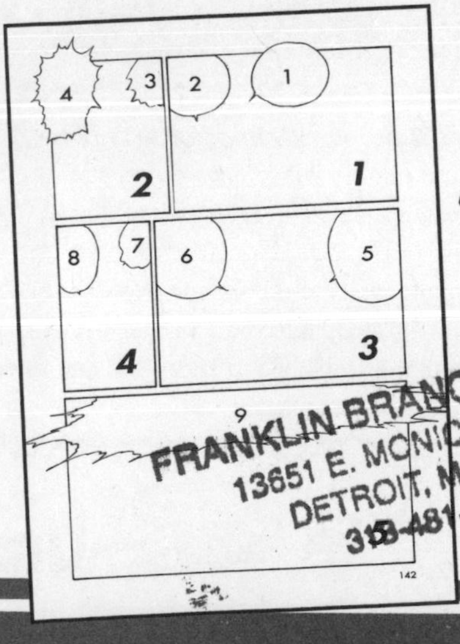
1
2
3
4
1
2
5
6
7
8
3
4
9
5
142